THE LUXURY ECONOMY AND INTELLECTUAL PROPERTY

The Luxury Economy and Intellectual Property

CRITICAL REFLECTIONS

Edited by Haochen Sun
Barton Beebe
and Madhavi Sunder

OXFORD
UNIVERSITY PRESS

OXFORD
UNIVERSITY PRESS

Oxford University Press is a department of the University of Oxford. It furthers the University's objective of excellence in research, scholarship, and education by publishing worldwide.

Oxford New York
Auckland Cape Town Dar es Salaam Hong Kong Karachi Kuala Lumpur Madrid
Melbourne Mexico City Nairobi New Delhi Shanghai Taipei Toronto

With offices in
Argentina Austria Brazil Chile Czech Republic France Greece Guatemala Hungary
Italy Japan Poland Portugal Singapore South Korea Switzerland Thailand
Turkey Ukraine Vietnam

Published in the United States of America by
Oxford University Press
198 Madison Avenue, New York, NY 10016

Library of Congress Cataloging-in-Publication Data

The luxury economy and intellectual property : critical reflections / edited by Haochen Sun, Barton Beebe, Madhavi Sunder.
pages cm
Includes bibliographical references and index.
ISBN 978-0-19-933570-1 ((hardback) : alk. paper)
1. Luxury goods industry—Law and legislation. 2. Intellectual property. I. Sun, Haochen, editor. II. Beebe, Barton Carl, 1969- editor. III. Sunder, Madhavi, editor.
K1406.L89L89 2015
346.04'8—dc23

2015004001

Note to Readers

This publication is designed to provide accurate and authoritative information in regard to the subject matter covered. It is based upon sources believed to be accurate and reliable and is intended to be current as of the time it was written. It is sold with the understanding that the publisher is not engaged in rendering legal, accounting, or other professional services. If legal advice or other expert assistance is required, the services of a competent professional person should be sought. Also, to confirm that the information has not been affected or changed by recent developments, traditional legal research techniques should be used, including checking primary sources where appropriate.

(Based on the Declaration of Principles jointly adopted by a Committee of the American Bar Association and a Committee of Publishers and Associations.)

Contents

Contributors

Ann Bartow is Executive Director of the Franklin Pierce Center for Intellectual Property and Professor of Law at the University of New Hampshire School of Law. She previously held tenured appointments at Pace Law School and the University of South Carolina School of Law. She specializes in intellectual property law, cyberspace law, privacy law, and feminist legal theory. She is an Advisory Board Member of the Electronic Privacy Center (EPIC) and a member of the American Law Institute. She spent the 2011–12 academic year as a Fulbright Scholar at Tongji University in Shanghai, China.

Barton Beebe is the John M. Desmarais Professor of Intellectual Property Law at New York University School of Law. He has been the Anne Urowsky Visiting Professor of Law at Yale Law School and a Visiting Professor of Law at Stanford Law School. In 2007, Professor Beebe was a Special Master in the case of *Louis Vuitton Malletier v. Dooney & Bourke, Inc.*, No. 04 Civ. 2990 (SAS) (S.D.N.Y.). His published works include *Intellectual Property Law and the Sumptuary Code*, 123 Harvard Law Review 809 (2010).

Sara T. Bernstein currently teaches film studies at Portland State University. Her research and teaching explore issues of representation, identity and power through fashion and mass media. She has authored and co-authored several articles that situate fashion in relation to other mass-representational forms—mainly film and television—but also novels, magazines, and new media. Sara received her PhD in Cultural Studies from the University of California, Davis, and her M.A. in Visual Culture: Costume Studies from New York University.

Mario Biagioli is Distinguished Professor of STS, Law, and History, and Director of the new Center for Science and Innovation Studies at the University of California at Davis. Prior to joining UCD, he taught history of science at Harvard and UCLA, and held visiting positions at Stanford and EHESS (Paris). He is the author of *Galileo Courtier* (Chicago, 1993), *Galileo's Instruments of Credit* (Chicago, 2006)), and the co-editor of *The Science Studies Reader* (Routledge, 1998), *Scientific Authorship* (Routledge, 2003), *Making and Unmaking Intellectual Property* (Chicago, 2011), and *Nature Engaged* (2013). He is currently completing a book on plagiarism in science.

Irene Calboli is the Deputy Director of the Applied Research Centre for Intellectual Assets and the Law in Asia, School of Law, Singapore Management University where she is also a Lee Kong Chian Fellow and Visiting Professor. She is also a Professor of Law at Texas A&M University School of Law, and a Transatlantic Technology Law Forum Fellow at Stanford Law School. Her research projects currently focus on overlapping intellectual property rights, the principle of intellectual property exhaustion, and the protection of geographical indications of origin. She has published many articles and chapters on intellectual property-related topics in English and Italian in leading journals and collective volumes. Her most recent publications include the books *Trademark Protection and Territoriality Challenges in a Global Economy* (2014, edited with E. Lee), *Diversity in Intellectual Property* (2015, edited with S. Ragavan), and *The Law and Practice of Trademark Transactions* (forthcoming 2016, edited with J. de Werra).

Anupam Chander is Director of the California International Law Center and Professor of Law at the University of California, Davis. A graduate of Harvard College and Yale Law School, he has been visiting professor at Yale, Chicago, Stanford, and Cornell. The author of *The Electronic Silk Road* (Yale University Press), he has published articles in the nation's leading law reviews. He practiced law in New York and Hong Kong with Cleary, Gottlieb, Steen & Hamilton. He is the recipient of multiple Google Research Awards and serves on the E15 expert group of the World Economic Forum and ICTSD.

Stacey L. Dogan is Professor and Law Alumni Scholar at Boston University School of Law, where she specializes in intellectual property and competition law. Professor Dogan has written numerous articles about IP and competition law, with a special emphasis on the challenges wrought by technology and the Internet. Before joining BU's faculty, she taught at Northeastern University School of Law and practiced with the law firm of Covington & Burling in Washington, DC. After graduating from Harvard Law School, Professor Dogan clerked with the honorable Judith Rogers on the U.S. Court of Appeals for the D.C. Circuit.

Joseph "Joe" H. Hancock, II teaches, publishes, and conducts scholarly activities at Drexel University in the Department of Design. He has twenty-year retailing background having worked for The Gap Corporation, The Limited, Inc., the Target

Corporation and continues to do publishing and merchandising consulting work on an international level. Joe earned his PhD from the Ohio State University focusing his research in popular culture as it relates to transnational mass fashion garments and world dress, aspirational fashion branding and experiential retailing, as well as men's fashion and lifestyles. He has published with Bloomsbury Publishers, Intellect Ltd, and University of Chicago Press. He released his book *Brand/Story: Ralph, Vera, Johnny, Billy and Other Adventures in Fashion Branding* (Bloomsbury, 2009) and the second edition is due out in 2016. He has published two edited books, *Fashion in Popular Culture* (2013) and *Global Fashion Brands* (2014) with Intellect Publishing and he is the principal editor of the peer-reviewed journal *Fashion, Style and Popular Culture* (Intellect Publishers) that debuted in October 2013.

Susan B. Kaiser is Professor of Women and Gender Studies and Textiles and Clothing, and Interim Dean of Humanities, Arts and Cultural Studies at the University of California at Davis. Her research and teaching bridge fashion studies and feminist cultural studies, with current interests in shifting articulations of masculinities; fashion and space/place; and possibilities for critical fashion studies. She is the author of *The Social Psychology of Clothing* (1997) and *Fashion and Cultural Studies* (2012), and ca.100 articles and book chapters in the fields of textile/fashion studies, sociology, gender studies, cultural studies, and consumer behavior.

Sonia K. Katyal is Chancellor's Professor of Law at the University of California, Berkeley. Previously, Professor Katyal served as Associate Dean for Research and Joseph M. McLaughlin Professor at Fordham University School of Law. Professor Katyal is the author of *Property Outlaws* (with Eduardo M. Penalver), published by Yale University Press in 2010, and a forthcoming book on advertising and trademarks, also to be published by Yale University Press. Her research focuses on civil rights and intellectual property law, with a special emphasis on gender, sexuality, and race.

Mark A. Lemley is the William H. Neukom Professor of Law at Stanford Law School and the Director of the Stanford Program in Law, Science and Technology. He teaches intellectual property, computer and internet law, patent law, trademark law, antitrust, and remedies. He is the author of seven books (most in multiple editions) and 144 articles on these and related subjects, including the two-volume treatise *IP and Antitrust*. Mark is a founding partner of Durie Tangri LLP. He litigates and counsels clients in all areas of intellectual property, antitrust, and internet law. He has argued 16 federal appellate cases and numerous district court cases, and represented clients including Comcast, Genentech, DISH Network, Google, Grokster, Guidewire, Hummer Winblad, NetFlix, and the University of Colorado Foundation in over 90 cases in his more than two decades as lawyer. Mark is a founder and board member of Lex Machina, Inc., a startup company providing data and analytics around IP disputes to law firms, companies, courts, and policymakers.

David Llewelyn is Professor (practice) & Deputy Dean of the School of Law at Singapore Management University and Professor of Intellectual Property Law at King's College London. Between 1999 and 2010 he was a partner of international law firm White & Case based in its London office. Professor Llewelyn is a co-author of *Kerly's Law of Trade Marks and Trade Names* (15th ed. 2011; Supplement 2014) and joint author of *Cornish, Llewelyn & Aplin on Intellectual Property: Patents, Copyright, Trade Marks and Allied Rights* (8th ed. 2013). His business book *Invisible Gold in Asia: Creating Wealth through Intellectual Property* (2010) explains the field of intellectual property to non-lawyers, using Asian examples throughout. Resident in Singapore since 2010, he is involved in international arbitration work and is consulted by governments and corporations on a range of intellectual property matters.

Yi Qian is Associate Professor of Marketing at the Sauder School of Business, University of British Columbia. Professor Qian's research interests shape around marketing strategies in the context of technology advancement and international trade. She applies this knowledge to propose successful business strategies to secure brand values and Intellectual Property Rights against counterfeits, and to suggest reasonable policies in adopting technology and absorbing foreign direct investments. She has also advanced methodology on causal inference and marketing analytics. Prior to joining the Sauder School, she taught courses on Advanced Econometrics and International Trade and Investments at Harvard University and Marketing Research and Applied Econometrics at Kellogg School of Management.

Kal Raustiala is Professor at UCLA Law School and the UCLA International Institute, where he directs the Burkle Center for International Relations. He is co-author, with Chris Sprigman of NYU, of *The Knockoff Economy: How Imitation Sparks Innovation* (Oxford 2012).

Susan Scafidi is the first professor ever to offer a course in Fashion Law, and she is internationally recognized for her leadership in establishing the field. She has testified regarding the proposed extension of legal protection to fashion designs and continues to work actively with members of Congress and the fashion industry on this and other issues. Her additional areas of expertise encompass property, intellectual property, cultural property, international law, trusts &estates, and legal history. Professor Scafidi founded and directs the nonprofit Fashion Law Institute, which was established with the generous support and advice of the Council of Fashion Designers of America and its president, Diane von Furstenberg, and is located at Fordham Law School. Prior to teaching at Fordham, Professor Scafidi was a tenured member of both the law and history faculties at Southern Methodist University, and she has taught at a number of other schools, including Yale, Georgetown, and Cardozo.

Christopher Jon Sprigman is Professor at the New York University School of Law, and Co-Director of NYU's Engelberg Center on Innovation Law and Policy. He is co-author, with Kal Raustiala (UCLA) of *The Knockoff Economy: How Imitation Sparks Innovation* (Oxford 2012), and he has authored or co-authored many academic and popular press articles on intellectual property and technology issues.

Haochen Sun is Assistant Professor of Law at the University of Hong Kong Faculty of Law. He teaches and writes in the areas of intellectual property and property law. He has been a Visiting Professor of Law at the University of California, Davis, School of Law. Professor Sun has organized a few leading international conferences on intellectual property and has taught courses on luxury brand protection. His recent publications include *Living Together in One Civilized World: How Luxury Companies and Consumers Can Fulfill Their Ethical Responsibilities to the Poor*, 46 UC Davis Law Review 547 (2013).

Madhavi Sunder is Professor of Law at the University of California, Davis, School of Law. Her work traverses numerous legal fields, from intellectual property to human rights law and the First Amendment. She has been Visiting Professor of Law at the Yale Law School, the University of Chicago Law School, and Cornell Law School. She was named a Carnegie Scholar in 2006. She is the author of *From Goods to a Good Life: Intellectual Property and Global Justice* (Yale University Press 2012).

Rebecca Tushnet is Professor of Law at Georgetown. She previously clerked for Associate Justice David H. Souter and worked in private practice. Her work focuses on copyright, trademark, and advertising law. With Eric Goldman, she publishes a casebook on advertising and marketing law. She helped found the Organization for Transformative Works, a nonprofit dedicated to supporting and promoting fanworks. Her blog, tushnet.blogspot.com, is one of the top intellectual property blogs, and her writings may be found at tushnet.com. She is also an expert on the law of engagement rings.

Diane Leenheer Zimmerman is Samuel Tilden Professor of Law Emerita at New York University where she has specialized in intellectual property and first amendment law. Professor Zimmerman is co-editor of *Expanding the Boundaries of Intellectual Property: Innovation Policy for the Knowledge Society* (2001) and *Working Within the Boundaries of Intellectual Property: Innovation Policy for the Knowledge Society* (2010). She has lectured in the United States and abroad, and written extensively, on topics including copyright, innovation policy and theory, publicity rights, commercial speech regulation, and libel and privacy law.

I Introduction

1 Introduction

Barton Beebe*

THE GLOBAL LUXURY goods market is enormous. Recent estimates peg its overall value in 2014 at $1 trillion, with personal luxury goods accounting for one quarter of that sum.[1] It is also enormously profitable. As the rich get ever richer in a global economy characterized by extraordinary concentrations of wealth, luxury goods companies are reporting surging profits, even in a time of overall economic malaise.[2] But perhaps the true measure of the significance of the luxury goods industry is found in its outsized impact on global culture. Global luxury brands rank among the most recognized symbols in the world, as familiar as the most prominent national flags or religious icons. Most of the billions of consumers around the globe will never be able to afford the products of the luxury goods industry, yet many will nevertheless immediately recognize names like Louis Vuitton, Mercedes-Benz, BMW, Gucci, Hermès, Cartier, Rolex, or Apple.

---

* John M. Desmarais Professor of Law, New York University School of Law.

[1] Claudia D'Arpizio, Federica Levato, Daniele Zito and Joelle de Montgolfier, *Luxury Goods Worldwide Market Study Fall-Winter 2014: The Rise of the Borderless Consumer*, http://www.bain.com/publications/articles/luxury-goods-worldwide-market-study-december-2014.aspx.

[2] *See, e.g.*, Nicola Clark, *LVMH, the Luxury Goods Giant, Posts a 64% Gain in Annual Profit*, N.Y. TIMES, Feb. 3, 2015, http://www.nytimes.com/2015/02/04/business/lvmh-theluxury-goods-giant-posts-a-64-gain-in-annual-profit.html.

As much as these brands rely on the creativity of their designers, the skill of their workers, and the cunning of their advertisers to maintain their vast economic and cultural power, so they rely just as much on their intellectual property lawyers and intellectual property law, particularly trademark law and design protection law in its various forms around the world. In recent decades, intellectual property law and its effective enforcement have emerged as necessary prerequisites to a viable luxury goods system. To maintain their brands' reputation for exclusivity and quality, luxury goods companies must constantly guard against all manner of intellectual property infringements, such as line-for-line counterfeits, closely similar knockoffs of protected designs, or confusingly similar trademark usages. This may help to explain why Louis Vuitton in particular has developed such a fearsome reputation around the world as being probably the most aggressive intellectual property litigant on the planet. And who can blame them? Their primary and perhaps their only truly significant asset is their brand, which was valued in 2014 at $22.5 billion.[3] Intellectual property protection is the sine qua non of the luxury brand and of the luxury goods industry.

Technological advances, specifically in technologies of simulation, have made the role of intellectual property law all the more significant. Though attention typically focuses on infringing simulations such as outright counterfeits and other clear intellectual property violations, perfectly legal forms of imitation and copying have arguably played an even greater role in pushing the industry toward the production—and consumers toward the consumption—of luxury goods that take the form of intellectual property. Consider the example of diamonds. Since the 1950s, engineers have produced ever more sophisticated methods of producing "cultured diamonds" that are now essentially indistinguishable from mined or "organic" diamonds. This represents a significant threat to the status of diamonds as the quintessential luxury good. The response by the De Beers cartel is highly indicative. In 2004, De Beers began literally to brand their diamonds with a laser-inscribed trademark that they have dubbed the "Forevermark." In the face of increasingly effective and altogether legal simulation technologies, De Beers can no longer rely on nature (or its own cartel) to enforce the rarity of what it offers for sale. Instead it has turned to intellectual property law to *create* the rarity that nature no longer provides, now in the form of a trademark. Rarity arguably constitutes a necessary characteristic of goods perceived to be luxurious. Intellectual property law has emerged as the most effective means of generating rarity and protecting it from imitation and overproduction. It is for this reason that so many luxury goods now essentially take the form of intellectual property,[4] and why recent decades have witnessed what might be called, for lack of a better term, the full-blown intellectual-propertization of the luxury economy.

---

[3] http://www.bestglobalbrands.com/2014/louisvuitton/.

[4] *See* Barton Beebe, *Intellectual Property Law and the Sumptuary Code*, 123 Harv. L. Rev. 809 (2010).

The conventional law-and-economics account of intellectual property law asserts that intellectual property protection promotes the luxury goods industry in the same way that it promotes any other industry. Trademark protection lowers consumers' "search costs" by allowing consumers to rely on trademarks as shortcuts to find the luxury products that they seek. Trademark protection also incentivizes luxury producers to produce high levels of product quality by reserving for these producers—and not for counterfeiters or confusingly similar competitors—the reputation-related rewards associated with that product quality. For their part, copyright and design protection incentivize the creation of new copyrightable expression and designs by providing short-term monopoly rights that allow luxury producers at least to cover the costs, if not to profit, from the development of new luxury goods. The happy result is greater economic efficiency and social welfare.

The law-and-economics story is simple and in that sense appealing, but as the chapters collected in this volume show, the relation between the luxury economy and intellectual property law is considerably more complicated—and controversial. Trademark law in particular does more than merely limit consumer search costs and incentivize product quality. As several of the chapters discuss, various trademark law doctrines can only be explained as designed to facilitate status consumption. For example, the doctrine of "post-sale confusion" in the United States prohibits the sale of imitation goods even when purchasers are perfectly aware that they are purchasing imitations; the doctrine does so on the ground that other people, even those who would never buy any of the goods at issue, may be confused after the point of sale.[5] Similarly, the prohibition against the taking of "unfair advantage" in the European Union has been used to suppress cheap smell-alike perfumes patterned after far more expensive luxury brands on the ground that doing so will protect the perceived exclusivity of these brands.[6] Importantly, intellectual property law protects not simply the kind of horizontal, hierarchical status consumption for which the luxury goods economy is notorious. The law also works to preserve vertical distinctions of status, mere signs of difference that enable the consumer to assert, to perform, some degree of uniqueness in an overall economy of industrialized sameness. Indeed, an effective use of trademark law, particularly antidilution doctrine, enables producers to cope with one of the fundamental challenges of mass production, which is how to produce countless copies of a product that will nevertheless confer on its consumers the experience of being or appearing distinctive.

Intellectual property law has also proven useful in defending luxury brands and the luxury goods industry against attacks on the very idea of luxury itself. Whether they take the form of for-profit parodies of luxury products or political and artistic commentary that incorporates references to luxury brands, such attacks constitute speech and

---

[5] *See, e.g.*, Mastercrafters Clock & Radio Co. v. Vacheron & Constantin-Le Coultre Watches, Inc., 221 F.2d 464, 465 (2d Cir. 1955).

[6] *See* L'Oréal SA v. Bellure NV, Case C-487/07, 2009 ECJ EUR-Lex LEXIS 532 (June 18, 2009).

are therefore privileged in most jurisdictions as expressions of their speakers' freedom of speech. But such attacks are also attacks on property and can cause considerable damage to that property. Thus is joined in the intellectual property realm the increasingly fraught battle between strong traditions of freedom of expression and equally strong traditions championing the sanctity of property rights. While U.S. courts are especially attentive to the importance of freedom of expression, they have nevertheless enjoined parodies, some very clever,[7] others very silly,[8] of luxury products even when those parodies were developed explicitly "for the purpose of casting ridicule upon the tastes and pretension"[9] of luxury consumers. Several of the chapters that follow invoke the story of the artist Nadia Plesner, whom Louis Vuitton sued for producing a painting that depicted among other things a naked, undernourished African child holding a fashionable lapdog and a handbag resembling Louis Vuitton's Monogram Multicolore handbag. As Sonia Katyal explains in her contribution to this volume, a Dutch trial court initially issued an injunction against Plesner but later ruled in her favor. But even when critical speakers can expect eventually to be vindicated by the courts, they may not have the resources to defend their rights all the way to final judgment. In a previous dispute between Louis Vuitton and Plesner, the artist had agreed to stop producing a T-shirt depicting the image of the African child rather than try somehow to cover the costs of litigating the issue. The mere threat of intellectual property litigation can chill oppositional speech that the law would nevertheless allow.

The chapters that follow engage these and many other themes on which conventional accounts of intellectual property law, be they grounded in law and economics or simply in efforts toward the more rational systemization of the doctrine, have traditionally remained silent. The chapters emerged out of two conferences, *Charting the New Frontiers of Intellectual Property Protection of Luxury Goods*, organized by Haochen Sun at the University of Hong Kong, and *Brand New World: Distinguishing Oneself in the Global Flow*, organized by Mario Biagioli, Anupam Chander, and Madhavi Sunder at UC Davis Law School in California. The conferences assembled leading historians, gender studies and media studies scholars, economists, law professors, and luxury industry lawyers and challenged them to critically reflect on the luxury goods economy, the intellectual property law foundations on which it is built, and the public interest and social concerns arising from this rapidly developing area of economy, culture, and law.

The chapters in Part II focus on one of the basic issues animating this critical inquiry, which is just how we define luxury and how intellectual property law both informs and

---

[7] Schieffelin & Co. v. Jack Company of Boca, 850 F. Supp. 232 (S.D.N.Y. 1994) ("Dom Popignon" popcorn infringing of DOM PERIGNON champagne).

[8] Grey v. Campbell Soup Co. 650 F.Supp. 1166, 1175 (C.D. Cal. 1986) (finding "Dogiva" and "Cativa" treats for animals infringing of GODIVA chocolate); Gucci Shops, Inc. v. R. H. Macy & Co., Inc., 446 F.Supp. 838 (S.D.N.Y. 1977) (finding "Gucci Goo" diaper bags infringing of GUCCI mark).

[9] Schieffelin & Co., 850 F.Supp. at 237.

disrupts that definition. In chapter 2, Susan B. Kaiser, Davis Joseph H. Hancock II, and Sara T. Bernstein range widely—and dialectically—across the landscape of critical fashion studies to explore the highly ambivalent, often internally contradictory concept of luxury. They address in particular the increasingly common efforts by luxury fashion producers to democratize fashion or at least to expand their customer base and so their profits. Such efforts displace the fashion producers and their products to new and contested locations along the dimensions of race, class, gender, sexuality, and other indicia of subjectivity, locations against which the fashion producers' own claims of exclusivity may at one time have been defined. In chapter 3, Irene Calboli invokes the theory and practice of trademark law to further the critique of the democratization of luxury. She notes the fundamental changes that overtook the luxury goods industry in the 1980s and 1990s as many small and independent luxury goods houses merged into a handful of giant luxury goods conglomerates eager to profit from brand extensions and bridge lines. Calboli describes how trademark law has evolved to facilitate this new luxury business model but questions whether luxury goods brands that have been extended to products of lesser quality should enjoy the benefits of certain kinds of trademark protection, particularly antidilution protection. Finally, in chapter 4, Yi Qian reviews the remarkable results of her field and lab studies of counterfeit purchases in the luxury shoe sector. Qian shows that in certain situations counterfeits may actually work to the benefit of the company whose products are being counterfeited. When the authentic goods are of very high quality, low-quality counterfeits will not substitute for authentics and may help to advertise them. But where authentics and counterfeits are of similar quality, producers of authentics will be negatively impacted.

Part III shifts its focus to the cultural dimensions of luxury brands and the intellectual property laws designed to protect them. Mario Biagioli, Anupam Chander, and Madhavi Sunder explore the significant limitations of the traditional law-and-economic theory of trademark law and urge the law to recognize that trademarks, beyond simply identifying the source of goods, facilitate consumer self-fashioning and identity performance. Trademarks perform this function through meanings that are collectively generated as much by consumers as by producers. Biagioli, Chander, and Sunder emphasize that as trademarks take on an ever-broader role in global culture, we must not make the category mistake of allowing trademark property rights to expand along with this role. Stacey Dogan and Mark Lemley also attend to the cultural workings of trademarks, particularly the manner in which trademarks can be both targets and vehicles of oppositional speech. Their concern is how to create doctrinal space for parodies that are themselves brands, such as those at issue in the remarkable 2007 case of *Louis Vuitton Malletier S.A. v. Haute Diggity Dog, LLC*,[10] in which the defendant produced parody dog toys and beds featuring brand names like Chewy Vuiton, Chewnel #5, Jimmy Chew, and Furcedes Bed. Rebecca Tushnet challenges the constitutionality in the United States

[10] 507 F.3d 252, 256 (4th Cir. 2007).

of trademark doctrines such as antidilution and post-sale confusion law that suppress non-false speech. She draws a compelling connection to *U.S. v. Alvarez*,[11] the Supreme Court case that found unconstitutional the Stolen Valor Act, a law that criminalized the act of falsely representing oneself as the recipient of any U.S. military decoration or medal. The Court ruled that the Act's failure to require any showing of harm beyond the falsity of the representation itself rendered the law unconstitutional. Tushnet asks why the same reasoning shouldn't apply to trademark laws prohibiting diluting third-party uses. Ann Bartow's chapter concludes Part III. It musters an enormous amount of evidence in support of the propositions that the luxury goods industry's branding practices demean and damage women, and that the current framework of intellectual property law only furthers this abuse.

Part IV explores the distributive justice dimensions of the luxury economy and the intellectual property law that underpins it. Diane Zimmerman situates her analysis within the context of global trends toward increasing wealth and income inequality, and suggests that Veblen's early-twentieth-century critique of status consumption, which fell out of fashion by the end of the century, has regained much of its relevance in recent years. She urges a recognition of the significant social, economic, and psychological benefits that flow to non-wealthy consumers in the form of knockoffs and other close adaptations of status clothing. Furthering this focus on status consumption, I discuss the implications of the rise of "shanzhai" imitative and counterfeit goods in China and consider the cultural dimensions of intellectual property law's role in their suppression. In an ambitious proposal, Haochen Sun outlines an "ethical responsibility initiative" in which luxury goods producers would agree to disseminate information about the substantial proportion of the world's population living in abject poverty. Sun suggests one means of incentivizing companies to participate: the degree to which luxury goods producers acknowledge and act on their ethical responsibilities could factor into a court's determination of their brands' qualification for antidilution protection. Finally, Susan Scafidi provocatively suggests that legal academics who are hostile toward luxury brands and critical of their impact on society and culture are motivated by envy of the creativity of those who produce and consume luxury fashion. Such feelings of *ressentiment*, rather than concerns for social justice, Scafidi suggests, are responsible for much of the legal academic critique of intellectual property law and the luxury economy.

Part V broadens the focus of the volume to consider more directly the global dimensions of the relation between intellectual property and the luxury economy. Kal Raustiala and Christopher Sprigman offer a nuanced interpretation of the phenomenon of counterfeiting in China. Building in part on Yi Qian's work, they show how, in certain situations, counterfeiting can strengthen rather than weaken a brand by, for example, helping to advertise the brand or providing an initial gateway to goods bearing the brand. David Llewelyn ranges widely across the landscape of global trademark law to expose the

[11] 132 S. Ct. 2537 (2012).

incoherence of much of the doctrine affecting luxury goods. In conclusion, Sonia Katyal charts the rise of "trademark cosmopolitanism" not just in how consumers and producers conceive of global brands or in how trademark law regulates these brands, but also in how transnational activists now create and deploy global antibranding campaigns.

Together, the collected chapters present a wide-ranging and sophisticated critique of the intersection of the luxury goods economy and intellectual property law. The discussion, however, is by no means comprehensive or definitive. Our hope, at the very least, is that the chapters show not just the extraordinary importance of intellectual property law to the global luxury goods system, but also the increasing impact the luxury goods system is having on the design of global intellectual property law. Neither of these two areas can now be properly understood without attention to the other, and as we hope these chapters reveal, neither can be properly understood without attention to the economic, cultural, and political implications of their interconnection.

II The Concept of Luxury

2 Luxury and Its Opposites

A CRITICAL FASHION STUDIES PERSPECTIVE

Susan B. Kaiser,* Joseph H. Hancock II,** and Sara T. Bernstein***

LUXURY AND BRANDING? Luxury and authenticity? Luxury and social justice? Each of the latter terms seems contradictory or oxymoronic—for various reasons—when paired with luxury. In this paper, we explore the contradictions in these pairings, as well as within the concept of luxury itself. Luxury is a loaded concept, with multiple layers and internal conflicts. The first definition of luxury in the *Oxford English Dictionary* is "lasciviousness, lust," and in some of the uses cited, luxury is also modified by terms such as "adulterous" and "shameless." Other definitions refer to "the habitual use of, or indulgence in, what is choice or costly," "refined and intense enjoyment," and a sumptuous form of enjoyment or comfort—that which is desirable but not necessary. A cited 1833 reference to luxury under the last definition as "selfish pleasure" reveals the extent to which luxury can hardly be described as a neutral concept. We might say that a picture of "comfort plus" emerges; there is space for excess embedded in the concept.[1]

* Susan B. Kaiser, PhD, Professor of Women and Gender Studies, and Textiles and Clothing, and Interim Dean, Humanities, Arts and Cultural Studies, University of California, Davis.

** Joseph H. Hancock, II, PhD, Associate Professor, Department of Design, Drexel University.

*** Sara T. Bernstein, Adjunct Assistant Professor, Film Studies, Portland State University.

[1] OXFORD ENGLISH DICTIONARY (2013).

In this chapter, we consider the view of luxury as "everything and its opposite," as proffered by the linguistic philosopher and fashion theorist Patrizia Calefato.[2] Using a critical fashion studies perspective, we attempt to unpack some of the layers of contradiction associated with luxury and its opposites. Drawing on case studies of contemporary luxury goods and controversies, interviews with consumers and producers of luxury goods, and following Calefato, we hope to contribute to a critical and creative discourse on luxury in fashion studies, as well as cultural studies, law, marketing, and other fields.

I. Luxury and Branding

If not polar opposites, the concepts of luxury and branding are at least in direct tension with one another, especially in the context of global capitalism's profit motivation. How can a company reconcile competing desires to sell "exclusive luxury" and to increase the market share of its brand? The process of branding itself involves storytelling and strategizing, presumably in hopes of selling more products.[3] Luxury branding, then, becomes a delicate dance between telling a special story about product exclusivity, on the one hand, and achieving profitability, on the other. As a case in point, Louis Vuitton—the flagship brand of the world's largest luxury conglomerate, LVMH (Moët Hennessy—Louis Vuitton)—capitalized on its prestige by marketing its heavily branded canvas handbags. These canvas handbags became the company's "bread and butter" product for decades. However, as reported by the business pages of the *New York Times*, the $900 canvas "Speedy tote ... lost cachet in recent years for being ubiquitous and affordable—not to mention vulnerable to knock-offs." As the annual profits at LVMH have fallen nearly flat, especially in its fashion luxury brands such as Louis Vuitton, the company has increased its focus on marketing fewer, higher-quality leather handbags costing thousands of dollars to extremely wealthy consumers.[4]

LVMH, like other luxury conglomerates, experienced the limits to the "massification" of luxury. This massification involves marketing an elite brand identity "downwardly" to aspirational consumers. It meshes with a neoliberal logic, through which—oxymoronically and tautologically—luxury is theoretically available to "all." James B. Twitchell, an anthropologist of consumer culture, has remarked that "the

---

[2] Patrizia Calefato, Luxury: Fashion, Lifestyles, Excess (translated by Lisa Adams, 2014).

[3] *See* Joseph H. Hancock Ii, Brand/Story: Ralph, Vera, Johnny, Billy, And Other Adventures In Fashion Branding (2009).

[4] Nicola Clark, *Annual Profit Nearly Flat for Luxury Group LVMH*, N.Y. Times (January 30, 2014). On its website, LVMH describes its mission as representing "the most refined qualities of Western 'Art de Vivre' around the world. LVMH must continue to be synonymous with both elegance and creativity. Our products, and the cultural values they embody, blend tradition and innovation, and kindle dream and fantasy" (http://www.lvmh.com/the-group/lvmh-group; accessed March 20, 2014). Undoubtedly, it is difficult to "kindle dream and fantasy" when highly recognizable, branded canvas bags have become so ubiquitous.

pleasure of spending just to spend is the dirty little secret of affluence. The rich used to do it: Now the rest of us are having a go at it."[5]

In addition to the widespread availability of counterfeited luxury brands (e.g., handbags on Canal Street in New York City—just a few blocks from the designer "originals"), limited numbers of luxury brands can be purchased on a daily basis through online websites such as Rue La La, Gilt, and MyHabit. Recent Rue La La's "Legend Luxe" and "Luxe Lounge," for example, highlight a few items sold at a deep discount: "Over the top opulence? You bet … Get in there and start indulging already." Within a few minutes of a flash sale in October of 2013, the three Andrew Marc men's black lamb leather jackets (with a wool-and-nylon-blend ribbed knit collar and removable bib), normally retailing at $795 but reduced to $349.90, disappeared. Only one AM "Camden" Olive Waxed Coat (100% polyester with decorative wool knit trim)—an outdoorsy style—remained. It normally retailed for $795 but was available on Rue La La's flash sale for $279.90. One two-button, dual-vent navy suit (73% wool, 27% mohair), from the Armani Collezioni and made in Italy, remains: only in a size 50. It had retailed for $1,995, but is available through the flash sale for $649.90. One brown plaid (rural-inspired) sport coat from the same collection, also in size 50, was available. The plaid was perfectly matched, including the angled pocket. The coat was 54% rayon, 27% wool, and 19% polyester.[6]

There are cracks, however, in the so-called democratization of luxury fashion: consumer credit card debt, intellectual property issues,[7] and tremendous gaps between consumer pleasure and the working conditions in garment factories. Further, as discussed in the last section of this paper, still-prevalent, racialized notions of which consumers "belong" in luxury retail settings are alive and well. Uncomfortable interactions in brick-and-mortar luxury retail settings may contribute to the appeal of both safe anonymity and the budgetary savings associated with shopping online. As Calefato notes, ultimately luxury divides as it unleashes power and passion. Yet it also offers a regime of identification and imitation (legal or otherwise).[8]

Fashion theorists, drawing on the German sociologist Georg Simmel,[9] frequently point to the dynamic interplay between imitation (identification) and demarcation (differentiation) as a driving social-psychological impetus underlying fashion change. That

---

[5] JAMES B. TWITCHELL, LIVING IT UP: OUR LOVE AFFAIR WITH LUXURY 8 (2002).

[6] We wish to thank Madhavi Sunder for raising provocative questions about online luxury shopping and the extent to which brand owners manage or police the circulation of their goods in online shopping sites featuring flash clearance sales. As she points out, if luxury companies do not do so, they may ultimately have fewer claims to define and protect the brand in their own terms. This is a topic that is ripe for further study.

[7] For helpful arguments about the need for better connections between intellectual property and social justice, see Haochen Sun, *Can Louis Vuitton Dance with HiPhone? Rethinking the Idea of Social Justice in Intellectual Property Law*, 15 UNIVERSITY OF PENNSYLVANIA JOURNAL OF LAW AND SOCIAL CHANGE 387 (2012); and MADHAVI SUNDER, FROM GOODS TO A GOOD LIFE: INTELLECTUAL PROPERTY AND GLOBAL JUSTICE (2012).

[8] CALEFATO, *supra* note 2, at 36.

[9] Georg Simmel, *Fashion*, 10 INT'L QUARTERLY 130–55 (1904).

is, fashion changes in an ongoing manner as a result of impulses to belong and to be unique. This both/and orientation flies in the face of modern western thought's insistence on binary (either/or) oppositions, and is consistent with the intersections between African American and feminist theorizing (i.e., "double consciousness").[10] Although Simmel's classic treatise on fashion dealt with social class as a major factor in imitation and demarcation (often interpreted reductionistically as the "trickle-down" theory), in fact his theory can be applied to a range of subject positions, including gender,[11] age/generation,[12] and place/space.[13] Further, the idea of a both/and framing, rather than an either/or framing melds with feminist and fashion theorizing on individual and cultural ambivalence as a source of fuel for fashion change.[14]

Diverse, or even conflicting, social-psychological factors as potential predictors of intention to purchase luxury goods have been the topic of a spate of consumer behavioral studies—often using sophisticated statistical methods—in recent years. There is some evidence, for example, that British "creative counter-conformists" are able to balance the desire to acquire status (e.g., "to wear what most high-status people buy") with the desire to be exclusive or unique, through their consumption of luxury fashion.[15] Because 85% of new luxury stores are in emerging markets (e.g., China, India, Brazil, Russia), there has been a lot of scholarly marketing interest in the interplay between cultural differences (e.g., individualist versus collectivist cultures) and social-psychological variables (e.g., self-monitoring behavior, need for uniqueness). The studies show mixed results. In a comparison of U.S. and Chinese female university students, for example, some of

---

[10] *See* the following for further background on African-American epistemologies: W. E. B. Du Bois, The Souls Of Black Folk (1903); Bell Hooks, Yearning: Race, Gender, and Cultural Politics (1990); Patricia Hill Collins, Black Feminist Thought (2008). For linkages between these authors' ideas and fashion theory, see: Susan B. Kaiser and Sarah R. McCullough, *Entangling the Fashion Subject through the African Diaspora: From Not to (K)not in Fashion Theory*, 14(3) Fashion Theory 361–86 (2010); and Susan B. Kaiser, Fashion and Cultural Studies (2012).

[11] Grant D. McCracken, *The Trickle-Down Theory Rehabilitated*, in The Psychology of Fashion (Michael R. Solomon ed., 1985).

[12] Kathleen Huun and Susan B. Kaiser, *The Emergence of Modern Infantwear, 1896–1962: Traditional White Dresses Succumb to Fashion's Gender Obsession*, 19(3) Clothing And Textiles Research Journal 103–119 (2001); Heike Jenβ, *Cross-Temporal Explorations: Notes on Fashion and Nostalgia*, 4(1/2) Critical Studies in Fashion and Beauty 107–24 (2013).

[13] Sara Tatyana Bernstein and Susan B. Kaiser, *Fashion Out of Place: Experiencing Fashion in a Small American Town*, 4(1/2) Critical Studies in Fashion and Beauty 43–70 (2013); Susan B. Kaiser, *Place, Time and Identity: New Directions in Critical Fashion Studies*, 4(1/2) Critical Studies in Fashion and Beauty 3–16 (2013).

[14] See: Elizabeth Wilson, Adorned in Dreams: Fashion and Modernity (2003); Susan B. Kaiser, Richard H. Nagasawa, and Sandra S. Hutton, *Fashion, Postmodernity and Personal Appearance: A Symbolic Interactionist Formulation*, 14(2) Symbolic Interaction 165–85 (1991); Fred Davis, Fashion, Culture, And Identity (1992); Susan B. Kaiser, *Place, Time and Identity: New Directions in Critical Fashion Studies*, 4(1/2) Critical Studies in Fashion and Beauty 3–16 (2013).

[15] Minas N. Kastanakis and George Balabanis, *Between the Mass and the Class: Antecedents of the "Bandwagon" Luxury Consumer Behavior*, 65(10) Journal of Business Research 1399–1407 (2012).

the results contradicted the prevailing wisdom that Chinese students would be more collectivist and U.S. students more individualistic with respect to luxury fashion consumption.[16] So, one might surmise that the global demand for luxury fashion challenges or complicates existing ideas about culture and social psychology (and their interplay).

Most likely, perceptions of luxury are contextual and relational, but not necessarily in ways that can be predicted by cultural or other stereotypes, as many of these quantitative studies suggest. Some of the mixed results may have much to do with changing conceptions of capitalism and global marketing. These studies collectively raise a number of intriguing questions about luxury consumption in a global economy. The sample sizes in many of these studies are large, but one can get a sense of disembodiment when trying to make sense of what luxury *means* to consumers. Which brands are considered luxury brands? What kinds of stories that brand marketers tell do consumers "buy"? What kinds of materials and material qualities figure into the concept of luxury? Do individuals actually use a discourse of "luxury" to characterize their consumption practices?

We submit that luxury, like many concepts or topics, demands a mixture of methods: qualitative as well as quantitative. To illustrate what consumers can tell us in their own words, we are sharing two portions of interviews from a larger study of fashion, subjectivity, and place/space. Although neither of these interviews involved the use of the term "luxury," we were struck by the ways in which brands (that may in one place/space or another be considered luxury brands: and who gets to decide?) figured prominently in the following discussions of place/space in consumers' everyday lives. Even consumers who do not have large incomes may nevertheless find ways to work what we might call "personalized luxury" items into their wardrobes. Both of these interviews were conducted in a non-urban area of the Pacific Northwest in the United States.

First, B.J., a white gay male in his 30s, discusses how his shopping habits and, in particular, his desire for certain designer brands has been financially problematic. He had recently moved back into his working-class parents' rural home in order to manage his debt. As he tells his story, one can sense both the pleasures and the pitfalls associated with "luxury branded" fashion items (especially accessories, which he can mix and match with less expensive items):

> B.J.: As fashion goes, I went through a phase where I was a total label whore. I would do trips to: my two favorite places to go shopping were Kenneth Cole and Neiman Marcus in San Francisco. Very evil thing. Never get a Neiman Marcus card. Their credit card is a 10 million dollar limit [he says facetiously]. And their finance charge is like 30%. That was ... eeeeyeah ... don't spend $9,000 at Neiman Marcus in one day. Lesson learned.... So I went through a phase where it was Kenneth Cole shoes. My dress shoes are Kenneth Cole. I have a black and

---

[16] Qin Bian and Sandra Forsythe, *Purchase Intention for Luxury Brands: A Cross Cultural Comparison*, 65(10) Journal of Business Research 1443–51 (2012).

brown pair. They're identical. I have a couple of Prada shoes. As far as fashion, high end, I like expensive shoes, expensive glasses, expensive bags. And I think that that complements my very simple pants and shirts. I have a Diesel bag that I'm wearing. A small handbag. Maybe 5X7 or so. It's purple. This was during my "I'm gay" phase. And I was at the Diesel store in Seattle and I only bought it because the guy was flirting with me. And it was the cheapest thing; I'd just spent like $200 at Kenneth Cole and so I was like I don't know how much is on my card. I know I have enough, but I should be good—like he's flirting with you; you have to buy something. So I was like there's a purple bag, and purple's my favorite color, so I was like, I'll take it. $35 for a Diesel bag? I thought it was worth flirting and—anyway.

S: It's all part of the experience. The shopping experience.

B.J.: And my sunglasses right now are Versace. And I actually got them here, in [his home town]. At the same store; they don't have them now, but they also carry Prada frames. And they had Christian LaCroix. And I was like there's Christian LaCroix. In real … like … yeah.

S: Was it like an eyeglasses—frame shop?

B.J.: [Says "yes" and goes on to describe his collection of glasses]: They have like Polo and Guess, which is fine. I have three pairs of sunglasses. One is a giant, 10-dollar pair of green Elton John-looking, you know like Jackie O-looking sunglasses from Old Navy. And those are my fun ones. I have a dark pair of brown Kenneth Cole that I use for bright days. And then for hazy days I have—trips to San Francisco are evil. I opened a Saks Fifth Avenue card so that I could buy a pair of pink Coco Chanel sunglasses. And before we leave—they're in my car, so …

S: Yeah. I'd like to see them.

B.J.: I like accessories. My keychain is a Prada keychain. I like the little things—I don't know if it's necessarily—there's times when I'm just annoyed with people here wearing Walmart. I'm [thinking] like, "You know what? My keychain costs more and is worth more than everything you have on right now." Which isn't saying much. I mean it's a hundred-dollar keychain. It's not like thousands and thousands.

The idea of mixing luxury items with other clothes also arose in another interview with two members of a Radical Faerie (gay) commune in the woods not far from B.J.'s home. Issues of desire also became intertwined with sexuality. In an interview, Dan and Hudson discussed the changes in their clothes since moving from larger cities to "The Land" (their commune). On The Land, they wear a lot of drag, mixing in higher-end and luxury items. Most of their clothes are free, but they splurge on their boots and appreciate being "gifted" luxury brands and accessories. Dan said "here … everybody's kind of got their drag closet side … it's like, 'Oh, that's pretty; that looks good.' Because everybody is more radical." Dan went on to note that "there's just something really special about … chopping wood in a tutu" from the free communal "drag closet," and wearing that tutu with one's own boots—which had been a splurge. Their consuming pattern is to invest in expensive items such as boots, but to spend almost nothing on other clothing items:

HUDSON: You thrift-store it, you find it, you get it from other people. You should not be spending money on it. You spend money maybe on like a few things that are really special.

DAN: I get like some clothes when I go to The Land … like my most recent one was I got a Vivienne Westwood T-shirt. You know, I've just read about Vivienne Westwood. I've looked at her pictures on the Internet. Little did I know I'd be getting this Vivienne Westwood T-shirt at The Land … that was pretty sweet. That was special. And it's always like, "OK, this is yours now." Like, "I have something special for you." You know, it's always a gift. I like that a lot.

HUDSON: I was given this bracelet of diamonds. Yes, real diamonds, not rhinestones.

DAN: Uh-huh. Rhinestone cowboy.

HUDSON: It's like a two-and-a-half-inch thick bracelet of diamonds that Darlene the Ambassador's wife just handed it to me one night, and was like, "Oh my god, you need this." And like took it off her arm and gifted it to me and was just like, "You need this for your outfit. It's yours."[17]

DAN: It's like the family jewels. You're getting heirlooms.

HUDSON: Yeah, it's like the Faerie godmother is passing on to the younger generation. Or—like us—it's interesting, sometimes I'll see someone and I'll be like, "I have something that you need." And it may be something that's really special and precious to me, but has just never felt like mine. Whether it be like a shirt or skirt or whatever. It's just never felt like mine. And I'll see someone and I'll know that it goes to him.

DAN: There's so much materials out there. There's so many clothes. That's why I say like there's no need to—OK, there is a need to buy a pair of $200 boots if they're special—but they will go great with the rest of your outfit that's been scrounged together and gifted.

HUDSON: It's like boots—these boots cost $200. The rest of this outfit cost $3.50.

DAN: Exactly. That's what it's about.

HUDSON: Including all the jewelry. I think the most I've ever spent on a piece of clothing is close to $300 on a pair of jeans. They were like $240 or something

---

[17] This interchange suggests the ways in which individuals are able to personalize luxury goods as they negotiate their own (and others') identities. For a cogent analysis of how individuals seek to develop their own sense of authenticity in a "brand new world," see: Mario Biagioli, Anupam Chander, and Madhavi Sunder, *Brand New World: Distinguishing Oneself in the Global Flow*, 47(2) UC DAVIS L. REV. 455–72 (2013).

> like that. Um and I may have like maxed out my credit card, or I overdrew my account or something when I got 'em? But that's four-and-half years ago and the jeans still look super fuckin' hot on me. They still fit. Like I needed it at that moment . . . like I needed that at the moment. So like I have no qualms spending a shit-ton of money on something if it's gonna be worth it. Because most of the eleven-and-a-half months out of the year, I don't spend any money on clothes. They're just free or I spend $2 at a thrift store.

Luxury goods do not necessarily circulate in ways anticipated by LVMH or other conglomerates. Individual consumers create their own stories, as they stretch their budgets in a variety of ways to work luxury goods into their wardrobes. They do so through spontaneous splurges, strategic approaches to mixing and matching more and less expensive items into their everyday looks, and so on. Consumers are *bricoleurs* who make use of what they have or can acquire inexpensively; the meanings of the luxury goods (at various price ranges, assuming luxury is contextual) become embedded into their own styles, but in some ways these goods retain their branded identities and special recognition, even within personalized spaces.

Presumably, from a marketing point of view, luxury producers want to increase their profit margins, but how do they simultaneously expand their appeal and remain exclusive? In the next section, we consider how the menswear luxury industry generates stories of authenticity, often deploying metaphors of outdoorsiness, rurality, and rugged individualism.

II. Luxury and Authenticity

Luxury fashion companies (and their advertisers) must attempt to construct authenticating stories in order to justify their existence and to generate some kind of what we might call an "originating aura" around their brands. This may be especially true with menswear, given the feminine-centric bias in modern western fashion.[18] In other words, more rationale or justification (and hence more storytelling) may be required to market menswear, which is still not as taken for granted as a norm as is women's fashion. In the process of reconciling the contradiction between exclusivity and mass marketability, luxury menswear companies, especially, use the "magic" of advertising[19] and store displays to authenticate their claims to luxury, as they navigate strategically between originality and profitability. New (and yet seasoned) narratives are required to generate a simultaneous illusion of distinctiveness, desire, and material superiority, along with the

---

[18] For a discussion of this female-centric bias in fashion studies, see Susan B. Kaiser, Fashion and Cultural Studies (2012).

[19] *See* Judith Williams, Decoding Advertising: Ideology and Meaning in Advertising (2002); Raymond Williams, Culture And Materialism (2005).

possibility of acquired status—or what Thorstein Veblen called "pecuniary consumption."[20] Commonly, storytelling around men's luxury apparel highlights claims to historical authenticity, rugged individualism, and outdoorsiness.

During the time of this writing, a "luxury clearance" online retail site, Gilt, features "rustic weekend essentials," including the Billionaire Boys Club Car Coat. Dancing around the interplay between urban and rural spaces, the site highlights how luxury becomes a common thread that can "move" from one site to another. The British upper-class luxury of having both "town and country" dwellings (including the time and space required for fox-hunting and other leisure pursuits) becomes reinforced by contemporary horse trials with their own luxury retail scene.[21] Recalling Veblen's concepts of "conspicuous consumption" and its association with "conspicuous leisure" (showing no signs of, or being impractical for, manual labor), however, we find it necessary to point to the ways in which "luxury storytelling" has deployed or appropriated metaphors of both working-class and rural (weekend or vacation) leisure activities to create tales of "truth" and authenticity. In the context of global counterfeiting of luxury logos and "design piracy" of visual styles that cannot practically be copyrighted (because that process would take at least two years of legal action, and fashion moves much faster) and are frequently not considered to be "patent worthy" as new inventions, it becomes all the more crucial for luxury brands to authenticate themselves with narratives of originality.

Paradoxically, Veblen's concept of "conspicuous leisure" is both more relevant than ever in the second decade of the twenty-first century *and* seems on the surface to be somewhat irrelevant in the context of the working-class and rural imagery in luxury storytelling. What perhaps gets skipped over in this imagining is the very bourgeois or upper-middle, merchant class that Veblen was theorizing. The working classes and the aristocratic classes come together in the visual imaginary; the down-to-earth (even dingy) retail props and settings somehow mystically (or mythically) turn ordinary objects into extraordinary items of luxury. The luxury fashion can afford to refer narratively to working-class imagery to achieve a sense of authenticity, because there is little chance that it will actually be *perceived* as working class by luxury consumers. At the same time, the aura of authenticity associated with the luxury lingers. In the process of establishing and nurturing that aura, luxury brands rely on narratives linked to historical roots, heritage, and rural spaces, in addition to working-class imagery. Here, there is a delicate balancing act: as Calefato[22] argues, luxury storytelling can easily slip into kitsch, or over-the-top sentimentality.

Ralph Lauren, a retail corporation known for their sumptuous, luxurious thematics, is a good example of a firm that has managed its luxury storytelling strategically.

---

[20] THORSTEIN VEBLEN, THE THEORY OF THE LEISURE CLASS (1899).

[21] Alison L. Goodrum and Kevin J. Hunt, *The Field as Mall: Redressing the Rural-Urban Divide in Fashion Theory through Equestrian Events*, 4(1/2) CRITICAL STUDIES IN FASHION AND BEAUTY 17–42 (2013).

[22] CALEFATO, , *supra* note 2, at 16.

The corporation has approximately seven divisions dedicated to selling their menswear collections. They include: Purple Label, Black Label, Polo Ralph Lauren, Denim & Supply, Big & Tall, Golf, and RRL. Their RRL division (which stands for Ralph & Ricky Lauren) focuses on rich quality and an aura of authenticity, with each garment being designed and manufactured (by U.S. workers) based on historical ideals of early to mid-twentieth-century working-class styles.[23] With garments such as denim jeans ranging from $250 to $490, this brand attracts a luxury customer.

Eddie Ochoa, a sales professional for the company, states that he prefers working for this division because it represents an exclusive heritage line of clothing that is produced with very few stock keeping units (skus) being produced: "This allows for his customers to feel that they are buying an exclusive garment that no one else will have and allows them to feel special."[24] Additionally, the RRL clothing line is sold in very few of Ralph Lauren's retail outlets in order to keep its exclusivity.

Like most fashion lines, RRL situates the garments by using recurring visual themes embedded in the roots of American culture. Vintage and rare clothing items are sold and intermixed with this line in order to give the new clothes the same authenticity as those that are truly from the days of mid-century manufacturing; a vintage barn jacket from the 1950s sells for $1,250 next to a new barn jacket for $790. Most of this clothing line utilizes styles from the army, the navy, blue-collar workers, ranchers, and the American cowboy. The use of these mimetic themes contextualizes the brand, allowing it to completely appear as if it is authentic and from the time period it represents.[25] In Figure 2.1, the visual interplay among visual props, images, vintage clothing, and new clothing creates new ideological connections regarding Western wear and the American cowboy. With the blatant use of the American cowboy featured prominently in the center, the consumer knows this display is about Western wear. But Ralph Lauren's mixing of garments allows for new interpretations for what his brand feels should be men's Western apparel. For example, in Figure 2.1, the body form seen on the left mixes men's fashion elements such as a straw cowboy hat, barn jacket, denim vest, print-inspired Navajo print T-shirt, and cargo shorts. While historically, a cowboy hat, denim vest, and barn jacket may have been worn together, Lauren's addition of a print-inspired Navajo T and white cargo shorts makes this particular look his own interpretation of contemporary urban cowboy fashion.

One way of fostering a sense of authenticity is through semiotic linkages and references to history. Another way of doing so is to highlight the materiality of the product itself, along with wearers' stories of use and functionality. This latter approach has been

---

[23] Ralph Lauren, Ralph Lauren (2007).

[24] Eddie Ochoa, personal communication (2013).

[25] Kevin Matthews, Joseph H. Hancock, and Zhaohui Gu, *Rebranding American Men's Heritage Fashions through the Use of Visual Merchandising, Symbolic Props and Masculine Iconic Memes Historically Found in Popular Culture*, 1(1) Critical Studies in Men's Fashion 39–58 (2014).

FIGURE 2.1 Ralph Lauren Double RL Company store in New York's Nolita Area. Note the various Western icons and the blatant use of the cowboy as a marker of acceptable men's fashion. Photo courtesy of Kevin Matthews and Joseph Hancock, 2012. All Rights Reserved.

employed by active sportswear companies. One example of a new (one-year-old) company using this approach effectively is Kitsbow, whose mixed shell jacket was cited by *Outdoor* as among the "top mountain biking gear for winter 2013"[26] and by *Bike Magazine* as "perhaps the greatest piece of mountain bike attire I've ever used ... The cut is sublime and the style is subdued ... The fabrics are superior, the cut is without comparison, and the attention to detail is phenomenal."[27]

In personal interviews, the Kitsbow founders talk about their product in very tactile, embodied ways, describing: the use of ultimate fabrics with functional properties (e.g., warm yet lightweight, water resistant, anti-microbial properties), superb fit (with multiple fit blocks designed for diverse body types), and attention to detail (e.g., cover-stitched, rearward-facing seams; seam finishes; reflective elements for visibility; and in the shorts, an articulated, quilted waistband, shown in Figure 2.2). The clothes are designed to feel pleasurable (and even to become so comfortable as to become un-noticed) when mountain biking.

---

[26] Aaron Gulley, *The Cycle Life: Top Mountain Biking Gear for Winter 2013*, OUTDOOR, http://www.outsideonline.com/outdoor-gear/cycle-life/The-Cycle-Life-Top-MTB-Gear-for-Winter-2013.html#gallery-photo-10

[27] Seb Kemp, Review, *Kitsbow Mixed Shell Jacket: Is It as Good as It Looks?*, BIKE MAGAZINE, http://www.bikemag.com/gear/review-kitsbow-mixed-shell-jacket/.

FIGURE 2.2 This image features the inside of Kitsbow's "Soft Shell A/M Shorts" ($269). The Swiss-produced (Schoeller) fabric has a "lightly brushed interior" and is abrasion-resistant, water-resistant, and highly breathable. The short seams are covered and finished, and the waistband is contoured, articulated and quilted: it "sits naturally above your pelvic bone" to ensure "complete coverage and comfort" (www.kitsbow.com). Photo by Rodger Hostetler. Photo courtesy of Kitsbow.

When asked about the concept of luxury, both Kitsbow founders, Zander Nosler and Charlie Cronk, express hesitancy: "It is sort of a difficult concept for us."[28] "It would make us sound a little full of ourselves."[29] They prefer to use other concepts to characterize their products through their relation to mountain biking: passion, quality, performance, and comfort. While the fabrics do have a "luxurious hand" or tactile feel,[30] Kitsbow does not tend to market itself as a luxury brand. Simply put, the company aims to provide the very best mountain biking apparel on the market, to improve the experience of the sport: a passion for both Nosler and Cronk. They attribute the relatively high price points ($269 for shorts, $369 for a mixed-shell jacket, $265 for a jersey) to the quality of the materials and the manufacturing (by a factory in Vancouver, British Columbia, with garment workers featured on the website), the excellent fit, and the attention to detail, rather than on luxury branding, which would be "a little frivolous."[31]

The authenticity of the Kitsbow products resides in the experiences of users, who the company hopes will discover the "hidden comfort" features for themselves. For example, in March 2013, Kitsbow sponsored a group of male mountain bikers, in their mid-thirties, on a "cycling adventure tour" in British Columbia. The bikers faced bad weather for ten days and spent six to eight hours per day in Kitsbow apparel. The feedback the company

[28] Zander Nosler, personal communication (2013).
[29] Charlie Cronk, personal communication (2013).
[30] Zander Nosler, personal communication (2013).
[31] Charlie Cronk, personal communication (2013).

received was that the bikers "felt great" and "at peace with nature"; they were not conscious of pulling or tugging, and they remained warm and dry in drizzly conditions. According to Cronk, they felt "respected as knowledgeable cyclists" when they went into bike stores and also felt comfortable wearing the jersey and jacket to dinner, given the classic menswear styling and the fabrics' resistance to taking on odors (due to the antimicrobial features). In other words, physically and psychologically, they felt comfortable wearing these clothes for days on end.

Kitsbow highlights value in terms of material functionality and user comfort, whereas Ralph Lauren Double RL tells stories of historical authenticity. Yet both brands offer consumers ideas or dreams about how to perform authentically. Of course, not everyone can afford the brands, so the audience or consumer base becomes limited by the costs of materials and labor, design expertise, and customer service. However, there still may be a space for sports or fashion enthusiasts to invest in pieces (e.g., one pair of shorts, one T-shirt, one pair of sunglasses) of what they might imagine as "luxury" on a personal level: doing what one loves to do or wants to become in the clothes that help to make this possible as a consumer.

To the extent that luxury "divides,"[32] however, there is still the question of who becomes "qualified" to consume luxury in the cultural imaginary. How do issues of class, "race," nation, gender, sexuality, and other subject positions intervene?

III. Luxury and Social Justice

In *From Goods to a Good Life: Intellectual Property and Global Justice*, Madhavi Sunder explores the link between goods and social justice.[33] Her discussion of social justice, together with issues of production, distribution, and consumption contribute to our understanding of the interplay between luxury and social justice. With some exceptions (e.g., Kitsbow and Ralph Lauren's Double RL line), "luxury" apparel companies may not really want consumers to think about material qualities, factories, garment labor and so on. A disconnect may exist between the conspicuous leisure of a luxury image and the (inconspicuous) labor required to make a luxury product.

Social justice issues also apply in the realm of consumption. For centuries, the elite or aristocratic classes (e.g., royalty) have passed sumptuary laws to confine luxury apparel (e.g., certain furs, laces, dyes, collars) to their own use.[34] So, even if an individual from the merchant class, for example, is able to obtain a certain luxury item, it would technically

[32] CALEFATO, *supra* note 2, at 36.

[33] MADHAVI SUNDER, FROM GOODS TO A GOOD LIFE: INTELLECTUAL PROPERTY AND GLOBAL JUSTICE (2012).

[34] *See* THE FASHION HISTORY READER: GLOBAL PERSPECTIVES (Giorgio Riello and Peter Mcneil eds., 2010).

be illegal. Although such laws have historically been difficult to enforce, they have made claims to "legitimate" luxury clear in terms of power dynamics.

Some semblance of the exclusionary logic surrounding sumptuary laws remains in contemporary luxury retail settings. The question of who luxury goods are "for" continues: at the time of this writing, a controversy is brewing regarding the luxury New York City retailer, Barneys, who made the news for racially profiling a young African American male customer. The customer, Trayon Christian, a college student, had purchased a $349 Salvatore Ferragamo belt (for which he had been saving from his part-time job) with his debit card at Barneys. Christian had been wanting the belt since he had seen Harlem rapper Juelz Santana wearing it. After Christian left the store with his belt, he was stopped and questioned by undercover officers: how could he afford to purchase such an expensive belt? The officers handcuffed him and took him to the police station while they checked his debit card, which the police found to be legitimate.

Coincidentally, Barneys had recently entered an arrangement with African American rapper Jay Z (born Shawn Corey Carter). Jay Z was curating a holiday collection of luxury clothes and accessories with Barneys, and a promotional launch of the collaboration was scheduled for November 20, 2013. The event would triple-bill Barneys, New York City, and Jay Z's fashion label (Shawn Carter). The luxury products curated by Jay Z ranged from a $70 T-shirt to a $33,900 watch (with Carter's logo on the face) manufactured by the luxury Swiss company, Hublot, part of the LVMT conglomerate:

> Let 2013 be remembered as the year that Jay Z's releasing a holiday collection in collaboration with Barneys, and also, the year young black men still couldn't go into Barneys to buy luxury items without being questioned by store employees and cops.[35]

In cultural studies terms, there was a "disconnect" in the circuit of culture:[36] between the cultural representation of the new "urban" luxury "brand" and consumption in the store ("shopping while black"). Barneys had indicated that its intent in collaborating with Jay Z was to expand its "urban" (i.e., hip hop) appeal and expand its customer

[35] Matt Welty, Foster Kamer, and James Harris. *Barneys and NYPD Falsely Accuse Black Teen of Fraudulent Luxury Belt Purchase*, COMPLEX STYLE, October 23, 2013, http://www.complex.com, accessed October 28, 2013. It may well be that the collaboration between Barneys and Jay Z was, in part, an attempt to render visibility to African-American luxury consumption (and to increase sales), but if this was the goal, something seems to have been missing in the delivery of the collaboration.

[36] In cultural studies, the circuit of culture analyzes the dynamic interplay among issues of production, representation, consumption, identity, and regulation for any cultural product or text. (*See* PAUL DU GAY, STUART HALL, LINDA JONES, HUGH MACKAY, AND KEITH NEGUS, DOING CULTURAL STUDIES: THE STORY OF THE SONY WALKMAN [1997].) For an adaptation of the circuit of culture model for fashion studies, including a discussion of the "disconnect" or rupture that occurs between production and consumption in the context of global capitalism, see SUSAN B. KAISER, FASHION AND CULTURAL STUDIES (2012).

base. Semiotically, branding Barneys, New York City, and Jay Z's fashion label (Carter) together (with a festive black, silver, and gold holiday color scheme) conveys that luxury transcends "race," but socially, racial profiling still exists. From a social justice perspective, one might ask: if luxury is about want over need, then who deserves (earns the right) to have their desires met? The everyday in-store regulatory practices (based on racist assumptions) harken back to the sumptuary laws of the fourteenth and fifteenth centuries, signaling that it is not sufficient to be able to afford certain luxuries; luxury is reserved for the select few with the power to demarcate their superiority. The idea (perhaps still?) is that one needs to be born into the culture of luxury, and cannot easily acquire it through democracy or meritocracy via capitalism, especially if one does not "look the part."

In London, the *Daily Mail* coverage of the story—complete with a video interview with Christian and his mother on the website—included an interview with the African American male supermodel Tyson Beckford, who became famous in 1993 when he became the face of Ralph Lauren's Polo line. Beckford indicated that despite having one of the most recognizable faces in this world, he still gets racially profiled when shopping at Barneys and other luxury stores.[37]

A London-based Indian and Jewish reader of the *Daily Mail* story comments online that the experience of racial profiling affects non-white shoppers in general and suggests: "Do your shopping online and maintain your dignity."[38] Yet, is cultural invisibility/anonymity the solution? Is it better for African American (and other) consumers, for example, to step up and confront situations of social injustice? Or, would it be better to boycott and shop online in ways that enable the preservation of a sense of dignity?

Face-to-face interactions become a key factor in brick-and-mortar retail luxury culture, if not in retail settings in general. A *Huffington Post Business* article details the "insider culture" at Barneys (and other high-end retailers), pointing to an institutionalized way of systematically labeling certain customers as (a) not worthy of attention (in a highly competitive environment, in which a significant portion of compensation is based on commission) and/or (b) "suspicious" and as not belonging in the setting (e.g., "shopping while black"; further, incentives may go to those retail workers who help to combat shoplifting or credit card fraud). Hence, the stage is set for racial profiling on one level or another. Nearly a thousand responders to the article wonder—alternatively and collectively—what motivates luxury-retail workers; why African American consumers would subject themselves to such scrutiny; why college students would desire, and invest

[37] Daily Mail Reporters, *Male Supermodel Tyson Beckford Says He Gets Racially Profiled "All the Time" in Barney's as Row Rumbles on Over Two Customers Who Say They Were Stopped Because They Were Black*, October 25, 2013, http://www.dailymail.co.uk/news/article-2476928/Male-supermodel-Tyson-Beckford-says-gets-racially-profiled-time-Barneys-row-rumbles-customers-say-stopped-black.html, accessed October 29, 2013.

[38] *Id.*

in, luxury goods in the first place; where the luxury goods are made and how much they actually cost to produce; and whether institutionalized racism in retail settings is confined to luxury contexts.[39]

Related to the question of in-store (and outside-store "stop and frisk") dynamics is the issue of Jay Z's collaboration with Barneys. If Barneys is trying to expand its profit margin through this partnership, then how is the luxury retailer planning to manage its interactions in the store? More than 16,000 individuals signed onto a petition demanding Jay Z's withdrawal from his collaboration with Barneys. Comedian Jon Stewart, on his nightly *Daily Show*, acknowledged that Jay Z was in an awkward predicament, but insisted that it is "not as awkward a position as sitting handcuffed in the back of a police car" after "shopping while black." Satirically, the *Daily Show*'s "black news correspondent" Larry Wilmore "defended" Jay Z, saying that he has a multi-million dollar brand to protect (as Jay Z is now "Jay Z Penney"), but then Wilmore went on to say: "Make up your mind, America. You can't tell brothers to pull up our pants [a reference to cultural anxieties about hip-hop-influenced "sagging" pants] and then arrest us when we buy a belt."[40]

Jay Z announced a few days before the holiday opening that he would continue the collaboration with Barneys under the condition that he would demonstrate leadership in the review of the store's policies. He planned to donate 100% of the sales to his charitable foundation, which funds education for under-privileged youth. Barneys also committed an additional 10% of all Barneys sales during the November 20, 2013, launch day, and guaranteed at least $1 million.[41]

IV. Conclusion: A Touch of Luxe?

Can luxury become an accessible, democratic concept? Perhaps it is because of the layers of cultural baggage associated with the concept that shopping websites such as Rue La La gingerly use the term French word "luxe" instead, to connote luxury without invoking its full weight in English. As we have seen, individual consumers may work "a touch of luxe" into their wardrobes with accessories (e.g., belts, sunglasses, boots) or individual garments (e.g., T-shirt, mountain bike shorts), even if they cannot afford head-to-toe "luxury."

---

[39] Kim Bhasin and Julee Wilson, *Barneys Racist Culture Deeply Ingrained in Store, Insiders Say*. Huffington Post Business, November 7, 2013, http://www.huffingtonpost.com/2013/11/07/barneys-racist_n_4225710.html, accessed November 7, 2013.

[40] Ginger Adams Otis, *"Daily Show" Belts Barneys Partner Jay Z Over Shopper Racial Profiling Claims*, New York Daily News, November 7, 2013, http://www.nydailynews.com/entertainment/daily-show-belts-bjay-z-barneys-profiling-claims-article-1.1510368, accessed November 8, 2013.

[41] Associated Press, *Jay Z Says He'll Continue Barneys Collaboration*, http://www.npr.org/templates/story/story.php?storyId=245505688, accessed November 18, 2013.

Ultimately, however, luxury is a difficult concept. Its inclusion of everything "and its opposite"[42] calls for both/and interpretations. What is the potential, for example, for shared space between desire, on the one hand, and extreme comfort/functionality, on the other? One such space, we contend, is performativity: the process of "doing" and constructing identity in a highly embodied way—whether styling on the street or in a nightclub, chopping wood in a tutu and boots, outfitting one's "kit" for a mountain biking adventure, or so on. Embodied performativity involves more than experiencing an "act" for others: it includes mind and body; personal comfort and tactile sensations in a given social situation and physical environment; and feelings of a certain degree of well-being, pride, and sense of belonging. Wearing "a touch of luxe" in one's own way, on one's own terms, may contribute to tactile as well as social pleasure. Mixing pieces of luxury-branded apparel into one's look may also have financial benefits over head-to-toe branding and help to avoid the rather decadent connotations of luxury introduced at the beginning of this chapter.

Producers/retailers cannot fully anticipate how consumers will aim to perform their identities and activities through their products—as a whole (head to toe) or in part (as a piece)—but they (together with their marketers) construct stories and scenarios to supply potential seeds for consumers' imaginations regarding what they can do and how they can be/become. There are still limits to the enactments of these imaginations, however, as in the case of "shopping while black."

In Calefato's book, she self-reflexively acknowledges her own ambivalence about luxury fashion: her love/hate relationship with it. Inasmuch as luxury both promises and divides, its incorporation of everything and its opposite (luxury and branding, luxury and authenticity, luxury and social justice) keeps luxury an ambivalent concept. Luxury becomes highly contextual as it circulates in a globalized economy across consumers' bodies and performances. In this sense, "pieces of luxe" occupy diverse and ambiguous spaces, the meanings of which are negotiated not only by luxury brand storytelling, but also by consumers seeking to derive pleasure, even as they navigate the ambivalent terrain of luxury.

---

[42] CALEFATO, *supra* note 2, at 15, 37.

3 The Story of Luxury Products and the (Broken) Promise of Superior Quality in a World of Prestige for the Masses

Irene Calboli*

I. Introduction

In this chapter, I address the legal protection of luxury trademarks. These marks are frequently protected not only against trademark infringement, but also against trademark dilution because (in several instances) they are considered to be famous marks. More specifically, I address the relationship between this protection (that is, against trademark infringement *and* dilution) and the promise of superior quality that luxury products generally convey to the public. Superior product quality represents indeed the foundation upon which the luxury industry built itself and the reason many luxury trademarks became famous, thus the reason that justifies, in theory, anti-dilution protection for these marks.[1] In my analysis I focus, however, on the evolution of the luxury industry

* Lee Kong Chian Fellow and Deputy Director, Applied Research Centre for Intellectual Assets and the Law in Asia (ARCIALA), School of Law, Singapore Management University; Professor of Law, Texas A&M University School of Law. I thank Barton Beebe, Madhavi Sunder, and Haochen Sun for their feedback on a previous draft of this chapter. I am also grateful to Graeme Dinwoodie and Dan Hunter for insightful comments on my research in this area. Additional thanks are due to Elizabeth Kendall, who provided excellent research and editorial assistance. Any mistake or omission remains my own.

[1] The Oxford Dictionary defines "luxury" as "a state of great comfort or elegance, especially when involving great expense," or "an inessential, desirable item which is expensive or difficult to obtain," and "a pleasure

and its progressive shift away from products of superior quality toward embracing also a culture of prestige for the masses, or "*masstige*"[2]—a certainly more profitable aim, but one less focused on a tradition of superior product quality, and in turn less deserving of anti-dilution protection.

As several scholars have noted, in the past decades, luxury trademarks have gradually transformed from the indicators of *objets de luxe*—meticulously made, frequently by hand, by master artisans—into the ambassadors, or often merely the advertisers, of the products mass-marketed worldwide by multinational luxury conglomerates. These conglomerates have replaced or swallowed many of the historic luxury *maisons* and, in turn, have fundamentally changed the business model and the traditional rules that governed the luxury industry in the past. In particular, besides producing high-end and superior-quality luxury products, these new luxury corporations have become increasingly more receptive to downward brand extension or "pyramidal" luxury. Thus, they have extended their operations to mid- and entry-level market sectors, and to collateral and promotional (luxury) products, catering to a continually growing consumer base of would-be luxury fans. As a result, instead of continuing to indicate the origin and superior quality of products meticulously and selectively produced as they did in the past, luxury trademarks have increasingly morphed today into messengers of an aura of luxury-at-large, and even into the objects of public desire in and of themselves (consumers dress in the logos, which are prominently displayed in the clothes, handbags, and so forth), often regardless of the actual quality of the products that the marks identify.

Yet, this transformation of luxury trademarks, from indicators of exclusive products of superior quality into messengers of an aura of luxury and into the objects of desire per se, begs some important questions regarding the legal protection granted to these trademarks, particularly with respect to anti-dilution protection. Notably, in this new luxury economy of luxury-at-large and *masstige*—in which the same trademarks identify both ultra-luxury products and ordinary items prominently displaying luxury trademarks on their packaging—what is left of the promise of consistently superior product quality that has traditionally represented the raison d'être of the additional legal protection granted to famous luxury trademarks?

---

obtained only rarely." *See Luxury*, Oxford Dictionaries, http://www.oxforddictionaries.com/definition/english/luxury. In this chapter I do not elaborate on the many nuances of the word "luxury" as applied to the luxury industry today. Instead, I consider luxury products those products that "have more than necessary and ordinary characteristics compared to other products of their category, which include their relatively high level of price, quality, aesthetics, rarity, extraordinariness, and symbolic meaning." Klaus Hein, *The Concept of Luxury Brands, in* LUXURY BRAND MANAGEMENT, 2012, http://www.conceptofluxurybrands.com/concept/luxury-product-definition.

[2] The word "*masstige*" was first used by Silverstein and Fiske to identify goods that "occupy a sweet spot between mass and class." *See* Michael J. Silverstein & Neil Fiske, *Luxury for the Masses*, 81 HARV. BUS. REV. 48, 49 (Apr. 2003). *See generally* MICHAEL J. SILVERSTEIN & NEIL FISKE, TRADING UP: WHY CONSUMERS WANT NEW LUXURY GOODS AND HOW COMPANIES CREATE THEM 1 (2005).

As noted by several scholars, the answer to this question is that the difference between luxury products and ordinary products today is most often negligent or nonexistent for mass-produced *masstige* products such as luxury eau de toilette, eyewear, smart-phone cases, and so forth. Only the difference in the quality of high-end luxury products and ordinary products remains considerable; for example, a Vacheron Constantin, a Patek Philippe, or a Jaeger-LeCoultre luxury watch continue to be exceptional timepieces in terms of craftsmanship, materials, performance, and duration compared to other watches. Still, in many instances, consumers are attracted to high-end luxury products also due to nonfunctional factors. This is due to the rise of the luxury trademarks as symbols of status and wealth per se. Consumers desire these products to dress in the logos regardless of whether these products are high-end or *masstige* products. In other words, consumers are attracted both to the luxury eyewear and luxury watch also, if not primarily because of the messages that these products, via the attached luxury trademarks, can communicate to third parties who see the buyers wearing these products.[3] Called the "Veblen effect" after the American economist and sociologist Thorstein Veblen,[4] this nonfunctional and status-signaling effect of luxury trademarks has been generally explained by recalling people's desire to signal wealth and social status "by conspicuous consumption," that is, by showing the possession of material wealth through products indicating superior social standing, such as the luxury products identified by these marks.[5]

Legal scholars have traditionally shown skepticism toward this status- and exclusivity-signaling function of luxury trademarks. More specifically, scholars have repeated that it is not the role of trademark law to protect this function.[6] Despite these objections, however, trademark law seems to have increasingly shifted toward (also) protecting this status with anti-dilution protection. Notably, due to the transformation of the luxury industry from one based on superior product quality to an industry based

---

[3] *See* Jeffrey L. Harrison, *Trademark Law and Status Signaling: Tattoos for the Privileged*, 58 FLA. L. REV. 195, 196 (2007); Laurie Simon Bagwell & B. Douglas Bernheim, *Veblen Effects in a Theory of Conspicuous Consumption*, 86 AM. ECON. REV. 349 (1996); Russell W. Belk, *Possessions and the Extended Self*, 15 J. CONSUMER RES. 139 (1988); William O. Bearden & Michael J. Etzel, *Reference Group Influence on Product and Brand Purchase Decisions*, 9 J. CONSUMER RES. 9 (1982).

[4] *See* THORSTEIN VEBLEN, THE THEORY OF THE LEISURE CLASS (Houghton Mifflin 1973) (1899); ROGER MASON, THE ECONOMICS OF CONSPICUOUS CONSUMPTION: THEORY AND THOUGHT SINCE 1700 (1998).

[5] The literature on this topic is extensive. *See, e.g.*, B. Curtis Eaton & Mukesh Eswaran, *Well-Being and Affluence in the Presence of a Veblen Good*, 119 ECON. J. 1088 (2009); Harvey Leibenstein, *Bandwagon, Snob, and Veblen Effects in the Theory of Consumers' Demand*, 64 Q.J. ECON. 183 (1950); Aron O'Cass & Hmily Frost, *Status Brands: Examining the Effects of Non-Product-Related Brand Associations on Status and Conspicuous Consumption*, 11 J. PRODUCT & BRAND MGMT. 67 (2002).

[6] *See* Harrison, *supra* note 3, at 210–26. Harrison states specifically that "[t]he movement of trademark law into the area of interpersonal signaling about status cannot be supported by notion of efficiency nor by appeals to moral rights consistent with either Rawlsian or Lockean theory." *Id.* at 227. *See also* Jeremy N. Sheff, *Veblen Brands*, 96 MINN. L. REV. 769, 794 (2012); Glynn S. Lunney Jr., *Trademark Monopolies*, 48 EMORY L.J. 367, 404–8 (1999).

also, if not primarily in certain instances, on an aura of luxury-at-large, the rationale for protecting famous luxury trademarks against dilution has clearly departed from the traditional objective of such protection—protecting the marks against the "whittling away" of their uniqueness.[7] Instead, anti-dilution protection has translated into also, if not primarily, protecting this status and exclusivity-signaling function.[8] Hence, where it was already challenging to justify anti-dilution protection for marks identifying selectively made products of superior quality—anti-dilution protection has always been an odd addition to the pro-competitive objectives of trademark law—it is even more challenging to justify this protection for symbols of pyramidal luxury and *masstige*.

In this chapter, I agree with the scholarly critique against this protection and argue that luxury conglomerates should not be entitled to claim protection against dilution of their marks when they themselves regularly "whittle away," or self-dilute, the uniqueness of their marks through numerous brand extensions to gain more profits.[9] Yet, I also posit whether this protection could be justified for marks that identify the products of those few luxury *maisons*, both old and new, that continue to invest in superior product quality and produce exclusively in high-end markets without engaging in brand extension. In particular, my considerations focus on the public benefits that these luxury *maisons* may offer to society as a whole with their business model of limited quantity and superior quality of their products compared to the business model of luxury conglomerates of pyramidal luxury and mass-produced *masstige* products.

More specifically, in section II, I recount the history of the luxury industry and the changes that have affected it after the rise of luxury conglomerates, the villains in this

---

[7] The expression "whittle away" comes from Frank Schechter, who famously defined "dilution" as "the gradual whittling away or dispersion of the identity and hold upon the public mind of the mark or name by its use upon non-competing goods." *See* Frank I. Schechter, *The Rational Basis of Trademark Protection*, 40 HARV. L. REV. 813, 825. (1926–1927). Schechter promoted in the United States the idea initially developed in Germany that "[t]he true functions ... are, then, to identify a product as satisfactory and thereby to stimulate further purchases by the consuming public." *Id.* at 818. For a detailed critique of Schechter's argument, see Barton Beebe, *The Suppressed Misappropriation Origins of Trademark Antidilution Law: The Landgericht Elberfeld's* Odol *Opinion and Frank Schechter's* The Rational Basis of Trademark Protection, *in* INTELLECTUAL PROPERTY AT THE EDGE: THE CONTESTED CONTOURS OF IP (Rochelle C. Dreyfuss & Jane C. Ginsburg eds., 2014) (stressing how Schechter intentionally omitted from his recount of the dilution doctrine in the United States the fact that the German court applied it as a course of action against conducts contrary to good morals).

[8] *See* Harrison, *supra* note 3, at 198. In general, the literature on trademark dilution is very extensive. *See, e.g.*, Sandra L. Rierson, *The Myth and Reality of Dilution*, 11 DUKE L. & TECH. REV. 212 (2012); Laura Bradford, *Emotion, Dilution, and the Trademark Consumer*, 23 BERKELEY TECH. L.J. 1227 (2008); Clarisa Long, *Dilution*, 106 COLUM. L. REV. 1029 (2006).

[9] For a detailed argument contending that a dilution cause of action should be unavailable to trademark holders who have extended their marks so broadly that they have diluted the distinctiveness of their marks, see Sara Stadler Nelson, *The Wages of Ubiquity in Trademark Law*, 88 IOWA L. REV. 731, 732 (2003); Lauranne Buchanan et al., *Brand Equity Dilution: Retailer Display and Context Brand Effects*, 36 J. MARKETING RES. 345 (1999); Elizabeth C. Bannon, *The Growing Risk of Self-Dilution*, 82 TRADEMARK REP. 570 (1992).

story. In section III, I review important changes in trademark law and policy in the areas of trademark transactions, the scope of trademark protection, as well as protectable subject matter, and I highlight how these changes permitted the construction of the new mass-market oriented luxury economy. In section IV, in light of the intentional choice of many luxury corporations to prefer quantity and mass profits, I argue that these marks, used to identify *masstige* products or varieties of luxury products across different levels of the luxury pyramids, do not deserve to be protected against dilution because they are no longer unique. In section V, I conclude the chapter and support that a grant of anti-dilution protection could still be justified for marks that identify high-quality products made by those few luxury *maisons* that continue the tradition of high-quality and selective production. Notably, I consider that these *maisons* bring a variety of benefits to society as a whole—they contribute to incentivizing a culture of high-quality materials and to conserving traditional manufacturing (including hand-made production) techniques while also pioneering innovative technologies and styles for the general industries. Still, also in these instances, the application of anti-dilution protection should remain a very seldom occurrence, as the traditional confusion-based infringement action is sufficient to protect also these luxury these marks in most instances. Likewise, anti-dilution protection should not foreclose unauthorized descriptive, comparative, and parody or other free-speech-related uses of these (or any other) luxury marks.

II. The Story of Luxury Products from Promises of Superior Quality to Symbols (Also) of Prestige for the Masses

The story of luxury products is the story of the making, selling, and owning of objects of desire.[10] The idea of luxury is as ancient as humans themselves, and luxury is an expression of the human desire to own beautiful and precious things. Since the appearance of the very first civilizations, kings and aristocrats—the rich and powerful of those times—attracted the best craftsmen to their palaces to create precious artifacts. They then used these artifacts, some of which we can admire today in museums across the globe, for both their personal hedonic satisfaction and for signaling wealth, status, and power to others. This model, based on luxury products made for the rich and fortunate few, continued throughout many centuries, even though the number of these fortunate rich slowly grew due to the rise of a less aristocratic but increasingly richer class of merchants, starting in the Middle Ages. The Industrial Revolution partially changed this idea of luxury that was reserved only for the elite few, because it brought changes to the

[10] For a historical reconstruction of the meaning of luxury throughout history, see CHRISTOPHER J. BERRY, THE IDEA OF LUXURY: A CONCEPTUAL AND HISTORICAL INVESTIGATION (1994). *See also* MICHAEL KWASS, LUXURY IN THE EIGHTEENTH CENTURY: DEBATES, DESIRES AND DELECTABLE GOODS (2002); THE FASHION BUSINESS. THEORY, PRACTICE, IMAGE (Nicola White & Ian Griffiths eds., 2000).

traditional division of social classes, in particular the creation of a larger and more affluent bourgeoisie, which became able and willing to purchase high-quality products.[11] It was precisely during the late 1800s and early 1900s that talented and innovative artisans, designers, and technicians conceived, created, and brought to the market innovative luxury products. The creations made by these new artists of fashion and design such as Coco Chanel, Guccio Gucci, Mario Prada, Louis Vuitton, Ferruccio Lamborghini, and Enzo Ferrari (who sold road cars to fund his dream, the Ferrari racing team or "Scuderia Ferrari") combined meticulous craftsmanship with high-quality materials.[12] Despite the new possibility of utilizing machines, many of these products were still made in whole or in part by hand, and to order. Thanks to the high quality of their products, their business savvy, and perhaps some luck, many of these artisans and designers established themselves as icons of post–Industrial Revolution luxury, and many of their brands continue to be acclaimed in today's luxury landscape.

Certainly, as the kings and aristocrats did before, members of the elite class purchased the products made by these new luxury designers not only because of their high quality but also to signal status and wealth. It was precisely during these times that economists and sociologists started to take note of and analyze this phenomenon, probably due to its growing influence on the purchasing behaviors (or purchasing desires) of a larger share of the population. As I mentioned in the introduction to this chapter, American scholar Thorstein Veblen labeled this phenomenon "conspicuous consumption" in his famous publication *The Theory of the Leisure Class*.[13] In his book, Veblen observed that individuals purchase luxury or similarly expensive products instead of more ordinary products of equivalent functionality as positional goods, that is, in order to signal economic power and accumulated wealth to others.[14] In the following and present centuries, academics debated and further analyzed this theory.[15] Trademark legal scholars in particular have generally supported the notion that trademark law has no place protecting this status-signaling function by granting extra protection to luxury trademarks, because trademark protection is supposed to focus on promoting efficiency in the market through protecting marks only when they provide consumers with information about the origin and quality of the marked products.[16]

---

[11] *See, e.g.*, Michael T. Ryan, *Consumption, in* The Blackwell Encyclopedia of Sociology 701 (George Ritzer ed., 2007).

[12] *See* Valerie Steele, Fashion Italian Style (2003); Luigi Settembrini, *From Haute Couture to Pret-a-Porter, in* The Italian Metamorphosis 482 (Germano Celant ed., 1994).

[13] Veblen, *supra* note 4.

[14] Veblen, *supra* note 4, at 42.

[15] *See, e.g.*, Wilfred Amaldoss & Sanjay Jain, *Conspicuous Consumption and Sophisticated Thinking*, 51 Mgmt. Sci. 1449 (2005); sources cited *supra* note 6.

[16] *See* Sheff, *supra* note 6, at 818–19; Harrison, *supra* note 3, at 198. *See also* Barton Beebe, *Intellectual Property and the Sumptuary Code*, 123 Harvard L. Rev. 809, 821–30 (2010) [hereinafter Beebe, *Sumptuary Code*]. Beebe notes, however, that "individuals seek a level of optimal distinctiveness that need not necessarily

Still, despite their undeniable Veblen effect, the products made by these early masters of modern luxury were of superior quality, in the higher attention to detail, longer product life, innovative designs and materials, and so on. This tradition of quality continued with the second generation of these luxury *maisons*. In most cases, the founding fathers and mothers of these *maisons* passed their businesses to family members who continued to produce the same, or largely similar or related products, with techniques that carefully balanced innovation and tradition. For several decades, these family-run luxury *maisons*, their products, and their trademarks have nurtured a culture of luxury products of superior quality and uniqueness. Throughout the years, other emerging designers joined this initial group—Giorgio Armani, Valentino Garavani, Gianni Versace, Domenico Dolce, and Stefano Gabbana are some of the new talents who have also established themselves as icons of high-quality and innovative designs.

Then, in the late 1980s and early 1990s, this business model based on individual designers and family-run luxury *maisons* was profoundly shaken by the emergence of large corporate actors in the luxury industry. The 1987 merger of the historical fashion house Louis Vuitton with Moët Hennessy—itself a merger between the champagne producer Moët & Chandon and the cognac producer Hennessy—signaled the beginning of a new era of luxury led by companies often listed in public stock markets and driven by the logic of short(er) term profits and accountability to shareholders rather than, or in addition to, superior product quality for consumers.[17] In this new era, family-run luxury *maisons* had to transform in order to survive within a global market, in which there is increasingly less space for a culture of small, artisanal, and traditional production. In particular, they had to convert to a process of fast(er) cycles and larger quantities in order to increase sales and profits. Unable to sustain this new rhythm, many family-run luxury *maisons* ultimately merged or sold control of their businesses, and their marks, to the emerging luxury mega-groups.[18] LVMH, led by luxury tycoon Bernard Arnault, established itself as one of the larger luxury groups, today controlling a number of luxury trademarks, including, among many others, Bulgari, Fendi, Loro Piana, Emilio Pucci, and TAG Heuer. Two other mega-groups also emerged: the French conglomerate Kering (formerly PPR)—today the owner of, inter alia, Gucci, Bottega Veneta, and Balenciaga—and the Swiss-based conglomerate Richemont, which controls luxury brands such as Cartier, Baume & Mercier, Jaeger-LeCoultre, and Officine Panerai. In addition to these luxury mega-corporations, other smaller national luxury groups formed during these years,

---

confer hierarchical status." Beebe, *Sumptuary Code*, at 822 (*quoting* ROBERT G. DUNN, IDENTIFYING CONSUMPTION 123 (2008)).

[17] A general overview of today's luxury industry is well presented in Claudia D'Arpizio, *Luxury Goods Worldwide Market Study Fall 2013*, BAIN (Oct. 28, 2013), http://www.bain.com/publications/articles/luxury-goods-worldwide-market-study-fall-2013.aspx.

[18] This appetite for existing labels continues to dominate the landscape today. *See* Astrid Wendlandt, *Small Labels Lure Big Bucks in Fashion's Latest Trend*, REUTERS (Mar. 13, 2013, 4:50 PM), http://www.reuters.com/article/2013/03/13/us-fashion-investment-idUSBRE92C0AV20130313.

such as the Valentino Fashion Group, which was created as a result of the transfer of the Valentino's fashion *maison*—first to the Italian conglomerate HdP in 1998 and later to the textile group Marzotto in 2002. Among the few luxury *maisons* that resisted mergers and takeovers, such as Prada and Ferragamo, some decided to list their companies in public stock markets in order to raise capital to expand and compete.[19] Others, such as Armani, Emenegildo Zegna, Chanel, and Dolce & Gabbana, resisted the attraction of public offering, and instead actively pursued a variety of brand extensions in order to market product lines under their trademarks in other sectors.[20]

As part of this general transformation of the luxury industry, the traditional role played by luxury trademarks also changed. Instead of indicators of the origin and quality of luxury products, luxury trademarks increasingly became assets per se, that is, a highly precious currency that luxury investors wanted to purchase (often in the stock market) to increase their luxury business portfolios. Luxury trademarks also became the vehicles through which luxury companies could conquer new markets, new consumers, and new profits. Gone was the traditional mentality of a few exclusive luxury products of superior quality; instead, luxury corporations started to seek new avenues in which to expand, and luxury trademarks facilitated this expansion through their ability to carry over the prestige embodied in the marks into larger and less exclusive market levels. Mid-level luxury lines such as Emporio Armani exemplified the trend of more accessible products that could attract a larger number of consumers who could not afford Giorgio Armani's high-end products, but who would choose Emporio Armani over similar clothes because the message that the name "Armani" still conveyed applied to these clothes.[21] Besides creating mid- or entry-level product lines, luxury corporations also branched off from their traditional sectors and began marketing accessory products—such as perfumes, eyewear, and office and home products. With these products, luxury corporations could increase their brand affiliation with existing customers—Giorgio Armani's customers could wear sunglasses and spray themselves with mists from their favorite designer—as well as meet new customers, who could now try and enjoy Armani's accessories and later buy his signature clothes or mid-level lines, or who could finally buy a piece of the Armani luxury thanks to the lower price of these accessories compared to the designer's clothes.

---

[19] *See* Kymberlee Fernandes, *Ferragamo, Prada Get IPO Valuations Worth Billions*, LUXPRESSO (June 2, 2011, 6:00 AM), http://luxpresso.com/news-lifestyle/ferragamo-prada-get-ipo-valuations-worth-billions/5395. When listed in Hong Kong, the Prada IPO was "five times oversubscribed." Garry White, *Prada's Hong Kong IPO Is "Five Times Oversubscribed,"* TELEGRAPH (June 12, 2011, 7:11 PM), http://www.telegraph.co.uk/finance/newsbysector/retailandconsumer/8571143/Pradas-Hong-Kong-IPO-is-five-times-oversubscribed.html.

[20] *See, e.g.*, Martin Roll, *Giorgio Armani—The Ultimate Fashion Brand*, VENTURE REPUBLIC, http://www.venturerepublic.com/resources/giorgio_armani_-_the_ultimate_fashion_brand.asp (last visited Feb. 19, 2014).

[21] *Id.*

In the past two decades, luxury companies (conglomerates and independent firms-turned-corporate entities) continued to follow this business model of expansion, both vertically with similar but less exclusive product lines and horizontally with new types of products. Still, under this redefinition of luxury, luxury conglomerates did not completely abandon the high-end side of the marketplace. Instead, they frequently adopted a pyramidal multilevel structure, with high-end exclusive goods at the top, and gradually less exclusive products, made with less detail, and sold less expensively to a larger number of consumers, at the mid- and lower-levels. Thanks to this pyramidal structure, luxury conglomerates could continue a tradition of prestige with only a few exclusive products of superior quality at the top of the pyramid, but also use this prestige to enhance the perceived value of their products across other market levels. Here again, luxury trademarks played a fundamental role in this process. By identifying luxury products throughout all levels of the luxury pyramid, they could carry the aura of luxury from the top of the pyramid down to the levels of *masstige* products. Still, luxury corporations use trademarks not only to unify their product lines, but also to differentiate them among the various levels of the luxury pyramid to avoid the negative effects of trademark vulgarization or overexposure of the luxury high-end marks. Giorgio Armani, Emporio Amani, Armani Junior, and Armani Casa identify very distinct product lines, gradually less prestigious and less expensive, but that are nonetheless united under the mark Armani. As I elaborate in the next section, luxury corporations very soon realized the power and importance of their marks in promoting their message of luxury into larger market sectors, and thus joined the calls from the rest of the business world for higher protection for trademarks in general.

III. The Journey of Trademark Law from Protecting Consumers to Facilitating Signaling Prestige for the Masses

As shown in section II, much of the transformation of the luxury industry, from individual and family-run luxury *maisons* (producing and distributing selective quantities of products, mostly directly) to luxury conglomerates (controlling the production of luxury goods made by a variety of licensees and destined to go to a variety of market sectors) heavily relied on a business model in which trademarks are considered business assets rather than merely indicators of commercial origin and quality. Not surprisingly, luxury trademark owners strongly supported trademark reforms focused on validating this business model through liberalizing the commercial exploitation of trademarks as well as enhancing trademark protection beyond the traditional confusion-based standard for trademark infringement.[22] In the present section, I highlight some of these reforms, particularly in the areas of trademark transactions, the scope of trademark protection,

[22] Throughout the years, individual luxury trademark owners as well as the International Trademark Association (INTA) have regularly supported positions favoring the expansion of trademark rights. *See, e.g.*, *Policy and Advocacy*, INTA, http://www.inta.org/Advocacy/Pages/main.aspx (last visited Feb. 19, 2014).

and the expansion of protectable subject matter.[23] Even though legal changes in these areas are known to trademark scholars, their analysis in this context is needed, as these changes invariably added legal support to the new luxury business model, in which exclusivity and superior product quality could be traded away for mass-production and profits, generally without any legal consequences for trademark owners.

In particular, even though trademark owners have historically desired to "trade in their trademarks" as independent business assets, trademark law traditionally subjected trademark transactions to specific requirements in order to avoid "trademark trafficking," which could result in consumer confusion as to the origin or quality of the products.[24] Notably, most national trademark laws prohibited trademark assignment "in gross" and required that trademarks be assigned along with the business, or the relevant part of the business, under which the products identified by the assigned marks were produced, or at least along with the goodwill of those marks.[25] In addition to restricting trademark assignment, many national laws and courts did not recognize the validity of trademark licensing for several decades, and when the practice finally became accepted they conditioned licenses' validity on trademark owners' control over the quality of the products produced by licensees.[26] Even more controversial was the practice of trademark merchandising, which still remains a source of heated debate. In particular, in several countries, the practice of using trademarks on promotional goods such as T-shirts or baseball hats without authorization was a common occurrence, and the courts often dismissed claims for trademark infringement, stating that consumers were not confused as to the origin of these products.[27]

Then, during the latter half of the past century, several of these requirements were abandoned as part of a wave of liberalization of trademark transactions, which included

---

[23] Trademark owners have also exercised pressure in other areas. For example, trademark owners oppose trademark exhaustion for luxury goods not only internationally, but also domestically when unauthorized sales can be prejudicial for the allure and prestige that is usually attached to the marks. *See* Irene Calboli, *Reviewing the (Shrinking) Principle of Trademark Exhaustion in the European Union (Ten Years Later)*, 16 MARQ. INTELL. PROP. L. REV. 257, 264 (2012). Additionally, trademark owners have supported the introduction of an ad hoc duty of care for intermediaries beyond the current standards for secondary trademark liability on the Internet. *See* the various contributions in the symposium *Who's Left Holding the [Brand Name] Bag? Secondary Liability for Trademark Infringement on the Internet*, 37 COLUM. J.L. & ARTS (2014).

[24] For more in this respect, see Nathan Isaacs, *Traffic in Trade-Symbols*, 44 HARV. L. REV. 1210, 1210 (1931); 2 J. THOMAS MCCARTHY, MCCARTHY ON TRADEMARKS AND UNFAIR COMPETITION § 18:3 (4th ed. 2013).

[25] *See generally* WORLDWIDE TRADEMARK TRANSFERS: LAW AND PRACTICE (Susan Barbieri Montgomery & Richard J. Taylor eds., 1992).

[26] *See generally* NEIL J. WILKOF & DANIEL BURKITT, TRADE MARK LICENSING (2005).

[27] For a critique of the practice in the United States, see Stacey L. Dogan & Mark A. Lemley, *The Merchandising Right: Fragile Theory or* Fait Accompli?, 54 EMORY L.J. 461 (2005). For an argument that marks used to identify promotional products still fulfill the distinctive trademark function, and thus should be protected as any other mark, see Irene Calboli, *The Case for a Limited Protection of Trademark Merchandising*, 2011 U. ILL. L. REV. 865 (2011).

legislative amendments or the gradual weakening of the existing requirements through broad judicial interpretations by national courts.[28] The adoption of the Agreement on Trade-Related Aspects on Intellectual Property Rights (TRIPs) in the early 1990s validated this system of flexible trademark transactions at the international level.[29] In particular, Article 21 of TRIPs removed the requirement that trademarks should be assigned with the related business and confirmed the validity of trademark licensing.[30] As I elaborate below, the adoption of Article 16.3, which prohibits the use of well-known marks, or similar signs, for non-similar products also helped validate the practice of trademark merchandising in all TRIPs members.[31]

In addition to liberalizing trademark transactions, recent legal reforms profoundly changed the scope of trademark protection, especially for famous marks. Famous marks have enjoyed some enhanced protection since 1925 with the Hague Revision of the Paris Convention for the Protection of Industrial Property, where member countries adopted Article *6bis*, which mandates that members refuse or cancel the registration, or prohibit the use of a mark that "constitute[s] a reproduction, an imitation, or a translation, liable to create confusion, of a mark considered by the competent authority of the country of registration or use to be well-known in that country."[32] Still, for decades, the business world pressured lawmakers to introduce protection against trademark dilution—the loss

---

[28] In previous works however, I have argued that these changes were necessary in order to permit businesses to remain competitive in a global market and, when needed, adapt to consumers' changing expectations. In particular, with respect to the United States, I have proposed that courts and legislators focus on the transactional result—whether consumers are confused or deceived because of changes in product quality—rather than on difficult to define and inconsistently applied requirements such as assignment with "goodwill" or licensing with "control." *See* Irene Calboli, *Trademark Assignment "With Goodwill": A Concept Whose Time Has Gone*, 57 FLA. L. REV. 771 (2005); Irene Calboli, *The Sunset of "Quality Control" in Modern Trademark Licensing*, 57 AM. U. L. REV. 341 (2007). Several of the transactions that today characterize the luxury economy remain nonetheless questionable under this approach, as consumers are often lured into purchasing products that frequently do not stand up to the promise of superior quality that the consumers expect.

[29] Agreement on Trade-Related Aspects of Intellectual Property Rights, Apr. 15, 1994, Marrakesh Agreement Establishing the World Trade Organization, Annex 1C, THE LEGAL TEXTS: THE RESULTS OF THE URUGUAY ROUND OF MULTILATERAL TRADE NEGOTIATIONS 320 (1999), 1869 U.N.T.S. 299 (1994) [hereinafter TRIPs].

[30] TRIPs, *supra* note 29, Art. 21. The provision states that that "[m]embers may determine conditions on the ... assignment of trademarks, it being understood ... that the owner of a registered trademark shall have the right to assign his trademark with or without the transfer of the business to which the trademark belongs." *Id. See also* DANIEL GERVAIS, THE TRIPS AGREEMENT: DRAFTING HISTORY AND ANALYSIS 183–84 (2003).

[31] TRIPs, *supra* note 29, Art. 16.3. *See generally also* DAVID S. WELKOWITZ, TRADEMARK DILUTION: FEDERAL, STATE, AND INTERNATIONAL LAW (2002).

[32] Article *6bis*, Paris Convention for the Protection of Industriasl Property, Mar. 20, 1883, last revised at Stockholm July 14, 1967, 21 U.S.T. 1583, 828 U.N.T.S. 305 [hereinafter Paris Convention]. The provision was introduced during the Convention's revision at The Hague Conference on November 6, 1925. *See* Marshall A. Leaffer, *Protection of Well-Known Marks: A Transnational Perspective, in* TRADEMARK PROTECTION AND TERRITORIALITY CHALLENGES 18 (Irene Calboli & Edward Lee eds., 2014).

of trademark distinctiveness due to blurring or tarnishment[33]—directly into the trademark statutes. For example, the legislative history of the 1946 United States Trademark Act (Lanham Act) shows that anti-dilution proposals were introduced, but ultimately rejected, in the proposals of the 1946 Act. Moreover, several States enacted variations of anti-dilution protection as a result of these pressures.[34]

Additional protection for well-known marks was eventually introduced into the final text of TRIPs in 1994. Notably, Article 16.3 of TRIPs expanded the reach of Article *6bis* of the Paris Convention, mandating that members prohibit the use or registration of signs that would indicate a connection with existing well-known marks "provided that the interests of the owners of the registered trademark are likely to be damaged by such use."[35] As result of Article 16.3 of TRIPs, all member countries had to implement this protection, which implied that the owners of famous marks, including many luxury trademarks (which are generally niche-famous, but frequently also famous to the public-at-large due to extensive advertising campaigns), could now prevent unauthorized uses of identical or similar signs on unrelated products in the market far beyond the traditional consumer confusion protection. Even though some scholars disagree, this essentially translated in mandating the adoption of anti-dilution protection at the national level.[36] Prior to the adoption of TRIPs, a similar provision was also introduced into the 1988 European Trademark Directive, Article 5(2) of which prohibits the unauthorized uses of a sign that is identical with or similar to a mark that has a "reputation in the Member State" when the use of "that sign without due cause takes unfair advantage of, or is detrimental to, the distinctive character or the repute of the trade mark."[37] Even though the European provision was optional for Member States to adopt, it was implemented in the law of all Members States.

---

[33] *See, e.g.*, Schechter, *supra* note 7, at 825–26.

[34] *See* Walter J. Derenberg, *Dilution and the Antidilution Statutes*, 44 CALIF. L. REV. 439, 449 (1956). Schechter himself drafted the Perkins Bill in 1932, which included a provision protecting any mark that was a "coined or invented or fanciful or arbitrary mark," as well as against uses that could "injure the good will, reputation, business, credit or securities of the owner of the previously used trademark." *Id.* (citing H.R. 11592, 72d Cong. (1st Sess. 1932)).

[35] TRIPs, *supra* note 29, Art. 16.3. In 1999, the World Intellectual Property Organization issued a *Joint Recommendation on the Protection of Well-Known Marks* in order to provide guidelines for the factors that should be taken into account when defining a mark as well-known. *See* World Intellectual Property Organization [WIPO], *Joint Recommendation concerning Provisions on the Protection of Well-Known Marks*, WIPO Doc. 833(E) (Sept. 29, 1999) [hereinafter Joint Recommendation on Well-Known Marks], *available at* http://www.wipo.int/about-ip/en/development_iplaw/pub833.htm.

[36] *See generally* FREDERICK W. MOSTERT, FAMOUS AND WELL-KNOWN MARKS: AN INTERNATIONAL ANALYSIS (1997). *But see* Paul J. Heald, *Trademarks and Geographical Indications: Exploring the Contours of the Trips Agreement*, 29 VAND. J. TRANSNAT'L L. 635 (1996) (stating that anti-dilution protection is not a requirement under Article 16.3 of TRIPs).

[37] Article 5(2), Council Directive 89/104, 1989 O.J. (L 40) 1 (EEC), now replaced by European Parliament and Council Directive 2008/95, 2008 O.J. (L 299) 25 (EC) [hereinafter EU Trademark Directive]. Article 5(2) is based on Article 13A(2) of the old Uniform Benelux Law. *See* Commission of the European Communities, *Memorandum on the Creation of an EEC Trade Mark*, SEC (76) 2462, BULLETIN OF THE EUROPEAN COMMUNITIES (July 6, 1976), *reprinted in* 7 INT'L REV. INTELL. PROP. & COMPETITION L. 367 (1976),

Besides the acceptance of anti-dilution protection, the interpretations of the traditional standard for trademark infringement—the "likelihood of consumer confusion" standard—also profoundly changed in the past decades. Not surprisingly, this change was in favor of a less stringent interpretation of the standard. Notably, from its original interpretation of confusion as to the source of the products in terms of actual product manufacturing, starting in the 1960s, this interpretation was expanded so as to include confusion also as to the "control," "sponsorship," "endorsement," or "affiliation/association" with the products. This revision paralleled, or rather was prompted by, the widespread use of trademark licensing. As trademark owners were no longer the "actual makers" of the licensed products, it was gradually accepted that the concept of source, including "confusion as to the source," had to be interpreted broadly.[38] As a result, the likelihood of confusion as to the "business control," which includes confusion as to the sponsorship, endorsement, and affiliation/association with the products, became a valid basis for a finding of trademark infringement.

In some countries, these expanded interpretations of source and confusion started as judicial doctrines and were later incorporated into the language of several trademark legislations. In the United States, for example, the 1988 Trademark Revision Act introduced "confusion as to the sponsorship" of products into Section 43(a) of the Lanham Act.[39] That same year, the adoption of the European Trademark Directive enacted the principle that trademark owners are entitled to prevent unauthorized uses of signs identical with, or similar to, their registered marks when "there exists a likelihood of confusion on the part of the public, which include a likelihood of association between the sign and the trade mark."[40] Not surprisingly, the adoption of this standard of consumer confusion at large additionally allowed luxury *maisons* to enforce their trademark rights against those who used identical or similar signs on unrelated products, which in turn promoted engaging in brand extensions through licensing agreements. In recent years, this broad interpretation of the confusion-based standard for trademark infringement has expanded even further in some jurisdictions—for example, the doctrines of initial interest confusion and post-sale confusion in the United States, which remain controversial but important addenda to the traditional standard.[41]

---

available at http://aei.pitt.edu/5363/1/5363.pdf; Charles Gielen, *Harmonization of Trade Mark Law in Europe: The First Trade Mark Directive of the European Council*, 8 EUR. INTELL. PROP. REV. 262 (1992); Peter Prescott, *Has the Benelux Law Been Written into the Directive?*, 3 EUR. INTELL. PROP. REV. 99 (1997).

[38] For a detailed reconstruction and criticism of the expansion of the concept of "confusion" in trademark law, see Mark P. McKenna, *Testing Modern Trademark Law's Theory of Harm*, 95 IOWA L. REV. 63 (2009).

[39] Lanham Act § 43(a), 15 U.S.C. § 1125(a) (2000).

[40] EU Trademark Directive, *supra* note 37, Article 5(1)(b); *see also* Charles Gielen, *Likelihood of Association: What Does It Mean?*, 84 TRADEMARK WORLD 21 (1996).

[41] For a detailed recount and critique of these doctrines, see Jennifer E. Rothman, *Initial Interest Confusion: Standing at the Crossroads of Trademark Law*, 27 CARDOZO L. REV. 105 (2005); Sheff, *supra* note 6, at 769.

Last, but not least, the business world also scored important victories toward yet again stronger trademark protection by expanding the traditional interpretation of what constitute protectable subject matter under trademark law. More specifically, the list of signs that can be protected or registered as trademarks grew considerably in recent decades to include colors and shapes or even smells and gestures, based on the rationale that these features are capable of distinguishing products and thus should be protected as trademarks. Historically, the Paris Convention has not mandated limitations on protectable subject matter, even though Article *6quinquies* provides that member countries should extend to foreign marks the same level of protection granted in the country of origin.[42] Yet, legislators and courts traditionally looked with suspicion at color, shapes, and other nontraditional trademarks. Ultimately, Article 15.1 of TRIPs accepted that "any sign, or any combination of signs, capable of distinguishing the goods or services of one undertaking from those of other undertakings, shall be capable of constituting a trademark."[43] Among these signs, the provision includes "figurative elements and combinations of colours as well as any combination of such signs," the only limitation being that "members may require, as a condition, that signs be visually perceptible."[44] In the meantime, national courts also accepted that color and shape could be protected as trademarks when they served to distinguish products' commercial origin,[45] even though they subjected such protection to the doctrine (or the statutory defense) of trademark functionality in order to attempt to avoid monopolies on utilitarian and aesthetically functional product features, as well as to prevent businesses from using trademark law as a species of mutant patents, copyrights, or industrial design after the expiration of these rights.[46] Luxury companies immediately took advantage of nontraditional trademark protection. Among the most famous color or shape marks are the red soles of Louboutin; the turquoise jewelry boxes of Tiffany; the decorative patterns used by Gucci, Louis Vuitton, and Burberry; and most recently (at least in the United States) the waved patterns of Bottega Veneta's handbags. Despite recent claims of functionality with respect to some of these marks in a few countries, these marks continue to be protected and enforced widely across the globe.[47]

---

[42] Paris Convention, *supra* note 32, Art. *6quinquies*.

[43] TRIPs, *supra* note 29, Art. 15.1.

[44] *Id.*

[45] *See, e.g.*, Wal-Mart Stores, Inc., v. Samara Brothers, Inc., 529 U.S. 205 (2000); Qualitex Co. v. Jacobson Prods. Co., 514 U.S. 159 (1995); Two Pesos, Inc. v. Taco Cabana, Inc., 505 U.S. 763, 765 (1992); Graeme B. Dinwoodie, *The Death of Ontology: A Teleological Approach to Trademark Law*, 84 IOWA L. REV. 611, 691 (1999).

[46] *See* TrafFix Devices v. Mktg. Displays, 532 U.S. 23 (2001); Brunswick Corp. v. British Seagull Ltd., 35 F.3d 1527 (Fed. Cir. 1994); Deere & Co. v. Farmhand, Inc., 560 F. Supp. 85 (S.D. Iowa 1982), *aff'd*, 721 F.2d 253 (8th Cir. 1983).

[47] *See* Christian Louboutin v. Yves Saint Laurent Am. Holding, Inc., 696 F.3d 206, 225 (2d Cir. 2012); Brief for Tiffany & Co. as Amici Curiae Supporting Appellants at 3–4, Louboutin S.A. v. Yves Saint Laurent Am., Inc., No. 11-cv-3303 (2d Cir. Oct. 24, 2011); Brief for International Trademark Association (INTA) as Amici Curiae at 26, Louboutin S.A. v. Yves Saint Laurent Am., Inc., No. 11-cv-3303 (2d Cir. Nov. 21, 2011); Joe Palazzolo, *Ruling against French Shoemaker Gives Tiffany the Blues*, WALL ST. J. L. BLOG (Oct. 26, 2011,

IV. Restoring the Promise of Superior Product Quality Part I: Denying Anti-dilution to the Symbols of Prestige for the Masses

In summary, today luxury corporations enjoy much greater freedom in trading and exploiting their luxury marks than ever before. As a result, the luxury industry has been allowed to depart from its tradition of superior product quality and selective product quantities. Instead, luxury corporations have been given legal license to follow a business model driven almost exclusively by profitability, in which brand extensions, larger production, and larger profits have frequently become staple features. Only a few remaining luxury *maisons* have not caved in to this model, and instead continue to create unique luxury products based primarily on traditional techniques, which continue to reflect superior product quality. However, corporate luxury and mega-luxury groups are the ones dominating the market and the news that feature the luxury business. For example, publications such as the *Financial Times*, the *New York Times*, *The Economist*, and many others, regularly report about the luxury economy;[48] the financial health of the luxury industry; the best and the worst mergers and acquisitions and luxury takeovers (in which luxury companies' CEOs, such as Bernard Arnault, are as much the celebrities of the day as the designers); the ups and downs of luxury stocks across financial markets in the various continents; and the economic relevance of "accessible luxury" as a "larger [and larger] piece of [the luxury profits'] pie."[49]

Yet, in this deeply transformed luxury industry, in which the definition of luxury has become increasingly more vague, and in which ultra-luxury, pyramidal luxury, and *masstige* often blur in the mind of the public, what remains of the original promise of luxury marks—that promise of consistent superior quality and uniqueness—in the marks that identify the luxury products that are sold today by most luxury *maisons*?

In many instances, it is true that luxury *maisons* continue to include high quality and sophistication as an important part of their market expansion. For example, when Giorgio Armani announced that his group had licensed the worldwide production and

6:51 PM), http://blogs.wsj.com/law/2011/10/26/ruling-against-french-shoemaker-gives-tiffany-the-blues. *See also* In re Bottega Veneta Int'l S.a.r.l. Serial No. 77219184 (T.T.A.B. Sep. 30, 2013) (giving applicant "the benefit of the doubt" on aesthetic functionality in the United States). *Cf.* Bottega Veneta International vs./ OHMI, Cases T-409/10 and 410/10, March 22, 2013 (in which the General Court of the EU denied Bottega Veneta the registration of two three-dimensional trademarks for purses and handbags).

[48] *See* Elizabeth Paton & Rachel Sanderson, *Luxury Brands Eye Trends for 2014*, FIN. TIMES, Dec. 30, 2013, *available at* http://www.ft.com/intl/cms/s/0/2abf5816-6f53-11e3-bc9e-00144feabdc0.html; *Business of Luxury*, FIN. TIMES, June 3, 2013, *available at* http://im.ft-static.com/content/images/205c26fe-c99c-11e2-9d2a-00144feab7de.pdf; Nicola Clark, *Luxury Goods Group Posts Flat Earnings*, N.Y. TIMES, Jan. 31, 2014, at B2. The list of the contributions in *The Economist* can be found at *Luxury Goods*, ECONOMIST, http://www.economist.com/topics/luxury-goods.

[49] Paton & Sanderson, *supra* note 48.

distribution of Armani Dolci to Venchi,[50] one of Italy's market leaders in the high-quality chocolate sector, chocolate lovers (including this author) praised Armani for his good choice in selecting one of the best *maître chocolatiers* for his chocolates. Still, in many other instances, the true difference in the quality between luxury lower-end products or accessories and equivalent ordinary goods is negligible or nonexistent. As I mentioned in the introduction to this chapter, there is often not much difference between luxury eyewear and ordinary quality glasses. The same can be said for placemats, smart-phone cases, bathroom tiles, and so on. Hence, these products marked by luxury trademarks are often preferred over similar ordinary products because the idea of luxury still attaches to the marks they carry, or because these marks indicate the affiliation of their users with a certain designer instead of another.

Still, from a legal standpoint, in this new world of *masstige* and pyramidal luxury, to what extent should trademark law continue to protect these luxury trademarks not only against consumer confusion, but also against trademark dilution, as the justification for such protection is based on the "whittling away" of the uniqueness of famous marks and not on the protection of the status-signaling function of these marks? As scholars have noted before, no reasonable argument has yet been raised to justify anti-dilution protection for luxury trademarks that are used ubiquitously on both high-end and ordinary products. Instead, the only argument that justifies this protection is the (increasingly predominant) assumption that, in today's economy, trademarks deserve to be protected as business assets—an argument that remains nonetheless incorrect and is incompatible with the pro-competitive objectives of trademark law.[51] In addition, anti-dilution has generally been centered on the need to "preserv[e] the uniqueness or individuality of the trademark,"[52] its "singularity,"[53] against the vitiation or impairment "by its use upon either related or non-related goods."[54] In this respect, trademark dilution laws have been generally drafted so as to protect trademarks against two specific types of harm to uniqueness through unauthorized uses: anti-tarnishment protection and anti-blurring protection. On the contrary, the marks used by luxury conglomerates are frequently anything but unique. Instead, these marks are applied to products spanning clothing, handbags, perfumes, eyeliners, key chains, pens, coasters, placemats, and so on—in other words, they are the antithesis of unique and singular marks.

[50] *See* Jessica Bumpus, *Armani Taste*, VOGUE NEWS (July 9, 2010), http://www.vogue.co.uk/news/2010/07/09/armani-group-signs-licensing-agreement-with--venchi.

[51] *See* Mark A. Lemley, *The Modern Lanham Act and the Death of Common Sense*, 108 YALE L.J. 1687 (1999); Kenneth L. Port, *The "Unnatural" Expansion of Trademark Rights: Is a Federal Dilution Statute Necessary?*, 85 TRADEMARK REP. 525, 552–59 (1995).

[52] Schechter, *supra* note 7, at 825. "[D]ilution is the 'destruction of the uniqueness of a mark by its use on other goods.'" *Id.* at 823.

[53] *Id.* at 831.

[54] *Id.*

Hence, this widespread use of the marks is difficult to reconcile with the claims presented by trademark owners that third parties may tarnish or blur the distinctive uniqueness of these marks by using similar signs on different goods without authorization, as trademark owners themselves self-dilute the uniqueness and singularity of their marks with these brand extensions.[55] Accordingly, these marks should not enjoy anti-dilution protection and should be protected only within the general consumer confusion theory, that is, against trademark infringement. As scholars have noted, withdrawing anti-dilution protection to these marks would not amount, in practice, to considerable changes in the protection that these marks will continue to enjoy. Notably, as I noted above, anti-infringement protection has expanded so dramatically in the past decades that it now offers essentially "as extensive a level of protection as does antidilution protection, particularly for ... famous marks."[56] In practice, luxury trademark owners would still be able to prevent most cases of subpar copies of luxury products as well as most unauthorized uses of famous marks by just relying on the general anti-infringement trademark protection. Still, to deny these marks anti-dilution protection would nonetheless make an important statement as to the ultimate function of anti-dilution protection: protecting trademarks' uniqueness rather than trademarks as symbols of status and wealth per se.

Naturally, luxury corporations would continue to argue that anti-dilution protection is necessary to protect their investment in the quality of their products, lest no company would invest in quality and consumers would be offered only "lemons"—cheap products of lesser quality.[57] Luxury trademark owners often invoke this argument to justify extra protection for their marks. Yet, although this argument could perhaps have some validity with respect to the quality investment by high-end niche-producers as I explain in section V, it becomes essentially moot with respect to the marks that are used by the luxury *maisons* that engage in brand extension, that is, *masstige* and pyramidal luxury. More specifically, the quality of *masstige* products is generally not better than that of ordinary mass-produced products.[58] Accordingly, it is simply not true that trademark owners truly invest in the quality of these mass-produced products, even though these products carry their luxury trademarks. Additionally, the current business model of luxury pyramids does not justify a grant of anti-dilution protection for those luxury *maisons* that produce high-end products primarily to maintain prestige across the levels of their

---

[55] *See* Nelson, *supra* note 9, at 791–92, 798–99.

[56] Barton Beebe, *The Continuing Debacle of U.S. Antidilution Law: Evidence from the First Year of Trademark Dilution Revision Act Case Law*, 24 SANTA CLARA COMPUTER & HIGH TECH. L.J. 449, 463 (2008).

[57] *See* George A. Akerlof, *The Market for "Lemons": Quality Uncertainty and the Market Mechanism*, 84 Q.J. ECON. 488, 489–92 (1970) (explaining the theory that if consumers could ask for an increasing discount because of information asymmetries, i.e., fears of being cheated, sellers of quality products would be driven out of the market and only sellers of low-quality products—lemons—would be willing to meet consumer demand for lower prices). *See also* Sheff, *supra* note 6, at 799–800.

[58] *See* discussion *infra* section V.

pyramids and also use their luxury marks on products mass-distributed in lower market levels. Here again, many of these luxury corporations (unfortunately) do not invest in the quality of high-end products to honor a tradition of excellence, uniqueness, local production, and conservation of traditional knowledge. Rather, they invest in high-end quality as a necessity to successfully leverage the prestige that they build in their top lines with respect to mass-produced profit-making lines. Therefore, providing anti-dilution protection to these luxury marks simply stretches anti-dilution protection beyond its already very broad conception, essentially offering absolute trademark control to luxury conglomerates, which in turn may not use this protection to promote high-quality and unique products, but rather to enforce even further the corporate model of brand expansion and market control that has characterized luxury conglomerates since the 1990s, all at the expense of the true tradition of superior product quality.

V. Restoring the Promise of Superior Product Quality Part II: The Case for Anti-dilution Protection for Only High-End and Niche-Market Luxury Products

Still, not all luxury *maisons* engage in downward brand extension and embrace the mentality in which superior product quality may yield to greater numbers of lesser-quality products and increased profits. Instead, a few luxury *maisons* continue the tradition of high quality, innovation, and limited production. Some of these *maisons* are famous worldwide, such as Bruno Magli, Testoni, or Manolo Blanik, and are known for the high quality of their products that are manufactured with meticulous detail and sold in company stores or in high-scale retailers. Others are niche-famous—such as the luxury handbag designer Maddalena Marconi in my native Bologna. However, these designers manufacture their products with high-quality (and often traditional) manufacturing techniques, frequently still make several of their products (or parts of their products) by hand, and use precious materials in their collections. Hence, it is precisely for the marks that identify the products manufactured by these designers (more established in the global market or in the local market) that anti-dilution protection should perhaps be granted, albeit with caution and with the support of evidence for the potential loss of the mark's uniqueness through tarnishment or blurring.

Still, also in these instances, anti-dilution protection should not be used to protect the status- and exclusivity-signaling function of luxury marks, or the hedonic sense of satisfaction that the consumption of the luxury products and their marks bring to their users.[59] Rather, anti-dilution protection should be used to promote a relevant public

[59] Elizabeth C. Hirschman & Morris B. Holbrook, *Hedonic Consumption: Emerging Concepts, Methods and Propositions*, 46 J. MARKETING 92 (Summer 1982). For an interesting analysis of the hedonic role of trademarks, see Irina Manta, *Hedonic Trademarks*, 74 OHIO ST. L.J. 241 (2013).

function, namely in order to protect the uniqueness and superior product quality of the products that these marks identify. This added protection should also correspond to effective superior product quality. Such superiority in products quality could be measured analyzing the materials, style, and techniques used in making these products compared to other products. In these instances, anti-dilution protection could ultimately incentivize the production of products of superior quality, and thus promote a culture of high quality, which could bring important benefits to society as a whole, both from an economic development and culture perspective.[60] Notably, these luxury *maisons* generally promote high-end products for the level-type products in question, whether on a global or local scale. Additionally, they frequently promote local business and highly specialized labor.[61] In many instances, these luxury *maisons* continue to utilize traditional artisanal manufacturing techniques as a staple feature of their products. This does not mean that these maisosn oppose innovation. In fact, these maisons also tend to invest in new and sophisticated technological innovation to perfect their creations. Still, these maisons generally try to reconcile innovation and traditional techniques and tend to consistently communicate to the public these changes, and the reasons for the changes, in their production (e.g., the adoption of eco-friendly techniques, the discontinuation of certain materials because of concerns of wildlife population, etc.).

Accordingly, protecting the marks that identify their products against dilution could further motivate these *maisons* to continue to meet high production standards, which would maintain the social capital that they have built in the marketplace with their marks. In contrast, the owners of luxury trademarks, such as Testoni or Maddalena Marconi, may not be able to prevent free-riders from making subpar, yet non-confusing, similar products, or from using similar marks for unrelated low-quality products. Hence, these subpar products could ultimately impact their markets and future sales, resulting in a lasting and detrimental impact on their ability to invest in product quality,

---

[60] This argument is not new and has been repeated by many distinguished scholars. *See* Edward S. Rogers, *The Lanham Act and the Social Function of Trademarks*, 14 LAW & CONTEMP. PROBS. 173, 175 (1949) (arguing that without trademarks, "[t]here could be no pride of workmanship, no credit for good quality, no responsibility for bad."); W.M. LANDES & R.A. POSNER, THE ECONOMIC STRUCTURE OF INTELLECTUAL PROPERTY LAW 168, 179 (2003) ("[A] firm with a valuable trademark will be reluctant to lower the quality of its brand because it would suffer a capital loss on its investment in the trademark.... [L]egal protection of trademarks encourages the production of higher-quality products.").

[61] *See, e.g.*, Annamma Joy et al., *Fast Fashion, Sustainability, and the Ethical Appeal of Luxury Brands*, 16 FASHION THEORY 273 (2012). "Luxury brands can become the leaders in sustainability because of their emphasis on artisanal quality." *Id.* at 291; *see also* Jean-Noël Kapferer, *Why Luxury Should Not Delocalize: A Critique of a Growing Tendency*, March–April, EUROPEAN BUSINESS REVIEW 28 (2012); LUCIEN KARPIK, VALUING THE UNIQUE: THE ECONOMICS OF SINGULARITIES (Nora Scoot trans., 2010); Jean-Noël Kapferer, *All That Glitters Is Not Green: The Challenge of Sustainable Luxury*, Nov./Dec. EUR. BUS. REV. 40 (2010). For an additional argument with respect to the social role of luxury *maisons*, see Hoachen Sun, *Living Together in One Civilized World: How Luxury Companies and Consumers Can Fulfill Their Ethical Responsibility to the Poor*, 47 U.C. DAVIS L. REV. 547 (2013) (advocating for a revision of trademark law to foster and promote the ethical responsibility of luxury companies).

or to be in business at all. Moreover, these luxury *maisons* frequently adopt high-end labor, environmental, and safety-related standards as part of their production choices. Accordingly, if third parties are permitted to tarnish or blur the goodwill associated with their marks, these *maisons* would find it difficult to continue to signal these positive benefits to the public, who may no longer trust the message conveyed by these marks. Ultimately, anti-dilution protection could motivate these luxury *maisons* to continue to adopt high manufacturing standards, which are environmentally friendly and respect high standards of labor protection.[62]

In addition, the luxury products made by these high-end niche-market *maisons* are expressions of the cultural identity of the localities, regions, and nations that produce them.[63] Even though using intellectual property law to promote culture-related interests has been criticized by some scholars,[64] this does not forestall the possibility of considering anti-dilution protection as a means to promote culture-related interests.

In particular, these few selectively made high-end luxury products, along with the techniques that are used to produce them, specifically fit within the definition of "intangible cultural heritage" from the 2003 Convention for the Safeguard of the Intangible Cultural Heritage adopted by the United Nations Educational, Scientific, and Cultural Organization (UNESCO).[65] Article 2(1) of the Convention defines "intangible cultural heritage" as "the practices, representations, expression, knowledge, skills—as well as the instruments, objects, artifacts, and cultural spaces associated therewith—that communities, groups and, in some cases, individuals recognize as part of their cultural heritage."[66] Under this framework, granting anti-dilution protection to the marks identifying these high-end niche-market luxury products against subpar imitations carrying similar, though non-confusing, trademarks could promote the continuing use

---

[62] *See* Kirsi Niinimäki, *Eco-Clothing, Consumer Identity and Ideology*, 18 SUSTAINABLE DEV. 150 (2010); Barbara Mihm, *Fast Fashion in a Flat World: Global Sourcing Strategies*, 9 INT'L BUS. & ECON. RES. J. 55 (2010); Donald N. Sull & Stefano Turconi, *Fast Fashion Lessons*, 19 BUSINESS STRATEGY REV. 4 (Summer 2008); Stephanie Clifford, *Some Retailers Reveal Where and How That T-Shirt Is Made*, N.Y. TIMES, May 9, 2013, at A1.

[63] I recently made the same argument with respect to the protection of geographical indications of origin. *See* Irene Calboli, *Of Markets, Culture, and* Terroir: *The Unique Economic and Culture-Related Benefits of Geographical Indications of Origin*, *in* RESEARCH HANDBOOK ON INTERNATIONAL INTELLECTUAL PROPERTY 433 (Daniel Gervais ed., 2015). In this context I emphasized the importance of niche-markets and local production as necessary counterweights against globalization, which frequently implies the elimination of cultural diversity in favor of mass-production and standardization, and which is increasingly more proven to negatively affect sustainable development and human rights. For a detailed analysis, including a criticism of this position, see Tomer Broude, *Conflict and Complementarity in Trade, Cultural Diversity and Intellectual Property Rights*, 2 ASIAN J. WTO & INT'L HEALTH L. & POL'Y 345 (2007). For another possible criticism, see Beebe, *Sumptuary Code*, *supra* note 16, at 868.

[64] *See, e.g.*, Tania Voon, *UNESCO and the WTO: A Clash of Cultures?*, 55 INT'L & COMP. L.Q. 635 (2006).

[65] UNESCO Convention for the Safeguarding of the Intangible Cultural Heritage, Oct. 17, 2003, 2368 U.N.T.S. 1, *available at* http://unesdoc.unesco.org/images/0013/001325/132540e.pdf.

[66] *Id.* Art. 2(1).

of the skills and knowledge necessary to make these products. Instead, if similar, yet non-confusing marks can be used on subpar, mass-produced copies, the products and also the cultural aspects that are encapsulated in the marks' goodwill, could succumb to the appropriation of mass production, and ultimately disappear. Simply put, by safeguarding these high-end products that are produced in niche-markets as unique artifacts, anti-dilution protection could promote the opposite of globalization and protect localized manufacturing that makes contemporary cultural artifacts through both traditional and innovative techniques—which would otherwise be wiped out by a pressing logic of mass-production, delocalization, short-termism, and mass profits.[67]

Of course, as scholars have noted before, anti-dilution protection does not come without costs for competitors even when it is applied to a select group of marks that identify superior-quality luxury products.[68] Hence, in response to this valid concern, it should be noted that anti-dilution protection for these marks does not prevent competitors from copying the type or style of the products (unless other protections apply). Instead, competitors can, and regularly do, imitate these products that are often the trendsetters for entire industries. Still, it remains true that, in most instances, the general confusion-based trademark protection is sufficient to protect these luxury trademarks against subpar copies and the threats to the marks' uniqueness. Accordingly, anti-dilution protection should be applied only in very limited instances also with respect to these marks, based on a careful analysis of whether the unauthorized uses of identical or similar signs could in fact lead to the dilution of the uniqueness of the marks in question.[69]

In general, the decisions to grant anti-dilution protection should be carefully weighed against the possibility that additional trademark protection could instead discourage further investment in product quality. For example, famous trademarks such as Gucci, Fendi, or Louis Vuitton have overinvested in their logos, specifically because of the additional protection granted to their trademarks in the past decades. These companies have transformed their logos into flagship patterns, which not only have become ubiquitous, but also have ultimately contributed to "lock in" these companies' creativity and innovative designs as consumers now expect to see these patterns, lest they would not recognize the products as coming from these companies. Even more problematic, these famous marks have standardized logo-patterns as a "fashion style," so that new entrants—such as Coach, Guess, or Michael Kors—have followed suit. This ultimately has reduced many luxury products to logo-patterned goods, in which even other product details—such as

---

67 For criticism on these aspects, see G. RITZER, THE MCDONALDIZATION OF SOCIETY (6th ed. 2011).

68 For example, the judiciary has resisted findings of dilution in many instances, perhaps because of the costs of such findings. In this respect see Beebe, *supra* note 56, at 450; Long, *supra* note 8, at 1032; MCCARTHY, *supra* note 24, § 24.15.

69 *See, e.g.*, Starbucks Corp. v. Wolfe's Borough Coffee, Inc., No. 12-364-cv (2d Cir. Nov. 15, 2013) (finding no dilution after twelve years of litigation in the case); Robert Brauneis & Paul J. Heald, *The Myth of Buick Aspirin: An Empirical Study of Trademark Dilution by Product and Trade Names*, 32 CARDOZO L. REV. 2533 (2011).

buttons, buckles, etc.—are now in the shape of the same logos in order to enjoy enhanced protection. Hence, this is not a good development for the luxury industry because such strategic uses of trademark protection has undermined these companies' creativity. Instead, these repetitive uses of marks as logo-based-patterns promote standardization in products' decorative elements and designs, thus undermining originality and adding less to cultural diversity in the world of luxury.

Finally, although anti-dilution protection could assist these luxury *maisons* in investing in high product quality, it should not be forgotten these *maisons* are not legally bound to continue to provide the same high quality in the future.[70] Notably, trademark law cannot force trademark owners to retain superior product quality apart from the requirement that trademarks cannot be used misleadingly, lest trademark registrations be canceled. In this respect, even though one may argue that changes in product quality may amount to a misleading use of the marks, trademark owners are nonetheless allowed to modify their products' quality as long as consumers are not deceived as to the actual quality of the products that they are purchasing.[71] Not surprisingly, this rule is precisely what has permitted the owners of luxury trademarks to adopt luxury pyramid structures and to use the same marks on products of lower quality and that are less unique. Still, under my considerations in section IV, if luxury *maisons* deviate from providing superior product quality and instead engage in brand extension or a watering down of the quality of their products, their marks should no longer enjoy anti-dilution protection because the trademark owners themselves would have engaged in self-dilution.[72] Last, but not least, granting anti-dilution protection to the marks identifying high-quality and niche-market products should also be balanced with the necessary permitting of unauthorized descriptive, comparative, noncommercial, and parody or free-speech related uses of these marks by third parties.[73] In other words, competitors should be able to compare their products with these luxury products by using the luxury marks, independent retailers should be able to advertise the sale of these products (perhaps obtained

---

[70] Changes in product quality are a normal occurrence in the business world, often not only because of business choices, but also due to business necessities to adapt to changes in technology or consumer preferences. Likewise, producers of high-end goods cannot be prevented from changing or decreasing the quality of their products. With respect to luxury goods, many luxury *maisons* are in fact perceived to have lowered the quality of their products compared to the past. *See* Erin Shea, *54pc of Affluent Consumers Think Luxury Brands Are Lowering Quality Standards: Ipsos*, LUXURY DAILY (May 2, 2013), http://www.luxurydaily.com/54pc-of-affluent-consumers-say-luxury-brands-lowered-quality-standards-ipsos/.

[71] For example, in the United States, section 2(a) of the Lanham Act prohibits the registration of marks that are deceptive. 15 U.S.C. § 1052(a) (2000). Deceptive trademarks are also subject to cancellation according to section 14(3) of the Lanham Act. 15 U.S.C. § 1064(3) (2000). Finally, section 14(5) of the Lanham Act states that "the Federal Trade Commission may apply to cancel any mark registered on the principal register established by this chapter." 15 U.S.C. § 1064(5) (2000).

[72] *See* discussion *supra* section IV.

[73] For a general discussion on these aspects, see Lisa P. Ramsey, *Increasing First Amendment Scrutiny of Trademark Law*, 61 SMU L. REV. 381 (2008).

via parallel imports) with the products' marks, and artists and parodists should be able to feature these marks in their works, as well as when these works are sold and replicated for commercial purposes. Ultimately, the adoption of this more compromising approach offers an even stronger argument supporting a grant of anti-dilution protection for these luxury trademarks in limited cases.

VI. Conclusion

In April 2013, in an interview with the Italian newspaper *La Repubblica*, Karl Lagerfield, the creative director of Chanel (one of the few remaining independent fashion *maisons*) and Fendi (one of the many signature brands of LVMH), stated that it is only thanks to a few ultra-rich "living in emerging countries far way," and "who know how the true luxury is European," that the artisan hearth of the luxury industry can still survive.[74] These ultra-rich, Lagerfeld said, know that "only in our old continent, in France, in Italy, still exist great artisans, artists of leather, fabrics, and embroidery" and "continue to give work to this marvelous industry based on a tradition of hand-made products that otherwise would disappear."[75] As Lagerfield observed, luxury—based on the tradition of meticulously made products, handmade or innovatively made by luxury masters, with high-end materials, unique attention to detail, and in few and selective quantities—is an important part of our society, tradition, and culture. Far more than being just an industry, this type of luxury is the result of the labor of niche-producers, who set styles and trends for entire industries and whose products also constitute a form of cultural heritage. Still, inasmuch as Lagerfield's observations are correct, the fact that he made them is in part paradoxical. As the creative director of Fendi, one of the early acquisitions of the LVMH group, Lagerfield himself is part of (and plays convenient roles in) that luxury conglomerate machine that has transformed the tradition of luxury, which was based on few products and superior quality, into an aggressive and profit-making business driven primarily by economies of scale. In this new luxury industry, quality is often sacrificed for machine-made products that may well be produced in low-cost countries under questionable labor standards (and these luxury company rarely produce evidence of the contrary by disclosing the location of their manufacturing plants, the working conditions of their laborers, their hourly salary, and so forth).

Certainly, this new luxury industry also continues to create exclusive artifacts on a selective basis for the ultra-rich, as Lagerfield noted in his remarks. These few and select products, however, serve, in many instances, primarily to continue to portray an image

[74] Natalia Aspesi, *Lagerfeld: "La mia vocazione e' farvi desiderare il superfluo,"* REPUBBLICA.IT (Apr. 8, 2013), http://www.repubblica.it/persone/2013/04/08/news/intervista_lagerfeld-56166099, translated at http://translate.google.com/translate?hl=en&sl=it&tl=en&u=http%3A%2F%2Fwww.repubblica.it%2Fpersone%2F2013%2F04%2F08%2Fnews%2Fintervista_lagerfeld-56166099%2F.

[75] *Id.*

of a tradition of prestige, which is frequently nothing more than an image. This image is necessary in order to sell more products at the lower levels of the luxury pyramids. In these pyramidal business structures, the spectrum of luxury easily spans from a Gucci Jackie crocodile handbag, produced in a handful of exemplars and sold for over $37,000 to a few ultra-rich consumers, to the new Jackie python handbag, which retails for $6,900 in the Gucci stores, to less expensive versions of a similar Gucci handbag made with less precious material, to a bottle of Gucci eau de toilette purchased on Amazon for $59.95, the packaging of which prominently displays the luxury trademark to assure the buyers that the essence shares the luxury magic associated with the Gucci tradition.

In this new luxury economy, luxury masters are allowed to sell the luxury tradition thanks to strategic transactions between the original designers and luxury conglomerates. Beside luxury conglomerates, private equity funds have also joined the "luxury pie" and own today's luxury brands that once upon a time belonged to revered designers. This, in turn, has triggered further races for fast profits and capitalization in the luxury industry. Not surprisingly, the new luxury masters rely on the selling power of luxury trademarks to continue to sell the luxury magic. As a result, luxury trademarks have taken on a life on their own, as the public is rarely aware of the actual ownership of luxury brands and often continues to rely on the name of the original designers who created those brands. For example, who would have known, in 1998, when Valentino Garavani decided to sell his company to the Italian group HdP, that the Valentino Fashion Group would have changed ownership four more times within a decade, to Marzotto Apparel in 2002, the private equity fund Permira in 2007, and finally Mayhoola, a Qatari investment group, in 2012?[76] Still, regardless of these changes, the group continues to sell Valentino products—from haute couture to ready-to-wear, women accessories, men's collection, fragrances, and eyewear—under the Valentino trademark. Certainly, many of the shoppers of the Valentino's products are not aware of the changes in the ownership of the firm. Almost paradoxically (and sadly for this author), the value of the Valentino's products may even have increased with the recent launch of the Valentino Garavani's Virtual Museum showcasing the masterpieces and the life of the designer, and the recent "Valentino Master of Couture Exhibition" featured at the Somerset House in London.[77]

Hence, this type of mass-produced and pyramidal luxury does not deserve special legal protection. This type of luxury promotes an idea of luxury based on status, wealth, and images rather than superior product quality. Moreover, it frequently promotes

---

[76] Nadya Masidlover & Jessica Hodgson, *Qatar's Royals Buy Valentino—Purchase of Fashion House Reflects Oil-Rich State's Pursuit of Luxury Brands*, WALL ST. J. (July 12, 2012), http://online.wsj.com/news/articles/SB10001424052702304373804577522821213020772 (highlighting that "[a] representative for Mayhoola said in a statement: 'Valentino is ideally suited to form the basis for a global luxury goods powerhouse'").

[77] *See* Suzy Menkes, *Valentino Virtual Fashion Museum Opens Its Doors*, N.Y. TIMES (Dec. 5, 2011), http://www.nytimes.com/2011/12/06/fashion/06iht-fvalentino06.html?_r=0; Sarah Karmali, *Valentino on Show*, VOGUE NEWS (Aug. 2, 2012), http://www.vogue.co.uk/news/2012/08/02/valentino-couture-exhibition-opens-at-somerset-house-in-london.

standardization by focusing excessively on logos and logo patterns (to emphasize status and identification with the brand), instead of fostering creativity and cultural diversity with new products and varying designs. Accordingly, the marks that are used to identify products sold in mass quantities or used across multiple market levels to attract consumers with an idea of luxury, which is often nothing more than a mark affixed on ordinary products, should not enjoy anti-dilution protection. To extend this protection would amount to offering a subsidy to luxury conglomerates by recognizing that these companies can dispose of their marks as property rather than as symbols of commercial origin and product quality. Instead, based on the consumer protection theories that are still the foundation of trademark law and policy, these marks should enjoy protection only within the limits of consumer confusion and trademark infringement. In practical terms, to withdraw anti-dilution protection to these marks would not considerably, if at all, affect luxury conglomerates, as today's interpretation of likelihood of confusion at large still allows these companies to prevent most unauthorized users of similar signs in most market sectors. Nevertheless, adopting this position would make a statement about the type of interests that we, as a society, would like to protect and ultimately subsidize. This should not include protecting marks as symbols of status and wealth, or just as images per se to be affixed on luxury, or *masstige* luxury, products.

Still, as I noted above, a few luxury *maisons* continue to operate in selective markets and have not sacrificed the tradition of superior quality for mass profits. This type of luxury—based on high-skilled labor and handmade or innovatively made products—perhaps deserves anti-dilution protection. In particular, this type of luxury should perhaps be incentivized because it contributes to maintain the traditional culture of high quality in the production of luxury products In turn, granting extra protection to these products and their marks could promote a culture of high quality for other products. Moreover, it could promote local development and better production standards in terms of labor standards and respect for the environment. Also in these instances, however, the benefits of anti-dilution protection should be carefully weighed, on a case-by-case basis, against the costs of such protection for competition and the public interest. Generally, anti-dilution protection should remain the exception and not the general rule. It should only apply to those few remaining marks that are still unique and would benefit from anti-dilution protection against the whittling away of their uniqueness.

4 The Economics of Demand for Counterfeiting

Yi Qian*

I. Introduction

Counterfeits are illegal products that infringe upon others' brands that the counterfeiters do not own. They affect many industries and can have large influences on brands' innovative incentives through affecting authentic sales. Given the growing popularity of counterfeits across many sectors and countries, it is not surprising that counterfeiting remains at the center of trade disputes. The year 2007 alone witnessed a G-8 summit recommending stronger enforcement of intellectual property rights (IPR), the initiation of a WTO dispute over China's IPR enforcement regime, and the launch of intergovernmental negotiations toward an Anti-Counterfeiting Trade Agreement (ACTA). In fiscal year 2009, the U.S. Customs and Border Protection seized more than $260 million worth of counterfeits, and counterfeit footwear accounted for 40% of the total seizures.[1]

* Associate Professor of Marketing at the Sauder School of Business, University of British Columbia.

[1] N. Schmidle, *Inside the Knockoff-Tennis-Shoe Factory*, N.Y. TIMES, Aug. 19, 2010. p. 2

While curbing counterfeiting by strengthening IPR protection has been a common practice worldwide to foster brand values, upholding the protection of IPR remains controversial.[2] Only a few research studies have directly examined the impacts of counterfeits. Grossman and Shapiro[3] theorize about the implications of counterfeits for international trade. An investigation involving premium brands in Thailand and India reveals that consumers of genuine items adopt one of three strategies when faced with the prospect of their favorite brands being counterfeited: flight (abandoning the brand), reclamation (elaborating the patronage of a brand), and abranding (disguising all brand cues).[4] Qian offers the first econometric study of the impacts of entry by counterfeiters on authentic price, quality (as proxied by unit production cost), advertising, and self-enforcement expenditures.[5] The study shows that authentic firms innovate and engage in self-enforcement in the face of counterfeits. In order to effectively guide priorities and directions of innovation and enforcement strategies, it is crucial to understand the sales impacts of counterfeits on authentic products of different quality tiers. However, this topic is largely unexplored in the past literature, partly due to lack of data.

Qian has significantly extended the brand-level panel data to footwear product-line details within each brand by obtaining product-line-level sales data for the first time and studying the sales impacts of entry by counterfeiters, a topic that directly sheds light on the incentives and directions of innovation and that is one managers and scholars care about deeply.[6] That study provides careful empirical identifications of the heterogeneous effects of counterfeits on sales of authentic products at different quality tiers. The dynamic heterogeneous effects over time are also charted there. In this chapter, I further probe into the heterogeneous sales impacts based on theories and data. The combination of theory and lab data generates insights at both the conceptual level and the individual- sampled consumer level. The theory formalizes rationales, and the lab experiments unravel such impacts at the consumer level. They generate findings that shed new light on linking different strands of theoretical literature on vertical differentiation and advertising. The framework proposed here helps provide theoretical foundations and generalizes the findings.

---

[2] J. Lanjouw & I. Cockburn, *Do Patents Matter? Empirical Evidence after GATT* (NBER Working Paper, W7495 2008); Phillip McCalman, *Reaping What You Sow: An Empirical Analysis of International Patent Harmonization*, 55 J. INT'L ECON. 161–86 (2001); J. David Hsu Gans & S. Stern, *The Impact of Uncertain Intellectual Property Rights on the Market for Ideas: Evidence from Patent Grant Delays*, 54 MGMT SCI. 982–97 (2008); ADAM JAFFE & JOSH LERNER, INNOVATION AND ITS DISCONTENTS (2004).

[3] G. Grossman & C. Shapiro, *Foreign Counterfeiting of Status Goods*, 103(412) Q.J. ECON. 79–100(1988) [hereinafter Grossman & Shapiro, *Foreign Counterfeiting*]; G. Grossman & C. Shapiro, *Counterfeit Product Trade*, 78 AM. ECON. REV. 59–75 (1988) [hereinafter Grossman & Shapiro, *Counterfeit Product Trade*].

[4] Suraj Commuri, *The Impact of Counterfeiting on Genuine-Item Consumers' Brand Relationships*, 73 J. MKTG. 86–98 (May 2009).

[5] Yi Qian, *Impacts of Entry by Counterfeiters*, 123(4) Q.J. ECON. 1577–609 (Nov. 2008).

[6] Yi Qian, *Counterfeiters: Foes or Friends?* MGMT. SCI. Lead article in Volume 60, Issue 10: 2381–400 (2014).

Last but not least, the discovery and understanding of the heterogeneous impacts at theoretical and empirical levels have important implications for guiding priorities for IPR enforcement policy. As a recent World Intellectual Property Organization study comments, "Governments are invariably resource constrained and completely eradicating violations of IPR law—like violations of other types of law—is out of reach for even the best-resourced states."[7] Advocates of IPR believe in the stimulating effects it would have on innovation, which would fuel faster economic growth. Such stimulating effects are shown to be very limited in practice[8] with a generalizable conditional importance of patent effects only in countries of higher development and education levels.[9] The debate over IPR culminated in the TRIPs (Trade-Related Intellectual Property) negotiations, which were largely motivated by the desire to reduce trade in counterfeit goods. This study therefore contributes to the broader literature on how firm responses to the legal environment could have important moderating effects on the impact of IPR protection.[10]

A number of insights emerge from this study. Counterfeit entry exhibits both negative substitution and positive spillover effects on authentic sales. The net effect is positive for high-end authentic products and negative for low-end authentic products, even within the *same brand*. These findings, together with the stated purchase motivations in the lab experiments, reveal the potential advertising mechanism underlying the counterfeiting effects. That is, the positive effect on high-end authentic products comes mainly from increased brand awareness and affinity due to the presence of counterfeits. Brands with less government protection seek to differentiate their products by moving up the quality ladder. Over time, these brands shift toward higher-end product lines and shrink their low-end product lines. Such heterogeneous sales impacts are directly linked to the corresponding impact of being exposed to counterfeits on a consumer's purchase intent for products of the three quality tiers. The experiment responses also suggest the double-edged effects of counterfeits in increasing brand awareness and in substituting for the authentic product.

These findings suggest that counterfeiters are not always damaging. A brand owner could optimize its self-enforcement efforts according to the particular adolescence stage the brand faces. At the early stages of the brand development, counterfeiters could help increase the brand awareness and penetrate the market, very much to the effect of buzz

---

[7] C. Fink, K. Maskus & Y. Qian, *The Economic Effects of Counterfeiting and Piracy: a Literature Review*, Advisory Committee on Enforcement WIPO (Sept. 3, 2010), World Intellectual Property Organization.

[8] J. Lerner, *The Empirical Impact of Intellectual Property Rights on Innovation: Puzzles and Clues*, 99(2) AM. ECON. REV.: PAPERS & PROCEEDINGS 343–48 (2009).

[9] Yi Qian, *Do National Patent Laws Stimulate Domestic Innovation in a Global Patenting Environment? A Cross-Country Analysis of Pharmaceutical Patent Protection: 1978–2002*, 89(3) REV. ECON. & STATISTICS (2007); Margaret Kyle & Anita McGahan, *Investments in Pharmaceuticals before and after TRIPS*, REV. ECON. & STATISTICS 94(4): 1157–72 (Mar. 2012).

[10] J. H. Mortimer, C. Nosko & A. Sorensen, *Supply Responses to Digital Distribution: Recorded Music and Live Performance* (Working Paper 2010); Qian, *supra* note 5.

agents. This also links to findings in Berger et al.[11] that no publicity is bad publicity. As the brand grows and becomes prominent, such benefits of counterfeits dwindles and the authentic producers can enhance enforcement against counterfeits to weed out their business-stealing effects. This was exactly Microsoft's strategy in China. Bill Gates told an audience at the University of Washington that "Although about 3 million computers get sold every year in China, people don't pay for the software. Someday they will, though. And as long as they're going to steal it, we want them to steal ours. They'll get sort of addicted, and then we'll somehow figure out how to collect sometime in the next decade."[12] Only after the majority of consumers were "locked into" Microsoft software did they engage in furious enforcement campaigns in collaboration with the government to crack down on piracy and make the Chinese market adopt legitimate Microsoft software. By that point, other producers such as Linux was far less of a competitor for Microsoft in China than it was in the United States.

The heterogeneous sales impacts of counterfeits on different product lines further imply that the optimal level of enforcement could vary across the product lines within each brand. For instance, brand owners need not concern themselves too much with counterfeits that have a wide quality gap below their authentic counterparts, as these counterfeits would capture a very different customer segment that would not have purchased the authentic products anyway. Brands could also devote relatively fewer enforcement resources in high-fashion product lines, as counterfeits could help set fashion trends and diffuse authentic innovations. This further promotes the product innovation cycle.

The rest of the chapter is organized as follows. First, I discuss the relationship between this research and the existing literature. Second, I propose a theoretical framework that builds on and synthesizes the literature. Third, I detail the theory model and predictions. Next, I document the lab experimental design and results. Finally, I draw out policy implications. Figures and tables are included in the end.

II. Literature and Theory

A. LITERATURE REVIEW

While proponents of IPR argue that counterfeits could undermine incentives to innovate by displacing authentic sales, it is not clear in theory or in practice whether counterfeits are always damaging. Based on her ethnographic research, Gosline[13] documented that

---

[11] J. Berger, A. Sorensen, & S. Rasmussen, 29(5) *Positive Effects of Negative Publicity*, MKTG. SCI. 815–27 (2010).

[12] C. Piller, *How Piracy Opens Doors for Windows*, L.A. TIMES, April 9, 2006, http://articles.latimes.com/2006/apr/09/business/fi-micropiracy9.

[13] R. Gosline, *Simultaneous Distinction, Democratization and Omnivorism Effects: A Longitudinal Analysis of Dynamic Symbolic Boundaries in Counterfeit Consumption Networks* (dissertation, Harvard Business School, 2009).

the purchasing of counterfeits stimulated consumers to purchase more branded purses. A stream of literature on online piracy has vigorously debated the effect of file-sharing on original music sales in recent years, and Liebowitz[14] and Oberholzer-Gee and Strumpf[15] provide excellent surveys. Several empirical studies point to a negative effect of piracy and file-sharing,[16] yet Oberholzer-Gee and Strumpf[17] conclude the opposite, based on a uniquely matched dataset of music downloads and purchases. Along the same lines, Mortimer et al.[18] find that illegitimate redistribution of digital goods increases revenue from nondigital complementary products, notably live performances. At the consumer level, Rob and Waldfogel[19] conducted surveys of undergraduate students. Although they found that the average drop in album purchases due to downloading was $.20, consumer surplus increased due to the lower prices.

In short, the literature has not provided generalizable guidance on the sales effects of counterfeits or the underlying mechanisms. Grossman and Shapiro theorize the implications of counterfeits in the context of international trade.[20] While their model yields interesting welfare guidance on trade policies, the industry and firm competitive dynamics remain largely unexplored. The theoretical predictions also call for empirical testing. Qian pioneers data collection efforts for under-the-table counterfeiting activities and studies the impacts of counterfeiting on authentic quality, prices, and other marketing norms.[21] However, sales implications remain unexplained due to lack of data. Qian[22] collected detailed sales data at the product-line level for each of the thirty-one branded companies and their counterfeits in the original sample in Qian's "Impacts of Entry by Counterfeiters."[23] These new data enable rich analyses of the sales impacts of counterfeits at the product-line level. This study starts with theoretical foundations to unify and generalize the earlier empirical findings. I then supplement with lab experiments in testing the heterogeneous effects and exploring mechanisms.

---

[14] S. J. Liebowitz, *File-Sharing: Creative Destruction or Just Plain Destruction?*, 29 J.L. & ECON. 1–28 (2006).

[15] Felix Oberholzer-Gee & Koleman Strumpf, *File-Sharing and Copyright*, *in* 10 INNOVATION POLICY AND THE ECONOMY Joshua Lerner & Scott Stern eds. 19–55 (2009).

[16] M. Givon & E. Muller, *Software Piracy—Estimation of Lost Sales and the Impact on Software Diffusion*, 59(1) J. MKTG 29–37 (1995); Hui Kai-Lung & Png Ivan, *Piracy and the Legitimate Demand for Recorded Music*, 2(1) B.E. Journal of Economic Analysis & Policy, De Gruyter 1–24, (September 2003); S. J. Liebowitz, *Economists Examine File-Sharing and Music Sales, in* INDUSTRIAL ORGANIZATION AND THE DIGITAL ECONOMY 145–74 (G. Illing & M. Peitz eds., 2006); S.-H Hong, *Measuring the Effect of Napster on Recorded Music Sales* (2008), manuscript available at https://netfiles.uiuc.edu/hyunhong/www/research.htm.

[17] Feli Oberholzer-Gee & Koleman Strumpf, *The Effect of File Sharing on Record Sales: An Empirical Analysis*, 115 J. POL. ECON. 29–37 (2007).

[18] Mortimer et al., *supra* note 10.

[19] Rafael Rob & Joel Waldfogel, *Piracy on the High Cs: Music Downloading, Sales Displacement, and Social Welfare in a Sample of College Students*, 49 J.L. & ECON. 29–62 (Apr. 2006).

[20] Grossman & Shapiro, *supra* note 3.

[21] Qian, *supra* note 5.

[22] Qian, *supra* note 6.

[23] Qian, *supra* note 5.

B. THEORETICAL FRAMEWORK

Assimilating advertising effects into a vertical differentiation model, I link these two strands of the theoretical literature in a stylized model to conceptualize and guide the empirical tests. Although I relegate the model details to the appendix, I summarize the key intuitions and insights of the model in this section.

I started with the vertical differentiation model pioneered by Gabszewicz and Thisse.[24] Counterfeiters usually imitate authentic products by reverse-engineering to different degrees.[25] The quality is hence below or, at best, equivalent to that of the authentic product. The vertical differentiation model provides an appropriate and useful framework for conceptualizing the competition between the authentic and counterfeit producers. I extended the model in the traditional single-product setting to one in which the incumbent branded producer has multiple products, as in the real world, and studied a market with a multi-product brand facing the threat of counterfeit infringements.

The model yields insights on two opposing effects of entry: substitution effect and demand-enlarging effect. Like any entrant competitor, a counterfeiter steals demand from the authentic brand as some consumers trade down to purchase the counterfeits. This substitution effect is more negative when counterfeits are closer substitutes for the authentic product.[26] The vertical differentiation model also informs us of an opposite positive effect of the entry of a lower-quality product: namely, it could help to capture a segment of consumers whose valuation of the product quality is so low that they are not willing to pay the higher price for the authentic product. With the introduction of counterfeits, these consumers now participate in the marketplace by enjoying lower-quality (or lower-authenticity) counterfeits at a lower price. I derived closed-form solutions for the negative substitution effect and the positive demand-enlarging effect.

Besides the demand-enlarging effect, illegal imitation can have other positive effects on authentic product sales. A commonly cited mechanism is network effects, where the consumer utility of a product is an increasing function in the size of the user base, and this argument is proposed particularly for software and book copyright cases.[27] Others suggest that

---

[24] J. Gabszewicz & J.-F. Thisse, *Price Competition, Quality and Income Disparities*, 20 J. ECON. THEORY 340–59 (1979).

[25] Schmidle, *supra* note 1.

[26] Here I focus on the case in which consumers knowingly purchase counterfeits. In the case of deceptive counterfeits, where consumers cannot discern counterfeits from authentic products, the business-stealing effect will be even stronger.

[27] L. N. Takeyama, *The Welfare Implications of Unauthorized Reproduction of Intellectual Property in the Presence of Demand Network Externalities*. 42(2) J. INDUST. ECONOM. 155–66 (1994); K. R. Conner & R. P. Rumelt, *Software Piracy: An Analysis of Protection Strategies*, 37(2) MANAGEMENT SCI. 125–39 (1991);

B.Z. Khan, *Does Copyright Piracy Pay? The Effects of U.S. International Copyright Laws on the Market for Books*, 1790–1920. NBER Working Paper 10271, National Bureau of Economic Research, Cambridge, MA (2004).

imitation could serve as a signal for the original product's or idea's high quality,[28] and that the copy could be a trial product for the authentic product.[29] All these mechanisms speak to the advertising effect of counterfeits.

I therefore incorporated advertising into the vertical differentiation framework to explain an additional positive effect counterfeits could exert on authentic demand. That is, counterfeits could recruit new customers to purchase authentic products by increasing brand awareness. Qian and Xie[30] note survey results in which Chinese consumers learned about their favorite brands initially through counterfeits. After the cultural revolution in 1976 and the opening up of the market economy, there is unleashed energy from both supply and demand sides. Chinese consumers have been delighted as well as overwhelmed by the booming brand and product varieties. The general lack of information about different brands does not match consumers' eagerness to use and associate with brands. Therefore, they often look to others or for marketplace "trends" to learn about popular brands.[31] In China, brand awareness has definitely been an increasing function in the number of times people see the brand being worn: that is, the size of the consumer base. My model fits this context very well too.

A recent study by Johnson and Myatt suggests a new taxonomy of advertising, distinguishing between hype, which shifts out demand, and real information, which rotates demand by altering the price elasticity for brands.[32] Unlike the traditional advertising literature, the potential spillover effect of counterfeits may be considered an "externality" to the branded firm. As the authentic branded companies do not internalize such advertising costs in their own optimizations, the advertising hype can lead to heterogeneous sales impacts for authentic products of different quality tiers. It can both shift and rotate demand functions for products of different quality levels. Notably, because counterfeits impose less competitive pressure on a high-end authentic product because of a wider quality gap between the two, the equilibrium sale quantity of the high-end authentic product primarily increases when counterfeits enter the market and boost the brand awareness. The equilibrium sales quantity of the low-end authentic product is influenced by the two opposing effects of counterfeits and declines when the substitution effect outweighs the advertising effect.

---

[28] J. Castro, D. Balkin, & D. Shepherd, *Can Entrepreneurial Firms Benefit from Product Piracy?*, 23(1) J. BUS. VENTURING 75–90 (2008); B. Biais & E. Perotti, *Entrepreneurs and New Ideas*, 39(4) RAND J. ECON. 1105–25 (Winter 2008).

[29] CARL SHAPIRO & HAL VARIAN, INFORMATION RULES: A STRATEGIC GUIDE TO THE NETWORK ECONOMY (1999).

[30] Yi Qian & Hui Xie, *Investigating the Dynamic Effects of Counterfeits with a Random Changepoint Simultaneous Equation Model* (NBER Working Paper w16692, 2001, available at http://www.nber.org/papers/w16692).

[31] JESSICA LIN, FAKE STUFF (2011)

[32] J. P. Johnson & D. P. Myatt, *On the Simple Economics of Advertising, Marketing, and Product Design*, 96(3) AM. ECON. REV. 756–84 (2006).

In sum, the theoretical framework outlined above yields a set of testable hypotheses:

1. Hypothesis 1: Authentic high-end product sales increase after massive entry of counterfeiters of the brand;
2. Hypothesis 2: Authentic low-end product sales decrease after massive entry of counterfeiters of the brand.

I conducted lab experiments to test the causal effects of counterfeit presence on consumers' purchase intent on the sample shoes of the three typical quality tiers as observed in the field data.

III. Model

Consumer preference is a function of the product quality s, brand awareness b, and its price P: $U = V^{*} s^{*} b - P$; where the consumer taste for quality s, as denoted by V, is uniformly distributed between $[V^L, V^H]$. We assume $V^H \geq 2V^L$ to ensure that the market is "covered," and consumer valuations are monotonic in product qualities. Similar to Connor and Rumelt,[33] parameter b here captures brand awareness and network externality, which is an increasing function of the number of users of the product: $b = f(N)$.

There is at first one original producer with products of two qualities: $s^H > s^L$. The unit costs of producing the two types of qualities are c^H and c^L, respectively. The producer attempts to maximize joint profits in the two segments of market: the upper segment who purchases s^H, and the lower segment who purchases s^L. The prices of these two products are set accordingly.

In a market with counterfeits, a counterfeiter enters with product of quality s^F and unit cost $c^F < c^L < c^H$. Let P^H, P^L, P^F be the prices for the original high- and low-quality authentic goods and the counterfeit good, respectively.

We first consider the case that the producer simply optimizes its prices. Before counterfeits enter the market, an indifferent consumer with valuation V is equally happy with consuming the high-quality product or the low-quality one if: $Vs^H * b - P^H = Vs^L * b - P^L$ $\Longrightarrow V = \dfrac{P^H - P^L}{(s^H - s^L)b}$; and the lowest valuation among the consumers who would still purchase the low-quality good is: $Vs^L * b - P^L = 0 \Longrightarrow V = \dfrac{P^L}{bs^L}$. Any consumers with an

[33] Conner & Rumelt, *supra* note 29.

even lower taste will not purchase because she would derive negative utility otherwise. It is then easy to get the demand for each type of products:

$$D^H(P^H, P^L) = V^H - V = V^H - \frac{P^H - P^L}{b(s^H - s^L)}$$

$$D^L(P^H, P^L) = V - V = \frac{P^H - P^L}{b(s^H - s^L)} - \frac{P^L}{bs^L}$$

The original producer maximizes total profits:

$(P^H - c^H)D^H(P^H, P^L) + (P^L - c^L)D^L(P^H, P^L)$ *w.r.t.* P^H *and* P^L, and yields:

$$P^{L^*} = \frac{bV^H s^L + c^L}{2}, \; P^{H^*} = \frac{bV^H s^H + c^H}{2} \tag{1}$$

$$D^{L^*} = \frac{c^H s^L - c^L s^H}{2bs^L(s^H - s^L)}, \; D^{H^*} = \frac{V^H}{2} - \frac{c^H - c^L}{2b(s^H - s^L)} \tag{2}$$

After counterfeits enter the market, the boundary condition becomes: $Vs^F * b - P^F = 0 ==> \underline{V} = \frac{P^F}{bs^F}$. I introduce another consumer with valuation V^F who is indifferent regarding whether to purchase the original or the counterfeit products. $V^F s^F b - P^F = V^F s^L b - P^L ==> V^F = \frac{P^L - P^F}{b(s^L - s^F)}$. The market is segmented into the following parts: consumers with the lowest tile valuations $[0, \underline{V}]$ do not purchase anything, consumers with slightly higher valuations $[\underline{V}, V^F]$ will purchase the counterfeits, consumers in the interval $[V^F, V]$ will purchase the low-quality product, and the consumers in the upper segment $[V, V^H]$ will enjoy the high-quality product. I thereby derive the demands for the high- and low-quality original products and that for the counterfeits:

$$D^H(P^H, P^L, P^F) = V^H - \frac{P^H - P^L}{b(s^H - s^L)}$$

$$D^L(P^H, P^L, P^F) = \frac{P^H - P^L}{b(s^H - s^L)} - \frac{P^L - P^F}{b(s^L - s^F)}$$

$$D^F(P^H, P^L, P^F) = \frac{P^L - P^F}{b(s^L - s^F)} - \frac{P^F}{bs^F}$$

The original producer maximizes $(P^H - c^H)D^H + (P^L - c^L)D^L$ $w.r.t.$ $P^i (i = H, L)$ and the counterfeit producer maximizes $(P^F - c)D^F$ $w.r.t.$ P^F. If the authentic company is the Stackelberg leader in the game, then I could solve the reaction function of the counterfeiter and then plug into the authentic profit function. The equilibrium prices and demand are solved to be:

$$P_c^{H*} = \frac{bV^H(2s^L s^H - s^F(s^H + s^L)) + s^L c^F + 2c^H s^L}{4s^L - 2s^F}$$

$$P_c^{L*} = \frac{s^L(c^L + c^F) + (2bV^H s^L + c^L)(s^L - s^F)}{4s^L - 2s^F}$$

$$D_c^{H*} = \frac{V^H}{2} - \frac{c^H - c^L}{2b(s^H - s^L)}$$

LEMMA 1 *b increases after being counterfeited as a result of a larger user base of the brand.*

PROOF: The total number of users for the brand under the multi-product monopoly condition is $N_m = V^H - \frac{P_m^L}{s^L}$, and that under the competitive market with the counterfeits is $N_c = V^H - \frac{P^F}{s^F}$. As derived in the model, the reaction function of the counterfeit price is $P^F = \frac{P_c^L s^F + c^F s^L}{2s^L}$. Rearranging the terms, we have $\frac{P^F}{s^F} = \frac{P_c^L}{2s^L} + \frac{c^F}{2s^F} < \frac{P_m^L}{2s^L} + \frac{c^F}{2s^F}$. With very low marginal cost of counterfeit products c^F, the last term is negligible. Hence, $\frac{P^F}{s^F} < \frac{P_m^L}{s^L}$. It follows that $N_c = V^H - \frac{P^F}{s^F} > V^H - \frac{P_m^L}{s^L} = N_m$. Since $b = f(N)$, with $f(.)$ increasing, $b_c > b_m$. The entry of counterfeits enlarges the total number of users of the brand, including authentic or counterfeit products, and increases the brand awareness.

PROPOSITION 1 *When b increases after being counterfeited, equilibrium sales of the high-end product increases, that is,* $\frac{\partial D^{H^*}}{\partial b} > 0$.

PROOF: $\frac{\partial D^{H^*}}{\partial b} = \frac{c^H - c^L}{2b^2(s^H - s^L)} > 0$. This proposition explains the increased demand and sales for the high-end authentic product due to the advertising effect of the entry of its counterfeits.

PROPOSITION 2 *Monopoly demand of low-end product* $\frac{\partial D^{L^*}}{\partial b} > 0$ *iff* $\frac{s^H}{c^H} = \frac{s^L}{c^L}$.

PROOF: $\frac{\partial D^{L^*}}{\partial b} = \frac{c^L s^H - c^H s^L}{2b^2 s^L (s^H - s^L)}$. This is greater than zero if and only if $c^L s^H - c^H s^L > 0$. This is equivalent to $\frac{s^H}{c^H} = \frac{s^L}{c^L}$. This suggests that increased brand awareness will raise low-end product demand if and only if the quality-cost ratio of the high-end product is higher than that of the low-end product. When the two types of products are sufficiently differentiated in their quality, then the increased brand awareness could expand market share for both branded products. Otherwise, the demand for low-end product may decline while its optimal price increases.

PROPOSITION 3 *When holding b fixed,* $D^{L^*} > D_c^{L^*}$ *iff* $\frac{c^F}{s^F} < \frac{c^L}{s^L}$.

When holding b fixed, I can compare the equilibrium demands of the low-end product in markets with and without counterfeits by taking the differences: $D^{L^*} - D_c^{L^*} = \frac{P_c^L - P^F}{(s^L - s^F)b} - \frac{P^L}{bs^L}$. We substitute in the reaction function of the counterfeiter $P^F = \frac{P_c^L s^F + c^F s^L}{2s^L}$ and the equilibrium prices P_c^L, P^L. After rearranging and canceling terms, I have $D^{L^*} - D_c^{L^*} = \frac{c^L s^F - c^F s^L}{4bs^L(s^L - s^F)}$. This difference is positive if and only if $c^L s^F - c^F s^L > 0$, which is equivalent to $\frac{c^F}{s^F} < \frac{c^L}{s^L}$. The condition says that the cost-quality ratio of counterfeits is less than that of the low-end authentic product. As counterfeiters copycat the authentic designs and use very inferior materials to produce their counterfeits, this condition often holds in practice. The proposition formalizes the substitution effects of counterfeits on the authentic products.

The above two propositions outline two opposing effects by the entry of counterfeits on the low-end authentic product: advertising effect to increase brand awareness and substitution effect to steal demand. As counterfeits impose less competitive pressure on the high-end authentic product due to the wider quality gap, the equilibrium sale quantity of the high-end authentic product increases when counterfeits enter the market and boost the brand awareness. The equilibrium sale quantity of the low-end authentic product is influenced by the two opposing effects of counterfeits, and will decline when the substitution effect outweighs advertising effect.

IV. Lab Experiments

While the heterogeneous sales impacts of counterfeits are well identified in the field data,[34] it is sometimes difficult to get a clear grasp of actual consumer purchase intents and motivations without disaggregated consumer-level data. I therefore further manipulated the exposure to counterfeits experimentally in order to test the causal effect of counterfeits on purchase intent of authentic branded shoes and to gain initial understandings on the motivations underlying the purchase intent. I conducted lab experiments using subject pools at the Northwestern University and the University of Illinois at Chicago.[35] The respondents consisted of masters' students in business administration, medicine, and statistics. Sixty-two responses were collected.

The first wave of experiments was designed for a between-subject study. The respondents were randomly assigned to take one of the two different surveys. The survey for the treatment group exposed the subjects to actual photos of a counterfeit shoe, together with three quality tiers of authentic shoes of a fictional brand name Muniao, and asked the participants to rate their purchase intent for each of the shoe stimuli. All the shoe stimuli were photos of actual shoes at the different quality tiers of a Chinese brand. These pictures were displayed with brief product descriptions and their real market prices. The respondents therefore rated their purchase intent based on full comparisons of all products, similar to the real-world condition where counterfeits coexist with authentic products in the market. The survey for the control group differed in the order of the questions and pictures. It first presented only the three quality tiers of authentic shoes for respondents to rate purchase intent. After they marked down purchase intent for the authentic shoes, they were exposed to a picture of the counterfeit shoe and asked

---

[34] Qian, *supra* note 6.

[35] The experiments have been approved by the IRB with code STU00001632.

to rate their purchase intent on this. Respondents in the control group were asked to rate the counterfeit at the end so I could ascertain whether the two groups differed systematically in their preferences for counterfeits.

Respondents had to answer questions in sequence and could not look ahead. The ratings on the authentic products in the control condition therefore reflected purchase intent without the presence of counterfeits. This study enabled between-subject comparisons of purchase intent across treatment and control groups. The purchase intent was measured by semantic differential scales in the experimental surveys, following the well-established social psychology literature.

None of the respondents has heard of the brand name before the experiments. The average purchase intents for the counterfeit stimuli are similar across the treatment and control groups, and so are the ratings on general attitudes toward counterfeits. The demographic information also shows that the two groups are rather comparable, thanks to the random assignments. The average purchase intents for the set of stimuli are tabulated in Figure 4.1. As compared to the control group, the treatment group (for whom the counterfeit was present in the consideration set when rating all products) exhibited higher average purchase intent for the high-end authentic shoes and lower average purchase intent for the low-end authentic shoes. Such differences account for at least half a point on a standard 5-point Likert scale and are statistically significant at the 6% and 5% levels. The difference in the average purchase intent for the medium-tier shoes is not significant either managerially or statistically across the groups.

The second wave of experiments was designed for a within-subject study to control for individual-specific effect and to check robustness of results from the first study. A follow-up study was conducted four weeks after these respondents took the first one. The follow-up survey was the same for all respondents. They saw actual photos of the three quality tiers of authentic Muniao shoes and the counterfeit, again with product

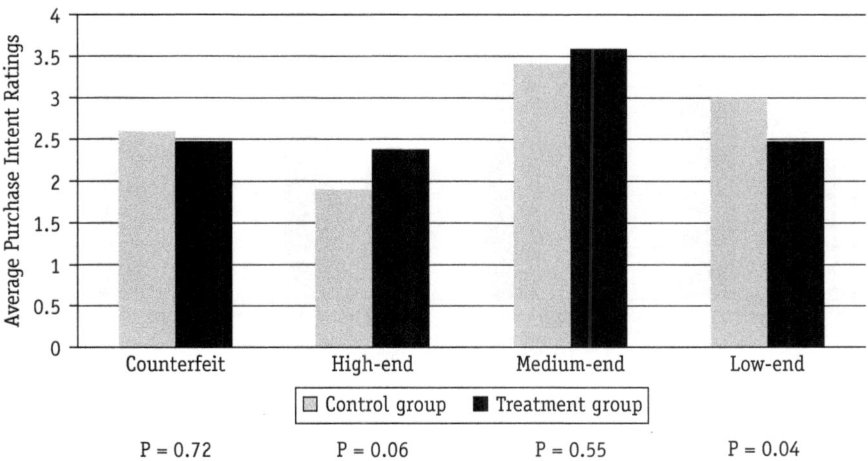

FIGURE 4.1 Purchase Intent Across Treatment and Control Groups

descriptions and real prices. They then rated their purchase intent for each and commented on their purchase motivations. The survey then asked a series of questions about their general attitudes toward counterfeits, using balanced Likert scales. Finally, each respondent copied down the serial number that was uniquely assigned to his or her first survey before exiting this follow-up survey. I used this number to match data for the two surveys by each respondent while allowing respondents to remain anonymous. By observing the purchase intent of respondents in the control group before and after seeing the counterfeit image, I could detect within-subject changes in purchase intent due to the exposure to counterfeits.

The average purchase intent for the counterfeit stimuli is not statistically different across the two surveys for the treatment and control groups, and neither are the ratings on general attitudes toward counterfeits. This suggests the consistency of respondent attitudes in the two waves of questionnaires on items under identical conditions. Figure 4.2 tabulates the average purchase intent of the respondents in the control group (who rated authentic shoes prior to seeing counterfeits in the first questionnaire while rating after seeing counterfeits in the second wave). Their purchase intent for the high-end authentic product was 0.35 higher on a 5-point Likert scale, on average, in the second survey. Such an increase in purchase intent due to having the counterfeit in the consideration set together with the authentic shoes is statistically significant at the 3% level, based on pair-wise t-tests. Exposure to the counterfeit, however, reduced the average purchase intent within subject for the medium- and low-tier authentic shoes, statistically significant at the 1% and 2% levels.

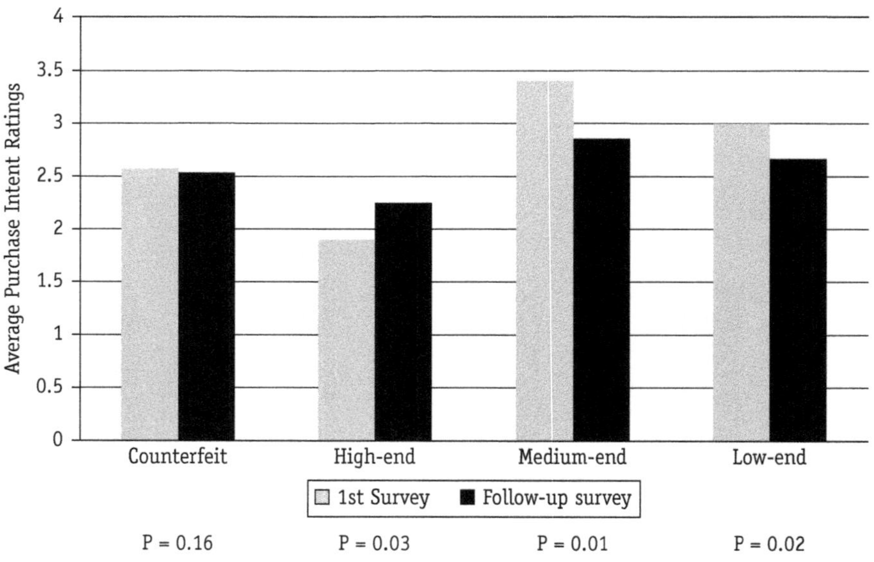

FIGURE 4.2 Purchase Intent Within the Control Groups

The surveys I designed explicitly asked respondents about their motivations for purchasing in the survey. Almost all respondents qouted the price-quality ratio or value of products as an important determinant. A number of respondents said they would like to purchase a variety of products, including counterfeits. This aligns with a strand of sociology theory on omnivorism, which predicts that high-status consumers can traverse a broad taste hierarchy because they possess knowledge of a diverse array of objects.[36] A majority in the treatment group wrote that counterfeits indicate that the brand is famous, and they rated high on the high-end authentic shoe stimulus. One respondent said, "Brand is a guarantee for quality. I don't know this brand, but it should be good if it has counterfeit followers." Respondents who lowered their ratings on the low-end authentic shoe stimulus after seeing counterfeits largely agreed with the following sentiment: "As long as the product fits my needs, I don't care if it is brand name or counterfeit." Several other respondents said they buy shoes for comfort and practicality.

I performed regression tests on the purchase intent for each type of authentic shoes and the counterfeit shoe against the treatment assignment and a series of general attitudinal ratings on counterfeits, controlling for a set of demographic variables and orders of the stimuli. Table 4.1 reports the results. The regression coefficients on the treatment indicator tell a story consistent with the t-test comparisons reported previously. The exposure to counterfeits significantly increased respondents' average purchase intent for the high-end authentic shoe but decreased it for the low-end shoe. The control and treatment groups were comparable in their average purchase intent for the counterfeit stimuli. In addition, subjects who thought that counterfeits could add variety to the market and believed they could distinguish counterfeits from authentic products had higher purchase intent for counterfeits as well.

TABLE 4.1

REGRESSION RESULTS FOR PURCHASE INTENT OF THREE QUALITY TIERS IN THE LAB

	Purchase Intent			
Variable	High-end	Medium-end	Low-end	Counterfeit
Treatment	**0.83**	0.07	**−0.67**	−0.04
	0.35	0.36	0.33	0.36
Counterfeit adds to variety	0.01	0.03	−0.04	**0.37**
	0.13	0.13	0.13	0.13

[36] B. H. Erickson, *Culture, Class and Connections*, 102 AMERICAN JOURNAL OF SOCIOLOGY 217–51 (1996); R. A. Peterson and R. M. Kern, *Changing Highbrow Taste: From Snob to Omnivore*, 61 AM. SOCIOL. REV. 900–907 (1996); R. Gosline, *supra* note 13.

	Purchase Intent			
Variable	High-end	Medium-end	Low-end	Counterfeit
Disallow fakes	−0.05	−0.02	−0.03	−0.27
	0.14	0.14	0.15	0.14
Switcher	−0.15	0.21	0.11	0.06
	0.12	0.12	0.13	0.12
Expert	−0.16	0.25	−0.15	**0.49**
	0.14	0.14	0.14	0.14
Negative Association	0.20	0.00	−0.05	0.30
	0.17	0.17	0.17	0.17
Household size	0.10	−0.07	0.06	−0.09
	0.08	0.08	0.08	0.08
Age	−0.19	0.09	−0.02	0.01
	0.18	0.19	0.19	0.19
Gender	−0.27	0.38	0.09	−0.09
	0.31	0.31	0.32	0.32
Income	0.11	0.17	0.04	0.05
	0.13	0.13	0.14	0.14
Race				
Asian	0.10	−0.14	0.24	−0.37
	0.39	0.40	0.41	0.40
Hispanic	0.76	−1.31	1.07	**−3.32**
	1.22	1.24	1.28	1.25
White	0.11	−0.62	0.49	−0.31
	0.47	0.47	0.49	0.48
Others	−1.14	−0.79	0.94	**−1.47**
	0.64	0.65	0.68	0.66
Single	0.48	0.48	−0.14	0.19
	0.33	0.34	0.35	0.34
Constant	2.69	1.09	2.75	0.63
	1.10	1.12	1.16	1.14
N	62	62	62	61

Notes: Each column reports one Seemingly Unrelated Regression equation. Point estimates are reported in the first row aligning with the corresponding product-line independent variable. Standard Errors are clustered at the level, and are reported in the second row for each corresponding independent variable.

V. Conclusion

Sales impacts of counterfeits are urgent concerns for business managers and policymakers. Senior U.S. senator for New York Charles E. Schumer introduced legislation at the beginning of August 2010 that would rewrite copyright law to cover fashion designs,[37] but he may not have had the positive effect of imitations in mind. This chapter provides a theoretical framework to conceptualize the potential sales impacts of counterfeiting. I model a branded firm with multiple product lines under both monopoly and competition conditions and derive the equilibrium demand for the authentic and counterfeit products.

The study uncovers heterogeneous effects of counterfeit entry on the sales of authentic products of three quality tiers among existing product lines. In particular, counterfeits have both advertising effects for the brand and substitution effects for authentic products. The advertising effect dominates the substitution effect for high-end authentic product sales, and the substitution effect outweighs the advertising effect for low-end product sales. The effects last for a few years before leveling off. Such differential effects reinforce incentives for authentic producers to innovate and move upward in the quality portfolio. The market shares for the higher-quality products increased post-entry and those of lower-end products declined. The model also predicts parameter ranges for product-line proliferation after the entry. Similar heterogeneous effects on the purchase intent of high-, medium-, and low-tier branded products were replicated in experimental settings. Responses in the experiments suggest that counterfeits signal brand popularity to at least some consumers, and a large number of consumers prefer to enjoy a variety of quality levels. Counterfeits therefore steal demand from the low-end authentic products while having positive spillover effects for high-end authentic products. These findings substantiate and enrich the discovery in prior research[38] that authentic firms' average prices and quality increase after entry by counterfeits. Combining these studies gives a deeper understanding of how counterfeit entry under weak intellectual property protection affects innovation incentives of firms and markets.

The theoretical and lab findings indicate priorities in enforcement against counterfeits. Although luxury companies such as Louis Vuitton are still very aggressive in enforcing their rights and attempting to weed out counterfeits, both governments and private sectors are resource constrained. The enforcement priority could be directed to counterfeiters that have closer quality proximity to the authentic products and hence pose higher substitution risks.

In sum, this chapter identifies through a combination of theory and lab experiments the heterogeneous effects of counterfeits on authentic product sales. The findings have

---

[37] K. Raustiala & C. Sprigman, *Why Imitation Is the Sincerest Form of Fashion*, N.Y. Times, Aug. 12, 2010, p. 5

[38] Qian, *supra* note 5.

important policy implications. As counterfeits hurt primarily low-end authentic products and have positive net effects on high-end ones, the focus of enforcement against counterfeits should be directed toward low-quality counterfeits or counterfeits that imitate lower-end authentic products. It seems not only socially beneficial to weed out low-quality counterfeits and to keep certain levels of higher-quality competition, but also privately efficient to the branded companies. In addition, the findings that the positive sales impact of counterfeiting is more pronounced for brands that were not yet well known at the time of infringment could imply that trademarks and IPR may be optimally enforced at different stages of brand or product adoption cycles. This is exactly what Microsoft did in China. It fiercely enforced measures against piracy only after the majority of the Chinese users had adopted its products (in either authentic form or pirated copies). The positive spillover effect of a low-quality entrant on the original brand is also identified in Qian, et. al. and Simester,[39] using the comprehensive scanner database by an American apparel company. Kuksov and Xie[40] also theorize the positive competition effect in the status goods market. The findings here, therefore, have applications beyond counterfeiting. Together, this body of research suggests that there is an optimal level of IPR protection, and the optimum varies from country to country,[41] sector to sector,[42] brand to brand, and even product to product. The optimum could also have a time dimension in light of the dynamic effects discussed in this study.

[39] Yi Qian, Eric Anderson, and Duncan Simester, *Multichannel Spillovers From a Factory Store* (Working Paper, Northwestern University and MIT 2013).

[40] D. Kuksov, Y. Xie, *Competition in a Status Goods Market*, 49(5) J. MARKETING RES. 609–23.

[41] Qian, *supra* note 10; Qian, *Are Intellectual Property Rights the Blossoming Rain?—Evidences from Innovations, Technology Transfer, and International Trade, in* THE DEVELOPMENT AGENDA: GLOBAL INTELLECTUAL PROPERTY AND DEVELOPING COUNTRIES (Neil Netanel ed., 2009).

[42] Qian, supra note 5.

III The Social Life of Luxury Brands

5 Brands R Us

Mario Biagioli,* Anupam Chander,** and Madhavi Sunder***

THE ORTHODOX ECONOMIC understanding of trademarks assumes that trademarks function to distinguish one good from another by identifying its maker, thereby conveying information about the quality of the good. But a luxury brand functions not just to provide information about the quality of the product, but to signal the discernment or income of its owner.[1] Where utilitarian brands focus on providing information to consumers seeking functional information about the *product*, luxury brands also focus on conveying information about the *buyer*.

* Director, Center for Science and Innovation Studies, Professor of Law, Science and Technology Studies, and History, University of California, Davis.

** Director, California International Law Center, Professor of Law, and Martin Luther King, Jr. Hall Research Scholar, University of California, Davis.

*** Professor of Law and Martin Luther King, Jr. Hall Research Scholar, University of California, Davis. This chapter is adapted from an article first published as the Introduction to the *UC Davis Law Review* symposium, "Brand New World: Distinguishing Oneself in the Global Flow" (December 2013). We are grateful to the *UC Davis Law Review*, its Editors-in-Chief Briana Fitzpatrick and Marissa Martin O'Connor, and Symposium Editors Nima Rahimi and Daniel Elefant for extraordinary work. We thank Jordy Hur for valuable research assistance.

[1] Barton Beebe, *Intellectual Property and the Sumptuary Code*, 123 HARV. L. REV. 809 (2010).

Branding practices stretch back into antiquity and demonstrate both continuity and change. Ancient physicians engaged in property disputes over the seals they impressed on the containers of their medications, making brand marks the oldest branch of intellectual property.[2] The antiquity of brand marks, however, has not helped their proper understanding by the law. While the conceptual and historical foundations of copyrights and patents continue to be part and parcel of contemporary legal debates, the full history and theorizing on business marks is largely external to trademark doctrine. Furthermore, with only a few and by now outdated exceptions,[3] whatever scholarship exists on these topics has been performed mostly not by legal scholars but by archaeologists, art historians, anthropologists, sociologists, and historians of material culture.

Such a striking imbalance suggests that the law is more eager to assume and state what trademarks should be rather than understand how they actually work today. Nor does the law often acknowledge the many different ways in which marks have always been deployed to distinguish both goods and their makers. This is not just a scholarly problem: given the extraordinary importance of brands in the global economy, the growing disjuncture between the way brands function in different contexts and cultures and trademark law's simplified conceptualization of that function has become a problem with increasingly substantial policy implications. Some new work, which we will describe herein, responds to an urgent need to realign the law with business practices and consumer culture and behavior. These studies can, however, only move toward that realignment. The disciplinary, geographical, and chronological scope of the new scholarship we will describe is a good indication of the complexity of the issues and of the range of perspectives needed to understand them. In this chapter, we begin to sketch a cultural approach to brands, informed by this recent interdisciplinary scholarship.

Brands represent the oldest branch of intellectual property, and yet modern law has focused on their conceptual instantiation in only one form: trademarks. To make an artificially narrow conceptualization even narrower, modern scholarship on trademarks has focused on one aspect of their role in commerce—the economics of information. In agreement with the assumptions of law and economics, marks have come to be seen as devices to reduce consumer search costs, thereby supporting investment by a producer in consistent quality over time and space.[4] This economic analysis elegantly coupled both consumer and producer interests in the legal protection of marks, but only recognized

---

[2] Danielle Gourevitch, *How Did Gallo-Roman Physicians Treat Their Patients? A Look into the Earliest Pharmacopoeias of France*, 34 MEDICOGRAPHIA 238, 245–47 (2012).

[3] *See, e.g.*, FRANK ISAAC SCHECHTER, THE HISTORICAL FOUNDATIONS OF THE LAW RELATING TO TRADE-MARKS (1925) (tracing the development of trademark law from medieval times to the early twentieth century).

[4] William M. Landes & Richard A. Posner, *Trademark Law: An Economic Perspective*, 30 J.L. & ECON. 265, 269 (1987) ("The benefits of trademarks in reducing consumer search costs require that the producer of a trademarked good maintain a consistent quality over time and across consumers. Hence trademark protection encourages expenditures on quality.").

certain features of business marks. It failed to recognize, for example, that brands were being used to supply information not just about the product or service, but about the user. It failed to see how clothes of a certain design or with a certain logo constructed the person who bought and wore them: woman or man, cool or reliable, energetic or sedentary, and so forth—that, in the eyes of many, clothes made the man or woman. The law also failed to recognize how users contributed to making and promoting the brand, thus giving it value. The relationship between the person and the brand has never been a unidirectional flow of information from good to buyer, but rather a dialogic process bordering on co-authorship.

The lacuna is greater still. *The psychological impact of brands is masked by the simple understanding of brands as information about the product.* The modern account failed to see the brand as an emblem of material culture, as zeitgeist, or a symbol of the times. Finally, the modern understanding obscures the relationship of brands to our station in life. Indeed, a popular song today has a girl in New Zealand reciting the luxury brands from the other side of the earth, even as she rejects them—simultaneously as being beyond her means and also outside her desires:

> We're driving Cadillacs in our dreams.
> But everybody's like Cristal, Maybach, diamonds on your timepiece.
> Jet planes, islands, tigers on a gold leash
> We don't care, we aren't caught up in your love affair
> And we'll never be royals.[5]

The economic approach underplays the complex social, psychological, and cultural role of brands, and how their production exceeds the agency of those who design, own, or control them. They also begin to consider how brands (when broadly construed as inscriptions conveying distinctive differences, as well as the performances through which those distinctions are displayed and made public) are in fact quite distinct from trademarks as lawyers understand them.

Our contribution to this book on luxury and brands describes a cultural approach to brands and its logic and contradictions. We largely take as our data points articles recently published in two issues of the *UC Davis Law Review*, collecting papers presented at the "Brand New World: Distinguishing Oneself in the Global Flow" conference at UC Davis School of Law in 2012. Our chapter proceeds as follows. In section I, we briefly sketch a cultural approach to brands, distinguishing our analysis from the economic theory that currently dominates the understanding of business marks. In section II, we anticipate future challenges to branding logics.

---

[5] LORDE, ROYALS (Lava Records 2013).

I. From Economics to Culture and from Goods to Performances

When you unbox an Apple iPhone today, you find inside an Apple logo sticker, not an instruction manual. The sticker is not to be affixed to the iPhone, which already has that mark etched on its back and on its screen upon powering up. The logo here is not designed to help inform the user that he or she has purchased an Apple product. Rather the hope is that the user might want to tell others that he or she has purchased an Apple product. (This act of signification may not even be performed by the buyer him/herself, but rather delegated to the "kinship network," like when children attach those stickers to their bike or school binder.) The Apple logo here seeks to inform the world about the buyer or those connected to the buyer, not the product. Furthermore, even while the buyer seems to endorse the product, *the product endorses the buyer back*. This was particularly evident in pre-Internet days, when certain luxury goods could not simply be purchased online by anybody armed with Google and a capacious credit card, but required some pre-knowledge, like knowing where or through whom one could buy them. This symmetry between buyers endorsing (or confirming the distinction of) goods and goods endorsing the distinction of the person who could buy them has been missed by the conventional economic view of trademarks. Economic theory saw the informational function of marks as unidirectional—from the product to the buyer. But, as Margaret Chon observes, trademark law is "devoid of a deep understanding of the communicative process underlying brand value."[6]

The brand is not just about expressive identity; it is a full-fledged *social* phenomenon, a sign of the times. Brand packaging, ads, and slogans are emblems of material culture that help us define and understand who we are, or who we were. To wit: imagine a visit to a Museum of Brands (there actually is one in London). Such a visit is a step back though history. It tells us about who we were through the products of the age and the lifestyles they enabled. The slogans of the age represent its zeitgeist. *Have it your way. I want my MTV. Think different. Rip. Mix. Burn.* Brand marks reflect the technologies and people of a time and place. In his fascinating account of the new plain packaging for cigarettes required under Australian law, for example, Alain Pottage describes retail packaging as "closely conditioned by ... the evolution of the technologies which determined what sorts of images or symbols could be printed, stamped, or inscribed on what sorts of materials."[7] Pottage writes, "[T]he look and feel of the package depended in

---

[6] Margaret Chon, *Slow Logo: Brand Citizenship in Global Value Networks*, 47 UC Davis L. Rev. (2014); *see also* Stacey L. Dogan & Mark A. Lemley, *Parody as Brand*, 47 UC Davis L. Rev. (2014) ("Brands shape our communities and define our values. And while the traditional economic account views brands as conveying information unidirectionally—from producer to consumer—brands also convey information about the consumer and allow members of the public to communicate to each other.").

[7] Alain Pottage, *No (More) Logo: Plain Packaging and Communicative Agency*, 47 UC Davis L. Rev. (2014).

part on the development of packaging materials such as corrugated cardboard or molded fiber."[8] At the same time, brands do not just convey a time period. Brands themselves have "agency," in Pottage's words—they act on the world, eliciting particular consumer responses and giving products qualities "they would not otherwise have."[9] Indeed, in the context Pottage is describing—the tobacco industry—brands have blood on their hands. Brands, for better or for worse, make a brand new world. At the same time, brands are also resources used by individuals and communities for contesting and reshaping the values of a time and place. Brands both shape and convey meanings. Indeed, we can recognize shifts in culture through changes in marks—for example, from the change in warnings on cigarette packages from "CAUTION: Cigarette Smoking May Be Hazardous to Your Health" to mandated plain packaging.[10] We may usefully apply Clifford Geertz's famous definition of culture as "webs of significance"[11] to similarly understand brands as evolving cultural meanings that change over time.[12]

In elaborating the cultural work that brands do, our argument is not that the conventional economic analysis of trademarks is wrong, but that it is certainly incomplete. It is not simply that advertising changes the nature of one's preferences, thus fouling the assumption of "*de gustibus non disputandum est*"—the economists' attempt to hold individual preferences exogenous from the analysis. We take the effect of brands to be far more profound: they are tools that allow buyers to construct and perform distinctive personae for themselves. Brands are not valuable to the buyer simply because of the information they convey, but because of the "identity performances" they enable. Paradoxically, buyers may be attracted to branded goods because of these goods' potential instability, that is, not so much because of their stability or reliability as products or the stability of the information they carry, but rather because they function as resources the buyer can use to do something with—something that is always to some extent new. Buyers mobilize brands as props in their performances of image construction, which means that the meaning of brands is modified by the very performances they make possible. This may take place through the juxtaposition of varied branded goods brought together in the buyers' homes, on their clothing, and so forth. Barton Beebe describes the phenomenon of "shanzhai," or elaborate mimicry of established brands, in China today as "performance art" on a national scale.[13] Individuals, towns, and companies engage, imitate, and play with well-known luxury brands and experiences as both

---

[8] *Id.*

[9] *Id.*

[10] *Id.*

[11] CLIFFORD GEERTZ, THE INTERPRETATION OF CULTURES 5 (1973) ("The concept of culture is essentially a semiotic one. Believing, with Max Weber, that man is an animal suspended in webs of significance he himself has spun, I take culture to be those webs").

[12] Madhavi Sunder, *Cultural Dissent*, 54 STAN. L. REV. 495, 511 (2001).

[13] Barton Beebe, *Shanzhai, Sumptuary Law, and Intellectual Property Law in Contemporary China*, 47 UC DAVIS L. REV. (2014) [hereinafter *Shanzhai*] (quoting YU HUA, CHINA IN TEN WORDS 181 (Allan H. Barr

commerce and comment. Sonia Katyal describes transnational "anti-brand" movements by which consumers seek to upend the "official" meaning of the brand.[14] Stacey Dogan and Mark Lemley identify ways that brands beget brands—how Starbucks precipitated Charbucks, and Louis Vuitton spawned Chewy Vuiton.[15] Indeed, in their identification and discussion of the phenomenon of "brand parodies"—branded products that also serve as commentary on well-known brands—Dogan and Lemley acknowledge many ways in which "[b]rand parodies … don't fit well within existing trademark infringement or dilution law."[16]

James Leach forces us to imagine the next conceptual step, that is, to go beyond the performative use of branded goods and brands and think of the performance itself as the process through which persons and cultural distinctions are created.[17] The lengthy and intricate initiation rituals that turn some Papua New Guinea teenagers into "men" do rely on all sorts of specific objects—from clothing to staging devices. They are also quite expensive and physically taxing (growing up looking cool has never been cheap or painless anywhere). But what matters there are not the objects and props as distinct and distinguishing objects, but rather the performances that construct these specific new persons by connecting them to things, persons, and cultural narratives. This is not a call to happily go back to times and places where cultural distinction was produced through expensive performances rather than expensive branded goods, but rather to realize that when we mention "performance art" in connection to brands, as Beebe invites us to do, we may in fact be speaking a lot less metaphorically than we think.

Branding is and has always been performative. Evelyn Lincoln and Pascale Rihouet, for instance, show how late medieval and early Renaissance Italian religious confraternities developed distinctive marks, which they had included in the paintings and ritual objects they commissioned as well as on the buildings they owned. These marks spread long-lasting signs of the confraternity's presence and virtuous activities for everybody to see in a much more permanent fashion than today's ads and billboards can. At the same time, several of these branded objects, as well as the distinctive uniforms that members wore during confraternity-related activities (including processions featuring self-flagellations) were obviously designed for, and part of, public performances. It was through such performances that the confraternity members, together with the attending public, displayed and confirmed their corporate identity and their place in the town's life. Their marks may have been attached to goods, but they functioned by moving

---

trans., 2012)); see also Haochen Sun, *Can Louis Vuitton Dance with Hiphone? Rethinking the Idea of Social Justice in Intellectual Property Law*, 15 U. Pa. J.L. & Soc. Change 389 (2012).

[14] *See* Sonia K. Katyal, *Trademark Cosmopolitanism*, 47 UC Davis L. Rev. 875 (2014).

[15] *See* Dogan & Lemley, *supra* note 6.

[16] *Id.*

[17] James Leach, *"We Will Make a Man Out of You": Taro "Brands" and Initiation "Styles" on the Rai Coast of Papua New Guinea*, 47 UC Davis L. Rev. (2014).

around together with the body of the confraternity member, by producing an "animated logo for the confraternity."[18]

We are finally learning to recognize the performative nature of branding practices and thus go beyond "object thinking." It is easy to understand why we have privileged objects over associations, especially the kind of performative associations between persons and things that are so important to understanding brands. Property needs its objects, and perhaps pursues them even more single-mindedly when they are elusive, as is certainly the case with intellectual property. IP always strives, necessarily so, to stabilize its constructs: work, author, invention, and so forth—a goal that is always approached but never fully achieved. But this process of objectification may be even more difficult in the case of trademarks because, as suggested by historical and ethnographic examples, sociocultural distinctions may be even more performative (and more visibly so) than other forms of cultural productions like literary works, art, inventions, and so on. And collectivity follows from performativity. Inventors and authors build on the work of their predecessors and of those around them, but in the case of brands, the notion of collaboration often goes well beyond borrowing from peers or predecessors. Especially with goods that are valuable a buyer because of the social distinction they bestow on him or her, the brand functions by establishing, expanding, and then maintaining associations and connections. That is an inherently collective—not just derivative—process.

Goodwill and brand recognition may be treated as intangible but they are inherently based on many interactions and associations between people, things, and signs. This web of associations, however, has been reduced by trademark law (and its roots in law and economics doctrine) to an object that is attributed "information" (instead of potentialities, associations, etc.) while treating its users as buyers with "taste" (that is, an inclination to buy objects rather than to produce new subjectivities and cultural assemblages with them). And, in any case, the "taste" of the potential purchaser or user is cast as having nothing to do with the user's engagement with that good. Networks are cut, sealed objects and self-contained subjects are created—precisely the kind of dichotomy that the humanities and social sciences have so convincingly questioned and sometimes undone.[19]

Some corporations, however, are smarter than the law. They try to channel the buyers' transformative uses of their brands in directions they can control, for instance, by inviting consumers to connect to the company through their social networks. This means that companies understand that buyers change the meaning of their brands, but companies try to direct that process of change in a direction they can represent as the "growth"—not dilution—of their brands. Customers change the brands, but that's fine insofar as, by doing so, they end up identifying even closer with the company whose

[18] Evelyn Lincoln & Pascale Rihouet, *Brands of Piety*, 47 UC Davis L. Rev. (2014).

[19] See, among many other interventions, Bruno Latour, Inquiry into Modes of Existence: An Anthropology of the Moderns (2013).

brands they are to develop. It thus makes sense, as Deborah Gerhardt suggests, that consumer investment in trademarks facilitates the rise of brands, a practice that has grown with the rise of social media.[20] Deven Desai observes that not only do consumers share information about a mark, but the mark-holder can seek to convey different messages simultaneously with the mark.[21] As Desai writes, "[T]he mark is a medium through which many messages flow."[22]

In the old world, marks on goods—from coins to Chinese silk[23] to medicines—sought to convey authenticity, which was typically coupled with assumptions about quality. If I can be sure that the sword I am considering buying is made in Toledo with Toledo steel, then chances are it is a good sword. If I can be sure that the stamp on this brick means that it was really produced in Argillopolis—a place famous for the quality of its clay, its brickmakers, and its kilns—then I can be reasonably confident that the house I have built with these bricks will not crumble before I put the roof on. And so on. In some cases, the "brand" did not need to be attached to the good or printed on it, but could be integral to how the good looked, tasted, or sounded.[24] A Toledo steel blade could be recognized by distinctive striatures and color patterns, and one could tell pewter cups of good provenance and quality by recognizing the specific sound they made when you tapped them.[25] Visual or aural, marks conveyed information, but one needed to know both what that information was—"Toledo blades are good"—and be able to read the brand off the object. That is, one needed the skill to tell that a certain pattern of striatures on a blade meant "Toledo." While modern brands work well only when they are easy to recognize, the detection of old branding marks could be a task that necessitated some expertise—expertise that had to be mobilized even *before* one could connect a certain mark to specific information about the quality of that good. One needed to be able to sound a word, not just understand what that word meant.

In the brand new world, the detection of brands no longer requires special skills. (Actually that's precisely the point: to lower the threshold of connoisseurship and hermeneutic skills required of buyers so that they do not need to "read the good" but simply recognize the brand.) At the same time, "brand new brands" do a lot more than their ancestors. The rise of brands marks a fundamental shift in the law and business

[20] Deborah R. Gerhardt, *Social Media Amplify Consumer Investment in Trademarks*, 90 N.C. L. Rev. 1491, 1505–9 (2012).

[21] Deven R. Desai, *Bounded by Brands: An Information Network Approach to Trademarks*, 47 UC Davis L. Rev. (2014).

[22] *Id.*

[23] Dagmar Schäfer, *Peripheral Matters: Selvage/Chef-de-piece Inscriptions on Chinese Silk Inscriptions*, 47 UC Davis L. Rev. (2014).

[24] Gary Richardson, *Brand Names Before the Industrial Revolution* 4 (NBER Working Paper Series, Working Paper No. 13930, 2008), *available at* http://www.nber.org/papers/w13930.

[25] *Id.*

practice of trademarks. Where trademarks have long protected marks that signal the source of a good or service to consumers, increasingly today customers value logos such as the Nike "Swoosh" in and of themselves. In the "experience economy," corporations sell (the potential for) identity and community, authenticity and auras, not products. Starbucks is "everything but the coffee"—it is billed as an experience, a place to connect with others. Brands mark one as adventurous, sensible, whimsical, glamorous, rugged, carefree, sophisticated, cosmopolitan, old school, and even anti-brand. At this point, advertisement professionals have a much better grasp than legal scholars of how brands work.

Of course, this division between the old world of marks and the new world of marks is too neat. That separation is not an essential but a contextual one, depending on the specific feature of the good, its uses, its durability, modalities and scale of circulation and display, the ease or difficulty to disseminate information about it, copy it, and so on. Even in the "olden days," marks served a multiplicity of functions, designed to evoke the sights and sounds of exotic places or the sturdiest and hardiest elements of nature. As Lionel Bently reveals in his historical account of one of the earliest English trademark cases, *Singleton v. Bolton*, Mr. Singleton, a manufacturer of a medicine called *Dr. Johnson's Yellow Ointment* in the eighteenth century, sought to use a trademark to control the distribution channels of his product, much the way that luxury brand makers seek to do today.[26] Dagmar Schäfer's paper reveals that while brands are becoming increasingly crucial to modern business, they are as old as language itself. Used to establish prestigious identities (for example, the hegemony of the Chinese Emperor as Schäfer describes[27]) or to connect goods with their makers, they have been found in signature seals, royal coins, artists' anagrams, coats of arms, goods stamps, chops, guild marks, and more. By revisiting historical branding landscapes, the scholarship surveyed here raises questions of what elements of these practices have been included, or excluded, from the object of modern trademark law, and why.

If there is one thing that appears different today, it is the scale of branding practices and their global spread. Branding has become ubiquitous. Even a generic drug retailer wants to distinguish itself through branding, as Cori Hayden points out in a delightful inversion.[28] Brands are so pervasive in middle-class America that one can often tell the story of one's day through one's encounters with brands. Every charity, organization, and social movement seeks to brand itself, that is, to cultivate and trade off its distinct identity. Entire countries seek to distinguish themselves through brands. South Africa has an official entity called "Brand South Africa," which is "charged with marketing the

---

[26] Lionel Bently, *The First Trademark Case at Common Law? The Story of* Singleton v. Bolton (1783), 47 UC Davis L. Rev. (2014).

[27] Schäfer, *supra* note 23.

[28] Cori Hayden, *Distinctively Similar: A Generic Problem*, 47 UC Davis L. Rev. (2014).

country abroad."[29] *Foreign Affairs* journal characterizes even China's ambassador to the United States as a "brand ambassador."[30] A non-profit group, Light Years IP, is helping East Africa's Maasai to win trademarks to their name and customs across the world.[31]

Brand creation, management, and licensing involve concerns distinct from those of traditional trademarks, less focused on consumer confusion and more akin to copyright law's concerns for storytelling and expressive control. Where trademarks focus on quality, brands focus on feeling. Deven Desai observes that while trademarks provide consumers with information about the identity of products, brands have an emotional or symbolic component.[32] Corporations now invest time and resources into leading the consumers to associate a certain brand with a certain image and, in the process, "to look beyond price when making purchasing decisions."[33] In short: the move from trademarks to brands heralds a shift from product identification to the appreciation of the cultural meaning of that good.[34] A brand, Mark McKenna notes, "is a comprehensive concept that encompasses all of its representations and all the associated meaning."[35]

The range of the meaning and societal values delivered by brands proves to be very broad and varied, and it becomes more so whenever scholars look carefully at specific cases. Nicole Aylwin and Rosemary Coombe argue, for instance, that intellectual property rights "are no longer regarded merely as tools to solve economic public-goods problems and advance capitalist accumulation."[36] Rather, these scholars observe, "they are implicated and deployed in agendas as seemingly unrelated as identity politics, rural development, ethical consumption practices, the preservation of biological and cultural diversity, and indigenous self-determination."[37] Marks also symbolize conditions of production, not just the identity, of the product. As Paul Duguid observes, California long ago began permitting the registration of union labels, "which determinedly, though not uniquely, sought to make the conditions of production evident to the consumer."[38]

---

[29] Robyn Dixon, *South Africa Stumbles While Looking to Market Itself Abroad*, L.A. TIMES (Oct. 25, 2013), http://www.latimes.com/world/worldnow/la-fg-wn-south-africa-economic-woes-zuma-20131025,0,1749866.story#axzz2inZgJZu3.

[30] Cui Tiankai, *Beijing's Brand Ambassador*, FOREIGN AFF., July–Aug. 2013, at 10, *available at* http://www.foreignaffairs.com/discussions/interviews/beijings-brand-ambassador.

[31] Olga Khazan, *The Maasai People Take Back Their Brand*, ATLANTIC (Aug. 14, 2013), http://www.theatlantic.com/magazine/archive/2013/09/big-in-kenya/309425/.

[32] Deven R. Desai, *From Trademarks to Brands*, 64 FLA. L. REV. 981, 994 (2012) (describing how economic view of trademarks does not allow for emotional or irrational aspect of purchasing behavior).

[33] *Id.* at 985.

[34] Alain Pottage's discussion of meaning in the context of mass communication is particularly helpful here. *See* Pottage, *supra* note 7.

[35] Mark P. McKenna, *Testing Modern Trademark Law's Theory of Harm*, 95 IOWA L. REV. 63, 93 (2009).

[36] Nicole Aylwin & Rosemary Coombe, *Marks Indicating Conditions of Origin in Rights-Based Sustainable Development*, 47 UC DAVIS L. REV. (2014).

[37] *Id.*

[38] Paul Duguid, *California Marketing & Collective Amnesia*, 47 UC DAVIS L. REV. (2014).

This point connects Duguid's essay to Aylwin's and Coombe's as they too observe the importance of what they call "Marks Indicating Conditions of Origin" (or MICOs).[39] MICOs signal the provenance of a product, including identifying which communities made the goods and under what conditions of market and social exchange. Aylwin and Coombe argue for a "commitment to rights-based criteria if [MICOs are] to avoid reproducing old forms of privilege or perpetuating new forms of injustice."[40] Chon's paper raises related questions:[41] Can marks serve as indicators of morality? Can they improve products and processes, policing international trade? Who watches the watchers? What does certification mean when one group's "fair trade" may not coincide with another group's "fair trade"?

In sum, trademark law over-objectivizes the brand, depriving it of its many cultural associations and performative and collaborative dimensions. But there are also suggestions that trademarks do not always deliver on even the narrow promise to convey information about the quality of a product. Dan Kevles's fine-textured essay on the nineteenth-century trademarking of plants and fruits by innovative U.S. breeders who could not rely, at that time, on patents, dwells on the very serious problem posed by the variability of any plant variety. One simply could not know with certainty the precise features of the plant that would grow from seeds one purchased from a nursery. There were, in sum, two closely intertwined and equally serious problems: breeders could not patent the new varieties they had bred, and the variety was not a stable object that bred true and continued to reproduce itself in the same form and features through each generation. The trademarking of plants and fruits, therefore, may be read as an attempt to use the only tool the law offered breeders to protect their "intellectual property" (if limited to names and logos), but it can also be seen, more obliquely but not less importantly, as an attempt to use trademark law to create the effect that there was a stable plant or fruit variety one could name, depict, and sell in the first place. The trademarked name of the fruit and the accompanying attractively colorful picture in the catalogue created the effect—the "reality effect"—of the fruit's stability as an object when it was, in fact, subject to substantial variations. The trademark, in sum, did not simply convey information about the quality of the fruit or plant as an object or good, but actually helped to construe those trademarked plants and fruits *as objects*. The trademark helped to create the stability it was supposed to be based on.[42] Little could the fruit growers of the nineteenth century have imagined that "Apple" would come to denote a computing device by the end of the next century.

---

[39] Aylwin & Coombe, *supra* note 36.

[40] *Id.*

[41] Chon, *supra* note 6.

[42] *See* Daniel J. Kevles, *A Primer of A, B, Seeds: Advertising, Branding, and Intellectual Property in an Emerging Industry*, 47 UC Davis L. Rev. (2014).

II. Brand Futures

Even as they increasingly dominate our lives, there are counter-movements at work. If brands were about conveying information, that function has been replaced in part by new kinds of reputation systems made possible by the Internet. Customer rankings and reviews, of the kind popularized by Amazon and eBay, now supply a great deal of comparative and continuously updated information about products. Yelp, Angie's List, and Google reviews go beyond reviews of goods to reviews of services. Internet intermediaries, from Amazon to eBay and from Facebook to Google, increasingly interact with the branding phenomenon. In many instances, these ranking systems supply more information than can be carried by the brand alone—for example, the usability of a good or service for certain functions of interest to a narrow subset of purchasers, or whether a specific product by a famous brand is really as good as we would have assumed based on the brand's reputation.

These trends may exceed the logic of trademark law and its justification, but are certainly not surprising to scholars external to the legal community who have approached marks on objects (in both the past and present, in the West and everywhere else) as ways to develop and maintain social relations, construct persons and personae, produce cultural and material distinction, standardize practices and goods, or even protect intellectual property when patents or copyrights are not available or do not seem to provide sufficient protection. Similarly, scholars interested in collaborative and collective forms of cultural and knowledge production have focused on brands as windows beyond the individualist view of the author and the inventor. (For instance, the role of brands and trademarks is central to studies of cultural and religious heritage, as well as to the development of new religious movements.)

Even these can perhaps be improved on. Facebook and Google have recognized that an individual's social graph can be mined for products and services that might be of special interest to one's friends. Madhavi and Anupam are more likely to trust Mario's restaurant recommendations than those of Yelp or OpenTable or even the *New York Times*.

There is another concern: if brands represent auras or stories, perhaps they have overreached and ought to be ratcheted back. Perhaps the law should try to ensure that trademarks serve a singular and narrow function to relate product to source. But we might find in the search for distinction an understandable effort for individualization in a world of mass production. Brands can lend meaning to markets. Markets after all are an expression of social relations, including a human desire to understand not only the source of their products, but also how a good is produced and the role of that object in our social and cultural lives.

Producers find brands crucial in a world of efficient supply chains made possible by modern transportation, communication, and global mass production. Thus, a brand strategy is at the same time the embodiment of, and the antidote to, global capitalism.

Brands then are the producer's response to the problem of commoditization hypercharged by a world of efficient worldwide production and distribution. When a product with reliable and attractive qualities can be mass-produced and distributed, the producer needs to change the way that product is understood or risk facing the relentless price-pressures of commoditization. The product must now "tell a story" to distinguish itself from what are otherwise functionally similar products. Rather than an engineer, businessperson, or manufacturer, a producer becomes a seller of a story—an author, a narrator, a designer, or an artist.

Storytelling may be a better rubric for understanding brands than the conventional one of brands as static vessels of information. As Rasmus Nielsen of the acclaimed Danish artist trio Superflex beautifully conveyed in his keynote address for the "Brand New World" conference delivered at UC Davis in October 2012, the issue is not simply what story a brand tells, but who has the power to tell the story—and to retell it. Stories can grow on, but also bounce off, each other. While brand producers are becoming artists, Superflex (echoing Andy Warhol in this respect) has recognized that brands can themselves become the material for art. When a beverage multinational showed little concern for the Brazilian indigenous farmers who cultivated an energizing ingredient called guarana, for example, Superflex encouraged the farmers to brand themselves through a kind of guerilla use of the multinational's trademark.[43] As Nielsen observes in his keynote, "we tend to communicate with things, as well, not just words and papers."[44] Nielsen adds that brands "mirror our desires and create our desires . . . they colonize our desires."[45]

Thus, there is at once a socially useful role for brands in which they help tell stories, but there is also a more disquieting role, through which they subtly shape ordinary people. In the latter mode, brand auras might be misleading or manipulative, a way to get a gullible consumer to part with a few more coins. Peter Menell reviews the psychological literature, observing the exploitative nature of advertising.[46] He warns of a totalitarianism wrought by corporations, not governments: "It is more Adam Smith and Facebook than Benito Mussolini or Joseph Stalin."[47]

Some have observed the capacity of marks to entrench social difference, to reinforce the existing social hierarchies, if not by titles of nobility, then by the clothes or fragrance one wears, the handbag one carries, or the car one arrives in. Barton Beebe reports that some governments in China have become increasingly concerned about the capitalist

---

[43] Anupam Chander, *Illegal Art? The Artists' Group Superflex Co-Opts Global Trademarks*, FINDLAW.COM, May 13, 2004, at http://writ.news.findlaw.com/commentary/20040513_chander.html.

[44] Rasmus Nielsen, Superflex, Keynote address at UC Davis Law Review Symposium: "Brand New World: Distinguishing Oneself in the Global Flow" (Oct. 4–5, 2012) in 47 UC DAVIS L. REV. (2014).

[45] *Id.*

[46] Peter S. Menell, 2014: Brand Totalitarianism, 47 UC DAVIS L. REV. (2014).

[47] *Id.*

class differentiation promoted by brands, as antithetical to "social harmony."[48] He notes, "Beijing is reported to have banned the use of such words as 'royal,' 'imperial,' 'supreme,' 'high class,' and, 'luxury' in billboard advertising."[49] Noting the "ethical crisis" faced by places such as Hong Kong, where Gucci stores proliferate alongside the misery of people who live as "cage dogs," Haochen Sun would offer luxury brands strong trademark rights only in return for efforts to educate their consumers about poverty.[50] Sun believes this is necessary to, as his title indicates, live "together in one civilized world" that goes from Victoria Peak in Hong Kong to more humble addresses.[51] Dagmar Schäfer also focuses on China's keen concern with the relation between brands and social hierarchy, but goes back to the Ming and Qing periods to show how extraordinarily intricate marking practices were applied to a wide variety of goods, straddling the line between trademarks and certification marks.[52] In diametrical opposition to their modern cousins, Schäfer shows that early Chinese marks were not about conveying the product differentiation so crucial to the production of value in a global capitalistic economy, but rather about reinforcing the central authority of the emperor by articulating and inscribing it through the goods that circulated in his domain. Early Chinese marks were not antithetical to "social harmony" (as some modern Chinese politicians take brands to be), but the "harmony" they sought to maintain was surely not one that either Mao or the neoliberals would have approved of.

There is yet another dialectic at work with brands, one that is internal to them. The more ubiquitous a brand becomes, the less it marks an individual as distinct. An Apple logo would become meaningless as a mark of distinction for any consumer, if all consumers owned Apples. So producers of brands that distinguish consumers, and not just producers, must manage their brands carefully to avoid losing this characteristic.

Indeed, the logic of brands is such that, in many circumstances, a brand is worth more the less visible it is. Gucci's new "Jackie" bag is monogram free.[53] A discreetly placed mark (or even no mark) on a good whose value is known only to the cognoscenti marks a discerning buyer. Such brands trade on the fact that such items are largely inaccessible, marking the buyer as one of the privileged few—even if that status is known only to the buyer himself or herself.

Does recognizing a mark's broader role in society necessarily enlarge the scope of a trademark holder's rights? No. By recognizing a mark as part of culture, a cultural theory

---

[48] Beebe, *Shanzhai, supra* note 13.

[49] *Id.*

[50] Haochen Sun, *Living Together in One Civilized World: How Luxury Companies and Consumers Can Fulfill Their Ethical Responsibilities to the Poor*, 47 UC Davis L. Rev. (2014).

[51] *Id.*

[52] Schäfer, *supra* note 23.

[53] Liao Danlin, *Discreet by Design*, Global Times (July 6, 2013, 7:13 PM), http://www.globaltimes.cn/content/789115.shtml#.UouyZmR4bNA; Erin Donnelly, *"Discreet Luxury" In, Flashy Logos Out*, StyleList (Aug. 10, 2010, 6:50 PM), http://main.stylelist.com/2010/08/10/logos-discreet-luxury/.

supports the rights of those outside the corporate mark holder to comment on it, to critique it, to deploy it as part of cultural conversation, and even to play with it. Two of us (Chander and Sunder) have responded to the concern of over-propertization in an earlier *UC Davis Law Review* intellectual property symposium as follows:

> Recognizing the diversity of values underlying intellectual property should lead us to share certain rights in intellectual products, rather than reserve them more closely. Recall that new theories of property, from personhood to social relations, enhanced our ability to explain and justify legal limits on property, even while they served to bolster some property claimants, such as tenants.[54]

Nicole Aylwin and Rosemary Coombe describe exactly this, noting efforts to assert "countervailing rights such as those of consumers, patients, communities, farmers, indigenous peoples, and the users of cultural goods more generally."[55] Sonia Katyal notes that "global luxury brands have become not just the lingua franca of transnational consumption, but also of the anti-branding activists who resist it."[56] Margaret Chon's "brand citizenship" would recognize "the fluid, pluralistic and open-ended construction of the value of a mark and its associated social spectacle."[57]

III. Conclusion

A focus on brands (as opposed to trademarks alone) helps us move beyond simplistic accounts of the value of marks as merely signaling source or conveying information about a static object. Brands move from the realm of logic to the realm of emotion. Recent scholarship demonstrates the agency of brands. Brands fashion brand new worlds: forming and reforming objects, collectives, hierarchies, lifestyles, meanings, and tangible material cultures that did not previously exist. At the same time, brands are tools for personal, social, and cultural performance and expression. In short: signaling source is just the beginning of the complex social and cultural work that brands and logos do. An interdisciplinary approach will thus remain necessary to understand the brand new world in which we live.

---

[54] Anupam Chander & Madhavi Sunder, Foreword: *Is Nozick Kicking Rawls's Ass? Intellectual Property and Social Justice*, 40 UC Davis L. Rev. 563, 578 (2007).

[55] Aylwin & Coombe, *supra* note 36.

[56] Katyal, *supra* note 14.

[57] Chon, *supra* note 6.

6 Parody as Brand

Stacey L. Dogan* and Mark A. Lemley**

PARODIES MAKE FUN of a thing by copying enough of it to make it recognizable while subverting the message of the original. Most people don't like being made fun of. Some of those people turn to intellectual property (IP) law in an effort to suppress those parodies.

When IP owners use copyright law to suppress parodies, the courts have generally rejected those claims. The Supreme Court in *Campbell v. Acuff-Rose Music, Inc.* gave parody a fairly wide exemption under the fair use doctrine, at least where the parody didn't substitute for the original work (as it almost never will).[1] More recently, the Seventh Circuit held in a case involving an episode in the *South Park* television series that parody could defeat a copyright claim on a motion to dismiss, because the court needed only to compare the copyrighted work with the parody in order to resolve the fair use issue.[2]

---

* Professor of Law & Law Alumni Scholar, Boston University.

** William H. Neukom Professor, Stanford Law School; partner, Durie Tangri LLP. This is an abridged version of an article that appeared in the University of California at Davis Law Review, 47 U.C. DAVIS L. REV. 101 (2013).

[1] 510 U.S. 569, 576–94 (1994).

[2] Brownmark Films, LLC v. Comedy Partners, 682 F.3d 687, 692 (7th Cir. 2012).

While copyright law gives broad rights of control over the creative work itself, trademark law protects consumers from confusion about the source of products. Given that, it might stand to reason that rejecting legal attacks on parodies is even more straightforward under trademark law; the interest of trademark law seems less connected to the suppression of parody than does copyright law.

Nonetheless, courts have struggled with the evaluation of parody under trademark law. While many trademark courts have protected parodies, there are a surprising number of cases that hold obvious parodies illegal. Our goal in this chapter is to understand why, and to think about what circumstances (if any) should lead courts to find parody illegal. We conclude that, despite increasing attention to speech interests in recent years, the law's treatment of parody reflects too much uncertainty, leaving would-be parodists vulnerable to threats of legal action by trademark holders. In particular, given the flexibility of likelihood of confusion analysis, parodists' fate is usually determined by the subjective judgment of courts, whose treatment of parody often seems to turn on instinct rather than trademark principles. We suggest some doctrinal tools that offer greater predictability and quicker resolution of parody cases, while avoiding some of the shortcomings of more traditional infringement analysis.

I. Parodies, Brand Parodies, and the Law

A. TRADITIONAL PARODIES

Parodies and their close kin, satires, are common in popular culture. So, too, are lawsuits filed against those parodies by irate trademark owners. Many of these cases involve classic examples of social commentary using—and targeting—brands. Courts have applied a variety of different theories to these cases, however.

One approach, first crafted by the Second Circuit in *Rogers v. Grimaldi*, allows the use of trademarks in expressive works as long as they have some artistic relevance to the work and do not explicitly mislead as to source.[3] *Rogers* itself involved the use of "Ginger and Fred" as the title of a fictional film about two cabaret dancers whose act—and nicknames—copied the famous dancers Fred Astaire and Ginger Rogers. Ginger Rogers sued, claiming that the film violated her publicity rights and falsely suggested her involvement in the film. The court denied both claims, concluding that the First Amendment protects the use of names in titles of expressive works "unless the title has no artistic relevance to the underlying work whatsoever, or, if it has some artistic relevance, unless the title explicitly misleads as to the source or the content of the work."

Courts have adopted the *Rogers* test rather than likelihood of confusion analysis in a variety of cases involving trademarks used in expressive works. In *Mattel, Inc. v. Walking*

[3] 875 F.2d 994, 999 (2d Cir. 1989).

Mountain Productions,[4] for example, the defendant was an artist who posed Barbie dolls nude in photographs in which they were attacked by vintage household appliances. The artist did not use the term "Barbie" (or the doll itself) to brand or sell goods; the art itself involved the trademarked doll, and the titles[5] reflected that fact. As with much modern art, what exactly the artist was saying was not entirely clear, but it certainly seemed to be a commentary on Barbie herself. The court found no liability for this parody because the use of the term "Barbie" was "clearly relevant" to the defendant's work, and "d[id] not explicitly mislead as to the source of the work." In another Barbie case, the court invoked *Rogers* to allow the use of "Barbie Girl" as the name of a song that poked fun at the plasticity of the famous doll.[6] And in *E.S.S. Entertainment 2000, Inc. v. Rock Star Videos, Inc.*,[7] the plaintiff—the "Play Pen" strip bar—sued to stop the depiction of a similar strip bar called the "Pig Pen" in the video game Grand Theft Auto. Although the allusion to "Play Pen" was peripheral to the video game's central theme, the court found it sufficiently relevant to the game's expression to justify use of the mark, absent anything explicitly misleading about the use.[8]

Other courts have reached similar results by reference to trademark law's standard likelihood of confusion test. In *Hormel Foods Corp. v. Jim Henson Productions, Inc.*,[9] for example, the court held that defendant's use of a character named "SPA'AM" in a Muppets movie was a permissible parody of plaintiff's "Spam" mark for potted meat. The female, porcine "Spa'am" character was designed to make at least some fun of Spam and its dubious relationship to more traditional forms of meat. But the court did not apply any sort of speech or parody-related test, instead finding that there was no likelihood of confusion or dilution in the use.[10]

Not all classic parody cases turn out well for the defendants, however. In *Mutual of Omaha Insurance Co. v. Novak*,[11] the court held that defendant's antinuclear T-shirts, featuring a funny picture and the words "Mutant of Omaha," were likely to confuse consumers into thinking the insurance company "Mutual of Omaha" had sponsored the shirts.[12] In *Anheuser-Busch, Inc. v. Balducci Publications*,[13] the court found illegal a

---

[4] Mattel, Inc. v. Walking Mountain Prods., 353 F.3d 792 (9th Cir. 2003).

[5] For example, "Malted Barbie," which featured "a nude Barbie placed on a vintage Hamilton Beach malt machine." *Id.* at 796.

[6] Mattel, Inc. v. MCA Records, Inc., 296 F.3d 894, 902 (9th Cir. 2002).

[7] 547 F.3d 1095 (9th Cir. 2008).

[8] *See id.* at 1100 ("[O]nly the use of a trademark with '*no* artistic relevance to the underlying work *whatsoever*' does not merit First Amendment protection.... In other words, the level of relevance merely must be above zero" (quoting *MCA Records, Inc.*, 296 F.3d at 902 and Rogers v. Grimaldi, 875 F.2d 994, 999 (2d Cir. 1989)).

[9] 73 F.3d 497 (2d Cir. 1996).

[10] *Id.* at 505–8. Barton Beebe found that a parody defense is rarely asserted, but when asserted tends to be successful. Barton Beebe, *An Empirical Study of the Multifactor Tests for Trademark Infringement*, 94 Calif. L. Rev. 1581, 1596 n.65 (2006) [hereinafter *Empirical Study of the Multifactor Tests*]; *see also* William McGeveran, *Rethinking Trademark Fair Use*, 94 Iowa L. Rev. 49, 68–70 (2008).

[11] 836 F.2d 397 (8th Cir. 1987).

[12] *Id.* at 398–401.

[13] 28 F.3d 769 (8th Cir. 1994).

fake advertisement in a humor magazine for "Michelob Oily," a purported new brand of beer. The ad was designed to make fun of both brand differentiation and water pollution.[14] In both cases, the court accepted (dubious) evidence that consumers were likely to be confused by the parodies despite their rather obvious parodic nature. In *Deere & Co. v. MTD Products, Inc.*,[15] the court rejected a competing tractor company's use of the John Deere deer logo to attack the company in a comparative advertisement.[16] The court found the use to be dilutive (perhaps by tarnishment, though the opinion suggests that the dilution might have been something other than tarnishment).[17] In any event, the court thought that the fact that the Deere logo was being used to advertise competing products was undesirable, distinguishing it from uses for "worthy purposes of expression."[18] And in *Coca-Cola Co. v. Gemini Rising, Inc.*,[19] the court also proceeded on a tarnishment theory. It held that a poster done in the style of a Coca-Cola ad that read "Enjoy Cocaine" infringed Coca-Cola's "Enjoy Coke" mark because it associated plaintiff's "wholesome beverage" with a "noxious substance" like cocaine.[20]

In our view, these cases illustrate a distinction that should be categorical: a parody that makes fun of a trademark without adopting it as a brand should not be actionable under trademark law. This includes comparative advertising—poking fun at your competitor through a tongue-in-cheek ad—as well as use in expressive products like books, movies, T-shirts, or the like. We have emphasized elsewhere the role of the trademark use doctrine in weeding out general trademark claims that are not directed—as trademark law is supposed to be—at an effort to brand or advertise products using a mark.[21] Trademark use is a logical filter to weed out cases that are about parodies featured in magazines, movies, TV shows, Twitter feeds, or any of a variety of other uses that don't involve branding. While judicial adoption of a trademark use requirement has been uneven, trademark law has other tools to achieve this result for defendants who don't use their parody as a brand. The Trademark Dilution Revision Act makes it clear that parody cannot be dilutive when it is used "other than as a designation of source."[22] As

---

[14] *Id.* at 773–77.

[15] 41 F.3d 39 (2d Cir. 1994).

[16] *Id.* at 44–45.

[17] *Id.* at 45.

[18] *Id.* at 44–45.

[19] 346 F. Supp. 1183 (E.D.N.Y. 1972).

[20] *Id.* at 1189. This finding was particularly remarkable given that the name "Coca-Cola" derives from the soda's inclusion of coca leaf derivatives more than a century ago. *See, e.g.*, Coca-Cola Co. v. Koke Co. of Am., 254 U.S. 143, 145–46 (1920).

[21] *See* Stacey L. Dogan & Mark A. Lemley, *Grounding Trademark Law Through Trademark Use*, 92 Iowa L. Rev. 1669, 1682 (2007) [hereinafter *Grounding Trademark*]; Stacey L. Dogan & Mark A. Lemley, *Trademarks and Consumer Search Costs on the Internet*, 41 Hous. L. Rev. 777, 785 (2004) [hereinafter *Trademarks and Consumer Search Costs*].

[22] 15 U.S.C. § 1125(c)(3)(A) (2012). In any event, as we have argued elsewhere, dilution generally requires that the defendant use the term as a mark. *See* Stacey L. Dogan & Mark A. Lemley, *The Trademark Use Requirement in Dilution Cases*, 24 Santa Clara Computer & High Tech. L.J. 541, 542–44 (2008).

for infringement, nominative fair use should protect comparative advertisers, and *Rogers v. Grimaldi* addresses expressive works: as long as the use of a trademark has some artistic relevance to an expressive product and does not explicitly mislead as to source, trademark law should not intervene.[23] Using these doctrinal tools, we shouldn't need to reach the likelihood of confusion inquiry in order to resolve cases in which a clear parody is used other than as a designation of source for a separate commercial product.

Nor should the fact that a mark appears in the title of an expressive work change the outcome. As *Rogers v. Grimaldi* instructs, trademarks in titles should not infringe, as long as they bear some relationship to the underlying expression and don't lie. The speech interest in access to expressive works extends to their titles; consumers, as well as creators, benefit from a culture that allows subtle references and wordplay that draws from a variety of cultural reference points. This is true even if the use causes some level of confusion. As the Second Circuit pointed out in *Rogers*:

> [M]any titles with a celebrity's name make no explicit statement that the work is about that person in any direct sense; the relevance of the title may be oblique and may become clear only after viewing or reading the work. As to such titles, the consumer interest in avoiding deception is too slight to warrant application of the Lanham Act. Though consumers frequently look to the title of a work to determine what it is about, they do not regard titles of artistic works in the same way as the names of ordinary commercial products... [M]ost consumers are well aware that they cannot judge a book solely by its title any more than by its cover. We therefore need not interpret the Act to require that authors select titles that unambiguously describe what the work is about nor to preclude them from using titles that are only suggestive of some topics that the work is not about.[24]

In effect, *Rogers* does for expressive works what a robust trademark use doctrine could do more generally: it takes judicial notice that certain uses of trademarks (in expressive titles) don't usually signal source, and it balances the slight risk of confusion against the benefits of allowing such uses. We agree with the Second Circuit that parodies in expressive products should generally be immune from liability, and we find it heartening that recent parody decisions reflect a trend toward the *Rogers* standard. From Ginger and Fred to Barbie Girl to Blender Barbie to the Pig Pen, courts have sanctioned the use of trademarks both within the works and in their titles.

Indeed, a closer look at the decisions that find parody infringing suggests that one of three things is going on. First, some of these cases are misled by poor evidence of confusion. In *Balducci*, for instance, only 6% of people surveyed thought that Michelob Oily

---

[23] *See, e.g.*, Mattel, Inc. v. MCA Records, 296 F.3d 894 (9th Cir. 2002).

[24] *Rogers*, 875 F.2d at 999–1000.

was actually a new kind of beer, though fully half of those surveyed understood that it was a parody but thought that the humor magazine should have to get a license.[25] That may be a form of confusion—specifically, confusion about what trademark law actually requires—but it is not confusion that causes the sort of harm trademark law cares about, and it should not be actionable.[26] Similarly, in *Mutual of Omaha,* the plaintiff's survey showed that 42% of respondents thought the "Mutant of Omaha" shirt "[called] to mind" Mutual of Omaha, and that 10% thought Mutual of Omaha "[went] along" with the shirt.[27] Those questions are not the ones trademark law traditionally does or should care about. These cases are misled by poor surveys or improper questions to find confusion where it is in fact unlikely.

Second, cases like *Deere* and *Gemini* are driven by a misunderstanding of the nature of dilution. The evil of trademark dilution (if there is one) is that it weakens the association in the minds of consumers between the brand and the product by introducing another association between a different product and that brand.[28] That's not what's happening in either *Deere* or *Gemini. Gemini* didn't involve product branding at all, and accordingly wouldn't be actionable under the federal dilution statute. And the use in *Deere* was a commercial use of the mark, but not one that branded the competitor's goods; it used Deere's mark to refer to Deere's goods. The courts in these cases seem to have misunderstood tarnishment as saying something bad about the trademark owner, rather than its proper meaning of branding your own inferior or noxious goods with the plaintiff's mark.

The third factor that leads courts astray in these cases is a general aversion to free riding. Some judges just don't like it when people make money from evoking someone else's mark. In *Hard Rock Cafe Licensing Corp. v. Pacific Graphics, Inc.*,[29] for example, the defendant sold "Hard Rain Cafe" T-shirts in rain-plagued Seattle. After a cursory analysis finding likelihood of confusion, the court rejected defendant's parody claim, concluding: "A defendant's claim of parody will be disregarded where the purpose of the similarity is to capitalize on a famous mark's popularity for the defendant's own commercial use."[30]

---

[25] Anheuser-Busch, Inc. v. Balducci Publ'ns, 28 F.3d 769, 775 (8th Cir. 1994).

[26] *See* Jessica Litman, *Breakfast with Batman: The Public Interest in the Advertising Age*, 108 YALE L.J. 1717, 1723 n.36 (1999); Mark A. Lemley & Mark McKenna, *Irrelevant Confusion*, 62 STAN. L. REV. 413 (2010) [hereinafter *Irrelevant Confusion*] (arguing that trademark law should concentrate on confusion that may affect purchasing decisions); Rebecca Tushnet, *Running the Gamut From A to B: Federal Trademark and False Advertising Law*, 159 U. PA. L. REV. 1305 (2011) [hereinafter *From A to B*] (arguing that trademark law should limit itself to confusion that actually matters to consumers).

[27] Mut. of Omaha Ins. Co. v. Novak, 836 F.2d 397, 400 (8th Cir. 1987).

[28] *See, e.g.*, Stacey L. Dogan, *An Exclusive Right to Evoke*, 44 B.C. L. REV. 291, 313 (2003) (contending that dilution law should limit itself to the loss of singularity of unique marks).

[29] 776 F. Supp. 1454 (W.D. Wash. 1991).

[30] *Id.* at 1462 (citing Grey v. Campbell Soup Co., 650 F. Supp. 1166, 1175 (C.D. Cal. 1986)).

Trademark law, however, does not and should not aim to prevent all free riding. The law targets harms that result from confusion and, at least in theory, from the loss of singularity of particularly famous marks. Parodies that conjure up a trademark for humor and turn a profit in the process are engaged in perfectly lawful behavior, absent confusion or dilution.

For traditional parodies, then, the legal rule should be simple, even if it is not always followed: making fun of a trademark owner by doing something other than using their mark to brand your own products does not violate the Lanham Act.

B. BRAND PARODIES

Increasingly, however, we've witnessed a new phenomenon: lawsuits against parodies that serve as brands, logos, or taglines for commercial products. Haute Diggity Dog sells "Chewy Vuiton" dog toys, and Louis Vuitton is not happy about it.[31] Macy's sells a diaper bag called "Gucchi Goo," and Gucci sues (and wins).[32] The Utah tourism bureau describes the state as having the "Greatest Snow on Earth," a play on the Ringling Brothers' "Greatest Show on Earth" mark.[33] Black Bear Roastery sells "Charbucks" coffee to poke fun at the famous brand's dark roast while cheekily offering its own dark-roast alternative.[34] A Vermont hippie invites people to "Eat More Kale," and Chick-Fil-A thinks he's making fun of its "Eat Mor Chickin" mark.[35] Hogg Wyld sells plus-size jeans under the name Lardache, and jeans maker Jordache is not amused.[36] A college student sells "South Butt" T-shirts with the tagline "Never Stop Relaxing," raising the ire of The North Face brand with its "Never Stop Exploring" slogan.[37] A bar owner names its kitschy establishment the "Velvet Elvis," and gets a visit from the King's trademark attorneys.[38] And so on.

In many ways, this new form of parody resembles the old. It's motivated by a desire to comment or criticize, and it's unlikely to confuse anyone about the source of the

---

[31] *See* Louis Vuitton Malletier S.A. v. Haute Diggity Dog, LLC, 507 F.3d 252, 256 (4th Cir. 2007).

[32] *See* Gucci Shops, Inc. v. R.H. Macy & Co., 446 F. Supp. 838, 839, 841 (S.D.N.Y. 1977).

[33] *See* Ringling Bros.-Barnum & Bailey Combined Shows, Inc. v. Utah Div. of Travel Dev., 170 F.3d 449, 451 (4th Cir. 1999).

[34] *See* Starbucks Corp. v. Wolfe's Borough Coffee, Inc., 588 F.3d 97 102–3 (2d Cir. 2009). *See generally What It's All About?*, BLACK BEAR MICRO ROASTERY, https://blackbearcoffee.com/Starbucks/What%27s_it_all_about.htm (last visited Sept. 11, 2013) (offering Black Bear's account of the reason for its choices of name).

[35] *See* James Lantz et al., *A Defiant Dude*, KICKSTARTER, http://www.kickstarter.com/projects/1674889308/a-defiant-dude (last visited Sept. 11, 2013).

[36] *See* Jordache Enters., Inc. v. Hogg Wyld, Ltd., 828 F.2d 1482, 1483–84 (10th Cir. 1987).

[37] *See* Kelsey Volkmann, *South Butt vs. North Face*, ST. LOUIS BUS. J. (Oct. 16, 2010), http://www.bizjournals.com/stlouis/blog/2009/09/south_butt_vs_north_face.html. The defendant was ultimately enjoined in a consent judgment and held in contempt of that judgment for selling a separate T-shirt that read "The Butt Face." *See* North Face Apparel Corp. v. Williams Pharmacy Inc., No. 4:09-CV-02029-RWS, 2012 U.S. Dist. LEXIS 145987, at *1–9 (E.D. Mo. Oct. 10, 2012).

[38] *See* Elvis Presley Enters., Inc. v. Capece, 141 F.3d 188, 191–93 (5th Cir. 1998).

parody-branded product.[39] In other ways, however, parody as brand differs from parody as product because the parody is being used as an indicator of source. Building a brand name around someone else's trademark looks, to some observers, like a classic case of free riding, with the parodist taking advantage of the allure of the targeted brand. Trademark holders, not surprisingly, abhor the practice and sue to prevent it.

But trademark law is not—and has never been—about preventing all forms of free riding. Trademark law, even as it has expanded to prevent dilution, has purported to focus on preventing *harm*, either to the trademark holder or to the public (and sometimes to both). Those who develop brands-as-parody may well be benefiting from the appeal of a famous brand, but if their use is an effective parody, it doesn't cause the kind of harm that trademark law is designed to address. These brands-as-parody, moreover, offer a valuable form of social commentary. Even more than non-commercial forms of parody, the subversive use of a parody *as* brand invites critical reflection on the role of brands in society and the extent to which we define ourselves by them.[40]

Brands that parody, in other words, offer a unique platform for expression and pose little threat to trademark law's core values. As a matter of doctrine, however, the fact that a parody is also a brand complicates the trademark analysis. The trademark use doctrine is no longer a bar to an infringement suit; Black Bear *is* in fact using the term "Charbucks" as a mark to brand its products. Nominative use becomes harder, though not impossible, for the same reason. "Charbucks" is in fact nominative use in a sense; buyers presumably understand that it is a reference to Starbucks. But it is not *only* a nominative use; it is simultaneously a brand in its own right, and if it is memorable it may serve the traditional function of cementing Black Bear's product in people's minds.[41] When a parody is also a brand, a number of courts have concluded that the analysis is the same as it is for any other trademark case: we ask

---

[39] The lines between the two types of parody also blur as trademark owners arrogate to themselves the right to control secondary markets for the sale of T-shirts, memorabilia, and the like. The use of a brand on a T-shirt is classically an expressive use, but trademark owners (and some courts) have increasingly treated this merchandising as a form of branding within the trademark owner's control. For criticism of this phenomenon, see Stacey L. Dogan & Mark A. Lemley, *The Merchandising Right: Fragile Theory or* Fait Accompli?, 54 EMORY L.J. 461 (2005) [hereinafter *Merchandising Right*]; Mark A. Lemley & Mark P. McKenna, *Owning Mark(et)s*, 109 MICH. L. REV. 137 (2010) [hereinafter *Owning Mark(et)s*].

[40] *See, e.g.*, Sonia K. Katyal, *Semiotic Disobedience*, 84 WASH. U. L. REV. 489 (2006) [hereinafter *Semiotic Disobedience*] (discussing brand parodies as a form of cultural disobedience); Rebecca Tushnet, *Looking at the Lanham Act: Images in Trademark and Advertising Law*, 48 HOUS. L. REV. 861, 891–95 (2011) (noting special need of commentators to access expressive aspects of visual marks); *cf.* Deven R. Desai, *From Trademarks to Brands*, 64 FLA. L. REV. 981, 999–1009 (2012) [hereinafter *From Trademarks to Brands*] (exploring personal role of brands in culture).

[41] For this reason, courts have given lower First Amendment protection to parodic brands than to other forms of trademark parodies. *See, e.g.*, *Tommy Hilfiger Licensing*, 221 F. Supp. 2d at 415–16 ("When a parodist makes trademark use of another's mark, it should be entitled to less indulgence, even if this results in some residual effect on the free speech rights of commercial actors").

whether confusion or dilution is likely, and if it is, the use is unlawful.[42] In other words, those courts do not give parody a defense or any special treatment.

Perhaps it doesn't matter. Most parodies are unlikely to confuse consumers or to dilute the singularity of a famous trademark. Black Bear customers who buy Charbucks coffee presumably understand that they are not buying coffee at a Starbucks; they also seem unlikely to think that Starbucks has authorized a new, self-parodying blend and let Black Bear sell it. Nor does Charbucks make Starbucks less distinctive as a brand of its own; to the contrary, it only enhances Starbucks' fame. The same goes for The Greatest Snow on Earth and Ringling Brothers, or Chewy Vuiton dog toys and Louis Vuitton. So maybe we don't need a defense to protect brand parodies; they will take care of themselves.

That answer seems unsatisfactory, and not merely because some brand parodies are in fact held illegal under questionable circumstances.[43] Confusion is a fact-specific inquiry, often heavily reliant on manipulable survey evidence and subject to an ever-expanding notion of what it takes to confuse.[44] If confusion over whether the defendant needed a license is actionable, then virtually any brand evocation invites an expensive and

---

42 *See, e.g.*, Dr. Seuss Enters., L.P. v. Penguin Books USA, Inc., 109 F.3d 1394, 1405 (9th Cir. 1997) ("[T]he claim of parody is not really a separate 'defense' ... but merely a way of phrasing the traditional response that customers are not likely to be confused as to the source, sponsorship or approval"); *Tommy Hilfiger Licensing*, 221 F. Supp. 2d at 415–16 (applying traditional likelihood of confusion analysis to case involving brand parody). The leading treatise endorses this position:

> Some parodies will constitute an infringement, some will not. But the cry of "parody!" does not magically fend off otherwise legitimate claims of trademark infringement or dilution. There are confusing parodies and non-confusing parodies. All they have in common is an attempt at humor through the use of someone else's trademark. A non-infringing parody is merely amusing, not confusing.

6 J. Thomas McCarthy, McCarthy on Trademarks and Unfair Competition § 31:153 (4th ed. 2013).

43 *See, e.g.*, Anheuser-Busch, Inc. v. VIP Prods., 666 F. Supp. 2d 974 (E.D. Mo. 2008) (finding "Buttwiper" T-shirts likely to be confused with "Budweiser" brand); Gucci Shops, Inc. v. R.H. Macy & Co., 446 F. Supp. 838 (S.D.N.Y. 1977) (granting a preliminary injunction on use of "Gucchi Goo" mark on diaper bags because mark could be confused with "Gucci" brand); PRL USA Holdings, Inc. v. Thread Pit, Inc., Cancelation No. 92047436, at 15 (T.T.A.B. 2012) (canceling clothing mark that depicted a polo player falling off a horse as likely to confuse consumers of the Polo brand, noting "parody is not a defense if the marks are otherwise confusingly similar").

44 In *Anheuser-Busch, Inc. v. Balducci Publications*, 28 F.3d 769 (8th Cir. 1994), for example, the court found infringement by the "Michelob Oily" parody, reversing the district court on likelihood of confusion, because even though only 6% of the public thought Michelob Oily was a new brand of beer, "over half" of respondents "thought Balducci needed Anheuser-Busch's approval to publish the ad." *Id.* at 775. In doing so, the court added a consumer's misunderstanding of the law to the kinds of confusion apparently actionable under the Lanham Act. *See also* Schieffelin & Co. v. Jack Co. of Boca, 725 F. Supp. 1314, 1317 (S.D.N.Y. 1989) (finding high degrees of confusion based on survey that asked consumers whether they thought trademark holder's permission was required for "Dom Popignon" popcorn); *cf.* Universal City Studios, Inc. v. Nintendo Co., 746 F.2d 112 (2d Cir. 1984) (rejecting survey that asked leading question about whether Donkey Kong manufacturer needed permission from the owner of the King Kong mark).

unpredictable trial. Even if the law could guarantee the right result at trial, many parodists are small companies without the will or resources to fight a case all the way to trial. Many will cave in and abandon their parodies rather than hire a lawyer.

Dilution presents a different problem for brand parodies. While there is an explicit defense for parody in the Trademark Dilution Revision Act, it expressly applies only to parodies that use the mark "other than as a designation of source."[45] Brand parodies, by contrast, do not benefit from the defense. That doesn't mean they are dilutive, of course; the Fourth Circuit found in *Louis Vuitton* that Chewy Vuiton was not. But it does mean that the parody is to be evaluated under the normal standards of blurring or tarnishment, a set of fact-intensive standards that map poorly to uses expressly intended to evoke a famous mark. The statutory factors focus on the strength and fame of the plaintiff's mark and the possibility of association between the two marks.[46] While some might worry about brands that draw strength from association with a famous mark, in the context of parody we should expect that the defendant both targets famous marks and does so by creating an association between the mark and the parody. Indeed, that's the essence of parody. Brand parodies, then, simply don't fit comfortably with the statutory dilution factors. It isn't that the blurring factors necessarily make brand parodies unlawful, though many of them may be primed to line up in favor of the trademark owner, but rather that the questions the statute asks are largely tangential to the issues that matter in evaluating a parody.

Unlike blurring, the statute is largely silent on what dilution by tarnishment means. We have argued elsewhere that courts must distinguish between a defendant's use that tarnishes by associating the brand name with the *defendant's* noxious product (actionable) and a defendant's use that "tarnishes" because it disparages the *plaintiff's* product (not actionable).[47] On this view, parody will generally not be dilution by tarnishment, except by accident. The point of a parody is to target the plaintiff's work. Even a branded parody is aimed primarily at making fun of the plaintiff's work, not at marketing unrelated products that are shoddy or offensive. That doesn't mean a brand parody can never tarnish,[48] but courts must be careful not to confuse making fun of the plaintiff with tarnishing.

---

[45] 15 U.S.C. § 1125(c) (2012).

[46] *See* 15 U.S.C. § 1125(c).

[47] *See* Stacey L. Dogan & Mark A. Lemley, *A Search-Costs Theory of Limiting Doctrines in Trademark Law*, 97 Trademark Rptr. 1223, 1230 n.26 (2007).

[48] The most likely context in which a brand parody could tarnish is when the "parody" appears on pornographic or drug-related products. Courts appear to be moving toward a presumption of tarnishment when a seller of such services adopts a mark that evokes a famous brand. *See, e.g.*, V Secret Catalogue, Inc. v. Moseley, 605 F.3d 382, 388 (6th Cir. 2010) (adopting "a kind of rebuttable presumption, or at least a very strong inference, that a new mark used to sell sex-related products is likely to tarnish a famous mark if there is a clear semantic association between the two"). We have our doubts about this precedent, especially to the extent that it reaches marks that evoke, without replicating, the famous brand. *See, e.g.*, Dogan, *supra* note 28 (criticizing precedent that finds tarnishment based on mere evocation of famous brands). For a critique of the presumption that a relationship with sex tarnishes, see Jennifer E. Rothman, *Sex Exceptionalism in Intellectual*

Brand parodies, then, don't fit well within existing trademark infringement or dilution law. Parodies generally don't confuse consumers, and because they refer back to the plaintiff's mark directly they will not generally blur or tarnish that mark in the way dilution law prohibits. True parodies thus cause none of the harms that trademark law seeks to avoid. But because neither law is structured with parodies in mind, rote application of infringement and dilution standards can result in a condemnation of even obvious parodies. Lacking tools specifically designed for parody, courts treat it in an ad hoc way that reflects their own subjective assessment of the value of parody and the morality of free rides. The fact-intensive nature of the inquiry, moreover, means a long and costly process, which alone may deter parodies.

The solution, we believe, lies in a more consistent and predictable approach to brand parodies under both infringement and dilution law. In contrast to copyright law, we have seen little convergence in the courts' treatment of even basic questions involving trademark parodies. Given the increasing prevalence of parody as brand, the time has come for a more considered analysis that balances legitimate (or at least plausible) trademark holder concerns against the public's interest in this form of critical speech.

II. The Value of Brand Parodies

Whether or not they believe that a particular parody deserves legal protection, courts and commentators seem to agree that parody has social value as critical speech. As the

---

Property, 23 STAN. L. & POL'Y REV. 119 (2012). If the growing presumption holds, however, we can imagine it applying to some arguably parodic brands. The use of "Live American Girl Dolls" on a strip club, for example, may constitute tarnishment, even if it was adopted in part as a sarcastic commentary on the wholesome image of the famous doll label. Similarly, consider *Dallas Cowboys Cheerleaders, Inc. v. Pussycat Cinema, Ltd.*, 604 F.2d 200 (2d Cir. 1979), involving a porn movie from the 1970s called "Debbie Does Dallas" that depicts the star in a Dallas Cowboys Cheerleaders outfit in one scene. *Id.* at 202–3. Under *Rogers v. Grimaldi* there is surely artistic relevance, and the comment on the Dallas Cowboys Cheerleaders as selling sexuality seems pretty obvious. At the same time, one can imagine why the Dallas Cowboys viewed the association as tarnishing. Still other examples of arguable parodies that may tarnish because of their offensive or sexual content include the sale of hats labeled "Cuntier" that imitate the "Cartier" brand, see Misty White Sidell *New Cartier Spoof Finds Itself in Hot Water with the Brand*, DAILY BEAST (Mar. 8, 2013), http://www.thedailybeast.com/articles/2013/03/08/new-cartier-spoof-finds-itself-in-hot-water-with-the-brand.html, and singer Chubby Checker's suit against a company that supplied a penis-size calculation app for a mobile phone that it called "The Chubby Checker." *See* Evans v. Hewlett-Packard Co., No. C 13-02477 WHA, 2013 U.S. Dist. LEXIS 115856, at *2-3 (N.D. Cal. Aug. 15, 2013). Full disclosure: Lemley's firm represents the defendant in this case.

As in copyright cases, part of the challenge is to determine how much of the use owes itself to critical commentary, and how much is simply a convenient way to capture attention through use of someone else's mark. If the commentary is insignificant and the use is likely to tarnish the famous mark through dual association with an unsavory product, then the balance may tilt in favor of the trademark holder. But where it is the commentary that the trademark owner objects to, the law should not give the trademark owner the power to restrict that commentary.

Supreme Court has explained, "Like less ostensibly humorous forms of criticism, [parody] can provide social benefit, by shedding light on an earlier work, and, in the process, creating a new one."[49] Parodies make us think while making us chuckle; they offer a funny and often biting lens through which to view our cultural icons. From Henry Fielding's "Shamela"[50] to Alice Randall's "The Wind Done Gone,"[51] from Tina Fey's parody of Sarah Palin[52] to the Simpsons' cracks about "Mapple,"[53] parodies have, for centuries, had an "unerring ability both to delight and to confound."[54]

Despite their general appreciation of parody, however, courts show distinctly less enthusiasm for parodies that serve as brands. To some extent, their objection is doctrinal: both First Amendment and trademark jurisprudence give special status to non-commercial speech.[55] But the trouble with brand parodies transcends doctrine; courts seem to struggle over their own intuitions about whether a defendant's commercial objectives undermine its speech interest in the parody.[56] Given the malleability of confusion and dilution analysis, these judicial instincts often dictate the outcome in trademark litigation.

Yet there's a strong argument that, at least in the trademark context, incorporating a parody into a brand serves expressive goals that could not be realized through ordinary, non-branding speech. Many—perhaps most—branding parodies have a doubly subversive message. They are using a brand not only to lampoon the targeted brand, but also to call attention to the pervasiveness of branding in our society. Parodies, in general, replicate the central features of a particular work to "reference and ridicule" the work.[57] Brand parodies do more: they not only borrow from the trademark itself, but they also appropriate the device of branding and employ it to make us think critically about the

---

[49] Campbell v. Acuff-Rose Music, Inc., 510 U.S. 569, 579 (1994); *see also* L.L. Bean, Inc. v. Drake Publishers, Inc., 811 F.2d 26, 31 (1st Cir. 1987).

[50] *See generally* CONNY KEYBER, AN APOLOGY FOR THE LIFE OF MRS. SHAMELA ANDREWS (1741) (writing under a pseudonym, Henry Fielding presents a parody of SAMUEL RICHARDSON, PAMELA (1740)).

[51] *See generally* ALICE RANDALL, THE WIND DONE GONE (2001) (presenting a parody of MARGARET MITCHELL, GONE WITH THE WIND (1936)).

[52] *E.g., SNL Tina Fey then Gov. Palin*, YOUTUBE (Oct. 28, 2008), http://www.youtube.com/watch?v=IE-OCDexYrU.

[53] *See The Simpsons—Steve Mobs*, YOUTUBE (Dec. 2, 2008), http://www.youtube.com/watch?v=CZGIn9bpALo.

[54] 78 LINDA HUTCHEON, A THEORY OF PARODY: THE TEACHINGS OF TWENTIETH-CENTURY ART FORMS, at xvii (2000 ed. 1985)

[55] *Tommy Hilfiger Licensing, Inc. v. Nature Labs, LLC*, 221 F. Supp. 2d 410, 415–16 (S.D.N.Y. 2002), for example, found no likelihood of confusion between "Timmy Holedigger" dog perfume and "Tommy Hilfiger" people perfume, but noted that because the parody was serving as a brand, it was not entitled to any special First Amendment treatment and instead required analysis under the likelihood of confusion test.

[56] *See, e.g.*, Hard Rock Cafe Licensing Corp. v. Pac. Graphics, Inc., 776 F. Supp. 1454 (W.D. Wash. 1991) ("[D]efendant's claim of parody will be disregarded where the purpose of the similarity is to capitalize on a famous mark's popularity for the defendant's own commercial use."); *cf.* White v. Samsung Elecs. Am., Inc., 971 F.2d 1395, 1401 (9th Cir. 1992) ("The difference between a 'parody' and a 'knock-off' is the difference between fun and profit.").

[57] Campbell v. Acuff-Rose Music, Inc., 510 U.S. 569, 583 (1994).

role of brands in our culture. The dog chew toy in *Louis Vuitton*, for example, "pokes fun at the elegance and expensiveness of a LOUIS VUITTON handbag" but also "irreverently presents haute couture as an object for casual canine destruction."[58] Or so thought the Fourth Circuit, at least.[59]

Trademark holders, of course, would prefer not to face this kind of ridicule of their brands or their branding practices. But trademark law does not exist to suit the needs of trademark holders; it aims to promote broader social objectives. As a result, whether or not trademark law should condemn brand parodies depends on whether they threaten trademark law's normative goals.

We have written elsewhere about the rationale for—and the costs of—laws protecting trademarks. Despite an active contemporary debate over its descriptive accuracy and desirability, the dominant theoretical justification for trademarks remains an economic one. By providing shorthand signals about products, trademarks lower the costs of transferring information between buyers and sellers. By protecting the integrity of this product information, trademark law can facilitate more transparent and competitive markets.

This account, however, comes with two important caveats. First, because fair competition remains the ultimate goal of trademark law, the law's information-related objectives must sometimes give way to competition concerns. Trademark rules like functionality, fair use (both descriptive and nominative), and genericide are all designed to promote competition and market access, even when it means losing some informational clarity for consumers. Second, even the most modest version of trademark law—say, one focused only on passing off—creates the opportunity for rent-seeking behavior and the risk of monopoly.[60] While trademarks do convey objective information about products, they can also serve as vessels of advertising-laden prestige, status, and brand personality that often bear little relation to any objective measure of product quality. This kind of artificial product differentiation can lead to higher prices and deadweight loss. Whether we view this as a fundamental problem or a minor glitch in the system, it is an inevitable effect of trademark protection, and it raises real economic concerns.

As trademark law grows increasingly immodest—by protecting product designs against fears of post-sale confusion, for instance—these costs associated with trademark protection grow. Producers can now differentiate their products not only through names, but also through their "branded" product attributes. Luxury brands, in particular, thrive on the very fact of their scarcity and its attendant high price. Consumers

---

[58] Louis Vuitton Malletier S.A. v. Haute Diggity Dog, LLC, 507 F.3d 252, 261 (4th Cir. 2007).

[59] *Id.; see also* Nike, Inc. v. "Just Did It" Enters., 6 F.3d 1225, 1231 (7th Cir. 1993) ("[S]ome purchasers might resent paying a premium to be a walking billboard and would relish the opportunity to mock trendy folks who wear labels on their sleeves.").

[60] *See* Mark A. Lemley & Mark P. McKenna, *Is Pepsi Really a Substitute for Coke? Market Definition in Antitrust and IP*, 100 Geo. L.J. 2055, 2059–66 (2012); Glynn S. Lunney, Jr., *Trademark Monopolies*, 48 Emory L.J. 367, 367–69 (1999) (describing intellectual, political, and legal history of trademark law, including early debates over the tension between its informational objectives and its monopolistic tendencies).

demand these brands at least in part because of the image of distinction and wealth that they convey. Product use and consumption, in turn, become a form of expression, in which wearers or users of luxury-branded products project to the world their exalted status. Wearing, consuming, or riding in a luxury-branded product conveys a very public message about the consumer's affluence and values.

Our goal here is not to pass judgment on these economic and cultural phenomena. Whether one believes that brand-based product differentiation promotes social welfare or reduces it, it undeniably plays a major role in our economy and our society. Brands shape our communities and define our values. And while the traditional economic account views brands as conveying information unidirectionally—from producer to consumer—brands also convey information *about* the consumer and allow members of the public to communicate to each other. By selling branded products, producers enable us to brand ourselves. Indeed, in the modern world of luxury brands this is arguably the primary function of brands. Traditional trademarks serve as the source of goods and therefore protect the customer from fake goods. By contrast, Nike swooshes, red shoe bottoms, and Chanel purse logos are not really about ensuring that purchasers make the right decision, but about allowing purchasers to tell the rest of the world about that decision. Were it otherwise, known counterfeits wouldn't be so popular. Brands, then, don't just help trademark owners speak; they help all of us speak. And that speech is so common that refusing to wear brand names is itself a recognized counter-cultural statement.[61]

Which brings us back to brand parody. As discussed above, brands that parody have a dual target: the brand itself and the phenomenon of branding. Given the prevalence of branding and its economic and social impact, commentary about both brands and branding is a matter of public concern. If they succeed in the market, moreover, these parodic brands most likely do so because they offer some value to consumers—because their message resonates with a substantial audience. Just as prestige brands confer value to consumers who want to project an image of exclusivity, so brand parodies bring utility to consumers seeking to project a more rebellious or sardonic message.[62] Absent some

---

[61] *See, e.g.*, NAOMI KLEIN, NO LOGO (1999) (recounting popular movements designed to counter the message of dominant brands by, among other things, exposing brand hypocrisy); MC LARS, NO LOGO (Horris Records & Oglio Records 2009) (mocking the mocking of brand hypocrisy). *See generally* Laura A. Heymann, *The Law of Reputation and the Interest of the Audience*, 52 B.C. L. REV. 1341 (2011) [hereinafter *The Law of Reputation*] (noting broader community interest in the construction of individual and corporate reputation); Mark P. McKenna, *A Consumer Decision-Making Theory of Trademark Law*, 98 Va. L. Rev. 67 (2012) (suggesting that persuasive, non-deceptive uses of marks by third parties can have social value). For a discussion of the act of subverting the meaning of a brand as itself speech-significant, see Katyal, *Semiotic Disobedience, supra* note 40, at 554–68.

[62] They also make life more fun by adding some levity to our lives. As Justice Sachs of the South African Constitutional Court proclaimed, in a case involving a parody of a beer brand:

> The Constitution cannot oblige the dour to laugh. It can, however, prevent the cheerless from snuffing out the laughter of the blithe spirits among us. Indeed, if our society became completely solemn

harm to the informational function of the underlying trademark, the availability of this new type of product likely increases social welfare.[63] Further, if brands are part of a conversation between consumers, not just with trademark owners, brand parodies allow others to participate in that conversation with a different, unapproved message. In so doing, it helps us define ourselves. As Salman Rushdie put it, "[t]hose who do not have power over the story that dominates their lives, power to retell it, rethink it, deconstruct it, joke about it, and change it as times change, truly are powerless, because they cannot think new thoughts."[64]

If the parody is effective, moreover—if consumers get the joke—it's hard to see how brand parodies pose any cognizable threat to trademark law's informational goals. Sure, the public might think less of the trademark holder as a result of the criticism, but trademark law has never addressed itself to that kind of harm. To the contrary, the fact that the defendant is using the plaintiff's brand to talk about the plaintiff, even for money, is a defense to infringement.[65]

Brand parodies, then, are a natural and desirable part of a social conversation that takes place through the phenomenon of branding. Trademark owners benefit from that conversation, but they are not the only ones with a right to speak.

III. A Defense for Brand Parodies

True brand parodies thus have social value and are unlikely to cause confusion or loss of distinctiveness of the targeted mark; trademark courts should rarely enjoin them. In practice, however, litigation against brand parodies can drag on for years, with courts equivocating over what rules to apply and how.[66] And some courts enjoin them based on questionable evidence of confusion. Both the equivocation and the misapplication of the law may well result from discomfort over the commercial nature of these parodies,

---

> because of the exercise of state power at the behest of the worthy, not only would all irrelevant laughter be suppressed, but temperance considerations could end up placing beer-drinking itself in jeopardy. And I can see no reason in principle why a joke against the government can be tolerated, but one at the expense of what used to be called Big Business, cannot.

Laugh It Off Promotions (1) SA at 63-64 para. 107 (Sachs, J., concurring).

[63] To be precise, the parodist and the people who view the parody generally benefit. There may be individuals who value the purity of brand integrity and oppose parody for its own sake. A utilitarian calculus would have to include their preferences too. *See* Irina Manta, *Hedonic Trademarks*, 74 Ohio St. L.J. 241, 261 (2013). But we are skeptical that the views of these few people are so strongly held that they will outweigh the value of parody to others, including the parodist.

[64] SALMAN RUSHDIE, *One Thousand Days in a Balloon*, *reprinted in* SALMAN RUSHDIE: A POSTMODERN READING OF HIS MAJOR WORKS 104 (Sabrina Hassumani ed., 2002).

[65] *See* Century 21 Real Estate Corp. v. Lendingtree, Inc., 425 F.3d 211, 217–18 (3d Cir. 2005); New Kids on the Block v. News Am. Publ'g, Inc., 971 F.2d 302, 308 (9th Cir. 1992).

[66] The Charbucks case, for example, has been up and down to the Second Circuit three times in the nine years it has been litigated so far, and there is no end in sight. *See* Starbucks Corp. v. Wolfe's Borough Coffee, Inc., 588 F.3d 97, 102–5 (2d Cir. 2009).

or from a perception of exploitation and free riding. Whatever the cause, the slipperiness of trademark doctrine gives courts room to find infringement or dilution, even under dubious circumstances, if they are motivated to do so.

We need more reliable protection for brand parodies under both trademark infringement and dilution law. A defense that can be litigated pre-trial would add great certainty to the process and protect speech. Even contemplating such a defense, however, raises a host of definitional and policy questions. What *is* parody, and why should we privilege it over other forms of critical speech such as satire? How should courts distinguish between real parodies and fakes? Assuming parody deserves some kind of legal protection, what form should the defense take? Should the defense be absolute once it is established that the defendant's brand is in fact a qualifying parody? Or should a brand parody be illegal if it causes enough confusion? We see no easy answer to these questions; in particular, we recognize the hazards of distinguishing between parodies and other forms of critical speech. Nonetheless, we believe that there is good reason to provide special protection for parodies, while at the same time preserving space for satire and other expressive uses of marks. The difficulty of drawing lines should not prevent us from protecting parodies that are clearly on the right side of the line, wherever drawn.

A. WHAT IS A PARODY? DOES IT MATTER?

To create a defense for brand parodies, we need either a definition of what a parody is or a general principle that encompasses brand parodies along with other forms of protected uses of a trademark.

In *Campbell v. Acuff-Rose Music, Inc.*,[67] a copyright fair use case, the Supreme Court sought to define parody. While it drew from classic and dictionary definitions a fairly broad definition of a parody that involved imitation of a work for the purpose of comic effect, the actual definition it adopted was narrower: "[T]he use of some elements of a prior author's composition to create a new one that, at least in part, comments on that author's works." Works that use elements from an original for comic effect but that do not comment directly on the original, by contrast, are classed by the Court as satire, not parody. The court reasoned that parody needs the original in order to work, but satire could use any work, not necessarily the plaintiff's.[68]

---

[67] Campbell v. Acuff-Rose Music, Inc., 510 U.S. 569 (1994).

[68] *Id.* at 580–81 ("Parody needs to mimic an original to make its point, and so has some claim to use the creation of its victim's (or collective victims') imagination, whereas satire can stand on its own two feet and so requires justification for the very act of borrowing"). In fact, however, there may be non-parodic uses that depend on a particular work. Machinima, for instance, makes videos out of content from individual video games, and fan fiction builds off of books or movies. While in theory the fan could build off of some other work, the entire point of machinima or fan fiction is to pay homage to a particular piece of culture. *See* Michael Choe, *The Problem of the Parody-Satire Distinction: Fair Use in Machinima and Other Fan Created Works*, 37 RUTGERS COMPUTER & TECH. L.J. 93, 114–16 (2011).

Campbell emphatically did not say that parody was protected and satire was not. Indeed, it strongly suggested that both satire and parody had claims to be fair use under copyright law where they did not substitute for the original goods.[69] But in the wake of *Campbell*, many courts in copyright and trademark cases have treated the parody/satire distinction not as a point of discussion, but as a bright line rule. Most notably, the Ninth Circuit in *Dr. Seuss* held that because The Cat NOT In the Hat was a satire, not a parody of Dr. Seuss's books, it was neither copyright fair use nor speech protected from trademark infringement.[70]

The result is that under existing law, there is a substantial benefit to having your work classed as a parody rather than a satire.[71] For many of the examples we discussed in section I, this is generally not an issue; most are pretty clearly targeting the brand owner at least in part. But other cases that clearly make reference to a trademark owner seem closer to satire—social commentary—than a parody of the trademark itself. In *L.L. Bean, Inc. v. Drake Publishers, Inc.*,[72] the court held that a pornography magazine that published a fake catalog called "L.L. Bea*m*'s Back to School Sex Catalog" was a lawful parody of L.L. Bea*n*'s Back to School Catalog.[73] Whatever commentary the Back to School Sex Catalog might be making doesn't seem to be about L.L. Bean per se. And in *MasterCard International, Inc. v. Nader 2000 Primary Committee, Inc.*,[74] the court held that Ralph Nader's political ad in the 2000 presidential campaign based on the

---

[69] *Campbell*, 510 U.S. at 580 n.14 ("[W]hen there is little or no risk of market substitution, whether because of the large extent of transformation of the earlier work, the new work's minimal distribution in the market, the small extent to which it borrows from an original, or other factors, taking parodic aim at an original is a less critical factor in the analysis, and looser forms of parody may be found to be fair use, as may satire with lesser justification for the borrowing than would otherwise be required."). By contrast, Justice Kennedy was alone in concluding that the court's analysis should be limited to parody and should not extend to satire. *Id.* at 597 (Kennedy, J., concurring) ("It is not enough that the parody use the original in a humorous fashion, however creative that humor may be. The parody must target the original, and not just its general style, the genre of art to which it belongs, or society as a whole...").

[70] Dr. Seuss Enters., L.P. v. Penguin Books USA, Inc., 109 F.3d 1394, 1405–6 (9th Cir. 1997) ("[T]he claim of parody is no defense 'where the purpose of the similarity is to capitalize on a famous mark's popularity for the defendant's own commercial use.'" (citation omitted)). For trenchant criticism of this decision, see Tyler T. Ochoa, *Dr. Seuss, the Juice, and Fair Use: How the Grinch Silenced a Parody*, 45 J. Copyright Soc'y U.S.A. 546, 585–633 (1998). For a contrary approach, see Blanch v. Koons, 467 F.3d 244, 259 (2d Cir. 2006). *See also* Madhavi Sunder, From Goods to a Good Life: Intellectual Property and Social Justice 23–44 (2012); Rebecca Tushnet, *Scary Monsters: Hybrids, Mashups, and Other Illegitimate Children*, 86 Notre Dame L. Rev. 2133, 2139 (2011).

[71] Indeed, several copyright cases bend over backward to find parody in what is really some other form of commentary or criticism. *See, e.g.*, Northland Family Planning Clinic, Inc. v. Ctr. for Bio-Ethical Reform, 868 F. Supp. 2d 962 (C.D. Cal. 2012) (edit of pro-choice video to intersperse anti-choice arguments was a "parody"; parody doesn't need to be humorous).

[72] 811 F.2d 26 (1st Cir. 1987).

[73] *Id.* at 34.

[74] No. 00 Civ.6068(GBD), 2004 WL 434404 (S.D.N.Y. Mar. 8, 2004). Full disclosure: one of us (Lemley) represented Nader in this case.

MasterCard "Priceless" ad campaign was a lawful parody.[75] But while Nader's ad was clearly social commentary, and while Nader argued that his ad was in fact designed in part to mock MasterCard, the ad was really satire, not parody. It was designed to use a well-known ad campaign to make a social commentary about something—campaign finance—unrelated to MasterCard. Indeed, one might question (as both Justice Kennedy's concurrence and the Sixth Circuit opinion did) whether 2 Live Crew's "Big Hairy Woman" song was really a parody of Roy Orbison's "Pretty Woman" or just a takeoff on it. Justice Kennedy worried in *Campbell* "that not just any commercial takeoff is rationalized *post hoc* as a parody."[76] But arguably a preference for parody over satire gives just such an incentive.

In many cases, therefore, the parties fight about whether a work is in fact a parody at all as a prelude to (or perhaps a proxy for) debating whether it is legal. For courts that focus on the parody/satire distinction, that requires them to make some tough choices in deciding what qualifies as a parody: Is a subsidiary purpose to make fun of the plaintiff enough, or must it be the primary focus of the defendant's use? How confident must we be that it is a parody? Does the defendant's intent to make a parody (or not) matter? Does it matter how the audience perceives it? Consider, for instance, Chick-Fil-A's complaint over "Eat More Kale" T-shirts.[77] Bo Muller-Moore, the maker of the shirts, said he didn't intend to make fun of Chick-Fil-A or its "Eat More Chikin" slogan.[78] But some people might see it that way, or at least see it as a takeoff that provides a humorous contrast with the fast-food mark. If we focus on the defendant's intent, the result would be that Muller-Moore's shirts would not be parodies, but identical shirts made by someone who sought to mock the fast food industry would be. If instead we focus on how consumers perceive the shirts, we face an expensive fact determination ancillary to the primary likelihood of confusion determination. And it is not clear what value that information has.

Perhaps we could use the court as a gatekeeper, bending over backward to perceive parody if at all possible and weeding cases out pre-trial. That's the approach copyright law takes, though copyright has always been less concerned than trademark with the reactions of individual consumers. A judicial judgment about whether something is a parody has advantages over both the defendant's belief and the public's, though it risks missing parodies that appeal to a younger or culturally different audience than tends to inhabit the federal bench. A number of people have worried that the Sixth Circuit in

---

[75] *Id.* at *2–9.

[76] Campbell v. Acuff-Rose Music, Inc., 510 U.S. 569, 600 (1994) (Kennedy, J., concurring).

[77] The fight over "Eat More Kale" is now the subject of an upcoming documentary, A DEFIANT DUDE.

[78] Bo Muller-Moore, EAT MORE KALE, http://eatmorekale.com/(last visited Sept. 7, 2013) ("I'm asked all the time, 'Hey Bo, what do you mean by "Eat More Kale" and where did the phrase come from?' . . . Most obviously, it's about eating healthier. Kale can be delicious and a SUPER FOOD! You *should* eat more of it. . . . Eat More Kale is about supporting small business, business that actually cares and hasn't been swallowed up by profit-hungry, corporate mentality").

Campbell simply didn't "get" 2 Live Crew's music; one might similarly worry about judges not "getting" the Enjoy Cocaine poster in *Gemini Rising* or a host of other modern parodies.

Perhaps there is a way for trademark law to avoid drawing this line altogether. It is not clear that trademark owners have any strong need to prevent satire. In *Campbell*, the Court focused on the defendant's need to use the plaintiff's work rather than any other work, suggesting that satire required more justification for copying because it didn't have to use the plaintiff's work. That argument has always rung a bit hollow even in copyright; if no one wants their works to be used as a basis for satire, the fact that there are many other potential plaintiffs whose works I can't use either is cold comfort indeed.[79] But the argument seems to have even less force in trademark law. Unlike copyright, which is designed to prevent copying and to give copyright owners control over the use of the work itself, trademark law cares only about the brand-product connection in the minds of consumers and how that might affect producer incentives. There is little reason to think that either parody or satire interferes with that connection; to the contrary, both will often reinforce the connection by calling to mind the famous brand or ad campaign they mimic.[80] And there is even less reason to think that satire will cause more interference with the connection than parody does.

A number of scholars, including one of the authors, have argued recently that trademark law needs a trademark injury requirement under which plaintiffs could block only uses that actually changed consumer perceptions or behavior.[81] Under a trademark injury filter, courts might not have to decide whether a particular referential use was parody or

---

[79] *See* Bruce P. Keller & Rebecca Tushnet, *Even More Parodic Than the Real Thing: Parody Lawsuits Revisited*, 94 Trademark Rptr. 979, 979–80 (2004) (making this point).

[80] Barton Beebe has made this point about tarnishment. *See* Barton Beebe, *A Defense of the New Federal Trademark Antidilution Law*, 16 FORDHAM INTELL. PROP. MEDIA & ENT. L.J. 1143, 1150–51 (2006). For general discussion, see Desai, *From Trademarks to Brands, supra* note 40, at 1007–8; Heymann, *The Law of Reputation, supra* note 61, at 1341.

We dealt above with a related argument—that satire will "overexpose" a mark and therefore weaken its value. For criticism of that argument, see generally Mark A. Lemley, *Ex Ante Versus Ex Post Justifications for Intellectual Property*, 71 U. CHI. L. REV. 147 (2004) [hereinafter *Ex Ante*]. Lemley notes:

> Where a work is truly iconic, even repeated debasement is unlikely to affect public perceptions. Justin Hughes observes that the Statue of Liberty, the Mona Lisa, Mount Rushmore, and the Eiffel Tower retain their iconic status despite repeated uses and abuses in many different contexts. So too do the works of Shakespeare and the characters Frankenstein (and his monster), Dracula, Scrooge, Uncle Sam, and King Arthur.

Id. at 146 n.63 (citing Justin Hughes, *"Recording" Intellectual Property and Overlooked Audience Interests*, 77 TEX. L. REV. 923, 961 (1999)).

[81] *See* Lemley & McKenna, *Irrelevant Confusion, supra* note 26, at 448–53; Lemley & McKenna, *Owning Mark(et)s, supra* note 39, at 188–89; McKenna, *Consumer Decision-Making Theory, supra* note 61, at 124–33; Tushnet, *From A to B, supra* note 26, at 1368–73; *cf.* CHRISTINA BOHANNAN & HERBERT HOVENKAMP, CREATION WITHOUT RESTRAINT: PROMOTING LIBERTY AND RIVALRY IN INNOVATION 176–81 (2012) (proposing an analogous copyright injury requirement).

satire, because the law should protect both of them in the ordinary case in which neither parody nor satire is likely to have any material impact on consumer purchasing decisions. While parodies and satires may well influence consumers' view of a brand, neither is likely to do so in a way trademark law should care about—by confusing consumers at the point of purchase or interfering with the uniqueness of the mark as signifier. Importing the *Rogers v. Grimaldi* test from the right of publicity may effect just such an end-run, depending on how broadly the courts define "artistic relevance." We can imagine a court concluding that Outkast's song "Rosa Parks" was artistically relevant to Rosa Parks because it contained the line "everyone move to the back of the bus," even though the song was not in fact about Rosa Parks at all.[82]

Under existing law, however, trademark holders can prevail if there's confusion about their sponsorship of a product, even if the confusion causes them no harm. As a result, it's at least theoretically possible to have consumer confusion in the case of satire; consumers could, we suppose, be confused over whether the trademark holder has made the satirical point. We think it's doubtful, but the possibility of such confusion may make it harder to resolve cases early, without resort to any likelihood of confusion analysis.

Parodies, however, by their very nature make confusion improbable, and dilution highly unlikely. Trademark holders are unlikely to develop brands that lampoon themselves, and consumers are unlikely to believe that they've done so.[83] And as the *Louis Vuitton* court recognized, parodies will rarely dilute, because their commentary calls attention to the famous trademark and reinforces its fame.[84] Classifying a use as a parody should therefore enable earlier resolution of cases even under current legal standards. In an ideal world, of course, courts would do a better job of handling expressive uses of trademarks more generally. But given the realities of existing law, we think that parodies, at the very least, present an attractive case for special treatment.

Doing so requires us to confront the definitional problem directly. It's not an easy task; because parody and satire have more commonalities than differences, courts reach decisions that sometimes leave us scratching our heads.[85] But at least in cases of clear parody, we see

[82] As it happens, the court found the issue to present a question of fact that could not be resolved on summary judgment. Parks v. LaFace Records, 329 F.3d 437, 459–60 (6th Cir. 2003).

[83] *Cf.* Campbell v. Acuff-Rose Music, Inc., 510 U.S. 569, 592 (1994) ("[T]he unlikelihood that creators of imaginative works will license critical reviews or lampoons of their own productions removes such uses from the very notion of a potential licensing market"). However, there is some evidence of both self-parody as an advertising strategy (Isuzu's "He's Lying" commercials) and even a willingness to license some parody, as Weird Al Yankovic does.

[84] *See* Louis Vuitton Malletier S.A. v. Haute Diggity Dog, LLC, 507 F.3d 252, 267 (4th Cir. 2007).

[85] The Second Circuit, for example, described "Charbucks" as "at most, a subtle satire of the Starbucks Marks." Starbucks Corp. v. Wolfe's Borough Coffee, Inc., 588 F.3d 97, 113 (2d Cir. 2009). We're not sure what the difference is between a subtle satire of a product and a parody of that product; according to the Supreme Court, at least, the use of a mark to poke even subtle fun at that mark would be parody rather than satire. The court seems to have thought that "Charbucks" was at most a joke about the dark roast of the Starbucks coffee (and therefore directed at dark roast generally), ignoring its rather more obvious implication that people are wasting their money buying expensive cups of Starbucks coffee. The fact that a court of appeals can garble the distinction in a case this easy gives us pause in endorsing it.

some value in carving out a separate defense. So we proceed here with the task even while understanding that at some level it is futile, because defining parody may enable us to take at least some easy cases out of court early.

We think a parody need not be intended solely as a parody; many brands seek to convey multiple messages at once. Nor should parody depend on the defendant's intent that something be a parody; it is worth noting that 2 Live Crew originally defended its song as a cover of the Orbison original, not as a parody. To focus on the defendant's intent would not only be unworkable but would cause similar uses to be treated differently depending on the defendant's state of mind and how careful they were in documenting their intent.

That leaves the public and the courts as possible arbiters of what is a parody. Both have their problems. Relying on the public simply falls back on the likelihood of confusion standard, here to determine not the fact of confusion but whether people thought the trademark owner or a third party was the target of the defendant's use. It would mean that it is essentially impossible to resolve parody cases pre-trial. The best (or least-bad) alternative may be to follow copyright and have judges make their own assessment of whether something is a parody, putting a thumb on the scale of finding parody in doubtful cases. That's not a perfect solution, because judges may not "get" the joke in many popular culture cases. But it may be the best we can do as long as courts are unwilling to put satire on equal footing with parody.

B. IMPLEMENTING A PARODY DEFENSE

The next question is how to implement such a defense. Should parody serve as a stand-alone defense that automatically defeats any likelihood of confusion? Or should courts inquire into confusion, allowing the parody only when confusion is impossible or highly unlikely? What kind of confusion, for that matter, should count?

It might seem logical to look to *Rogers v. Grimaldi*, given its value in non-brand parody cases. As discussed above, *Rogers* allows use of trademarks in expressive products as long as the mark has artistic relevance to the work and does not expressly mislead. But *Rogers* offers little guidance outside the expressive work context. A rule that considers a trademark's relationship to a movie, book, or video game does not apply readily to names of commodities such as coffee or dog toys. At the same time, parodies match up with the Second Circuit's core insight—that the risk of confusion with some sorts of uses might be so small, and countervailing speech interests so substantial, that courts should dispense with analysis of likelihood of confusion.[86] The trick is finding the doctrinal vehicle for analyzing parodies.

The Second Circuit ultimately affirmed a finding that Charbucks was not dilutive, using the ordinary dilution test rather than relying on parody. Starbucks Corp. v. Wolfe's Borough Coffee, Inc., No. 12-354-cv, 2013 WL 6037227 (2d Cir. Nov. 15, 2013).

[86] *See* Rogers v. Grimaldi, 875 F.2d 994, 999 (2d Cir. 1989).

We think that trademark's nominative fair use doctrine—with some tweaking—could serve as an adequate tool for resolving most brand parody cases without resort to likelihood of confusion. In cases in which the nominative fair use defense does not apply, courts should turn to a full analysis of likelihood of confusion and dilution. When this happens, however, they must take care to avoid some of the pitfalls that have led courts to find obvious parodies infringing. We offer some preliminary thoughts about how that analysis ought to proceed.

1. Nominative Fair Use

Nominative fair use is a common law doctrine that allows certain uses of trademarks to refer to the mark holder itself, or its products. The two primary tests used in nominative fair use cases come from the Ninth and Third circuits. The Ninth Circuit, which first formally devised the test, allows a nominative use if the defendant meets three conditions:

> First, the product or service ... [is] not readily identifiable without use of the trademark; second, only so much of the mark or marks may be used as is reasonably necessary to identify the product or service; and third, the user must do nothing that would, in conjunction with the mark, suggest sponsorship or endorsement by the trademark holder.[87]

The Third Circuit applies a similar test, but its third prong asks whether "defendant's conduct or language reflect[s] the true and accurate relationship between plaintiff and defendant's products or services."[88]

Admittedly, both of these tests turn in part on consumer expectations; courts cannot assess whether a defendant's use of a mark is "accurate"—or whether it improperly suggests endorsement—without some reference to how consumers will perceive the use.[89] As a result, critics have complained that nominative fair use simply re-entangles courts in the same likelihood of confusion inquiries that define infringement in the

[87] New Kids on the Block v. News Am. Publ'g, Inc., 971 F.2d 302, 308 (9th Cir. 1992); *see also* Toyota Motor Sales, U.S., Inc. v. Tabari, 610 F.3d 1171, 1175–83 (9th Cir. 2010); *cf.* Swarovski Aktiengesellschaft v. Bldg. No. 19, Inc., 704 F.3d 44 (1st Cir. 2013) (recognizing and applying nominative fair use but without adopting any particular definition).

[88] Century 21 Real Estate Corp. v. Lendingtree, Inc., 425 F.3d 211, 222 (3d Cir. 2005); *see also id.* at 223 & n.4 ("Fairness is a distinct concept from confusion, and it should be measured through a distinct inquiry."). The court also fiddled a bit with the other *New Kids* factors. In full, the Third Circuit's nominative fair use standard requires the defendant to show:

> (1) that the use of plaintiff's mark is necessary to describe both the plaintiff's product or service and the defendant's product or service; (2) that the defendant uses only so much of the plaintiff's mark as is necessary to describe plaintiff's product; and (3) that the defendant's conduct or language reflect the true and accurate relationship between [the parties].

Id. at 222.

[89] *See, e.g., Tabari*, 610 F.3d at 1176 (noting that the third prong of nominative fair use—whether defendant has improperly suggested sponsorship or endorsement—should be assessed from the perspective of the

first place.[90] Yet the role of consumer expectations is quite different in the two contexts. In the general likelihood of confusion context, consumer perception is the very heart of the inquiry: the factfinder must assess whether, given the nature of the parties, their products, and the marks at issue, consumers might mistakenly perceive a source- or sponsorship-oriented relationship between the parties. The defendant does not ordinarily have any particular reason for using the plaintiff's trademark, so the factfinder has no purpose against which to measure the nature of the use. In nominative fair use, in contrast, the defendant has a reason to use the mark; the factfinder's task is to assess how the use measures up against that legitimate purpose. This at least admits the possibility of a textual inquiry that relies on the court's objective assessment of whether the defendant's use promotes valid referential goals or instead appears intended to mislead. As a result, judges may be able to resolve nominative fair use issues without prolonged factual inquiries into consumer perceptions.[91]

In essence, the nominative fair use inquiry asks whether the defendant had a legitimate reason to use the mark to evoke the trademark holder; if so, the doctrine considers how the actual use matches up against that purpose. The doctrine recognizes that certain forms of communication require use of trademarks to achieve their expressive goals. You can't really compare a new product to an entrenched market leader without using the leader's trademark. It's hard to tout the sale of after-market parts without naming the cars that they were designed to repair. A news channel can't convey which sporting event it is covering without using the event's name.[92]

Indeed, it is often virtually impossible to refer to a particular product for purposes of comparison, criticism, point of reference or any other such purpose without using the mark. For example, reference to a large automobile manufacturer based in Michigan would not differentiate among the Big Three; reference to a large Japanese manufacturer

---

"reasonably prudent consumer"); *Century 21*, 425 F.3d at 231 (considering whether defendant's behavior "rendered the use inaccurate or was somehow misleading as to any endorsement or relationship").

[90] *See, e.g.*, McGeveran, *supra* note 10, at 88–97 (arguing that the substitution of fair use requirements for likelihood of confusion analysis is a significant problem that prejudices fair uses and prolongs litigation); *see also, e.g.*, Mark P. McKenna, *Trademark Use, supra* note 21 (making the point more generally).

[91] *See Century 21*, 425 F.3d at 224 ("Our test for nominative fair use considers distinct factors that are readily susceptible to judicial inquiry."). Importantly, the Third Circuit approach, unlike the Ninth Circuit, treats nominative use as a defense even in the face of confusion, while the Ninth Circuit could be read as saying that if consumers are confused as to sponsorship or affiliation the defendant is disentitled to a defense. So understood, the Ninth Circuit test wouldn't be a defense at all, but collapses into the confusion inquiry. Indeed, some circuits, like the Sixth Circuit, view nominative fair use as redundant because, they believe, it protects uses that are inherently unlikely to cause confusion. *See, e.g.*, PACCAR Inc. v. TeleScan Techs., LLC, 319 F.3d 243, 256 (6th Cir. 2003) ("This circuit has never followed the nominative fair use analysis, always having applied [the circuit's likelihood of confusion] test."), *abrogated by* KP Permanent Make-Up, Inc. v. Lasting Impression I, Inc., 543 U.S. 111 (2004). For criticism of the Ninth Circuit on this ground, see Greg Lastowka, Nominative Fair Use Makes No Sense (Oct. 9, 2013) (working paper), *available at* http://papers.ssrn.com/sol3/papers.cfm?abstract_id=2338296.

[92] *See* WCVB-TV v. Bos. Athletic Ass'n, 926 F.2d 42, 46 (1st Cir. 1991).

of home electronics would narrow the field to a dozen or more companies. Much useful social and commercial discourse would be all but impossible if speakers were under threat of an infringement lawsuit every time they made reference to a person, company or product by using its trademark.[93]

In all of these contexts, the nature of the defendant's communicative goals requires use of the trademark; the question for the court is really whether the defendant's use of the mark is coextensive with those goals, or whether it has exceeded its justification.

If, as we believe, trademark parodies are a unique and non-replicable form of speech about trademark holders, then they resemble the sorts of uses that nominative fair use seeks to protect. They involve speech about the trademark holder, and they cannot serve their inherent function—indeed, they can't be a parody—without borrowing from the original.[94] Nominative fair use thus offers a ready framework for analyzing trademark parodies. But how do we analyze the critical third factor (i.e., whether the defendant's actions match up to its legitimate speech-related objectives)?

In many ways, the considerations underlying nominative fair use mirror those at issue in copyright law's treatment of parody. As the Supreme Court has recognized, to do its job, a parody must borrow substantially from the target of its scorn.[95] It must borrow at least enough to evoke the work in the mind of the observer. Yet that's not all—the borrower can take *more* than necessary to evoke the work, as long as it's done to further the parody and doesn't come so close to the original that it morphs into a substitute (rather than a parody) of the original work.[96]

This logic folds nicely into trademark analysis of nominative fair use. First, in order to present an effective parody of a trademark, it is necessary to borrow substantially from that mark. As long as a parodic character can "reasonably be perceived," the necessity kicks in. Second, the court must examine the defendant's use of the mark to determine whether it goes too far beyond the parodic purpose. If the parody pervades the defendant's use, then substantial taking is justified; if, however, the parody is hard to perceive and the taking is substantial, then this requirement might not be satisfied. Finally, the court should consider the overall context of the use to determine whether the defendant

---

[93] New Kids on the Block v. News Am. Publ'g, Inc., 971 F.2d 302, 306–7 (9th Cir. 1992).

[94] *See* Mattel v. Walking Mountain Prods., 353 F.3d 792, 810 (9th Cir. 2003) (applying nominative fair use when defendant "used Mattel's Barbie figure and head in his works to conjure up associations of Mattel, while at the same time to identify his own work, which is a criticism and parody of Barbie").

[95] *See* Campbell v. Acuff-Rose Music, Inc., 510 U.S. 569, 587–89 (1994). In fact, the line between parody and satire isn't as clear here either. Haute Diggity Dog could have chosen to parody a brand other than Louis Vuitton, so it didn't *need* the Vuitton mark in a strict sense.

[96] *See id.* at 588 ("Once enough has been taken to assure identification, how much more is reasonable will depend, say, on the extent to which the song's overriding purpose and character is to parody the original or, in contrast, the likelihood that the parody may serve as a market substitute for the original").

did anything *beyond* mere use of the mark that suggests source-affiliation or sponsorship by the trademark holder. Precision on this last point is critical: as noted above, a reading of the Ninth Circuit test that permits evidence of confusion to defeat the defense would render nominative fair use a nullity. The third factor must refer to acts *beyond the parody itself* that cause confusion.

2. Trademark Standards When Nominative Fair Use Doesn't Apply.

The above analysis should resolve most cases involving trademark parodies. In some cases, however, the court might believe that the parodist went well beyond what was necessary to achieve its expressive goals, creating at least the possibility of confusion or dilution by doing something other than parodying the mark. Or it might conclude that the defense doesn't apply because the defendant's brand is purely satire or other humor rather than parody. When this happens, the court must move beyond nominative fair use and tackle, head-on, the questions of likelihood of confusion and dilution. We have some thoughts about the appropriate analysis in these expressive non-parody cases.

First, to the extent that the court perceives a parodic purpose but believes that the defendant's use of the mark exceeds that purpose and risks confusing the public, the court should resist the call for a complete injunction in favor of one that addresses the excesses while preserving the parody. Here, too, nominative fair use offers useful precedent. As the Ninth Circuit held in *Toyota Motor Sales, U.S.A., Inc. v. Tabari*,[97] courts considering nominative fair use cases should tailor injunctive relief to the particular excesses that create the risk of confusion. "At the very least," the court held, injunctions must be crafted to allow the defendant to achieve its nominative objectives. "Trademarks are part of our common language, and we all have some right to use them to communicate in truthful, non-misleading ways."

Second, courts should absolutely reject the notion that *confusion as to permission* is ever actionable as a matter of trademark law. For all we know, some substantial portion of the public may assume that trademark holders have a legal right to prevent *any* unauthorized use of their mark. It would be odd lawmaking indeed if courts defined legal rules by what the public *thinks* the law is, regardless of how misguided those perceptions may be. Of course, some amount of circularity is endemic in trademark law; the fact that infringement turns on the risk of consumer confusion makes it inevitable that the law will sometimes over-protect marks. But at least in the ordinary case, the claim of confusion has some plausible relevance to trademark law's goal of protecting consumer expectations about who makes or stands behind products. The fact that a consumer might mistakenly believe that a trademark holder gave permission to make fun of itself has nothing to do with that kind of confusion. It is a quintessential example of "irrelevant confusion."[98]

---

[97] 610 F.3d 1171 (9th Cir. 2010).

[98] *See* Lemley & McKenna, *Irrelevant Confusion, supra* note 26, at 427.

Third, in cases in which a brand use is also making an expressive statement, the expressive nature of the defendant's use should influence the entire inquiry into likelihood of confusion and dilution, just as it does for fair use in copyright law. Strength and similarity of marks, for example, should not serve its ordinary role of cutting in favor of confusion. If anything, for more famous marks, the satire will arguably be more recognizable; and, as discussed above, significant borrowing of the trademark may be important to the message being conveyed even if the defendant is not directly parodying the brand. Analysis of similarity should operate on a sliding scale, in which the stronger the expressive nature, the closer the marks may come to one another without this factor weighing in favor of confusion.

The dilution inquiry should likewise recognize that the very nature of expressive works will often require deliberate use of a recognizable mark. As a result, factors such as the mark's renown and the intent to create an association between the marks cannot serve their usual function of cutting in favor of dilution. Indeed, as the Fourth Circuit recognized in *Louis Vuitton*, several of the dilution factors arguably cut in opposite directions. The more famous the mark, for example, the less likely that a parody will impair its distinctiveness.[99] Courts in dilution cases should consider the factors in light of the ultimate question: whether the defendant's use affects the famous mark's ability to serve as a "unique identifier of its source."[100]

Fourth, given the value of even non-parodic but expressive uses, such as satire, small amounts of confusion should not justify an injunction. While trademark law generally finds infringement if even a small minority of consumers are confused,[101] it does so because there is no countervailing interest on the other side. By contrast, where there are consumer interests on both sides of the ledger, trademark law has tended to require higher confusion thresholds. To prove a mark generic, for instance, the law requires that a substantial majority of the public thinks it is, because the consumers who don't think so will be injured.[102]

---

[99] Louis Vuitton Malletier S.A. v. Haute Diggity Dog, LLC, 507 F.3d 252, 267 (4th Cir. 2007) ("[B]ecause the famous mark is particularly strong and distinctive, it becomes more likely that a parody will not impair the distinctiveness of the mark."); *see also* Lemley, *Ex Ante, supra* note 80, at 145–48 (offering examples of famous icons that retain their status despite constant dilution).

[100] *Louis Vuitton*, 507 F.3d at 267.

[101] *See* Henri's Food Prods., Co. v. Kraft, Inc., 717 F.2d 352, 358–59 (7th Cir. 1983) (holding that 7.6% confusion was insufficient to establish likelihood of confusion, but collecting authorities finding likelihood of confusion based on surveys showing as low as 8.5% confusion among consumers); Exxon Corp. v. Tex. Motor Exch. of Hous., Inc., 628 F.2d 500, 507 (5th Cir. 1980) (stating that 15% was sufficient); Jockey Int'l, Inc. v. Burkard, No. 74 123 S, 1975 WL 21128, at *7 (S.D. Cal. Feb. 21, 1975) (discussing survey evidence that "11.4 percent of the universe … would associate defendants' JOCK SOCK underwear package with plaintiff"); Grotrian, Helfferich, Schulz, Th. Steinweg Nachf. v. Steinway & Sons, 365 F. Supp. 707, 716 (S.D.N.Y. 1973) ("[O]f 520 people canvassed … 7.7% … preceived [*sic*] a business connection between the two companies and 8.5% confused the names."), *modified on other grounds*, 523 F.2d 1331 (2d Cir. 1975).

[102] *See* Murphy Door Bed Co. v. Interior Sleep Sys., Inc., 874 F.2d 95, 101–2 (2d Cir. 1989); King-Seeley Thermos Co. v. Aladdin Indus., Inc., 321 F.2d 577, 579 (2d Cir. 1963). Descriptive fair use does the same, providing a partial defense that can be overcome in some circumstances, but only with a higher showing of confusion. *See* KP Permanent Make-Up, Inc. v. Lasting Impression I, Inc., 543 U.S. 111, 121–23 (2004).

A parody or satire gives consumers who get the joke an interest in the defendant's brand that an injunction would stymie. Before we impose that injunction, we should be significantly more confident that harm to the confused consumers outweighs the harm to those who have an interest in the defendant's speech. The fact that there are interests on both sides may also affect the choice of remedy. Trademark law generally gives little shrift to disclaimers,[103] but parody and satire may be circumstances where the appropriate response to all but the highest levels of confusion is not an injunction or a change to the defendant's brand, but merely requiring the defendant to make clear that they are not associated with the plaintiff.

Doing so may also avoid conflicts with the First Amendment. The Ninth Circuit has emphasized the significant risks trademark law poses to speech in cases like "Barbie Girl."[104] And it has done so even in cases that have no arguable claim to parody, such as a football player objecting to his depiction in a football video game.[105] Laura Heymann has explained how the low confusion threshold makes the problem worse.[106] And as one of the authors has argued, that risk is heightened when the remedy is an injunction against the protected speech.[107] In the absence of a pure defense for brand parodies or satires, the combination of a higher confusion threshold and limited remedies may end up providing at least some speech protection.

IV. Conclusion

Brand parodies serve useful social purposes and are unlikely to interfere with any legitimate interests of trademark owners. But the fact that they are both parodies and brands means that their legal status is unclear. We think brand parodies deserve clear legal protection, and that existing law can provide that protection if it is properly understood.

---

[103] *See* JR Tobacco of Am., Inc. v. Davidoff of Geneva (CT), Inc., 957 F. Supp. 426, 437 (S.D.N.Y. 1997) ("[G]enerally, a disclaimer is ineffective to cure a literally false statement."). As the Callman treatise puts it, "[e]xperience has taught that a business acquires a material advantage over its competitors if it arrests the attention of the prospective purchaser. Deception followed by enlightment [*sic*] and explanation does not negate this initial advantage." LOUIS ALTMAN & MALLA POLLACK, CALLMAN ON TRADEMARKS, UNFAIR COMPETITION, AND MONOPOLIES § 5.31 (4th ed. 2013). For a discussion of trademark disclaimers, see generally Laura A. Heymann, *Reading the Product: Warnings, Disclaimers, and Literary Theory*, 22 YALE J.L. & HUMAN. 393 (2010).

[104] *See* Mattel, Inc. v. MCA Records, Inc., 296 F.3d 894, 902–7 (9th Cir. 2002); *see also* Mattel, Inc. v. Walking Mountain Prods., 353 F.3d 792, 801 (9th Cir. 2003).

[105] Brown v. Electronic Arts, Inc., 724 F.3d 1235, 1239–41 (9th Cir. 2013) (applying *Rogers* test to non-parodic use of a brand, and noting that the rule was the same whether the defendant's use was in the title or body of the work).

[106] *See* Laura A. Heymann, *The Public's Domain in Trademark Law: A First Amendment Theory of the Consumer*, 43 GA. L. REV. 651, 702–3 (2009).

[107] *See* Mark A. Lemley & Eugene Volokh, *Freedom of Speech and Injunctions in Intellectual Property Cases*, 48 DUKE L.J. 147, 216–24 (1998).

7 Stolen Valor and Stolen Luxury

FREE SPEECH AND EXCLUSIVITY

Rebecca Tushnet*

THE U.S. SUPREME Court has given extensive constitutional protection to speech, including false noncommercial speech and truthful commercial speech. Yet existing precedent is relatively unconcerned by the scope of a trademark owner's rights to control others' commercial speech, including rights to suppress nondeceptive but "dilutive" uses of trademarks. This paper explores trademark exceptionalism in free speech law, which it relates to variance in conceptions of harm and courts' willingness to give trademark owners control over the emotional resonance of marks, even as American constitutionalism rejects the offense of lèse-majesté in every other form.

Each era perhaps has its sufficient justifications for suppressing speech: fear of armed rebellion in the late eighteenth and early twentieth century, then fear of communist subversion in the mid-twentieth century. Attacks on the American system of government were thought to threaten the very basis of freedom. Today, however, sufficient justification for suppressing speech more readily comes from fear of attacks on the American way of business.[1]

---

* Professor, Georgetown Law. Thanks to the 2014 Intellectual Property Works in Progress conference, the Boston University Intellectual Property Seminar, the Georgetown Faculty Workshop, and the Washington College of Law's Trademark Roundtable.

[1] Even the U.S. statutory protections for online intermediaries reflect the special status of intellectual property. Online intermediaries are immune from any liability for hosting user-provided defamation and other

Criticize or mock the government—even for profit—and the First Amendment provides almost total protection. Criticize or mock a public figure—even for profit—and only knowing or reckless factual falsity can justify defamation liability (though the ever-growing right of publicity, with its strong similarities to dilution law, threatens the constraints put on defamation law over the past half-century). Criticize or mock a famous brand for profit, and risk an adverse trademark verdict.

Is this simply an extreme version of corporate capitalism, where all other values are dissolved and the only offense is to challenge the power of the wealthy to continue in their dominance? A failure to examine the harms of dilution and new varieties of infringement with a critical eye has allowed courts too easily to equate claimed harm to brand value with the harms of fraud, perjury, and other causes of action that survive First Amendment scrutiny. Courts have not deeply investigated the epistemological theories by which they presume that dilution, post-sale confusion, and the like do harm.[2] Instead, they make assumptions consistent with distaste for free riding. However, when truthful, nonmisleading commercial speech is involved, such assumptions should not be constitutionally sufficient, especially once we recognize that many of the claimed harms in trademark come from changing audiences' preferences rather than distorting their factual beliefs.

The real puzzle is why such lightly evidenced and antidemocratic theories have so readily justified suppressing nonfalse speech. Courts are often hostile to free riders; I will suggest that this hostility has effects on courts' willingness to find that copying is harmful, not just offensive.

I. Luxury as Value

Legislators and courts are willing to protect luxury brands, and even to note that their value comes from the ability to exclude other people from having them. But they have not defended that value as socially beneficial, rather than beneficial to the trademark owner's relative position, and they have not squared that exclusionary source of value with general First Amendment doctrine, which in other areas protects the right of speakers to challenge existing hierarchies and authorities. As Barton Beebe has written, trademark law has become a means of preserving the creation of distinction, creating a modern sumptuary code.[3]

Trademark's protections for exclusivity are not limited to dilution. Courts also use the language of "infringement" to protect "brand value," which is to say the aura of

---

speech that may lawfully be suppressed, including speech whose utterance constitutes a state crime, under § 230 of the Communications Decency Act. 47 U.S.C. § 230. But §230 specifically excludes intellectual property offenses from that complete immunity.

[2] *See* Mark McKenna, *Testing Modern Trademark Law's Theory of Harm*, 95 Iowa L. Rev. 63 (2009).

[3] Barton Beebe, *Intellectual Property Law and the Sumptuary Code*, 123 Harv. L. Rev. 809 (2010).

distinction and uniqueness claimed by a trademark owner.[4] In *Lois Sportswear, U.S.A., Inc. v. Levi Strauss & Co.*, for example, the influential Second Circuit enjoined a copyist of Levi's stitching, ostensibly on confusion grounds, because otherwise Levi's sales would be "affected adversely by ... buyers' ultimate realization that the pattern is no longer exclusive."[5] Other cases similarly find infringement because trademark owners' prestige—and the prestige of their customers—is at stake.[6] Trademark owners are thus allowed to aggregate insults to their customers' prestige, while third-party beneficiaries of copiers are rarely considered to have valid interests.

Indeed, purchasers of counterfeits, though not always confused themselves, are condemned for that very fact: their enjoyment of a simulated product is understood by courts to do damage to the buyers of the "real" thing, who find their exclusive status threatened and their signals of wealth and judgment blurred by the presence of imposters. As one oft-cited case held, a copyist was infringing because some of its customers would buy its cheaper product "for the purpose of acquiring the prestige gained by displaying what many visitors at the customers' homes would regard as a prestigious article."[7] The condemnation of the copyist's consumer is an important part of a finding of infringement by the copyist *because* the consumer is not confused, but rather deviously plotting to pose as wealthier or more tasteful than she actually is.[8] Trademark law understood this way is consumer protection law, but not because it protects against purchaser deception. Rather, it protects elite consumers of *other* products against competition for the status signals they wish to send.

Intriguingly, the infringement cases protecting prestige are not limited to classic "luxury" goods in the sense of goods that are both expensive and limited in production so that only the lucky few can have them. Dilution law's definition of "fame" likewise covers household names, whether or not the brand appears in most households. It seems that protections for relative distinction and privilege can't be too bald-faced, which

---

[4] Beebe, *Id.* at 851.

[5] 799 F.2d 867, 875–76 (2d Cir. 1986).

[6] *See, e.g.*, General Motors Corp. v. Keystone Auto. Indus., 453 F.3d 351, 358 (6th Cir. 2006) ("[T]he purchaser of an original may be harmed if the widespread existence of knockoffs decreases the original's value by making the previously scarce commonplace."); Hermès Int'l v. Lederer de Paris Fifth Avenue, Inc., 219 F.3d 104, 108 (2d Cir. 2000) ("[T]he purchaser of an original [luxury good] is harmed by the widespread existence of knockoffs because the high value of originals, which derives in part from their scarcity, is lessened."); Ferrari S.P.A. Esercizio v. Roberts, 944 F.2d 1235, 1237 (6th Cir. 1991) (protecting Ferrari's "image of exclusivity" and using harm to uniqueness to justify finding of infringement). Not all of these are luxury brands, but the aura of exclusivity or "uniqueness" is now apparently possessed by any popular brand.

[7] Mastercrafters Clock & Radio Co. v. Vacheron & Constantin-Le Coultre Watches, Inc., 221 F.2d 464, 466 (2d Cir. 1955). As Beebe notes, this rationale has been widely followed. Beebe, *supra* note 3, at 855.

[8] Gucci Am., Inc. v. Daffy's Inc., 354 F.3d 228, 235 (3d Cir. 2003) ("An underpinning of Gucci's post-sale confusion argument is that Daffy's customers are posing as true Gucci wearers, free-riding on Gucci exclusivity at a Daffy's price."); Jeremy Sheff, *Veblen Brands*, 96 Minn. L. Rev. 769, 803 ("[T]he failure that this line of cases guards against is not in the market for any particular class of goods, but in the market for social status. Put simply, the "lemons" in the status-confusion cases are not used cars, and they are not really even clocks or handbags or watches; they are people.").

I hypothesize is related to American reluctance to discuss class. In trademark, the result is a broadening of protection for any brands whose absolute value is large enough. In effect, wealthy brands can be treated as royalty. The hierarchy protected is specifically an economic hierarchy, even as the rationales for the legal rules appeal to concepts of exclusivity and prestige. This is only one of the conceptual difficulties of modern trademark law, and it magnifies the speech-restrictive effects of that law.

II. The General Protection for Nonfactual Statements and Trademark's Reversal of the Rule

Trademark protection in the absence of consumer confusion at the point of sale has been justified, at least in part, as a means of making consumers of "true" luxury products feel better about themselves. In other areas of First Amendment law, however, fixing meaning and protecting other people from threats to their self-images are not considered acceptable justifications for limiting speech.[9] For example, the *deliberate* infliction of emotional distress on specific targets is regularly protected by the First Amendment.[10] The pain of lost distinction may well be a true psychic harm—but so is the pain of seeing Nazis march, or protestors at one's child's funeral claiming that he deserved to die.[11]

When the harm sought to be avoided is change in third parties' opinions (as opposed to, for example, physical violence), defamation law has provided a detailed map of what the law may not suppress. Defamation requires a false statement of *fact*, even though derogatory opinions can cause harm, including economic harm. Some theorists have claimed that only factual claims can affect reputation,[12] but this is implausible, not to mention inconsistent

---

[9] I do not here criticize other theories of harm from post-sale confusion, though my later discussion of how harm might be proved bears on those theories as well.

[10] Snyder v. Phelps, 131 S. Ct. 1207, 1219 (2011) (public speech on a matter of public concern "cannot be restricted simply because it is upsetting or arouses contempt. 'If there is a bedrock principle underlying the First Amendment, it is that the government may not prohibit the expression of an idea simply because society finds the idea itself offensive or disagreeable.' Indeed, 'the point of all speech protection ... is to shield just those choices of content that in someone's eyes are misguided, or even hurtful.'") (citing Texas v. Johnson, 491 U.S. 397, 414 (1989), and Hurley v. Irish-American Gay, Lesbian and Bisexual Group of Boston, Inc., 515 U.S. 557, 574 (1995)); Nat'l Socialist Party of Am. v. Vill. of Skokie, 432 U.S. 43, 43–44 (1977) (reversing denial of stay pending appeal for American Nazi party, which was enjoined from marching through an Illinois village).

[11] *See* Wendy Gordon, *The Concept of "Harm" in Copyright*, in INTELLECTUAL PROPERTY AND THE COMMON LAW 452, 480–82 (ed. Shyamkrishna Balganesh, 2013) (arguing that subjective distress from others' copying, however strongly and powerfully felt, should not count as the kind of harm justifying a prohibition on copying). Well-known brands are also not the types of speakers who might be silenced by vicious attacks, given their incentives to stay in the market; equality-based justifications for rebalancing the speech market do not apply here.

[12] *See, e.g.*, Laura A. Heymann, *The Law of Reputation and the Interest of the Audience*, 52 B.C. L. REV. 1341, 1394, 1398 (2011) (distinguishing reputation, based in facts, from status, based on associations); Joseph H. King, *Defamation Claims Based on Parody and Other Fanciful Communications Not Intended to Be*

with the modern understanding of trademarks and branding, which accepts that emotion and stories sell much more readily than facts.[13] Consider, from the realm of electoral speech, Ronald Reagan's entirely nonfactual but devastating "There you go again," which helped sum up an entire line of political criticism. An ad depicting a competitor's logo as a pitiful, frightened creature similarly denigrates without being in any way understandable as a factual claim.[14]

First Amendment case law nonetheless teaches that only the falsifiability line sufficiently protects speakers.[15] But if the foundation for protecting speech is the importance of breathing room for truth,[16] then there's no particular reason to protect plainly nonfactual opinions. Why would an audience have any rational interest in taking nonfacts into account in forming their judgments? Although nonfactual claims do affect reputations and behavior, the falsifiability line serves a structurally speech-protective role. The requirement that harm-causing speech must be false, not just derogatory, substantially narrows the potential scope of law regulating speech, insulating speech from suppression by juries or judges unwilling to tolerate deviation from the majority opinion.[17] Freedom for nonfalsifiable claims also frees speakers and audiences to develop their own value systems and judgments. When we allow trademark law to avoid that fact-based constraint, we are returning to the protection of the powerful against lèse-majesté, a concept rejected throughout the rest of First Amendment law.

Thus, Laura Bradford's description of the posited harm of trademark dilution is at once a plausible account of some consumer behavior and a catalog of motivations for regulation otherwise prohibited in First Amendment law:

> Trademark dilution law is so difficult to understand because it aims at emotion and only indirectly at information. The emotion referred to here is of the most basic kind: "affect" or the automatic negative or positive response that a mark generates when viewed by a consumer. Research on brands and emotion teaches that familiar

---

Understood as Fact, 2008 UTAH L. REV. 875, 877, 882 (asserting that reputational harm requires others to accept false information).

13 See Laura R. Bradford, *Emotion, Dilution, and the Trademark Consumer*, 23 BERKELEY TECH. L.J. 1227 (2008).

14 *See* Deere & Co. v. MTD Prods., 41 F.3d 39, 41 (2d Cir. 1994).

15 Gertz v. Robert Welch, Inc., 418 U.S. 323, 339–40 (1974).

16 Heymann, *supra* note 12, at 1418; *see also id.* at 1424 (discussing risks posed to audience's decision-making by untrue information, but not by true information).

17 *Compare* Films of Distinction, Inc. v. Allegro Film Prods., 12 F. Supp. 2d 1068, 1078–79, 1081 (C.D. Cal. 1998) (allowing infringement and dilution actions to proceed in case involving a film's use of a television network's trademark, but dismissing defamation claims because there were no "factual assertions") *with* Hustler Magazine, Inc. v. Falwell, 485 U.S. 46 (1988) (holding that, when jury decided that a *Hustler* "parody could not 'reasonably be understood as describing actual facts about Falwell or actual events in which [he] participated,'" Falwell couldn't claim defamation or intentional infliction of emotional distress); Milkovich v. Lorain Journal Co., 497 U.S. 1, 19 (1974) (statements that aren't falsifiable, including opinions, are entitled to full First Amendment protection).

> trademarks offer value to consumers by lowering the amount of effort required in purchasing decisions. Consumers experience positive feelings from the ease of evaluating familiar marks and accordingly infer positive qualities for the brand and the underlying product.... Those who use famous marks in ways inconsistent from the owner risk making the marks more costly to evaluate, and thus may cause consumers to automatically feel more negatively toward the original brand and affiliated products. Dilutive conduct can thus undercut the reliability of trademarks as sources of information for buyers. This, in a nutshell, is the harm caused by "blurring" famous marks.[18]

Bradford recognizes that this account of dilution is a poor justification for legal protection of brand values. Trademark value is generally accumulated in exactly the same noncognitive, affect-based ways, and it has no special claim to continue unchanged. But dilution's proponents don't mind this tension. For example, Jerre Swann, a leading proponent of dilution protection, explicitly conflates emotion and information when he describes the qualities he believes trademark owners should be able to control through law:

> Many brands are upward ladders of attributes, functional and psychosocial consequences, and value satisfiers. They can best be understood as pyramidal structures: at the base are the features of a product or service, including perceptions as to its quality; a level up are the emotional benefits the brand affords to consumers; and at the peak are the self-expressive, self-esteem and cultural values that a brand may provide. "Successful trademarks are [thus] valuable [today] because of the information [and emotion] they convey." The "source and quality" brands of Schechter's day no longer provide the "added attributes and content that consumers now want, demand and need." Consumers today do not buy commodities, but "*experiences*... whose contents are largely image driven, intangible and symbolic."[19]

Dilution, it's posited, interferes with the communication of the brand's chosen attributes. Yet making audiences think harder and forcing them to choose from a variety of competing meanings, "experiences," and opinions, even when they don't want to, is generally a First Amendment value, not a harm to be avoided.[20] In nontrademark areas

---

[18] Bradford, *supra* note 13, at 1233–34 (footnotes omitted).

[19] Jerre B. Swann, *The Evolution of Dilution in the United States from 1927 to 2013*, 103 TRADEMARK REP. 721, 754–55 (2013) (footnotes omitted) (bracketed reference to emotion inserted by Swann).

[20] Cohen v. California, 403 U.S. 15, 25–26 (1971) (speakers have the right to use offensive means to communicate messages, thus triggering heightened emotions in the audience). *Cf.* Bradford, *supra* note 13, at 1237 (offering this description of dilutive conduct: "Typically interlopers that evoke famous marks in advertising subtly reveal to consumers alternative understandings such as that some segment of the public thinks the brand is pretentious, a bad value, or simply over-exposed. Even if consumers process the new message only subconsciously, automatically, and involuntarily, as they do with much authorized brand advertising, a resulting increase in negative feelings about the dominant brand may well be welfare-enhancing and efficient" (footnote omitted)).

of law, courts consider making the audience change its attitudes a standard function of speech—and one that has the power to change the world.

Consider "Pepsi is the choice of a new generation." It's nonactionable puffery, but it also positions Coke as uncool. If successful, it will change Coke's relative status in brand hierarchies. In common parlance, it will change—damage—Coke's reputation. Yet the fact that this kind of posited harm works at an emotional, perhaps unconscious level doesn't make it distinguishable from other speech regulations that have been reined in by the First Amendment. The Supreme Court has clearly stated that vicious, even unfair emotional assaults are fully protected by the First Amendment, in the absence of factual falsity, and that this is true whether the law's aim is to protect a reputation or to prevent emotional distress.[21] In nontrademark causes of action, the First Amendment requires us to assume that the reputational harm done by nonfactual statements—including statements that elicit negative emotions about the target—is not sufficient to justify speech restrictions. This is why political caricatures are protected speech: their slashing attacks are often unfair, but unfairness is not defamation.[22]

The mismatch between trademark and other regulations targeting speech-generated economic harm can be seen most clearly in the case of celebrities. Well-known individuals can claim trademark protection for their names and other aspects of their identities. Nonetheless, they shouldn't be able to evade the fact/nonfact distinction by bringing trademark causes of action any more than Jerry Falwell could evade the law of defamation by suing *Hustler* for publishing an offensive cartoon about him under the label "intentional infliction of emotional distress."[23] Loss of brand reputation from dilution or obvious counterfeit occurs—if it does—by changing consumers' emotional responses, not their factual beliefs.[24] And the First Amendment question posed is whether emotional responses can be the basis of a lawsuit against expression if (we believe) the changed emotions have a definable pecuniary impact on a plaintiff.

III. Is Commercial Speech Different?

Perhaps dilution law's limitation to "commercial speech" sufficiently protects it against First Amendment invalidity. Consider the following case: during the post-game show

[21] *Hustler*, 485 U.S. 46, 51–53; *see id.* at 55 (citing "our longstanding refusal to allow damages to be awarded because the speech in question may have an adverse emotional impact on the audience"); *see also* Texas v. Johnson, 491 U.S. 397 (1989) (upholding the First Amendment right to burn the American flag to express contempt for American values); Cardtoons, L.C. v. Major League Baseball Players Ass'n, 95 F.3d 959, 974 (10th Cir. 1996) (holding that the free speech interest in mocking famous baseball players outweighed the publicity rights of the players).

[22] *Hustler*, 485 U.S. at 56.

[23] *Id.* at 48 (Falwell, a prominent minister, was portrayed as stating that his "'first time' [having sex] was 'during a drunken incestuous rendezvous with his mother in an outhouse'").

[24] Bradford, *supra* note 13, at 1233–34.

of the 2010 Super Bowl, Hyundai ran a 30-second commercial that its counsel later described as "a humorous, socio-economic commentary on luxury defined by a premium price tag, rather than by the value to the consumer." It consisted of brief vignettes that show "policemen eating caviar in a patrol car; large yachts parked beside modest homes; blue-collar workers eating lobster during their lunch break; a four-second scene of an inner-city basketball game played on a lavish marble court with a gold hoop; and a ten-second scene of the [Hyundai] Sonata driving down a street lined with chandeliers and red-carpet crosswalks." The inner-city basketball game scene included a one-second shot of a basketball decorated with a pattern resembling Louis Vuitton's toile LV monogram on a chestnut-brown background. The court granted summary judgment in LV's favor on trademark dilution.[25]

Hyundai's expressed motive was to contrast its offer of "luxury for all" with "the silliness of luxury-as-exclusivity" through "juxtaposing symbols of luxury with everyday life (for example, large yachts parked beside modest homes)." But the court found this deliberate evocation of LV's mark as one of the examples of "old" luxury to be dilutive: it was Hyundai's attempt to fight its own lower-quality brand image by grabbing on to LV's image. Hyundai's survey showed that no respondent thought less favorably of LV because of the ad, and only 2% believed there was any affiliation between the two, but the court was more impressed by tweets reacting to the ad, such as, "I think a Louis vuitton football or basketball would be gangsta."[26] In addition, the ad's creators testified in marketing-speak that the ad was "definitely laddering and borrowing equity from Louis Vuitton."[27]

The court also rejected a fair use defense, because Hyundai lacked an intent to parody, criticize, or comment on LV specifically. Hyundai argued that the presence of the design reflected a broader social commentary designed to "challenge consumers to rethink what it means for a product to be luxurious." But Hyundai didn't have anything to say about LV specifically and the court therefore ruled that, as a matter of law, Hyundai could not invoke fair use. In some sense, the idea that LV could stand in for luxury brands generally, and be subject to commentary on luxury brands generally, was inherently offensive to LV's supposedly unique status. And yet LV does very much want to be known as a luxury brand.

The court did not allow Hyundai to criticize or comment on the genus of "luxury" by identifying actual members thereof. But First Amendment principles generally allow speakers to choose their own examples. As the Supreme Court held in a case allowing a man to wear a vulgar slogan on his jacket in a courthouse, "we cannot indulge the facile assumption that one can forbid particular words without also running a substantial

[25] Louis Vuitton Malletier, S.A. v. Hyundai Motor Am., 2012 WL 1022247 (S.D.N.Y.).
[26] *Id.* at *11.
[27] *Id.* at *13.

risk of suppressing ideas in the process."[28] By contrast, the *LV* court explicitly rejected a First Amendment defense, because the commentary was "subtle" and because the ad only offered a "broader social critique," which was "unworthy of protection."[29] This reasoning turns the First Amendment on its head. Broad commentary on matters of public interest generally deserves more protection rather than less—even when coming from self-interested commercial speakers.

Given the nonfalse, nonfalsifiable message about LV and luxury in the Hyundai ad, dilution's rationale—preserving status—does not justify the outcome, even for commercial speech. To let LV monopolize the *meaning* of its brand, not just its source signification, leads to discrimination against certain commercial speakers merely because of the cultural side on which they deploy emotion. LV gets to use imagery and emotional appeals to enhance its brand reputation, but Hyundai doesn't get to do the same to challenge that reputation. It thus enacts the very structural tilt against dissenters—here, cultural dissenters, pranksters, and those who don't respect a famous brand's aura of exclusivity—that the falsifiability line is supposed to protect against. The Supreme Court said this in a case about hate speech:

> [A] State may choose to regulate price advertising in one industry but not in others, because the risk of fraud (one of the characteristics of commercial speech that justifies depriving it of full First Amendment protection) is in its view greater there. But a State may not prohibit only that commercial advertising that depicts men in a demeaning fashion.[30]

LV does not obviously deserve more protection than human beings, but the *LV* court nonetheless believed that the commercial nature of the use disabled Hyundai from offering any defense grounded in free speech. This result is presaged by the dilution statute itself, which carves out extra protections for noncommercial speech.[31]

In defense of a commercial/noncommercial distinction, one could argue that the economic injury targeted by dilution law is different from emotional injury, making dilution more appropriate in the commercial realm. Emotions can be the mechanism of harm that is not restricted to the emotional sphere but that has economic consequences for individuals (regardless of the overall efficiency effects, which may be nil or even positive). Emotional effects on consumers could arguably someday lead to reduced sales for LV. Yet, as noted above, this theory has already been rejected by First Amendment doctrine

---

[28] Cohen v. California, 403 U.S. at 26.

[29] *Louis Vuitton*, 2012 WL 1022247 at *26.

[30] R.A.V. v. City of St. Paul, 505 U.S. 377, 389 (1992) (citations omitted).

[31] Even when LV lost a similar case against a commercial speaker, the court didn't see the issue as a question of free speech, but rather as a failure of proof of likely dilution. See Louis Vuitton Malletier S.A. v. Haute Diggity Dog, LLC, 507 F.3d 252 (4th Cir. 2007).

as applied to other business tort claims. The case law on intentional interference with economic advantage, for example, has assimilated the general First Amendment rule requiring factual falsity.[32]

If dilution is constitutional because it targets economic harm, though, it would seem possible to reconceptualize defamation in *every* case as dilution, or intentional interference with economic advantage, if defamation plaintiffs purported to seek only economic damages resulting from nonfalse statements. The better position is that, even if nonfalse use of a trademark results in economic injury, regulation of that speech should have to satisfy the constitutional standard for banning truthful commercial speech.[33]

A full commercial speech analysis would, in addition, consider the weight of the government's interest in suppressing nonfalse commercial speech, as well as the costs of such suppression. One might compare truthful, or even nonfalse, comparative advertising, which can clearly inflict economic damage. The government's interest in preserving the success of existing brands is unlikely to justify suppressing such advertising when the government could further its goal by directly subsidizing current winners without regulating speech.

However, in trademark cases, free riding—"laddering equity," in Hyundai's words—has substituted for harm analysis. But the presence of a profit motive and a desire to attract attention by using existing symbols doesn't differentiate diluters from other speakers, such as *Hustler* when it mocked Jerry Falwell. The *New York Times* also has a profit motive and an incentive to get our attention in the quickest way possible. Symbolic shortcuts are endemic to modern communication. Nadia Plesner, for example, made a poster showing a malnourished African child holding a Louis Vuitton bag in order to make the point that Western news would rather report on Paris Hilton's fashion choices than on conflict and starvation in Africa.[34] In other contexts, the Supreme Court has given unauthorized speakers' use of well-known symbols, such as the American flag,

---

[32] *See, e.g.*, Nanavati v. Burdette Tomlin Memorial Hospital, 857 F.2d 96, 109 (3d Cir. 1988) (stating that "the defenses applicable to defamation claims retain their full status for tortious interference claims if such tortious interference claims are based on verbal conduct"); Blatty v. N.Y. Times Co., 728 P.2d 1177, 1184–85 (Cal. 1986) (stating that claims for interference with prospective economic advantage that have "as their gravamen the alleged injurious falsehood of a statement ... must satisfy the requirements of the First Amendment"; "[i]f these limitations applied only to actions denominated 'defamation,' they would furnish little if any protection to free-speech and free-press values: plaintiffs suing press defendants might simply affix a label other than 'defamation' to their ... claims").

[33] *See* Central Hudson Gas & Elec. v. Pub. Serv. Comm'n, 447 U.S. 557, 565 (1980) (restrictions on truthful commercial speech are constitutional if they're sufficiently tailored to a substantial government interest); Rebecca Tushnet, *Gone in Sixty Milliseconds: Trademark Law and Cognitive Science*, 86 TEX. L. REV. 507, 554–55 (2008).

[34] *Art Student Nadia Plesner's Giant Louis Vuitton Copyright Suit*, NEW YORK MAGAZINE (May 6, 2008), http://nymag.com/thecut/2008/05/art_student_nadia_pelsners_gia.html.

special constitutional protection because those shortcuts make speech more powerful.[35] Given the communicative value of "free riding," the government's interest in suppressing only a fraction of emotionally manipulative commercial speech, and only when it harms strong brands, is insufficient to support trademark liability in the absence of material consumer deception.

There is a deep irony here, as Mark McKenna and Laura Bradford have noted.[36] Critics of commercial speech doctrine have repeatedly claimed that much commercial speech is nonfactual, and for that reason is not especially hardy or distinguishable from noncommercial speech and needs the same constitutional protection as political speech.[37] Supporters of the First Amendment value of advertising have also argued that image advertising, and advertising that simply makes people feel good about buying brand name products, is utility-enhancing. To then contend that Hyundai's nonfalsifiable speech about someone else's trademark can be banned because it's only used to get attention, build image, or amuse consumers contradicts those propositions, though mere irony is unlikely to deter trademark owners.[38] More than inconsistency, it is the resulting inequality—the special positional advantages given to now-dominant brands—that should concern us.[39]

In other areas of the law, truthful commercial speech is protected by default, whereas in dilution and post-sale confusion cases courts seem to put the burden on defendants to show the value of their "free riding" speech. Why is the risk of error on the defendant? Perhaps it's because, deep down, we don't really believe that commercial speech, speech serving primarily the speaker's desire to profit through sales of a noncommunicative

---

[35] *See* Spence v. Washington, 418 U.S. 405, 410 (1974) (holding unconstitutional an improper-use statute as applied to a student who displayed a modified American flag, noting that "the communicative connotations of the use of flags" were "a form of symbolism" and "a short cut from mind to mind") (citations omitted).

[36] *Cf.* Bradford, *supra* note 13, at 1279 ("[P]roponents of dilution law cannot have it both ways. If 'involuntary' alteration of consumer preferences is wrong, then the positive feelings generated by persuasive advertising are at least as problematic as any negative ones stimulated through dilutive conduct. If persuasive advertising can be valuable even if consumers don't understand how they use it, then perhaps the same might can be said for dilution by blurring. Because the law has no inherent interest in product preference per se, dilution regulations must stand or fall on whether they implicate societal interests in promoting competition by allowing effective communication about products and services."); Mark P. McKenna, *The Rehnquist Court and the Groundwork for Greater First Amendment Scrutiny of Intellectual Property*, 21 WASH. U. J.L. & POL'Y 11, 26 n.63 (2006).

[37] *See, e.g.*, Alex Kozinski & Stuart Banner, *Who's Afraid of Commercial Speech?*, 76 VA. L. REV. 627, 635 (1990).

[38] Deven R. Desai, *Speech, Citizenry, and the Market: A Corporate Public Figure Doctrine*, 98 MINN. L. REV. 455 (2013).

[39] Bradford, *supra* note 13, at 1284 ("Dilution regulation in practice treats advertising designed to appeal to affective biases differently depending on whether such communications come from an established producer or a market newcomer. Although other areas of the law offer precedent for excluding affectively biasing information in the interest of accurate decision-making, such rules are usually applied consistently to every party engaging in persuasion"). Indeed, the special protection for famous marks raises the prospect of another disparity: while symbols of nationhood like the American flag are free for all to use and abuse, privately owned trademarks can be protected from contests over meaning. See Katya Assaf, The Dilution of Culture and the Law of Trademarks, 49 IDEA 1 (2008).

product or service, is that important. Even so, present trademark law still represents a particularly bad application of that devaluation because of its uneven, discriminatory effects on different commercial speakers. Essentially, dilution, post-sale confusion, and similar concepts target a constitutionally protected outcome—changed beliefs, not violence or other harmful conduct—and a constitutionally protected mechanism—persuasion, not deception. It's possible that the free flux of meaning would change the relative economic positions of particular actors in the system. But that's a good, not a bad, in a system that protects freedom of speech; dilution represents a disagreement with this core commitment to communication-driven change.

IV. Alvarez *and Concepts of Harm*

The previous discussion accepted the economic harm theory of dilution and non-point-of-sale confusion such as post-sale confusion. Weaknesses in the harm theory, however, strengthen the constitutional case against such extensions of trademark protection. The Supreme Court's recent decision in *US v. Alvarez* offers another chance to look at trademark harm in a First Amendment framework.[40] Unfortunately, the Court's shallow and confused understanding of what trademark law is suggests that there's much more work to be done before courts take First Amendment challenges seriously in many trademark cases.

Alvarez involved a man who falsely claimed to have received a Congressional Medal of Honor, in violation of the Stolen Valor Act. The Act prohibited such lies, but didn't require any further showing of harm beyond the falsity itself. The Supreme Court invalidated the law, holding that falsity in itself was not enough to prohibit this type of speech. The plurality didn't explicitly discuss trademark law, though it did distinguish the Stolen Valor Act from the special statutory protection for the Olympic trademarks: the former law bars lies "entirely without regard to whether the lie was made for the purpose of material gain," and the latter protects the "commercial magnetism" of the Olympic marks.[41] The plurality failed to explain how the Olympic statute required any showing of harm to the marks' commercial magnetism, or why the defendant's material *gain* would matter in identifying constitutionally significant *harm*. The government's basic theory of harm—that lies about medals degraded the value of the medal and harmed the true recipients of the medal by diminishing their specialness—was structurally the same as the argument that counterfeit Louis Vuitton bags harm Louis Vuitton's brand and harm the legitimate consumers by making them less special.[42]

---

[40] U.S. v. Alvarez, 132 S. Ct. 2537 (2012).

[41] *Id.* at 2547.

[42] It is perhaps of interest that the harm to the purchasers of LV bags comes from something we don't ordinarily consider "commercial speech"—that is, it comes from the behavior of the counterfeit bags' purchasers, not from the conduct of the seller itself.

Justice Breyer's concurrence did no better. He identified a range of laws prohibiting false speech, with various levels of particularization in the harms targeted. "Those [other] prohibitions, however, tend to be narrower than the statute before us, in that they limit the scope of their application, sometimes by requiring proof of specific harm to identifiable victims; sometimes by specifying that the lies be made in contexts in which a tangible harm to others is especially likely to occur; and sometimes by limiting the prohibited lies to those that are particularly likely to produce harm."[43] Fraud statutes are an example of the first category, requiring proof of materiality, reliance, and injury. But all the interesting work happens in the second and third categories, where legislators decide that categories of misrepresentations, or specific contexts, make harm particularly likely—as the government argued was the case for the Stolen Valor Act. *Alvarez* suggests that a majority of the Supreme Court is skeptical of such findings, even though it accepts them as applied to perjury, misrepresentations that a private party comes from the government, and a few others, including trademark.

Turning to trademark analogies, Breyer treated confusion and dilution as equivalent and presumptions as proof of harm:

> Statutes prohibiting trademark infringement present, perhaps, the closest analogy to the present statute. Trademarks identify the source of a good; and infringement causes harm by causing confusion among potential customers (about the source) and thereby diluting the value of the mark to its owner, to consumers, and to the economy. Similarly, a false claim of possession of a medal or other honor creates confusion about who is entitled to wear it, thus diluting its value to those who have earned it, to their families, and to their country. But trademark statutes are focused upon commercial and promotional activities that are likely to dilute the value of a mark. Indeed, they typically require a showing of likely confusion, a showing that tends to assure that the feared harm will in fact take place.[44]

The references to "typical[ity]" and "likel[ihood]" indicate Breyer's casualness about who makes the harm determination and at what level of generality. And "confusion and dilution cause dilution of value" as an explanation of harm is not really a rigorous definition of the harm.

The dissent by Justice Alito made the most of the trademark analogy to the Stolen Valor Act, specifically the analogy to luxury goods. He endorsed the idea that trademark law should protect exclusivity and guard the status of purchasers:

> It is well recognized in trademark law that the proliferation of cheap imitations of luxury goods blurs the "'signal' given out by the purchasers of the originals." In

---

[43] *Alvarez*, 132 S. Ct. 2537, 2554 (Breyer, J., concurring).

[44] *Id.*

> much the same way, the proliferation of false claims about military awards blurs the signal given out by the actual awards by making them seem more common than they really are, and this diluting effect harms the military by hampering its efforts to foster morale and esprit de corps. Surely it was reasonable for Congress to conclude that the goal of preserving the integrity of our country's top military honors is at least as worthy as that of protecting the prestige associated with fancy watches and designer handbags.[45]

It's telling that Justice Alito identified the signal of exclusivity as coming from *purchasers*, not from the purchased products or associated marks. Human hierarchy, not individual experience, is the endgame of branded luxury.

In a footnote, the dissent made a very important point: there is a potentially big difference, for First Amendment purposes, between "each case must show individualized harm" and "the legislature can reasonably decide that a situation poses so much risk of harm that it may be banned or criminalized."[46] The Court's skepticism of blanket legislative determinations of risk ultimately produced the "clear and present danger" standard for antigovernment speech, rather than the earlier "bad tendency" test that allowed the state to punish all antigovernment speech. That doctrinal evolution came from the recognition that an individualized proof requirement can substantially constrain the scope of a law, and even deter unmeritorious and speech-chilling suits. Such a rule forces the system to err on the side of allowing, rather than suppressing, speech in certain cases.

Thus, falsity that causes specific harm may lack First Amendment protection, but the key move is whether legislative predictions can be substituted for case-by-case litigation about specific harm. As the dissent pointed out, many categories of prohibited speech don't require individualized proof of harm—perjury is unlawful even if no one believed the lie; damages can be presumed in some defamation actions; reliance need not be shown to prosecute someone for lying to a federal agent. The Justices who voted to strike down the law simply didn't believe that lies about receiving the Congressional Medal of Honor were so likely to be harmful that they could be categorically banned.[47]

But why, then, did every Justice seemingly accept the constitutionality of dilution law? The Court has rarely been careful about trademark law, using a property framework to

---

[45] *Id.* at 2559 (Alito, J., dissenting) (citing William M. Landes & Richard A. Posner, *Trademark Law: An Economic Perspective*, 30 J.L. & ECON. 265, 308 (1987) and San Francisco Arts & Athletics, Inc. v. United States Olympic Comm., 483 U. S. 522, 539–541 (1987) (rejecting First Amendment challenge to law prohibiting certain unauthorized uses of the word "Olympic" and recognizing that such uses harm the U. S. Olympic Committee by "lessening the distinctiveness" of the term)).

[46] *See id.* at 2562 n.14 (distinguishing between types of bans on false speech, some of which don't require showing of specific harm caused by the defendant's lies).

[47] *Cf.* Brown v. Entm't Merchs. Ass'n, 131 S. Ct. 2729, 2770 (2011) (Breyer, J., dissenting) ("This Court has always thought it owed an elected legislature some degree of deference in respect to legislative facts of this kind, particularly when they involve technical matters that are beyond our competence, and even in First Amendment cases").

skip over significant questions about trademarks' role in communication.[48] In *Friedman v. Rogers*, for example, the Court held that a trade name is "a form of commercial speech that has no intrinsic meaning" and thus is distinguishable from statements about the price and quality of products or services.[49] This distinction, the Court continued, allows greater regulation because of the possibility that a mark will be used to mislead[50]—but of course, if a trademark can "mislead" then it has meaning, "intrinsic" or not, like statements about price and quality. Nonmisleading price and quality claims receive significant constitutional protection, unlike nonmisleading trademarks.

One way this devaluation of the speech value of trademarks plays out is that most courts presume harm in dilution and confusion cases without any showing of actual, present harm—indeed, the statutory standard is explicitly only that confusion or dilution must be "likely." Congress might have determined that false negatives pose too much risk to the public and false positives are sufficiently rare that likely rather than actual confusion/dilution ought to be the standard. But it doesn't seem that Congress had specific or rigorous evidence before it, especially with dilution. With the most recent revision to the dilution provisions, what Congress had instead was testimony that actual dilution was hard or even impossible to prove. Nor did the legislature explicitly mandate the new theories of "confusion" courts have adopted in recent decades, such as affiliation confusion, initial interest confusion, and post-sale confusion leading to decreased prestige. The common-sense appeal that confusion causes harm, which makes sense as applied to classic point-of-sale confusion between competitive goods, has been extended to other types of harm without sufficient thought or justification.

V. Desert as Substitute for Harm?

The use of vague, conversation-stopping terms like "reputation," "goodwill," and "brand value" to describe what trademark owners own has contributed to the failure to theorize harm. Robert Post has analyzed concepts of reputation that operate in defamation law, and his model can usefully be applied to trademark. Post describes three

[48] Even nuanced and sophisticated discussions of trademark have sometimes fallen into the trap of the true/false binary. *See* Heymann, *supra* note 12, at 1343–44 (identifying falsehood as the common thread among many causes of action, including trademark law, and using true/false dichotomy without discussing statements that affect reputation while being neither true nor false); *id.* at 1347 (noting that celebrity endorsements help sellers by virtue of the emotional transfer between the celebrity's aura and the endorsed product's reputation, then returning to the idea that reputation stems from facts).

[49] Friedman v. Rogers, 440 U.S. 1, 12 (1979).

[50] In non-trademark areas, the Court has said that speech that is only potentially misleading can't simply be banned; further disclosures and disclaimers must apparently first be tried. In re R.M.J., 455 U.S. 191, 203 (1982). But the distinction between inherently misleading and potentially misleading speech is so undertheorized that it's probably not worth trying to sort out what the Court's jurisprudence could mean.

conceptualizations of reputation: reputation as property, as honor, and as dignity.[51] The last only applies to humans, and applies to them automatically as persons deserving equal treatment in a democratic community. As he defines it, dignity is not generally relevant to trademark owners' claims, though they may well speak in anthropomorphized terms about the respect to which their marks are entitled.[52]

The core justification for protecting trademarks' prestige against dilution and post-sale confusion is based in concepts of desert: trademark owners earn their reputations rather than inheriting them (at least if we believe the fiction that each iteration of a corporation or its successor is legally identical). A corporation's interest in its reputation is purely economic—a good reputation produces economic benefits[53]—and would seem to slot neatly into the "reputation as property" category.[54] But, as explained above, reputation in trademark exclusivity cases is protecting what Post calls honor: the distinction earned by being seen as better than others. Honor is relative, just as distinctiveness in trademark is relative, and some people have more than others, as some marks have more protection than others (especially via dilution).[55] The ability of famous marks to rest on their laurels is therefore in deep tension with the idea of reputation as property, which, as Post notes, implies that reputation is always changeable depending on market conditions.[56] Reputation as property should in theory be egalitarian, in that each entity is entitled to exactly that reputation it can carve out.[57] By contrast, reputation as honor is attributed

---

[51] *See* Robert C. Post, *The Social Foundations of Defamation Law: Reputation and the Constitution*, 74 CAL. L. REV. 691, 719–20 (1986).

[52] Individuals can bring trademark claims, as well as right of publicity claims. Whether an individual could assert a dignity interest *as a trademark owner* is an interesting question, bringing us back to balancing of individual interests in avoiding insult against the First Amendment interests of others in expressing their own opinions.

[53] Meiring De Villiers, *Quantitative Proof of Reputational Harm*, 15 FORDHAM J. CORP. & FIN. L. 567, 578–79 (2010).

[54] Eric Barendt, *What Is the Point of Libel Law?* 52 CURRENT LEGAL PROBLEMS 110, 115 (1999) ("The concept of reputation as property may explain.... why corporations can sue to protect their good name, an entitlement which is much harder to justify if reputation is considered in terms of personal honour or dignity"); Heymann, *supra* note 12, at 1342 (identifying property concept as often dominant in reputation discourse); Post, *supra* note 51, at 727 ("From the constitutional point of view, the concept of reputation as property is the least problematic of all justifications for defamation law").

[55] Heymann, *supra* note 12, at 1369–70 ("In this conception, reputation is neither earned nor intrinsic but rather is conferred as a result of one's position relative to others.... [A]s a result, certain social benefits derive from that recognition that are not available to individuals elsewhere in the hierarchy").

[56] Post, *supra* note 51, at 695–96 ("[B]ecause the concept of reputation as property requires defamation law to protect only those aspects of an individual's reputation that the market can measure, the concept assumes that the worth of a person's reputation will vary with market conditions. Reputation is thus not an absolute, a matter of either honor or dishonor. It is instead envisioned as a smooth and continuous curve of potential value. The legally protected interest in reputation will rise or fall depending upon an individual's productivity and upon fluctuations in market conditions") (footnote omitted).

[57] *Id.* at 696.

to a role: kingship, in the past, or fame now.[58] Yet harm to honor has become economic in a modernity that considers market share and merit to be equivalent. Famous luxury brands abhor the instability of markets, and leverage law to preserve their places.

It's compelling to claim that famous or well-known marks deserve their distinction, unlike kings, whose institutional merit is generally thought to reside in the distant past. But why do they deserve to be protected from competition over meaning, to which all others in the market are subjected? Moreover, the desert rationale too easily conflates investment and effort with harm: free riding by a copier isn't harm or loss[59]—it's not even a theoretical loss of licensing revenue, since the trademark owner would almost certainly never license the kinds of uses it tends to challenge.[60]

Nor can the idea of desert square dilution with the rest of First Amendment law. Reverend Falwell also "earned" his reputation, which *Hustler* brutally maligned.[61] The wealth of meaning the American people invested in the American flag wasn't enough to allow the government to ban flag burning. Likewise, even if a reputation was "legitimately" earned through convincing people that a trademark signifies luxury, that does not establish that it deserves protection against emotional assaults. Once protected from competition in the marketplace of emotional appeals, such a reputation is no longer earned but rather artificially sustained.

Even assuming the correctness of the harm story, then, one key insight in Post's analysis is that legal protection for reputation as honor puts far too many ways of changing reputation off limits. While reputation as property means that owners have to fight for status in the market, subject only to the constraints of truth, reputation as honor recognizes mere insults as damaging because of the higher status of the attacked entity. This protection of status hierarchies is inconsistent with the autonomy protected by the First Amendment, which should include the right to contest hierarchies.[62]

One might nonetheless argue that preserving status, at least economic status, could still be a legitimate government interest. As long as *Lochner* is still bad law, the government is entitled to pick economic favorites. But that does not mean that government

---

[58] *Id.* at 700. Honor, unlike property, requires stratification and subordination. *Id.*

[59] Mark A. Lemley, *Property, Intellectual Property, and Free Riding*, 83 TEX. L. REV. 1031, 1051 (2005).

[60] *Cf.* Ty, Inc. v. Publ'ns Int'l, Ltd., 292 F.3d 512, 520 (7th Cir. 2002) (noting that Ty "doesn't like criticism," that it licensed collectors' guides only when it could reserve a right to veto text, and that it challenged a guide that was "quite critical").

[61] Consider Learned Hand's explanation of why copying a trademark is actionable, even if the copying doesn't result in any lost sales or reputation: "If another uses [a mark], he borrows the owner's reputation, whose quality no longer lies within his own control. This is an injury, even though the borrower does not tarnish it, or divert any sales by its use; for a reputation, like a face, is the symbol of its possessor and creator, and another can use it only as a mask." Yale Elec. Corp. v. Robertson, 26 F.2d 972, 974 (2d Cir. 1928). Now imagine this rationale applied to *Hustler*'s mock ad in the voice of Reverend Falwell.

[62] Post, *supra* note 51, at 722–23 ("[T]he concept [of honor] is inconsistent with the egalitarian principles of American democracy. The Constitution itself disapproves of official honorific status in explicit terms. . . ."); *id.* at 737–38.

can constitutionally preserve current economic configurations through the mechanism of suppressing nonmisleading speech that could change consumers' opinions about trademarks.[63]

It's also noteworthy that a pure property rationale would seem to justify barring explicitly political uses of trademarks, such as Nadia Plessner's poster featuring a LV handbag or Ronald Reagan's appropriation of Wendy's "Where's the beef?" slogan. Usually we don't excuse trespassers who lack economic motivations. American jurisprudence generally holds that trademark owners shouldn't control such uses; this suggests that the label "property" can't itself explain the scope of trademark rights.

VI. Presumptions of Harm from Dislike of a Practice

I have argued that certain kinds of harm are not constitutionally cognizable. One might also ask whether they even exist. Though reputations clearly can suffer, it's far less settled that the reputations of well-known brands can be harmed by the kinds of behaviors our expansive trademark law targets. Since dilution and confusion are actionable without evidence of actual harm, the pecuniary impact is hypothetical, which leads to speculation piled on speculation. This should be relevant to the free speech analysis.

The empirical evidence that dilution and non-point-of-sale confusion cause noticeable harm to trademark owners when actual purchasers aren't confused is extremely weak.[64] Jerre Swann, for example, attempting to prove that dilution is a real threat, identifies acts of *self*-tarnishment by General Motors, Cadillac, and McDonald's—failing to make his point two times over, as missteps that consumers correctly attribute to the trademark owner aren't anything like nonconfusing third-party uses, and, separately, this self-tarnishment doesn't seem to have resulted in long-term harm to the brands.[65] Yet owners of "strong" brands fear that they are in fact weak and vulnerable to destruction by the smallest of incursions, even if they can't prove it.[66] Likewise, the black-letter doctrine has long been that actual harm from confusion is so hard to show that it can simply be

---

[63] Rodney A. Smolla, *Information, Imagery, and the First Amendment: A Case for Expansive Protection of Commercial Speech*, 71 TEX. L. REV. 777, 780–81 (1993) ("In classic First Amendment terms, however, the one thing the government may not do is regulate speech because it "sells" a lifestyle, fantasy, ethos, identity, or attitude that happens to be regarded by most as socially corrosive") (footnote omitted).

[64] *See* Paul J. Heald & Robert Brauneis, *The Myth of Buick Aspirin: An Empirical Study of Trademark Dilution by Product and Trade Names*, 32 CARDOZO L. REV. 2533 (2011); Sheff, *supra* note 8, at 781–82; Tushnet, *supra* note 33, at 528.

[65] Swann, *supra* note 19, at 760–61.

[66] Christine Haight Farley, *The Feminine Mystique of the Brand in Trademark Law Today* (Aug. 11, 2008). Available at SSRN: http://ssrn.com/abstract=1217875. In *Alvarez*, the dissenters seemed to fear the same thing about the "strength" of the Medal of Honor. Indeed, the current Court may feel that corporations in general are fragile and at risk, especially in terms of their own speech. *Citizens United* shows a Court concerned that corporations are not getting their due in the public arena; this may also be connected to ideas of effort and merit. Having earned their money, corporations are entitled to spend it effectively.

presumed for purposes of granting injunctive relief.[67] Courts rarely explore the alternative hypothesis: maybe harm is often hard to show in noncounterfeiting cases because harm is uncommon.

As Laura Heymann noted, decision-makers who think of reputation as something with commercial value can easily translate that belief into findings of likely harm, even without a sound factual basis.[68] Decision-makers may worry that other people are more easily swayed by negative, nonfactual messages than they themselves would be, increasing a bias toward finding harm.[69] These problems fit into a larger body of research about cognitive bias: people who dislike something are likely to consider it harmful.

This feature of human thought poses a significant challenge for First Amendment doctrines that allow regulation when speech causes tangible harm, but disallow it when speech only causes offense. It's common to find statements in the legal literature such as "free speech jurisprudence does not allow government-sanctioned punishment of speech solely because others find the message offensive. It allows regulation of speech only if the speech contains objective indicia of harm, such as speech accompanied by physical or aural invasions, threats, or violence."[70] This rule supposedly protects unpopular, challenging, disrespectful speakers.[71]

Research on the relationship between disagreement with viewpoints and perceptions of harm, however, suggests that the two are tightly linked: "[I]ndividuals tend selectively to credit empirical information in patterns congenial to their cultural values.... And they are more likely to note, assign significance to, and recall facts supportive of their cultural outlooks than facts subversive of them."[72] A person who finds speech offensive will therefore be

---

67 *See, e.g.*, Omega Importing Corp. v. Petri-Kine Camera Co., 451 F.2d 1190, 1195 (2d Cir. 1971) ("Yet to prove the loss of sales due to infringement is also notoriously difficult.... Furthermore, if an infringer's product is of poor quality, or simply not worth the price, a more lasting, but not readily measurable injury may be inflicted on the plaintiff's reputation in the market").

68 Heymann, *supra* note 12, at 1367 ("The risk [of treating reputation as property] is that the ease of administrability on the damages side will spill over into the determination of liability, such that courts or juries will be more likely to see harm to reputation when the plaintiff is involved in commercial activity"); *see, e.g.*, James Burrough, Ltd. v. Sign of Beefeater, Inc., 540 F.2d 266, 276 (7th Cir. 1976) ("Though economic harm per se is not required, this court has pointed out that the owner of a mark is damaged by a later use of a similar mark which places the owner's reputation beyond its control, though no loss in business is shown").

69 Heymann, *supra* note 12, at 1433 ("Moreover, decision makers may be susceptible to what communications scholars have called the 'third-person effect'—the concept that 'people feel media messages will have more influence on others than on themselves' and so overestimate the reputational harm of a given statement") (footnote omitted).

70 Christina Wells, *Regulating Offensiveness: Snyder v. Phelps, Emotion, and the First Amendment*, 1 CAL. L. REV. CIRCUIT 71, 72 (2010) (footnotes omitted); *see also* Steven G. Gey, *The Brandenburg Paradigm and Other First Amendments*, 12 U. PA. J. CONST. L. 971, 988–89 (2010) ("Social disorder, political change, vociferous debate, the undermining of traditional values, or even threatened change in the very nature of government itself are not even counted as cognizable risks of the [commonly recognized] paradigm").

71 *See, e.g.*, Cohen v. US, 403 U.S. at 21 (punishment of offensive speech "effectively empower[s] a majority to silence dissidents simply as a matter of personal predilections").

72 Dan M. Kahan et al., *"They Saw a Protest": Cognitive Illiberalism and the Speech-Conduct Distinction*, 64 STAN. L. REV. 851, 859 (2012).

likely to perceive that it also creates significant risks of harm.[73] Thus, in one study by Dan Kahan et al., the researchers told subjects either that they were viewing an anti-abortion protest at an abortion clinic or a protest against anti-gay policies at a military recruiting event. Conservative subjects were more likely to report seeing peaceful protest (protected speech) when they thought they were watching an anti-abortion protest, and the imminent threat of violence and intimidation (regulable conduct) when they thought they were watching an anti-discrimination protest. Liberal subjects were more likely to report seeing exactly the opposite. But the subjects saw the same video footage each time; it was the *meaning* that changed.[74] The speech/conduct distinction, then, was more of a "speech I like"/"conduct I don't like" line. The harm requirement serves the same function as the speech/conduct distinction in First Amendment law, and is likely to have the same weaknesses.[75]

In general, factfinders' orientations toward "hierarchical" values that favor order and power or "egalitarian" ones that resist hierarchy, as well as crosscutting individualist versus communitarian orientations, affect harm determinations.[76] Today's individualist/hierarchical Supreme Court routinely upholds property rights but allows individuals to do what they want when there's no assertion of property rights on the other side. Trademark's property rhetoric thus helps insulate it from the otherwise antiregulatory thrust of modern Supreme Court jurisprudence. To a hierarchical individualist, free riding for profit will appear more harmful than buying politicians for profit: one is illegitimate use of another's reputation (defying hierarchy) and one is use of legitimately obtained power (hierarchy). For example, as noted above, the Court found the Amateur Sports Act's prohibitions on unauthorized uses of the Olympic marks to be a reasonable way to protect the USOC's "legitimate property right."[77] The Court held that Congress could reasonably have determined that an explicit likelihood of confusion requirement is unnecessary because most commercial uses of the Olympic marks

---

[73] Dan M. Kahan, *"Ideology in" or "Cultural Cognition of" Judging: What Difference Does It Make?*, 92 MARQ. L. REV. 413, 417–18 (2009) ("The phenomenon of cultural cognition refers to the tendency of individuals to conform their views about risks and benefits of putatively dangerous activities to their cultural evaluations of those activities. Psychologically speaking, it's much easier to believe that behavior one finds noble is also socially beneficial and behavior one finds base is dangerous rather than vice versa"); Dan M. Kahan et al., *supra* note 72, at 854–55, 883 (experiment showed that factfinders tasked with distinguishing between protected "speech" and unprotected, dangerous "conduct" varied depending on whether or not they believed the protest they witnessed conformed to or conflicted with their own political views).

[74] Kahan et al., *supra* note 72, at 883–84. People with hierarchical and communitarian orientations, and thus likely to be anti-abortion, saw the protest as peaceful when they believed it was in front of an abortion clinic; but people with the same orientations thought that the protest was intimidating and dangerous when they believed that it was a protest against discrimination in the military. And the results reversed for egalitarian and individualistic subjects: they were likely to see threat in the "abortion" protest and no threat in the "military" protest.

[75] Kahan et al., *supra* note 72, at 887.

[76] *See* Dan M. Kahan & Donald Braman, *Cultural Cognition and Public Policy*, 24 YALE L. & POL'Y REV. 149, 150–57 (2006) (defining "cultural cognition" as "the psychological disposition of persons to conform their factual beliefs about the instrumental efficacy (or perversity) of law to their cultural evaluations of the activities subject to regulation").

[77] San Francisco Arts & Athletics, Inc. v. United States Olympic Comm. 483 U.S. 522 (1987).

are likely to be confusing or at least to harm the distinctiveness of the marks (that is, to dilute them).[78] It did not examine the evidence Congress had used to conclude that these were real problems.

When the supposed property rights of a respected institution are not implicated by a government regulation, by contrast, the Court is likely to scrutinize the evidentiary record with greater care. *Alvarez* is but one example. In *Brown v. Entertainment Merchants Association*, the Court was much more skeptical about the link between violent video games and increased aggression in minors, despite dozens of studies supporting a link.[79] Likewise, the Court demanded much more in the way of proof of a connection between speech and harm when striking down a ban on "virtual" child pornography.[80] The common-sense claim that sexual images of unreal children will lead viewers to act against real children seems no more tenuous than the claim that a local business's use of "Victor's Little Secret" could someday lead to fewer purchases from Victoria's Secret, especially since the latter is explicitly framed as a mere likelihood of dilution and dilution's harm is always posited to occur sometime in the future, after a thousand other businesses have engaged in their own acts of dilution.

VII. Conclusion

Decades ago, Robert Denicola noted the empirical weakness of harm claims in many trademark cases, and suggested that First Amendment jurisprudence needed to catch up with trademark's expansion.[81] Unfortunately, it still has not done so, and judges' preconceptions about harm are likely to present great barriers to change, unless and until

[78] *Id.* at 539 & n. 19.

[79] 131 S. Ct. 2729, 2738 (2011) (finding that "ambiguous" evidence was insufficient to regulate otherwise protected speech; existing evidence was mostly based on correlation rather than causation and studies had methodological flaws; moreover, magnitude of effect was very small and indistinguishable from effects produced by other media). The evidence for dilution is much weaker; *See also* Heald & Brauneis, *supra* note 64, at 2561–62 (attempting an empirical study of actual dilution and finding no persuasive evidence that it happened); Tushnet, *supra* note 33, at 545 (criticizing dilution studies).

[80] Ashcroft v. Free Speech Coal., 535 U.S. 234, 250, 253–54 (2002) ("While the Government asserts that the images can lead to actual instances of child abuse, the causal link is contingent and indirect. The harm does not necessarily follow from the speech, but depends upon some unquantified potential for subsequent criminal acts.... The Government has shown no more than a remote connection between speech that might encourage thoughts or impulses and any resulting child abuse. Without a significantly stronger, more direct connection, the Government may not prohibit speech on the ground that it may encourage pedophiles to engage in illegal conduct") (citation omitted).

[81] Robert C. Denicola, *Trademarks as Speech: Constitutional Implications of the Emerging Rationales for the Protection of Trade Symbols*, 1982 WIS. L. REV. 158, 194 ("In view of the uncertain economic underpinnings of the misappropriation and dilution rationales, however, the 'substantialness' of this regulatory interest might well be questioned when the use causes no deception. Such a judgment must surely depend in part upon the extent to which speech interests are in fact being sacrificed to attain the desired end") (footnote omitted).

advocates can retell the stories of infringement and dilution and show how they are more like claims to avoid offense than they are like claims to avoid injury from defamation.

Recent developments surrounding injunctive relief hold out some hope for more serious interrogation of trademark's harm stories. *eBay Inc. v. MercExchange, LLC*, held that courts couldn't presume irreparable harm based only on a finding of likely success on the merits in patent cases, despite common characterizations of patents as property.[82] Instead, a court must find irreparable harm based on a case-specific inquiry. Despite considerable resistance from trademark lawyers,[83] courts have increasingly recognized that *eBay* applies in trademark cases as well.

In 2013, for example, the Ninth Circuit held that "cursory and conclusory" invocations of irreparable harm, not based in any specific evidence before a court, would be insufficient to justify an injunction. Further, "citation to a different case with a different record does not meet the standard of showing 'likely' irreparable harm."[84] Following this case, a district court recently rejected the argument that confusion about plaintiffs' responsibility for the defendant's product could harm the plaintiffs' reputations when defendant delivered a shoddy product. Although this "lost control over reputation" theory has long been accepted by courts as a reason that consumer confusion is always harmful, the district court pointed out a logical and factual gap: plaintiffs didn't provide any evidence of shoddy manufacturing by the defendant, making their theory of irreparable harm "purely speculative."[85] While presented as a matter of equitable principles, this demand for an individualized, evidence-based showing of harm can also be speech-protective.

eBay, however, is not a constitutional doctrine, and doesn't give weight to free speech concerns as such. A more constitutionally sensitive doctrine would look at harm as an element of a plaintiff's case, not merely as a question of available relief. One possibility would be to keep the likelihood standard, but tighten our definition of harm. Association between the plaintiff's mark and the defendant's mark alone would not be sufficient to find either dilution or confusion, but a likely change in consumer behavior could be.[86]

For confusion, this change could draw on the concept of materiality: whether any confusion is the kind of confusion that is likely to affect consumers' behavior. Materiality has both a historical basis and a present existence in the Lanham Act as applied to trademark's

---

[82] 547 U.S. 388 (2006).

[83] *See, e.g.*, David H. Bernstein & Andrew Gilden, *No Trolls Barred: Trademark Injunctions after* eBay?, 99 Trademark Reporter 1037 (2009).

[84] Herb Reed Enterprises, LLC v. Florida Entertainment Management, Inc., 736 F.3d 1239, 1250 (9th Cir. 2013); *see also id.* ("Evidence of loss of control over business reputation and damage to goodwill could constitute irreparable harm. Here, however, the court's pronouncements are grounded in platitudes rather than evidence").

[85] Purdum v. Wolfe, No. C-13-04816, 2014 WL 171546 (N.D. Cal. 2014).

[86] My constitutional objections to dilution as discriminatory would remain, but at least the magical thinking that governs many likely dilution findings could be improved.

cousin, false advertising law.[87] Materiality could limit trademark's scope just as the concept of defamatory falsehood limits the scope of defamation law. Defamation recognizes that not all false statements, even intentionally false statements, are likely to do real harm to a person's reputation. While some kinds of negative statements are presumed to be harmful, they are a limited subset and real damage must otherwise be shown. Similarly, point-of-sale confusion could be presumed material and harmful, while courts could require more evidence of harm in other instances—evidence that is likely to be unavailable.

For dilution, the statutory language already at least purports to target association that impairs the distinctiveness of the famous mark, not just any association; the doctrine of constitutional avoidance could encourage courts to give this language force.[88] European definitions of dilution have moved in this direction, at least formally: the ECJ has clarified that the burden is on the senior user to provide "evidence of a change in the economic behaviour of the average consumer of the goods or services for which the earlier mark was registered consequent on the use of the later mark, or evidence of a serious likelihood that such a change will occur in the future."[89] That is a much higher standard than the inference of dilution from mere association that many US courts have been willing to make. It's not clear that likely change in consumer behavior could ever be shown for dilution, whose empirical foundations are so weak. Indeed, many theories of trademark harm that rely on consumers thinking differently, but not necessarily behaving differently, would not survive this kind of scrutiny.

Renewed attention to the structural similarities—and disparities—between trademark doctrine and other speech regulations could push courts to be more careful in evaluating trademark harm stories, especially those related to the preservation of distinctions among people. A focus on specifying the harms of infringement and dilution would at least clarify the issues. In many cases, replacing invocations of presumed harm with more detailed narratives would make clear that harm is merely theoretical, and that some of the posited harm—the part that comes from emotional appeals—should be constitutionally off limits even when an individualized harm determination has been made. American free speech doctrine formally promises that all our values are up for debate. As long as trademark law overprotects prestige, however, luxury items such as Louis Vuitton's leather goods will remain our sacred cows.

---

[87] *See* Rebecca Tushnet, *Running the Gamut from A to B: Federal Trademark and False Advertising Law*, 159 U. PENN. L. REV. 1305, 1351–52, 1356–69, 1366–67 (2011).

[88] *Cf.* Starbucks Corp. v. Wolfe's Borough Coffee, Inc., 736 F.3d 198, 211 (2d Cir. 2013) ("[T]he ultimate question is whether the Charbucks Marks are likely to cause an association arising from their similarity to the Starbucks Marks, *which impairs the Starbucks Marks' tendency to identify the source of Starbucks products in a unique way*") (emphasis added).

[89] Case C-383/12 P, Environmental Manufacturing LLP v. Office for Harmonisation in the Internal Market (Trade Marks and Designs) (OHIM), November 14, 2013 (noting that this proof has to come from objective elements and "cannot be deduced solely from subjective elements such as consumers' perceptions," and "the mere fact that consumers note the presence of a new sign similar to an earlier sign is not sufficient of itself to establish the existence of a detriment or a risk of detriment to the distinctive character of the earlier mark").

Living in the lap of luxury isn't bad, except that you never know when luxury is going to stand up.[1]

8 The Gender of Trademarks and Luxury Branding

Ann Bartow*

IN MOST CONTEXTS, women are less visible and less present than men in the performing arts, and in any commercial enterprise that exploits creative endeavors. Female creative output commands less attention and less money than the creative works of men, and women are less visible and receive less compensation than male counterparts when they collaborate in the production of creative works with men. Male writers, male singers, male visual artists, male actors, male directors and producers, male composers, male architects, and other male authors of almost any form of copyrightable work dominate the cultural terrain, and acquire and control a substantial majority of the financial resources that creative works accrue.[2]

* Executive Director of the Franklin Pierce Center for Intellectual Property and Professor of Law at the University of New Hampshire School of Law.

[1] Orson Welles, *available at* http://thinkexist.com/quotation/living_in_the_lap_of_luxury_isn-t_bad-except_that/167619.html.

[2] To confirm this point, look at the "bestseller" lists for books and music and listen to which artists are in heavy rotation on commercial radio. Look at what male actors earn versus female actors, look at who writes and directs the plays that are produced on Broadway. Look at who wins the Academy Awards in almost every category. Look at who wins architectural awards. Look at who works in Hollywood as screenwriters, directors, even camera operators. Look at the masthead of every major newspaper or magazine. Evidence of the dominance of men in commercially successful creative fields is omnipresent.

One exception, however, is found in the enormous body of work generated by commercial branding practices. Whether a product is being marketed to women or to men, or to consumers across gender, images of women are disproportionately deployed in advertisements. In the context of luxury goods that are pitched to men these images are usually highly sexualized, depicting women as aroused by the associated goods or services and craving physical congress with consumers. For example, consider an advertisement for used BMWs, which has the tag line: "You know you're not the first. But do you really care?" The clear implication is that just as you wouldn't turn down sex with a beautiful woman simply because she was not a virgin, you shouldn't turn down the chance to own a fabulous car simply because it had a prior owner.

Products themselves may also be unnecessarily gendered. Though a few products such as bras and jock straps are logically linked to one gender or the other, biological differences between the sexes do not require the distinctions to be nearly as severe and widespread as they are. Usually male is the default gender, while the female iteration is tagged with a feminizing signal such as the color pink or the words "for women."

Defining what a woman is can be fairly complicated. Whether gender identities should be linked to a person's chromosomes, genitals, lived experiences, or other factors is a rich and interesting debate.[3] For the purposes of this chapter, however, I simply acknowledge the omnipresence of social pressures to conform to gender binaries[4] and assume that everyone who self-identifies as female in response is indeed a woman.[5] The same goes for the category of men.

At least when described in English (rather than a language that designates the gender of every noun), most goods and services do not need to be assigned a gender to be understood or used. The gendered natures of marketing, branding, product configuration, and consumption are instead overwhelmingly consequences of the propaganda dissemination and manipulative socialization that provide the bases for branding practices. And these are harmful. Individually and as a class, women are demeaned and damaged by branding practices, especially those associated with luxury goods.

---

[3] Gender can be a matter of chromosomes, or of genitalia, or of lived experiences, or of societal perceptions. While people are in theory free to define themselves as any gender they please, as a practical and normative matter gender is a fairly rigid binary in most legal, social, and political contexts. Physical spaces such as bathrooms and locker rooms normatively require people to declare themselves female or male. Linguistic conventions for first names, titles (Mr. versus Miss, Ms., or Mrs.), descriptors (daughter versus son or sister versus brother), and third-person singular pronouns generally require speakers to assign genders to anyone who is a topic of conversation. Legal constructs such as sexual harassment, discrimination, and civil rights also sometimes demand gender designations from one of two categories. *See, e.g.*, Sonia Katyal, *The Intellectual Commons of Gender*, FORDHAM LAW LEGAL STUDIES RESEARCH PAPER (2007) No. 976648.

[4] Buzuvis, Erin, *Reading the Pink Locker Room: On Football Culture and Title IX*, 14 WM. & MARY J. WOMEN & L. 1 (2007).

[5] This is not to undermine the efforts of folks who choose to opt out of the traditional "female or male" gender binary constrictions. It is just to explain that for the purposes of this article, "women" are people who consider themselves women, and "men" are those who self-identify as men.

I. Public Participation in Brand Making

In 1948 Ralph Brown wrote an influential article about trademark law entitled "Advertising and the Public Interest: Legal Protection of Trade Symbols."[6] His death occasioned a 1999 volume of the *Yale Law Journal* dedicated to lauding and positioning his scholarly contributions. One of the best articles it contains is "Breakfast with Batman," written by Jessica Litman.[7] Litman observes that trade symbols can be extraordinarily valuable even when they are disambiguated from particular goods and services, but argues that this independent value does not justify protecting them under the trademark laws.[8] She persuasively asserts that "legal protection for trade symbols, in the absence of confusion, disserves competition and thus the consumer."[9]

Litman also explains that the value of well-known trade symbols results from mutual investments of time, attention, and money by producers of both goods and services, and the consumers who purchase them.[10] This is a theme that has been expanded upon by scholars such as Sonia Katyal, who has posited that trademarks function like public goods,[11] and Barton Beebe, who tells the story of the emergence of the modern trademark as a "floating signifier," and has observed that "while the economic account continues to profess that trademarks do little more than minimize consumer search costs, much of modern trademark law is now directed towards the commodification of semiotic 'sign value.' "[12]

Since "Breakfast with Batman" was published, and particularly over the past decade, legal academics have written numerous outstanding scholarly articles about the state of contemporary trademark law in the United States. Many of the astute analyses contained in these works apply globally. The most important observation, articulated in various contexts by almost every credible trademark law specialist, is that in its current form trademark law has very little to do with informing or protecting consumers.[13]

Trademark law has become (or perhaps always was)[14] a legal tool that producers of goods and services use to secure control over communicative terrain in the public sphere, which is used to facilitate the growth and expansion of private brand management. Stacey Dogan has warned against granting trademark holders an exclusive right

---

[6] Ralph S. Brown, *Advertising and the Public Interest: Legal Protection of Trade Symbols*, 57 YALE L.J. 1165 (1948).

[7] Jessica Litman, *Breakfast with Batman: The Public Interest in the Advertising Age*, 108 YALE L.J. (1999).

[8] *Id.* at 11–14.

[9] *Id.* at 2.

[10] *Id.* at 16.

[11] Sonia Katyal, *Trademark Intersectionality*, 57 UCLA L. REV. 1601 (2010).

[12] Barton Beebe, *The Semiotic Analysis of Trademark Law*, 51 UCLA L. REV. 621 (2004).

[13] Jennifer Rothman, *Initial Interest Confusion: Standing at the Crossroads of Trademark Law*, 27 CARDOZO L. REV. 105 (2005).

[14] Mark McKenna, *The Normative Foundations of Trademark Law*, 82 NOTRE DAME L. REV. 1839 (2007).

of evocation, asserting that expressive freedom encompasses a right to evoke trademarks communicatively.[15] Barton Beebe has observed that trademarks have grown stronger as consumers have become weaker, more easily manipulated and less relevant to calibrations of trademark scope.[16] And Rebecca Tushnet has intrepidly explained that current legal practices advantage the most powerful companies,[17] even though underlying assumptions about consumers may have no basis whatsoever in the teachings and findings of cognitive science.[18]

Mark McKenna has argued that liability under trademark law should be limited to circumstances in which the defendant's use of a mark is likely to deceive consumers in ways that will interfere with purchasing decisions.[19] An article he co-authored with Mark Lemley emphatically states that trademark law should focus its attention on confusion that is actually relevant to purchasing decisions,[20] paralleling Rebecca Tushnet's demand for a materiality threshold that restricts unlawful trademark claims to "those that actually matter to consumers."[21]

These scholars all argue in favor of putting a reasonably intelligent, rationally acting consumer back into a central analytic position in trademark law. Many courts, however, adopt a conception of people as easily confused fools, unable or unwilling to discern brand differences even when heavy advertising campaigns try to make and enforce brand distinctions.[22] This negative take on citizen astuteness positions strong trademark protection as a paternalistic form of kindness to the dumb and gullible. It ignores the conscious role that consumers can play in making or keeping brands popular or rendering them shunned, of which trademark holders are keenly aware. One advertising professional wrote of branding: "Quality is important, but not as important as the perception of quality."[23] Sometimes perceived quality is a function of perceived value for money, or of perceived wholesomeness. Other times the crucial cognitive link is to luxury.

Companies producing goods and services for the luxury market try to build associations between their trademarks and the perception of design, quality, durability, or performance that are remarkably superior to less expensive substitutes. Using images of elegant yet sexy-looking women to signify luxury is a common practice deployed to this

---

15 Stacey L. Dogan, *An Exclusive Right to Evoke,* 44 B.C. L. Rev. 291 (2003).

16 Barton Beebe, *Search and Persuasion in Trademark Law*, 103 Mich. L. Rev. 2020 (2005).

17 Rebecca Tushnet, *Running the Gamut from A to B:Federal Trademark and False Advertising Law*, 159 U. Pa. L. Rev. 1305 (2011).

18 Rebecca Tushnet, *Gone in 60 Milliseconds: Trademark Law and Cognitive Science*, 86 Tex. L. Rev. 507 (2008).

19 Mark McKenna, *A Consumer Decision-Making Theory of Trademark Law*, 98 Va. L. Rev. 67 (2012).

20 Mark A. Lemley & Mark McKenna, *Irrelevant Confusion*, 62 Stan. L. Rev. 413 (2010).

21 Rebecca Tushnet, *Running the Gamut from A to B: Federal Trademark and False Advertising Law*, 159 U. Pa. L. Rev. 1305 (2011).

22 Ann Bartow, *Likelihood of Confusion,* 41 San Diego L. Rev. 1 (2004).

23 Greg Stine, *The Nine Principles of Branding,* Polaris, Inc., http://www.polaris-inc.com/assets/pdfs/9_principles_of_branding.pdf.

end.[24] And just as trademarks and logos can themselves become product-like,[25] so too can women. Branding practices urge men to acquire luxury goods so that they will have access to attractive women.[26]

II. Authenticity Matters

One trademark concern that is relevant and material to consumers is the ability to distinguish between legitimate goods and fake ones.[27] Consumers value authenticity.[28] They favor a legal regime that provides some assurance that they are buying authentic luxury goods when they make expensive purchases.[29]

---

[24] Of course sex is also used to sell a multitude of products that are not luxury brands; *see, e.g.*, Abby Rogers & Aimee Groth, *13 Brands That Use Sex To Sell Their Products,* BUSINESS INSIDER (Feb. 3, 2012, 5:11 PM), http://www.businessinsider.com/13-brands-that-use-sex-to-sell-their-products-2012-2?op=1.

[25] *See, e.g.*, Jon Caramanica, *The Return of Logo Culture,* N.Y. TIMES, Nov. 21, 2013, at E1. ("In fashion, logos are the simplest way to turn a consumer into a billboard, and we are all inexorably branded now. With each passing year, it becomes more difficult to live out of the reach of corporate influence, and each successive generation has less of an idea of what life was like back when opting out was more of a possibility.

So maybe it's not a shock that this time is also seeing the arrival of the logo as a forward-looking fashion staple, a William Gibson and Milton Glaser fantasy come to life.

This is happening in the hands of a group of young designers who accept the ubiquity of logos and who work within that framework to turn their purpose and effect on their head. The logo becomes the canvas, whether it's their placement on a garment, the juxtaposition of several of them together or a rendering with an unconventional treatment. In all cases, the logo becomes a graphic element that can be mined for its familiarity, but is at least in part stripped of its corporate purpose.") *See also* Sonia Katyal, *Trademark Intersectionality*, 57 UCLA L. REV. 1601 (2010). *cf* Stacey L. Dogan & Mark A. Lemley, *The Merchandising Right: Fragile Theory or* Fait Accompli?, 54 EMORY L.J. 461 (2005).

[26] Rob M. A. Nelissen & Marijn H.C. Meijers, *Social Benefits of Luxury Brands as Costly Signals of Wealth and Status*, 32 EVOLUTION AND HUMAN BEHAVIOR 343 (2011).

[27] Kambiz Heidarzadeh Hanzaee & Sara Ghafelehbashi, *The Role of Product Involvement, Knowledge, and Perceptions in Consumer Purchase Behavior of Counterfeits: Perspective Islamic Country*, 2(1) J. BASIC. APPL. SCI. RES. 418 (2012); Celso Augusto de Matos et al., *Consumer Attitudes toward Counterfeits: A Review and Extension*, 24(1) JOURNAL OF CONSUMER MARKETING 36 (2007). Amir Foroughi et al., *Exploring the Role of Brand Image in Explaining Consumer Shopping Behavior of Counterfeits*, 51 ELIXIR MARKETING MGMT. 10771 (2012).

[28] *See, e.g., How to Spot Counterfeits: Inspect Deals on Designer Goods Before You Buy,* CONSUMER REPORTS MONEY ADVISER (Jun. 2012); http://www.consumerreports.org/cro/2012/06/how-to-spot-counterfeits/index.htm *cf Counterfeit Wine Maker Makes Typos, Gets Attention of Federal Prosecutors,* NORTH CAROLINA CONSUMERS COUNCIL http://www.ncconsumer.org/news-articles/counterfeit-wine-maker-makes-typos,-gets-attention-of-federal-prosecutors.html; *The 16 Rules to Avoid Being Fooled by Counterfeit/Copies Products,* AIMPOINT http://www.aimpoint.com/us/products/counterfeitscopies/16-tips/; Sean, *Nine Ways to Avoid Being Fooled by Counterfeits,* THE DEEP ROUGH (Aug. 4, 2007) http://www.deeprough.com/index.php/2007/08/04/is-my-golf-club-fake/; *Don't Be Fooled by Software Pirates: Five Myths of Software Piracy,* MICROSOFT (Apr. 1, 2010). http://news.microsoft.com/2010/04/01/dont-be-fooled-by-software-pirates/

[29] Jason M. Carpenter & Karen Lear, *Consumer Attitudes toward Counterfeit Fashion Products: Does Gender Matter?* 7(1) JTATM (2011) http://ojs.cnr.ncsu.edu/index.php/JTATM/article/view/993; James W. Gentry et al., *The Effects of Counterfeiting on Consumer Search*, 5(3) JOURNAL OF CONSUMER BEHAVIOUR 245 (2006).

Among trademark law scholars and trademark lawyers alike, the most defensible deployment of a strong and vengeful trademark law is against straight up counterfeiting.[30] A mark that many consumers recognize due to heavy advertising and/or market dominance of the marked goods or services is both strong and, because it is commercially effective, likely to attract putative "free riders." Where the free riding takes the form of counterfeiting, the mark holder is unequivocally entitled to a legal remedy.

It is true that under the Lanham Act the actionability of counterfeiting depends doctrinally on an assumption that the consumers purchasing counterfeit products have been deceived, which surely isn't always the case.[31] Nevertheless, few trademark law critics have categorized the illegality of counterfeiting as an overreaching or inappropriate attribute of the Lanham Act. When trademark law facilitates a monopolistic connection between a specific source identifying trademark and a singular product, there is a general consensus that it is behaving justly.[32]

Trademark laws may incentivize but do not require the production or distribution of high-quality goods or services. Quick trademark changes can help a source hide from the bad will it might otherwise reap when it fails to meet consumer expectations of performance or value.[33] Authentically trademarked pharmaceutical products can be ineffective or even harmful, foods may be produced under unhealthy conditions, and ordinary household goods can prove defective or dangerous.

Nevertheless, consumers' health and safety-based interests in having the trademark laws provide protection from counterfeiting can be compelling.[34] At the very least, legitimately trademarked goods connect harms to a commercial entity that can be held legally responsible for its misdeeds and from which financial compensation for injury can sometimes be procured. Counterfeiters generally do not have commercial reputations to protect, nor do they typically carry products liability insurance.

Consumers have another interest in authenticity that is less wholesome or socially beneficial. People who are keenly aware of the monetary value of material goods make assessments about economic class based in part on trademarks, and they like these judgments to be accurate. Turning once again to Barton Beebe's work, he has trenchantly described trademark law as being "capable of protecting forms of class distinction from imitation and overproduction," writing:

> Simply stated, while many characteristics of goods may now be both technologically and legally imitated (for example, the physical structure of diamonds), those

---

30 Ann Bartow, *Counterfeits, Copying and Class*, 48 Hous. L. Rev. 707 (2012).

31 William McGeveran & Mark P. McKenna, *Confusion Isn't Everything*, 89 Notre Dame L. Rev. 253 (2013).

32 Jeremy Sheff, *Marks, Morals and Markets*, 65 Stan. L. Rev. 761 (2013).

33 *Badwill*, Note, 116(6) Harv. L. Rev. 1845 (2003).

34 Daniel Langlois, *The Deadly Impact of Counterfeit Products*, IAEI Magazine (Sep. 7, 2012); Alfadl et al., Scale Development on Consumer Behavior toward Counterfeit Drugs in a Developing Country: A Quantitative Study Exploiting the Tools of an Evolving Paradigm, Bmc Public Health (2013).

> characteristics protected by intellectual property law, while they may be technologically imitated, may not be legally imitated (for example, brands of diamonds). While intellectual property law will not directly control which class of consumers may consume which distinctive goods, as did previous forms of sumptuary law, it does provide us with the means to govern the modern sumptuary code indirectly, by facilitating the private control of the production of such goods through the prevention of the unauthorized copying of them.[35]

Jeremy Sheff has vociferously and correctly criticized the court-made doctrine of post-sale confusion in trademark law, arguing that mistakes about source made by third parties should not be a basis for trademark infringement liability.[36] Sheff has concluded:

> [T]he information asymmetry that trademarks are called on to mitigate in the status-confusion cases is not between buyers and sellers of goods bearing Veblen brands—genuine or counterfeit. Rather, the asymmetry is between purchasers of goods bearing Veblen brands—genuine or counterfeit—and their social audience. The information as to which the asymmetry exists is not ultimately about the product at all, but about the social status of the person consuming it. And consequently, the failure that this line of cases guards against is not in the market for any particular class of goods, but in the market for social status. Put simply, the "lemons" in the status-confusion cases are not used cars, and they are not really even clocks or handbags or watches; they are people.[37]

Sheff convincingly asserts that status confusion borne of a post-sale expectation of or interest in trademark authenticity by third parties is an inappropriate justification for imposing trademark liability. But he stops short of criticizing the trademark law precepts underlying the illegality of counterfeiting more generally. Even when counterfeit products do not confuse consumers, undermine reputations for quality, nor divert sales of authentic goods, few legal scholars have advocated a trademark law regime that does not allow the legitimate mark holder to stop their production or distribution. The most circumscribed approaches to trademark law will still enforce some degree of exclusivity for an exact source-identifying mark that is linked through sales and advertising to a particularized good or service.

By one estimate "counterfeit goods account for nearly 10 percent of worldwide trade, an estimated $500 billion annually."[38] The intersection between counterfeiting and luxury goods is a profound one. According to a 2011 U.S. Customs and Border Protection report, luxury goods make up a significant portion of counterfeit goods imported into

[35] Barton Beebe, *Intellectual Property Law and the Sumptuary Code*, 123 HARV. L. REV. 809 (2010).

[36] Jeremy N. Sheff, *Veblen Brands*, 96 MINN. L. REV. 769 (2012).

[37] Jeremy N. Sheff, *Veblen Brands*, 96 MINN. L. REV. 769 (2012).

[38] David Wright & Brandon Baur, *LAPD, US Customs Battle Counterfeit Goods Market, Multi-Billion Dollar Industry More Lucrative Than Drugs*, ABC NEWS, Oct. 21, 2013, NIGHTLINE.

the United States from foreign countries.[39] In 2009 luxury footwear, wearing apparel, handbags, wallets, and backpacks comprised over half the counterfeit commodities seized, and in 2010 almost half.[40] Consumer demand for counterfeit luxury goods is driven by the desire to appear affluent and fashionable.

III. Branding and Gender

People are required to identify as female or male in many contexts of everyday living, and from our gender designation flows a host of social and legal consequences. Though women and men typically share bathrooms in their homes, the bathrooms in public spaces are usually segregated by sex.[41] Passports, drivers' licenses, birth certificates, and other official documents usually announce the bearer's gender.

Like pronouns in most languages, nouns in many languages, and definite articles in some, brands have gender. A few products are understandably linked to females: tampons, as well as items directly related to pregnancy and giving birth. In most cases, however, gender distinctions are spurious from a utilitarian perspective. Women's and men's bodies are neither so alike within gender nor so different across gender that gender-specific food, clothing, housewares, health and beauty aids, transportation devices, or entertainment products are necessary or even logical. Branding and marketing practices, however, create and reify sharp gender divides for instrumental, profit-based purposes.[42]

In her groundbreaking book *The Second Sex*, feminist philosopher Simone de Beauvoir described the way in which men are the standard of all things, and women are the Other, deviating from the proper way of being, and therefore assumed deserving of second-class treatment.[43] The answer to the question, "Why can't a woman be more like a man," may be in some part biological, but the reply proffered by de Beauvoir is "because men will not allow it." Agency, the power to think and do for oneself, is taken for granted by the Default group in a society, usually heterosexual white men, but it is less available to the Other. Standards

---

[39] U.S. Customs and Border Protection & U.S. Immigration and Customs Enforcement, Intellectual Property Rights: Fiscal Year 2010 Seizure Statistics—Final Report (2011).

[40] *Id.*

[41] Mary A. Case, *Why Not Abolish the "Laws Of Urinary Segregation"? in* Toilet: Public Restrooms and the Politics of Sharing (Harvey Molotch & Laura Noren eds., 2010). http://chicagounbound.uchicago.edu/book_chapters/569/.

[42] P. Alreck & R. B. Settle, *Gender Effects on Internet, Catalogue and Store Shopping*, 9(2) The Journal of Database Marketing 150 (2002); Lara O'Reilly, *Facebook's Sandberg: "Brands That Bridge Gender Gap Have an Advantage,"* Marketing Week, Nov. 21, 2013; Kathy Oneto, *Crossing the Gender Divide: A Brand's Ability to Speak to Women and Men*, Popsop (Apr. 12, 2012); *cf* Martha Engel, *Leaning In on SATURDAY: The Trademark Gender Gap*, Duets Blog (Aug. 15, 2013).

[43] Simone de Beauvoir, The Second Sex (1949). ("Now, what peculiarly signalises the situation of woman is that she—a free and autonomous being like all human creatures—nevertheless finds herself living in a world where men compel her to assume the status of the Other.")

are centered around the Default so ubiquitously, this is perceived by Default group members as the natural state of things. Feminist legal scholar Catharine MacKinnon has written:

> Men's physiology defines most sports, their needs define auto and health insurance coverage, their socially designed biographies define workplace expectations and successful career patterns, their perspectives and concerns define quality in scholarship, their experiences and obsessions define merit, their objectification of life defines art, their military service defines citizenship, their presence defines family, their inability to get along with each other—their wars and rulerships—defines history, their image defines god, and their genitals define sex.[44]

Consider clothing. The Default owns comfort and control, while the Other's role is to be decorative and ornamental. Think about the last formal social function you attended. The men's legs were loosely covered by pants and their arms were covered by shirtsleeves and sport coats or suit jackets. Their shoes fit the shapes of their feet. Most of the women, however, had bare arms; wore body-conscious dresses; wore stockings that revealed the contours, if not the skin, on their legs; and balanced on high-heeled shoes that damaged their bodies with every step. The garments people wear signal gender, and women are normatively expected to wear uncomfortable outfits that reveal a lot more about body shape than comparable men's attire.

Some women express preferences for dressing in ways that men view as sexy, while others would rather wear clothing that does not reveal the specific geographies of their bodies. On the surface, it looks as though women have more options than men in how they present themselves publicly. However, unlike men, who can simply follow the prevailing clothing norms of their male peers, the illusion of choice is really a trap. Every self-aware woman continually negotiates where she wants to fall along the femininity continuum, under the shadow of the knowledge that women who appear too sexy are sanctioned for it, as are women who are deemed insufficiently attractive. One feminist commentator explained this as "a femininity tightrope that all public women are forced to walk," writing:

> Public women should be X amount feminine, X amount motherly, X amount hot, X amount beautiful, X amount young, X amount confident, X amount helpless, X amount exotic, X amount educated, X amount intelligent (required: the last two values < the men in the office), X amount gay (the last value almost always = 0). The ratios are fluid, shifting from day to day at the whim of public sentiment, so that a woman may think she's got it pretty well sewed up, only to wake up one fine spring morn to discover that the parade being thrown in her honor has suddenly vanished. Later she finds out it's because she stupidly forgot she was a member of the sex class,

---

[44] Catharine A. MacKinnon, *Difference and Dominance: On Sex Discrimination, in* FEMINIST LEGAL THEORY: READINGS IN LAW AND GENDER 81, 84 (Katharine T. Bartlett & Rosanne Kennedy eds., 1991).

and had dared to imagine that she would be judged on merit rather than her ability to do femininity right.[45]

For women, our gender is like our "house mark,"[46] and our looks are our individual trademarks, manufactured by our bodies and the goods that we adorn them with. An attractive female body (or body part) augmented with expensive or at least expensive-appearing attire can itself take on the appearance of a luxury good. Attractive women with polished, upscale looks are often integrated into advertisements for expensive products primarily being marketed to men, or for men (by making women more appealing): luxury automobiles,[47] high-tech items,[48] cigars,[49] scotches[50] and whiskeys,[51] razors,[52] clothing,[53] cologne,[54] yachts[55], wristwatches,[56] and real estate.[57]

---

[45] Jill, *Hugs, Twisty: Woman's Sex Appeal Is Unbearable to Knob Coworkers*, I BLAME THE PATRIARCHY, Jun. 5, 2010, http://blog.iblamethepatriarchy.com/2010/06/05/hugs-twisty-womans-sex-appeal-is-unbearable-to-knob-coworkers/.

[46] See K. C. KAILASAM, LAW OF TRADE MARKS & GEOGRAPHICAL INDICATIONS 43 (2003) and P. NARAYANAN, LAW OF TRADE MARKS & PASSING OFF 370 (2004).

[47] Julie Zeilinger, *TrueCar Ad Called Out for Implying Women Need Help Buying Cars without a Man*, HUFF. POST, Jul. 23, 2013.http://www.huffingtonpost.com/2013/07/23/truecar-ad-sexist-women-buying-cars_n_3636242.html?

[48] Andrea Peterson, *Is This ad for Gmail's New Inbox Sexist?*, WASH. POST, Aug. 14, 2013. http://www.washingtonpost.com/blogs/the-switch/wp/2013/08/14/is-this-ad-for-gmails-new-inbox-sexist/.

[49] Cleveland Chick, *Cigars and Sexism in Ohio City*, BLOGGER.COM (Feb. 15, 2014, 6:54 PM), http://www.happinessisahotpierogi.com/2014/02/cigars-and-sexism-in-ohio-city.html/.

[50] Becky Paskin, *Dewar's "Sexist" TV Commercial Angers Viewers*, THE SPIRITS BUSINESS, Dec. 10, 2013 http://www.thespiritsbusiness.com/2013/12/dewars-sexist-tv-ad-angers-women/; James Wilmore, *US: Bacardi Pulls Dewar's Ad after "Sexist" Charge*, JUST-DRINKS, Dec. 11, 2013 http://www.just-drinks.com/news/bacardi-pulls-dewars-ad-after-sexist-charge_id112305.aspx.

[51] Fred Minnick, *Dewar's Sexist "Meet The Baron" AD Degrades Women, Puts Whisky Industry at Risk*, FRED MINNICK'S BLOG (Dec. 10, 2013), http://fredminnick.com/dewars-sexist-meet-barron-ad-degrades-women-puts-whisky-industry-risk/.

[52] http://sexistads.tumblr.com/post/12015018846/nauseating-new-razor-ad-campaign-by-gillette, Tim Nudd, *Retro Razor Ad Doesn't Have Legs to Stand on*, ADWEEK (Sep. 23, 2010, 11:43 AM), http://www.adweek.com/adfreak/retro-razor-ad-doesnt-have-legs-stand-12188/; see also *Sexist Veet Ads Pulled from Internet*, AUSTRALIAN WOMEN'S WEEKLY, April 10, 2014.

[53] Joanna Douglas, *JC Penney's New Sexist Men's Clothing Ad*, YAHOO SHINE (Sep. 29, 2011, 6:45 PM), https://shine.yahoo.com/fashion/jc-penneys-new-sexist-mens-clothing-ad-video-2572120.html/; Elizabeth Plank, *Think American Apparel Isn't Sexist? Maybe This Will Convince You*, POLICYMIC (May 17, 2013), http://www.policymic.com/articles/42717/think-american-apparel-isn-t-sexist-maybe-this-will-convince-you/; Soraya Roberts, *The Rise of Sexist Fashion, From Plain Jane Homme to Disney*, THE DAILY BEAST, Sep. 5, 2013. See http://www.thedailybeast.com/articles/2013/05/09/the-rise-of-sexist-fashion-from-plain-jane-homme-to-disney.html.

[54] Katrina Pedrazaa, *Unforgivable Women's Perfume*, SEXIST ADS (Dec. 2, 2009, 7:14 PM), http://sexistads.blogspot.com/2009/12/unforgivable-womens-perfume.html/.

[55] http://www.therichest.com/luxury/yachts-luxury/10-sexy-yachts-to-impress-any-woman/.

[56] Simon Boyle, *Clock These Photos: Stunning Bond Girl Berenice Marlohe in Sexy Ads for Omega Watches*, MIRROR, Nov. 27, 2012. http://www.mirror.co.uk/3am/celebrity-news/berenice-marlohe-in-sexy-omega-watches-1458695.

[57] Gwen Sharp, *Over-the-Top Sexist Australian Real Estate Ad*, THE SOCIETY PAGES (Mar. 14, 2011, 12:24 PM), http://thesocietypages.org/socimages/2011/03/14/over-the-top-sexist-australian-real-estate-ad/.

IV. Branding and the Color Pink

Colors are often coded for gender, and one signifier of arch femininity is the color pink. Pink can transform any ordinary consumer product into something specifically linked to femaleness and functions as the social trademark of gender. One model of the "Fisher Price Kid Tough Digital Camera" is a boy. We know this not because it has a penis, but because it is blue.[58] The girl camera is of course pink.[59] There is no gender-neutral option. Other toys have special versions for girls differentiated by color from those intended for normal people, which is to say boys. Examples include pink Legos,[60] pink sports equipment, and pink consumer electronics.

Goods and services targeted at women also often use the color pink as a signifier. Pink gives gender to otherwise asexual adult goods and services, linking them semiotically to women. Commentator Vicky Frost noted that pink has become more fully intergenerational, writing:

> Not so long ago, pink was a colour reserved for little girls. It was the colour of Barbie and bubblegum, of plastic tat that parents were pestered into buying, of pre-teen bedrooms and pocket-money accessories. Then, suddenly, it was everywhere—and being targeted at grown women. Next month, for instance, sees the launch of Fly Pink, a "boutique airline designed especially for women" which plans to operate from Liverpool's John Lennon airport. The airline will offer flights to Paris for "shopping breaks" in customised pink planes, and, to complete the experience, will also provide pink champagne and complementary manicures before take-off. Which just underlines the fact that it is now possible for women to experience their entire day in pink. You can work out with a pink yoga mat and weights; adorn your windscreen wipers with pink wiper wings; cook dinner on a pink George Foreman grill and style your hair with hot-pink hair straighteners. You can even see off would-be attackers with a powder-pink Taser gun.[61]

Pink is the color marker of the Other, an outsider who is normatively expected to buy and use marked, specially designated consumer products. Camel cigarettes are available in pink packaging,[62] as was the failed beverage Tab Energy, which was marketed as

---

[58] Fisher-Price, *Fisher Price Kid Tough Digital Camera-Blue,* AMAZON, http://www.amazon.com/Fisher-Price-Tough-Digital-Camera/dp/B000QULFQC/ref=sr_1_1?ie=UTF8&s=toys-and-games&qid=1206028389&sr=1-1/.

[59] Fisher-Price, *Fisher Price Kid Tough Digital Camera-PINK,* AMAZON, http://www.amazon.com/Fisher-Price-Tough-Digital-Camera/dp/B000QUJKFU/ref=sr_1_2?ie=UTF8&s=toys-and-games&qid=1206028389&sr=1-2/.

[60] Jake Wallis Simons, *Pink Lego Is an Abomination. End This Gender Fascism,* TELEGRAPH, Apr. 3, 2013.

[61] Vicky Frost, *La Vie en Rose,* GUARDIAN, Jun. 8, 2007.

[62] Stuart Elliott, *A New Camel Brand Is Dressed to the Nines,* NEW YORK TIMES, Feb. 15, 2007. http://www.nytimes.com/2007/02/15/business/media/15adco.html?_r=0.

"The deliciously pink 5 calorie energy drink created especially for women with a sense of style and purpose."[63] The word "pink" is similarly deployed by products such as Victoria's Secret's "Pink" line of underwear and other clothing items (which come in a variety of colors). Other textual marks for clothing incorporating the term pink include Electric Pink, Pink Ops, Pink Stuff, Pink Republic, Pink Memories, U.S. Pink, Team Pink, Parker Pink, Under Armour's Power In Pink and Ralph Lauren's Pink Pony. According to the USPTO trademark database, over 3,500 trademarks include the word pink, and over 21,000 trademark registrations reference the word or the color. [64]

Pink is deployed culturally as a way to encode "authentic" gender in people, and also binds people to particular goods and services that have been gendered by instrumental uses of the color. Erin Buzuvis has explained:

> Individuals who have internalized the gender binary are genuinely uncomfortable when they cannot decode an individual's sex. Even before it has any biological relevance, another individual's sex is the subject of scrutiny. Pre-adolescents (especially babies) present a particular challenge, because they do not yet have visible sex characteristics. To overcome this ambiguity and the discomfort that results, we rely on a color convention: pink for girls and blue for boys. This has become effective symbolism through widespread repetition over time. By dressing girls in pink, parents encode femininity onto their daughters who, at least when wearing clothes, would otherwise be gender-ambiguous (and thus, subversive). In other words, the color convention of pink-for-girls and blue-for-boys is one aspect of the cultural symbolism that interpellates the gender binary as the dominant ideology.[65]

Studies show that across cultures and across gender, the most preferred color is blue.[66] It can hardly be a coincidence that in many nations, blue is the contemporary color associated with boys and men.[67] However, while blue may indicate maleness among infants and

---

[63] *Pink Power: TaB Is Back, Sort of,* FOX NEWS, Mar. 1, 2006.

[64] Basic search of the USPTO's Trademark Electronic Search System on April 11, 2014, by author.

[65] Erin K. Buzuvis, *Reading the Pink Locker Room: On Football Culture and Title IX*, 14 WM. & MARY J. WOMEN & L. 1 (2007).

[66] Satyendra Singh, *Current Research Development: Impact of Color on Marketing*, 44(6) MANAGEMENT DECISION 783 (2006); Kay E. R. Vandergrift, *Color Preference And Gender Research, C.O.P.E.*; Sean Work, *True Colors—Breakdown of Color Preferences by Gender*, Kissmetrics; Valérie Bonnardel et al., *Color Preferences: A British/Indian Comparative Study*, AIC 2012 INTERIM MEETING, TAIPEI—IN COLOR WE LIVE: COLOR AND ENVIRONMENT 306.

[67] See Natalie Wolchover, *Why Is Pink for Girls and Blue for Boys?,* LIVESCIENCE (Aug. 1, 2012, 02:06 PM), http://www.livescience.com/22037-pink-girls-blue-boys.html and Meong Jin Shin et al., *Colour Preferences For Traditional Korean Colour*, JOURNAL OF THE INTERNATIONAL COLOUR ASSOCIATION (2012), *available at* https://www.google.com/url?sa=t&rct=j&q=&esrc=s&source=web&cd=18&cad=rja&ved=0CF0QFjAHOA0&url=http%3A%2F%2Faic-colour-journal.org%2Findex.php%2FJAIC%2Farticle%2Fdownload%2F126%2F106&ei=REyzUu6iI4jTsATOx4CgCg&usg=AFQjCNFIhDw-8rFV35ezVQwPU4huNwQd9g&bvm=bv.58187178,d.cWc.

small children lacking secondary sex characteristics, it is not as strongly associated with adult males or masculinity generally. This is because as the baseline humans, men have dominion over all colors. While women are incorporated within the category of "men" for some purposes, for others their differences from men are instrumentally highlighted. The term "blue collar," refers to employees across gender who lack a college education and/or perform manual labor for a living. Jobs that are disproportionately performed by women are sometimes referred to as "pink collar," as a way to subcategorize these workers, separating them from mainstream occupations offering higher salaries or more prestige.

In addition to maleness, blue's myriad societal associations include oceans, the sky, night, depression, "off-color" humor, and, in ribbon form, a first-place win. Pink is associated with good health. There is nothing inherently female about pink, or inherently pink about females. The connection is socially constructed,[68] and trademarks both make and sustain this association. An enormous proportion of the marks using the word or color pink have some nontrivial association with women. Pink marks are intended to signal otherness: (1) this is for women, (2) buying this helps women, or (3) this is a woman- and sex-related product for men.

As discussed in section I above, trademark owners free-ride on the existing meaning of symbols and appropriate them for private use. And every time pink is used to designate femaleness in some way, the semiotic attachment grows stronger, across marks. Though thousands of registered trademarks make use of the cultural connection between femaleness and the color pink, no entity has succeeded (or even attempted) to own it in singular fashion. The color pink functions like a public domain trademark that is copiously used by a multiplicity of companies and organizations to either feminize goods and services or commoditize women themselves. It is deployed by commercial actors in advertisements, used in product packaging, embedded in products, and integrated into trademarks themselves, all with little apparent fear of consumer confusion or trademark dilution. Its omnipresence is powerfully illustrative of the strength that semiotic signifiers can have, and of how effectively they can be used in commerce across a broad range of products and services, by a large variety of manufacturers and distributors.

Because it is a common practice in many nations for pink to be used as the color delineating female spaces and possessions, girls begin to internalize this constructed preference as babies, creating a self- reinforcing loop between the encoders and decoders of cultural texts. A toy manufacturer makes girls' toys pink because girls ostensibly prefer pink toys; girls may prefer pink toys because that is what is given to them and in turn is what they are given approval for choosing.[69] Pink is the trademark of girls who have been successfully feminized.

---

[68] Maria Popova, *The Pink and Blue Projects: Exploring the Genderization of Color*, BRAIN PICKINGS (Dec. 11, 2009), *available at* http://www.brainpickings.org/index.php/2009/12/11/pink-and-blue-project/.

[69] *Id.*; Erin K. Buzuvis, *Reading the Pink Locker Room: On Football Culture and Title IX*, 14 WM. & MARY J. WOMEN & L. 1 (2007).

The Disney Company markets a very successful line of clothing and toys under its "Princess" imprimatur. A significant proportion of the Princess products are pink, and the targeted consumers are clearly female. Disney didn't create the demand for pink among girls, but it exploits the affinity for pink among females quite deftly. The desires of girls who would prefer Princess toys in colors other than pink may be ignored by Disney, and girls who dislike pink may have to forgo the Princess line altogether. Disney doesn't have any obligation to cater to the pink-adverse consumer, but the societal messages it sends to girls who dislike pink are strong ones. Every girl wants to be a princess. Princesses surround themselves with pinkness. If you don't want to be a pink princess, something is wrong with you. Staying afloat in mainstream girlhood requires one to embrace pink products. Forgoing pink requires self-denial or overt cultural nonconformity. Pink is for girls, and girls are supposed to be for pink. Writer Peggy Orenstein expressed confusion and concern about the popularity of Disney princess merchandise and the princess meme generally that is apparently wildly popular with girls in the United States, observing that "to call princesses a 'trend' among girls is like calling Harry Potter a book," and that "'Princess,' as some Disney execs call it, is not only the fastest-growing brand the company has ever created; they say it is on its way to becoming the largest girls' franchise on the planet."[70] Orenstein has theorized that the princess phenomenon may be a backlash against feminism, and an effort to embrace traditional femininity. Orenstein described, in somewhat convoluted fashion, the classic double bind for feminists: women who embrace "princessism" are vapid and materialistic and rejecting feminism while embracing their shallow, fragile feminine femaleness. However, women who reject "princessism" are actually rejecting women-identified things and are therefore being sexist themselves, which is hypocritical and self-hating, and also drives women away from feminism. No matter what, feminism is apparently on the wrong side of the princess issue.

There is nothing inherently bad about pink as a color when it is freely chosen by women in exercises of agency, though how much agency individuals actually have, given the societal pressures that shape their actions, is debatable. It is the invocation of pink as a proxy for inferiority based on its identification with females that is the most troubling. In her book "Pink Think: Becoming a Woman in Many Uneasy Lessons," author Lynn Peril described a related phenomenon she labeled "pink think" as "a set of ideas and attitudes about what constitutes proper female behavior" that "assumes there is a standard of behavior to which all women, no matter their age, race or body type, must aspire."[71] Peril wrote:

> [P]ink think is more than a stereotyped vision of girls and women as poor drivers who are afraid of mice and snakes, adore babies and small dogs, talk incessantly on the phone and are incapable of keeping secrets. Integral to pink think is the belief

---

[70] Peggy Orenstein, *What's Wrong with Cinderella?*, The New York Times, Dec. 24, 2006. See also Peggy Orenstein, Cinderella Ate My Daughter (2012).

[71] Lynn Peril, Pink Think: Becoming a Woman in Many Uneasy Lessons (2002).

> that one's success as a woman is grounded in one's allegiance to such behavior. For example, a woman who fears mice isn't necessarily following the dictates of pink think. On the other hand, a woman who isn't afraid of mice but pretends to be because she thinks such helplessness adds to her appearance of femininity is toeing the pink think party line.[72]

To follow that analysis out to one logical conclusion, some women may pretend to prefer pink products, even though they might actually prefer other colors, because wearing pink and owning pink things is expected of her. Choosing pink against her own inner wishes constitutes consummate pink think by a female, reflecting self-sacrifice, conformity to gender norms, and acquiescence to the dictates of mainstream consumer culture.[73]

There are certainly contexts in which the use of pink, while still Othering, may persuade some girls to participate in activities from which they might otherwise feel excluded. For example, sporting goods stores feature child-sized pink batting helmets and bright pastel fielding gloves. The availability of these accoutrements in what are unequivocally "girl colors" may signal that baseball is a "girls' sport" in a way that attracts participation by people who guide their behavior by societal expectations and their perceptions of prevailing gender norms. If pink draws girls into sports, and pink sports equipment legitimizes their participation in organized athletics to parents who encourage their children to conform to constricted visions of gendered behaviors, this is arguably a socially beneficial use of the pink trademark. On the other hand, the adoption of pink sports equipment tends to instantiate equipment in "regular" or "normal" colors in widespread use as being male, rather than gender neutral. When a group of parents, mothers specifically, noticed that available hockey equipment was "designed for boys," they sought to remedy this by launching a company that made hockey equipment that was tailored to females. The design "problem" was not one of sizing or fit, but of colors. Manufacturing hockey equipment in pink and purple was supposed to make girls feel more comfortable participating in a boy-dominated sport, because they wouldn't have to "dress like boys." But as one feminist observer noted:

> [This just reifies] the impossible dilemma women who have entered traditionally masculine or more physically aggressive sports constantly face: you can be girly or you can be sporty. Making pink socks and sticks is not going to eradicate that binary. Is this really the way we want to attract girls to ice hockey anyway? Telling them, don't worry, you can play hockey and still wear pink? That may work for a

---

[72] *Id.* at 7–8.

[73] *See, e.g.*, http://www.thestate.com/125/story/58535.html ("Think pink: This Mother's Day, give mom a plate full of feminine color (and good health)").

> while with 5- and 6-year olds but those girls will still face the be girly or be sporty dilemma as they get older; except that "sporty" frequently slips into dyke-y as girls become teenagers.[74]

When pink is applied to a product, the product has been feminized, and this makes it perceptually inferior. Girls were already playing baseball and hockey before companies decided to market pink sports gear to them. But it is the rare boy indeed who will select a pink bat, helmet, or hockey stick. When Vassar College began admitting men, by some accounts it changed the school colors from pink and gray (symbolizing "the rose light of the dawn of women's education breaking through the grey of former years") to maroon and gray, at the request of male students.[75] According to an official Vassar website:

> With the move to coeducation in 1969, the "rose" part of the equation became an embarrassment, especially to Vassar's male athletes. "Legend has it that when the men's rugby team, suited in their pink and grey striped jerseys, stepped out onto the field to face Army, the game was over before it even started" (Lillian Reuman, The Miscellany News, September 16, 2009). The pink gradually darkened to maroon, at least for athletic uniforms.[76]

When men affirmatively adopt pink, it is often socially interpreted as either boldly transgressive[77] or as a signifier of homosexuality.[78] When Major League Baseball players decided to use pink bats as a Mother's Day 2006 effort to provide publicity to fundraising efforts of the

---

[74] Ken, *Can Polka Dots Build Confidence?,* AFTER ATALANTA (Dec. 28, 2007, 8:17 AM), http://afterata.blogspot.com/2007/12/can-polka-dots-build-confidence.html.

[75] Vassar Historian, *Vassar Myths & Legends*, VASSAR ENCYCLOPEDIA, http://vcencyclopedia.vassar.edu/vassar-myths-legends/index.html. ("In the early seventies, around the time that men were first admitted to the college, Vassar changed its school colors from "the rose light of the dawn of women's education breaking through the grey of former years" to a darker maroon and grey. The story goes that a group of male athletes, feeling too effeminate wearing pink athletic gear, circulated a petition to change the color, and the administration caved. Colton Johnson, Dean of Studies at the time of the switch, maintains that the colors were changed because of budget cuts; ordering custom-made pink uniforms was much more costly than the readily-available maroon, and so the school made the switch.")

[76] The Vassar Chronicle, *Flourishing for Founder Takes Fluctuating Forms,* VASSAR COLLEGE STUDENT HANDBOOK (May 5, 1956), http://vcencyclopedia.vassar.edu/traditions/.

[77] Ky Louisville, *Pink Bats Are Part of Fund-Raiser for Cancer Foundation*, Assoc. Press, May 10, 2006; *Real Men Wear Pink T-Shirt,* THE PLANET SHOPS, http://www.wackyplanet.com/remenwepit.html. But see Allen Salkin, *Pink Shirts Welcome,* NEW YORK TIMES, May 6, 2007.

[78] *Opponents Seeing Red Over Iowa's Pink Locker Room*, ASSOC. PRESS, Sep. 28, 2005; http://www.msnbc.msn.com/id/9517000/; http://www.siouxcityjournal.com/articles/2005/09/25/news/iowa/27c028c39eaea709862570870000e5232.txt http://www.pinknews.co.uk/news/index.php. *But see* Sally Jenkins, *Tickled Pink by Iowa's Locker Room*, WASH. POST, Oct 1, 2005, and Ann Althouse, *About That Pink Locker Room*, ALTHOUSE (Oct 1, 2005, 6:39 AM), http://althouse.blogspot.com/2005/10/about-that-pink-locker-room.html and David Burge, *Little Pink Footballs*, IOWAHAWK (Sep. 23, 2005), http://iowahawk.typepad.com/iowahawk/2005/09/little_pink_foo.html.

Susan G. Komen Breast Cancer Foundation, media coverage included observations like: "The thought of these big macho men, swinging pink bats to help women with breast cancer ... what a novel idea," and "It takes a big man to swing a pink bat in a major league game."[79] Using the Other's inferior color was thus interpreted as an act of both charity and courage.

Pink is the color at the crossroads between misogyny and homophobia, both offensively and defensively, when it is associated with men. Pink is used to insinuate the undesirable trait of femininity. The locker room for visiting teams at the University of Iowa's Kinnick football stadium has pink paint on its brick walls, as well as pink metal lockers, carpeting, sinks, showers, and urinals, in an effort to "soften" opponents.[80] Pink clothing is frequently used to punish male prisoners,[81] to make them feel involuntarily feminized, and also because it may make them more vulnerable to sexual assault by other inmates.[82]

Pink is also a color widely associated with pornography and prostitution.[83] Given its status as the color of commoditized sex, the fact that the color simultaneously signifies "little girls" and femaleness generally is no coincidence, given the "barely legal" or "Lolita" emphasis of significant sectors of the sex industries.[84]

Sometimes pink is affirmatively re-signified.[85] Pink triangles have become a symbol of gay liberation, through positive reclamation of the symbol used to denote homosexuality in the concentration camps of Hitler's Germany.[86] The color pink was probably chosen

---

[79] http://sports.espn.go.com/mlb/news/story?id=2439502.

[80] http://www.kcci.com/sports/5011621/detail.html; http://www.msnbc.msn.com/id/9517000/; Erin E. Buzuvis, *Reading the Pink Locker Room: On Football Culture and Title IX*, 14 WM. & MARY J. WOMEN & L. 1 (2007).

[81] Ron Barnett, *Pink a Punishing Color for Prisoners*, USA TODAY, Sept 14, 2007 http://usatoday30.usatoday.com/news/nation/2007-09-13-prisonpinksuits_N.htm; *South Carolina Prisons Director Defends Putting Inmates in Pink Jumpsuits*, ASSOC. PRESS, Aug. 22, 2007 http://www.foxnews.com/story/2007/08/22/south-carolina-prisons-director-defends-putting-inmates-in-pink-jumpsuits/; Amanda Lee Myers, *Inmates Convicted of DUI at Arizona Jail Wear Pink*, ASSOC. PRESS, Dec.12, 2007 http://www.policeone.com/community-policing/articles/1639596-DUI-inmates-don-pink-in-Ariz-chain-gang/; Seth Mydans, *To Punish Thai Police, a Hello Kitty Armband*, NEW YORK TIMES, Aug. 7, 2007 http://www.nytimes.com/2007/08/07/world/asia/07cnd-thai.html.

[82] *South Carolina Prisons Director Defends Putting Inmates in Pink Jumpsuits*, ASSOC. PRESS, Aug. 22, 2007 http://www.foxnews.com/story/2007/08/22/south-carolina-prisons-director-defends-putting-inmates-in-pink-jumpsuits/; Dave Ward and Gina Gaston, *Is Pink Prison Policy A Problem?*, ASSOC. PRESS, Aug. 22, 2007; http://www.charleston.net/news/2007/aug/21/its_not_easy_being_pink13565/; http://blogs.thestate.com/bradwarthensblog/2007/08/crystal-pink-pe.html

[83] *See, e.g.*, AutoAirColors, *Auto-Air Colors 4584 Sparklescent Porn Star Pink*, YOU TUBE (Dec. 8, 2011), http://www.youtube.com/watch?v=r7yCsfxIYio; *Pink World Free Porn Picture and Movie Galleries*, PINK WORLD, http://www.pinkworld.com/; *AG Busts "Detroit Pink" Prostitution Ring*, CBS DETROIT, Nov. 30, 2011; Andrea, *Pink is for Prostitutes*, RANTCHICK, Mar. 10, 2009, http://rantchick.com/pink-is-for-prostitutes/.

[84] Hugo Schwyzer, *Why Do Men Love "Barely Legal" Porn?*, JEZEBEL, Aug. 2, 2012, http://jezebel.com/5881335/why-do-men-love-barely-legal-porn.

[85] See Sonia Katyal, *Semiotic Disobedience*, 84 WASH. U. L. REV. 489 (2006).

[86] *Symbols of the Gay, Lesbian, Bisexual, and Transgender Movements*, LAMBDA GLBT COMMUNITY SERVICES, http://www.lambda.org/symbols.htm; Channel 4 http://www.channel4.com/history/microsites/H/history/n-s/pink.html; http://www.pinktrianglepark.net/.

by the Nazis to signal "gay" because of its feminized associations in that culture.[87] It is now used by some advocacy groups to show gay pride.[88]

Similarly, Code Pink[89] "is a women-initiated grassroots peace and social justice movement working to end the war in Iraq, stop new wars, and redirect our resources into healthcare, education and other life-affirming activities."[90] The name "Code Pink" was chosen in part as a play on the Bush Administration's Department of Homeland Security's color-coded "Threat Level" Advisory System.[91] Members participating in Code Pink events normally wear pink to identify themselves and declare their organizational association.[92] They also use alternative social meaning behind pink quite playfully, such as by issuing "pink slips" to politicians they would like to see fired.[93]

Nevertheless, pink is firmly entrenched in the culture as, metaphorically, the color of girl germs, and this has consequences. As one observer noted:

> Male and female stereotypes are established early: It is not hard to see a connection between girls playing with dolls and boys playing with cars, and the widespread segregation of labor markets into "female" and "male" professions. Nurses, primary school teachers and caregivers of most kinds are overwhelmingly female. Engineers, computer scientists and mechanics tend to be male.
>
> This segregation matters: It helps explain a stubborn pay gap between men and women, as the caregiving professions generally pay less than technical jobs. Women earn on average 16 percent less than men in the member countries of the Organization for Economic Cooperation and Development. They account for more than 70 percent of health, social and education workers but make up less than a quarter of employees in mining, manufacturing and construction.
>
> Stereotypes also help explain why few women have made it into leadership positions even in countries that have gone furthest in leveling the playing field at home: In Sweden, where parents can share 13 months of paid baby leave and are guaranteed a place in a subsidized preschool thereafter, women still make up only 23 percent of senior managers. Leadership is associated with "male" qualities like aggressiveness and risk-taking.

---

[87] http://www.triangles-roses.org/inmate_buchenwald.htm.

[88] Triangles, *Swade's GLBT Symbols Gallery*, SwadePages, http://www.swade.net/gallery/ptri.html Pink; *Gay Symbols Lambda*, StoneWall Society, http://www.stonewallsociety.com/gaysymb.htm.

[89] *See* CodePink Women For Peace at http://www.codepink4peace.org/.

[90] *Id.* at http://www.codepink4peace.org/article.php?list=type&type=3.

[91] http://www.dhs.gov/xinfoshare/programs/Copy_of_press_release_0046.shtm; Code Pink Women For Peace, *Women's Peace Activism: Forward into the Past?*, Jo Freeman.com, http://www.uic.edu/orgs/cwluherstory/jofreeman/photos/CodePink.html.

[92] *Id.*

[93] http://www.dallasnews.com/sharedcontent/dws/dn/latestnews/stories/062307dnnatcodepink.34f0383.html

> Which brings us back to Hamleys, where these qualities were on ample display on the blue-coded fourth floor: Amid miniature soldiers and plastic sabers, little boys were seen sparring noisily. Two floors down, girls were rocking baby dolls to sleep. On the store's Web site, the drop-down menu under "Dolls" is pink, while the drop-down menu under "Action Toys" is blue. Both categories offer "Roleplay & Dress-Up," but if the pink section touts princess dresses and "My First Dolly's Tea Set," the blue section sells a police officer outfit and a "Build Your Own Screwdriver" set.[94]

Academic books that further explain the negative consequences of "pink" socialization include *Delusions of Gender*, by Cordelia Fine; *Pink Brain, Blue Brain*, by Lise Eliot; and *Pink and Blue*, by Jo Paoletti.

A. PINK RIBBONS AND THE COMMODITIZATION OF BREAST CANCER

Pink is also the color of a particular women's affliction and is deployed as a mechanism for extracting money from women in the guise of soliciting compassion and helpful awareness-raising. The best-known gendered, cause-related, trademark-like icon is the pink ribbon. It is not exclusively held by any particular commercial or nonprofit entity. Instead, it is owned by an illness, and linked to a fundraising phenomenon. Pink is the color of female, and pink ribbons are a symbol of breast cancer, a disease that primarily affects women.[95] Massive advertising campaigns condition the populace to wear or display pink ribbons as a mechanism for signifying support for, and solidarity with, breast cancer sufferers. There is no social equivalent for heart disease or diabetes, two diseases that afflict women at high rates, nor for other uniquely woman-identified diseases such as cervical cancer. Female breasts are more valued than cervixes, a social good in part because men like to look at them, and pink ribbons are a visual reminder that breasts can be disfigured or lost.

The pink ribbon–related logos and slogans promote products and services for sale. The emphasis on consuming as a way of raising money, "shopping for the cure," arguably embraces a very conventional view of women. One fundraising organization, the Susan G. Komen Breast Cancer Foundation,[96] claims a trademark in the phrase "Passionately Pink for the Cure™!" Komen is a dominant breast cancer charity, and the foundation's name is often seen in conjunction with pink ribbons, but it does not "own" them.

---

[94] Bennhold, *Toys Start the Gender Equality Rift*, NEW YORK TIMES, Jul. 31, 2012. http://www.nytimes.com/2012/08/01/world/europe/01iht-letter01.html

[95] See SUSAN G. KOMEN BREAST CANCER FOUNDATION, http://www.komen.org/marketplace/, http://www.cancersocietystore.com/; ORIENTAL TRADING, http://www.orientaltrading.com/application?origin=page.jsp&namespace=search&event=button.search&Ntx=mode%2bmatchallpartial&Ntt=pink%20ribbon&N=0&Ntk=all; THE PINK RIBBON SHOP, http://www.pinkribbonshop.com/.

[96] http://cms.komen.org/komen/index.htm.

Komen solicits "corporate partners" to produce authorized products, and then requests that they donate money to the foundation in return for the public relations benefits.[97] The rhetorical pitch is not subtle: give us money and we will bring you new customers who think your company cares about women.[98] This is sometimes referred to as "pink washing."[99] In a certain sense, a pink ribbon converts objects into luxury items. People will pay more for an item linked by a pink ribbon with an aura of philanthropy; they may justify purchases of luxury goods or services in part because some of the proceeds go to charity. Examples of upscale pink-ribboned and pink-ribbon-related products with a past or present Komen link include the Dyson pink vacuum cleaner,[100] Wilson golf clubs,[101] and the Little Pink Tools toolkit.[102] The vacuum cleaner is a woman's appliance rendered even more femininely, the golf clubs lose their unisex veneer, and the toolkit is framed as affirmatively transgressive, since females who don't usually own tools now have special pink ones made "just for them."

The automotive company BMW organized "Ultimate Drive" events in which potential customers were invited to test-drive various car models that are decorated with pink ribbons.[103] The only link to breast cancer is that the company donates some money in a fairly transparent exchange for this goodwill-soaked marketing opportunity. The Ford Motor Company has offered a "Warriors in Pink Mustang Package."[104] Ford noted that: "Included with the package will be a pink ribbon and pony fender badge, pink Mustang rocker tape striping, charcoal leather seats with pink stitching, aluminum spoke steering wheel with pink stitching and charcoal floormats with pink ribbon and contrast stitching."[105]

Komen's corporate affiliates also include products within the realm of traditional femininity.[106] The Mattel toy company has marketed a Komen edition[107] of its Pink Ribbon Barbie Fashion Doll.[108] Breast Cancer Barbie has both of her plastic, nipple-less

---

97 http://cms.komen.org/komen/Partners/BecomeaPartnerorSponsor/index.htm.

98 *But see* Wency Leung, *Pink Makes Women Donate Less to Breast-Cancer Causes: Study*, THE GLOBE AND MAIL, Jul. 27, 2011.

99 *Pinkwashing*, URBAN DICTIONARY, http://urbandictionary.com/define.php?term=pinkwashing.

100 http://www.bcrfcure.org/part_cur_dyson.html.

101 http://www.wilson.com/wilson/corp/hope/index.jsp.

102 http://www.littlepinktools.com/.

103 http://www.bmwusa.com/BmwExperience/EventsandPrograms/UDSK/.

104 Matt Rigney, *Ford Unveils 2008 Warriors in Pink Mustang Package*, MOTOR AUTHORITY, May 13, 2007.

105 *Id.*

106 *Cancer Centre*, EVERYDAY HEALTH MEDIA LLC, http://www.thecancerblog.com/2006/08/18/breast-cancer-barbie-doll/.

107 Mattel, *Susan Komen Breast Cancer Foundation Pink Ribbon Barbie Doll Mattel*, AMAZON, http://www.amazon.com/Breast-Cancer-Foundation-Ribbon-Barbie/dp/B00FZ0J58S.

108 Mattel, *Barbie Collector Pink Ribbon Barbie Doll*, AMAZON, http://www.amazon.com/Barbie-Collector-Pink-Ribbon-Doll/dp/B000ERVLV6/ref=pd_sim_sbs_t_1.

breasts intact, if you were wondering. She has not undergone a mastectomy. Apparently Mattel's solidarity with cancer survivors only goes so far.

Some corporations reap the goodwill of breast cancer charity without affiliating with Komen. The Hooters restaurant chain used the occasion of its 10th Annual Hooters International Swimsuit Pageant in Las Vegas Hooters to announce a breast cancer research grant "in honor of former Hooters Calendar Cover Girl, Kelly Jo Dowd."[109] After she died the company issued a press release[110] and said in pertinent part:

> "She is our Susan G. Komen," explained Mike McNeil, Vice President of Marketing for Hooters of America. "Kelly Jo helped us break through the barriers of political correctness for Hooters with respect to breast cancer and ignited a passion for this noble cause. Because of her we have been able to address this serious women's health concern without people thinking we are insincere or opportunistic."[111]

What the "barriers of political correctness" were is never explained. Whether the company would ever hire a woman who had lost one or both breasts to the disease to work as a server is artfully avoided.

Other companies simply make money by selling mundane products adorned with pink ribbons. The Oriental Trading catalog has a range of products that include "Pink Ribbon Rubber Duckies,"[112] "Breast Cancer Awareness Buttermints,"[113] and "Breast Cancer Awareness Can Insulators."[114] If people purchasing the latter item make traditional trademark associations, they must think, "Wow, thanks to breast cancer, my beer has remained deliciously chilled." All that the catalog vaguely promises on its pages is that the company will donate "a percentage of the profits" to "breast cancer research initiatives."[115]

Breast cancer's pink-ribbonization has provoked scathing denouncements by Barbara Ehrenreich in "Welcome to Cancerland: A Mammogram Leads to a Cult of Pink

---

[109] http://www.hooters.com/news_and_events/news/2006/2006-08-04_kelly_jo.asp.

[110] http://prn.newscom.com/cgi-bin/pub/s?f=PRN/prnpub&p1=20070525/CLF060&xtag=PRN-prnphotos-62349&redir=detail&tr=1&row=1.

[111] Hooters of America, Inc., *Hooters Symbol Kelly Jo Dowd Passes*, PR NEWSWIRE, May 25, 2005.

[112] *Pink Ribbon Rubber Duckies IN-16/836*, ORIENTAL TRADING, http://www.orientaltrading.com/pink-ribbon-rubber-duckies-a2-16_836.fltr?Ntt=pink%20ribbon%20rubber%20duckies.

[113] *Breast Cancer Awareness Buttermints IN-K836*, ORIENTAL TRADING, http://www.orientaltrading.com/breast-cancer-awareness-buttermints-a2-_K828.fltr?Ntt=breast%20cancer%20awareness%20buttermints.

[114] *Breast Cancer Awareness Can Cover IN-3/807*, ORIENTAL TRADING, http://www.orientaltrading.com/breast-cancer-awareness-can-covers-a2-3_807.fltr?Ntt=breast%20cancer%20awareness%20can%20insulators.

[115] *Breast Cancer Awareness*, ORIENTAL TRADING, http://www.orientaltrading.com/occasions-and-events/breast-cancer-awareness-a1-550493-2-0.fltr?categoryFromSearch=true&rd=pink%20ribbon.

Kitch,"[116] in the book *Pink Ribbons, Inc.: Breast Cancer and the Politics of Philanthropy*, by Samantha King,[117] and via the Breast Cancer Action Network's web-based admonition to "Think Before You Pink."[118] The general theme of these critiques is that under the guise of pink philanthropy, corporations link product sales and self-promotion campaigns to the curing of the disease, while drawing attention away from public health prevention efforts and squelching calls for investigations into why and how breast cancer rates are so high and the extent to which these pink-ribbon corporations themselves are placing carcinogens into our air, food and water supplies, and the environment generally.[119]

The pink ribbon serves in some ways as a publicly held certification mark, ostensibly promoting breast cancer awareness, and projecting caring, while simultaneously harnessing the emotional power of the symbol for fundraising and commercial profit. Like traditional trademarks, it can also be used to deceive. The "Abortion Breast Cancer" organization uses the pink ribbon to draw attention to its scientifically unproven assertion that abortions cause breast cancer.[120] Thus, where a symbol is a social signifier rather than a true trademark, as is the case with breast cancer's pink ribbon, one facet of its uncontrolled commoditization can include the seeming legitimization of demonstrably false speech.

B. THE INESCAPABLE PINK LINK

Though thousands of registered trademarks make use of the cultural connection between femaleness and the color pink, no entity owns it in singular fashion. Nor is this likely to occur, absent a "famousness" finding that triggers dilution protections for color alone related to a color-alone mark registration. The color pink functions like a public domain trademark that is copiously used by a multiplicity of companies and organizations to either feminize goods and services or to commoditize women themselves. It is deployed by commercial actors in advertisements, used in product packaging, embedded in products, and integrated into trademarks themselves with little apparent fear of consumer confusion or trademark dilution. Its omnipresence is powerfully illustrative of the strength that semiotic

---

116 Barbara Ehrenreich, *Welcome to Cancerland: A Mammogram Leads to a Cult of Pink Kitsch*, HARPER'S MAGAZINE, Nov. 2001.

117 SAMANTHA KING, PINK RIBBONS, INC.: BREAST CANCER AND THE POLITICS OF PHILANTHROPY (2008).

118 *Think Before You Pink*, BREAST CANCER ACTION, http://thinkbeforeyoupink.org/; see also Twisty, *Cure for the cure*, I BLAME THE PATRIARCHY (Sep. 19, 2006), http://blog.iblamethepatriarchy.com/2006/09/19/crunch-for-the-cure/.

119 *E.g.*, Threadingwater, *Pink Porn*, THREADINGWATER (Oct. 3, 2006), http://threadingwater.wordpress.com/2006/10/03/pink-porn/; *but see, e.g.*, http://www.texassports.com/index.php?s=&url_channel_id=33&url_article_id=8181&url_subchannel_id=&change_well_id=2 (pink as expression of support).

120 COALITION ON ABORTION BREAST CANCER, http://www.abortionbreastcancer.com/.

signifiers can have and of how effectively they can be used in commerce without strong trademark protections.

Thinking about trademark law in connection with the color pink draws attention to the widely instantiated Othering of women and to how difficult it can be for individual consumers to avoid the double bind that pinkification presents. Embracing pink might mean someone is proud of being a woman, and that she cares about breast cancer awareness, but it also may mean she has succumbed to corporate and social manipulation. Eschewing pink may mean that a woman has liberated herself from constricting and manipulative social norms, but it also simultaneously suggests she is unfeminine, self-hating, ungrateful for "special treatment" accorded her based on her gender, judgmental and ungenerous toward women who freely choose to surround themselves with pink, and generally unsuccessful at womanhood. Pink or the absence of pink will unavoidably be a visible component of every woman's brand.

V. Luxury and the Social Control of Women

Femininity is a powerful benchmark against which women continually must choose how to brand and rebrand themselves, using or forgoing trademarks associated with luxury goods and services in the process. Luxury brands are trademarks or families of trademarks that are culturally associated with affluence. Both women and men may choose to advertise their affluence by visually associating themselves with particular trademarks, or they may try to create the illusion of affluence with counterfeit luxury goods.

Yet when one compares the manner in which upscale consumer goods are advertised to women with the ways that other luxury goods are marketed to men, it's hard to miss the starkness of the differences. Luxury goods coded for woman are pitched as necessary adjuncts or components of personal attractiveness.[121] Advertisements for luxury goods directed at men often position beautiful women as commodities that can be acquired by wealthy male consumers.[122]

According to an organization that calls itself The Luxury Institute, "Jeweler Tiffany & Co. and U.S. label Michael Kors are the most widely purchased jewelry and fashion brands by ultra-affluent women in the United States."[123] It also reports that "the top three most widely purchased jewelry brands by ultra-affluent women are Tiffany, David Yurman and Cartier" and "other top ranked brands are Prada, Burberry, Louis Vuitton, Chanel, Gucci

---

[121] One academic study of consumption posits that "women's luxury products often function as a signaling system directed at other women who pose a threat to their romantic relationships." Carlson School of Management, *University of Minnesota Research Reveals Luxury Products' Role in Relationships*, UN IVERSITY OF MINNESOTA (Jul. 24, 2013), http://www1.umn.edu/news/news-releases/2013/UR_CONTENT_450739.html.

[122] For an academic study related to this point see http://www.carlsonschool.umn.edu/assets/165659.pdf.

[123] Erin Shea, *Tiffany, Michael Kors Are Most Purchased Luxury Brands by Ultra-affluent Women: Luxury Institute*, LUXURY DAILY, Jul. 1, 2013.

and Marc Jacobs," while "Ralph Lauren and Brooks Brothers have the largest market share in ultra-affluent men's luxury fashion purchases."[124] An unscientific but easily replicable online survey of the advertising run in support of these top luxury brands demonstrates that women are expected to be consumers of luxury goods, but are also sometimes portrayed as luxury goods themselves, readily obtainable by men who are affluent and possess the proper trademarks.

When one moves beyond the realms of clothing, handbags, and jewelry, the role of gender in the advertising of luxury goods is completely unbalanced. Rare indeed is the advertisement that markets yachts, expensive automobiles, or top-shelf alcoholic beverages to women. Women appear in the advertisements for "masculine" upscale goods not as prospective consumers but either as part of the bounty associated with luxury brands[125] or as an obstruction to the male's full enjoyment of the product.[126] In advertisements for yachts, men are almost always the captains. In advertisements for elite sports cars, men are almost always the drivers. In advertisements for upscale liquors, men are portrayed as sophisticated consumers, for whom the beautiful women who imbibe are rendered instantly sexually available.[127]

By number of items and by dollar spent, the majority of luxury goods are purchased and owned by men: in addition to acquiring expensive clothing, shoes, briefcases, watches, and other personal accessories,[128] men purchase high-priced technology items, luxury cars,[129]

---

[124] *Id.*

[125] Jerod, *The Greatest Used Car Ad of All Time*, Pic Chore (Nov. 10, 2010) http://picchore.com/clever/the-greatest-used-car-ad-ever/.

[126] Stefan Christoff, *Why Is CBC Running Sexist Volkswagen Ads?*, Art Threat (Dec. 7 2011) http://art-threat.net/2011/12/cbc-volkswagen-passat-ad-sexist/.

[127] Mad World Virtual Symposium, *What Liquor Ads Teach Us About Guys*, Bitch Magazine (Jun. 22, 2010), http://www.feministfrequency.com/2010/06/what-liquor-ads-teach-us-about-guys/; Copyranter, *13 of the Most Sexist Beer Ads of All Time*, BuzzFeed (May 6, 2013), http://www.buzzfeed.com/copyranter/13-of-the-most-sexist-beer-ads-of-all-time; result of Google Search with search term "sexist liquor ads" at https://.google.com/search?q=sexist+liquor+ads&espv=210&es_sm=93&tbm=isch&tbo=u&source=univ&sa=X&ei=inmzUtLoMbOwsATxm4CICA&ved=0CCsQsAQ&biw=1280&bih=922; Simon O'Connell, *Why Men Are So Important to China's Luxury Market*, Luxury Society (Feb. 5, 2013); Tara Mogan, *Sick of Sexist Booze Ads*, Boise Weekly (Aug. 7, 2009, 4:51PM), http://www.boiseweekly.com/Cobweb/archives/2009/08/07/sick-of-sexist-booze-ads.

[128] *See, e.g.*, Simon O'Connell, *Why Men Are So Important to China's Luxury Market*, Luxury Society (Feb. 5, 2013); Olivier, *Chinese Men Buy More Luxury Goods Than Chinese Women*, Marketing China (Jun. 13, 2013), http://marketingtochina.com/chinese-men-buy-more-luxury-goods-than-chinese-women/; Peter Skeadas & Michael Ghory, *The American Male's Evolving Taste for Luxury Goods*, Columbia Business School MBA White Paper Series (2012), *available at* http://www8.gsb.columbia.edu/globalbrands/sites/globalbrands/files/images/American_Males_Evolving_Taste_for_Luxury_Goods.pdf; Ned Smith, *Men Snapping Up Luxury Goods Online, Study Shows*, BusinessNewsDaily, May 2, 2012.

[129] Mark Pereira, *Study Reveals Surprise Car Buying Differences Between Men and Women*, Autoblog Canada, Jan. 28, 2014; *Male New-Car Shoppers Prefer Luxury Automakers While Females Favor Import Brands, Reports Kelley Blue Book*, PR Newswire, May 25, 2005.

private airplanes,[130] and hyper-expensive pieces of real estate[131] at rates that vastly exceed those held by women.

Yet when the luxury goods economy is criticized, it is women who are given most of the blame, as if luxury goods intended for women made up the majority of items purchased by wealthy consumers. When the wife of North Korean leader Kim Jong-un was seen in designer clothing, she was described in the *New York Times* as having a style that "magnifies how disconnected the ruling Kim family remains from the public." Though the same article mentioned Kim Jong-un's private train, French wine collection, live lobsters, and personal chef, it was a photo of his wife toting a Christian Dior handbag that was used to illustrate the couple's debauchery in an article entitled "In a Starving Nation, Luxury for a Few."[132] When a law professor sought to compare higher education with other high-priced objects of conspicuous consumption, he chose a "$31,500 ... Louis Vuitton PM Showgirl handbag."[133]

Even the seemingly well-intentioned fall into this sexist trap. When a sympathetic observer wrote an essay explaining why poor people sometimes choose to purchase designer goods to signal the status they aspire too, her examples were overwhelmingly focused on women's clothing, jewelry, and handbags.[134] In an article decrying the "gender arbitrage" that results in the exploitation of poorly paid female workers in places like China, Romania, and Saudi Arabia, luxury women's fashions are pinpointed as the primary driver of this evil, which the author acerbically describes as "the ascendancy of the designer purse."[135] When she created a T-shirt to be sold in 2008 to raise money for victims of violence in Darfur, artist Nadia Plesner depicted an African child holding a

---

130 *Private Jets*, BORNRICH RICHFILES, at http://www.bornrich.com/richfiles/private-jets/.

131 *See, e.g.*, Morgan Brennan, *$130 Million River House Residence Is Now NYC's Most Expensive Home For Sale*, FORBES, Sep. 28 2013; Jenny Pisillo, *The Three Most Expensive Real Estate Transactions of 2012*, SFGATE, Jan.14, 2014; *see generally* Stanley A. Sedo & Sherrie A. Kossoudji, *Rooms of One's Own: Gender, Race and Home Ownership as Wealth Accumulation in the United States*, THE INSTITUTE FOR THE STUDY OF LABOR (2004), *available at* http://ftp.iza.org/dp1397.pdf; http://gencen.isp.msu.edu/documents/Working_Papers/WP296.pdf; Lightstone Property, *Growth in Luxury Black Property Ownership Soars*, LIGHTSTONE PROPERTY NEWSLETTER (March 2013), *available at* http://www.lightstone.co.za/Portal/uploads/newsletters/Property_Newsletter_March_2013.pdf; Malcolm Riddell, *China's New Marriage Law May Exacerbate Gender Wealth Gap: By Leta Hong Fincher*, CHINA DEBATE, Sep. 5, 2011, *available at* http://www.chinadebate.com/2011/09/china%E2%80%99s-new-marriage-law-may-exacerbate-gender-wealth-gap-by-leta-hong-fincher/; Lorna Fox, *Re-Possessing "Home": A Re-Analysis of Gender, Homeownership, and Debtor Default for Feminist, Legal Theory*, 14 WM. & MARY J. WOMEN & L. 423 (2008); Shelly Kreiczer Levy & Meital Pinto, *Property and Belongingness: Rethinking Gender-Biased Disinheritance*, 21 TEX. J. WOMEN & L.119 (2011).

132 Choe Sang-Hun, *In a Starving Nation, Luxury for a Few*, NEW YORK TIMES, Aug. 8, 2012.

133 Paul Campos, *How a Louis Vuitton Bag Can Explain the Higher Education Bubble*, THE WEEK, Feb. 26, 2014.

134 *Why Do Poor People "Waste" Money on Luxury Goods*? TPM, Nov. 1, 2013, http://talkingpointsmemo.com/cafe/why-do-poor-people-waste-money-on-luxury-goods Tressie Mcmillan Cottom.

135 Michael B. Likoshy, *Gender Arbitrage: Law, Luxury and Labor*, 23 WIS. J.L. GENDER & SOC. 293 (2009), http://hosted.law.wisc.edu/wjlgs/issues/2008-fall/likosky_format.pdf.

Louis Vuitton-style handbag and a Chihuahua wearing a pink shirt,[136] signaling that wealthy, status-conscious women were somehow responsible for a desperate political situation that was in fact overwhelming caused by the leadership (or lack thereof) and warmongering of men.[137] Although Plesner's point, that the public pays more attention to celebrities that it does to a human rights crisis was an important one, it is telling that she felt that luxury items associated with women best communicated superficiality.

To the extent women are depicted as vapid, materialistic, and superficial luxury consumers, our claims to equality in the workplace and society generally are undermined. When we are portrayed as passive objects that affluent men can acquire, our social standing is compromised further still. While sexist advertising is hardly limited to luxury brands, it hits particularly hard at both wealthy and aspirational demographics: people who aspire to wealth and the trappings of success that money can buy, and people who have the actual wealth and its emblems of success. Luxury branding practices are therefore a particularly powerful tool of gender subordination that can be used not only against women who are wealthy and successful but also against those women who hope to create the illusion that they have those same attributes.

---

[136] http://boingboing.net/2011/03/28/louis-vuitton-sues-a.html.

[137] *See generally* Jeevan Vasagar and Ewen MacAskill, *180,000 Die From Hunger In Darfur*, The Guardian, Mar. 16, 2005; *Darfur Genocide*, Jewish World Watch, *available at* http://www.jewishworldwatch.org/conflictareas/sudan/overview/sudan-genocide; *Conflict as a Cause of Hunger*, United Nation University, *available at* http://archive.unu.edu/unupress/unupbooks/uu22we/uu22we0j.htm. See also http://hyperallergic.com/21392/nadia-plesner-vs-louis-vuitton/

IV Law for the 1%? Concerns from Distributive Justice

NYC: Tolerant of your beliefs, judgmental of your shoes.[1]

9 Upstairs/Downstairs, Fashionwise

A VIEW OF DESIGN PROTECTION FROM LOWER DOWN THE FOOD CHAIN

Diane Leenheer Zimmerman*

I. Introduction

The claim that fashion designers need intellectual property protection to thrive and maximize their creative output is one that has prompted sharp disagreements for decades, particularly in the United States. Under American law, the stuff of fashion must grab its scant protections higgledy-piggledy under trademark law, design patents, and from the fringes of copyright.[2] To some, that result is just fine. Jonathan Barnett has hypothesized that even frankly counterfeit fashion items of obviously lower quality may actually benefit the designers of the originals by increasing the "snob value" of the designer

* Samuel Tilden Professor of Law Emerita, New York University School of Law.

[1] Advertisement for Manhattan Mini-Storage Company, 2012. A copy of the advertisement can be found at http://observer.com/2013/05/do-manhattan-mini-storage-ads-count-as-literature/.

[2] Because copyright does not protect "useful articles," 17 U.S.C. §102(b), clothing, except for separable decorative elements, is not covered by that body of law. See Copyright Office, Registrability of Costume Designs (1991), at http://www.copyright.gov/history/mls/ML-435.pd, excerpted from 56 Fed. Reg. 56530 (Nov. 5, 1991) for a discussion of the issue. The available intellectual property protections in the United States for fashion design are discussed in Linna T. Loangkote, *Note, Fashioning a New Look in Intellectual Property: Sui Generis Protection for the Innovative Designer*, 63 HASTINGS L. J. 297, 303–7 (2011).

good, and by encouraging people to buy the "real thing."[3] Raustiala and Sprigman have concluded that the lack of comprehensive protections for designers, net-net, has been generally beneficial: we have enjoyed gains to innovation, they argue, from allowing the fashion cycle to be driven at high speed, at least in significant part by the absence of serious intellectual property protection.[4]

Others, as one might expect, vigorously disagree.[5] Many countries, they point out, do offer such protection, a strong hint to the skeptical that, once more, the United States is behind the international curve in modernizing its law. The interests of established designers and new ones are delineated at length. Even the claim of wealthy consumers not to have their distinctive brands imitated by the lower classes is given credence as a reason to maintain design exclusivity.[6] The success of major copyists—Forever 21, Zara's and H & M—is put forth to illustrate the damage designers face from dilution of the relative inaccessibility to ordinary folk of their output.[7] Advocates of protection less sympathetic to the snob value of fashion nevertheless may remain convinced that designers need (and deserve) more comprehensive coverage under intellectual property law. Fashion design, they remind the reader, is akin to the kinds of creativity that go into the creation of formal artworks or literature.[8]

It is not my aim in this chapter to enter the fray over the merits of the fashion debate on the same terms in which it has been framed thus far. Rather, my purpose is to suggest another reason for Congress to exercise caution in changing the existing regime.

---

[3] Jonathan M. Barnett, *Shopping for Gucci on Canal Street: Reflections on Status Consumption, Intellectual Property, and the Incentive Thesis*, 91 VA. L. REV. 1381, 1399–408 (2005)

[4] *See generally* Kal Raustiala & Christopher Sprigman, *The Piracy Paradox: Innovation and Intellectual Property in Fashion Design*, 92 VA. L. REV. 1687 (2006); KAL RAUSTIALA & CHRISTOPHER SPRIGMAN, THE KNOCKOFF ECONOMY at 19–55 (2012). Indeed to some scholars, the constant change in style is what defines fashion. Svendsen says that "something is fashion only if it functions in a socially distinctive way and is part of a system that replaces it relatively quickly with something new." LARS SVENDSEN, FASHION: A PHILOSOPHY 14 (trans. John Irons, 2006) (2004).

[5] Among the more notable of the numerous proponents of fashion design protection are Susan Scafidi and co-authors C. Scott Hemphill and Jeannie Suk. C. Scott Hemphill & Jeannie Suk, *The Law, Culture and Economics of Fashion*, 61 STAN. L. REV. 1147 (2009); Susan Scafidi, *F.I.T.: Fashion as Information Technology*, 59 SYRACUSE L. REV. 69 (2008). See also Loangkote, *supra* note 2.

[6] Kristin L. Black, *Crimes of Fashion: Is Imitation Truly the Sincerest Form of Flattery?*, 19 KANSAS J. L. & PUB. POL. 505, 524 (2010). She says once the Burberry plaid was adopted by lower-class British, garments using it ceased to be sufficiently distinctive to appeal to many of Burberry's wealthy consumers. Nizar Souiden, Bouthaina M'Saad, & Frank Pons, *A Cross-Cultural Analysis of Consumers' Conspicuous Consumption of Branded Fashion Accessories*, 23 J. INTERN'L CONSUMER MARKETING 329, 339–40 (2011) (mass marketing by luxury fashion houses would hurt sales of their goods to individuals engaged in conspicuous consumption).

[7] Laura Howard, *An Uningenious Paradox: Intellectual Property Protections for Fashion Designs*, 32 COLUM. J. L. & ARTS 333, 341–44 (2009).

[8] "The right to intellectual property ownership is crucial for encouraging innovation among our country's artist and scientists, and the exact same reasoning applies to fashion design." Sara R. Ellis, Comment: *Copyrighting Couture: An Examination of Fashion Design Protection and Why the DPPA and IDPPA Are a Step Towards the Solution to Counterfeit Chic*, 78 TENN. L. REV. 163, 186 (2010).

What I refer to is an interest that thus far has surfaced only in the briefest and most tangential way in this debate: the consumer's stake in "knockoff" fashion.[9] This chapter makes no attempt to address the issue of counterfeits, fashion articles that, by using fake labels or trademarks, falsely purport to come from a particular designer or design house. Rather, I focus on "knockoffs," copies or close adaptations of "status" clothing and accessories, that do not pretend to be produced by famous designers but because of their lower purchase prices are accessible to consumers with widely varying degrees of purchasing power. I suggest that positive social benefits flow from a legal regime that allows ready access to knockoffs, and that these benefits deserve considerable weight in deciding how to proceed. This position will undoubtedly seem odd to some—akin perhaps to suggesting that we should not enforce copyrights if the public would benefit from acquiring the works of authors for free. The immediate counter-argument would be that even if they benefit from lower prices, in the long run, people will be harmed because, deprived of sufficient reward, creators will lack the incentive to produce new works.

But that argument does not work well here. The issue is whether to create new protections where they previously did not exist and where the target industry is already doing quite well. The designs for articles of clothing, except for unusual cases where patent law applies, or where only the decorative overlays and textile patterns are at issue, have never been protected in the United States. Nevertheless, clothing designers continue to compete for fame and customers in that country. Although French copyright law has covered clothing design since the eighteenth century,[10] elsewhere in the world designers of clothing, shoes, and handbags generally have made do with no, or with largely ineffective, intellectual property protection, aside from trademarks, throughout much of the modern era. Protection, to the extent it has existed, has been a work in progress—ratcheted up mostly in the latter half of the twentieth century, well after the development of a modern, mass-manufactured clothing industry. Sweden, for example, did not include fashion under its intellectual property laws at all until 1960.[11] Clothing protection in most countries is lumped under the general category of design protection, along with washing machines and kitchen gadgets. The impetus for the earliest form of design protection in Japan, which did not widely adopt Western-style clothing (and with it the so-called fashion cycle) until the mid-twentieth century,[12] was for textiles

---

[9] Social justice concerns in intellectual property have been raised by numerous scholars, most significantly in the fashion and luxury goods area by Haochen Sun. Haochen Sun, *Can Louis Vuitton Dance with HiPhone? Rethinking the Idea of Social Justice in Intellectual Property Law*, 15 U. PA. J. L. & SOC. CHANGE 389 (2012).

[10] France has protected the design of clothes since its first copyright act in 1793. Tedmond Wong, *Comment, To Copy or Not to Copy, That Is the Question: The Game Theory Approach to Protecting Fashion Designs*, 160 U. PA. L. REV. 1139, 1149–50 (2012).

[11] Marianne Dahlén, *Copy or Copyright Fashion? Swedish Design Protection Law in Historical and Comparative Perspective*, 54 BUSINESS HISTORY 88, 100 (2012).

[12] TOBY SLADE, JAPANESE FASHION: A CULTURAL HISTORY 7 (2009) ("In terms of making that ultimate self-identification as modern, donning Western-style clothing, the majority of the population waited until well into the twentieth century.")

rather than the clothes made from them.[13] As the scope of design protection expanded, it nevertheless tended to be weak and rarely much enforced.[14] Not until the Design Act of 1959 was a heightened level of design protection with a modernized registration system put into place.[15] Although Britain, like Japan, had long offered special protection to its textile industry, for a very long time fashion seems not to have been a particular focus of its interest. Even after a comprehensive design registration system became available in 1949,[16] the fashion industry felt under-protected; as a result, more particularized protection was enacted in 1988 in the form of the Copyright, Designs and Patents Act.[17] The European Union, in fact, was sufficiently concerned about the spottiness and inconsistencies in its members' national law on the subject of design to propose a directive requiring more uniform protection in 1991.[18] The scheme went into effect in 1998.[19]

In short, the reliance of designers on intellectual property protection has, historically, been weak, if it existed at all, and coverage has only made major inroads in recent years. Nevertheless, the market for designers' work remained robust, leaving the empirical evidence of the need for a serious regime of legal protection murky at best. If the United States Congress finally decides to adopt protection for fashion design after decades of first considering and then tabling design protection generally, its position—given the uncertainties—will be based on conjecture rather than solid evidence about whether going that route will lead to a more favorable outcome for designers.

In the face of the uncertain factual predicate for such legislation, legislative deliberation should be careful to take account of all the players with an interest in the

---

[13] Christopher Heath, *Intellectual Property and Anti-Trust* in HISTORY OF LAW IN JAPAN SINCE 1868 at 459 (ed. Wilhelm Röhl, 2005).

[14] *Id.* at 406.

[15] *Id.* at 459. See Design Act, Act No. 25 of 1959, available in an unofficial translation at http://www.cas.go.jp/jp/seisaku/hourei/data/DACT.pdf. The law was amended in 2006 to extend the term from 15 to 20 years. http://www.wipo.int/wipolex/en/details.jsp?id=7080.

[16] Intellectual Property Office, History of Designs, at http://www.ipo.gov.uk/types/design/d-about/d-whatis/d-history.htm.

[17] British Copyright Council, Protection of Designs in the UK: Fashion Design (Information Sheet 17), *available at* http://www.britishcopyright.org/pdfs/info/infosheet017.pdf (last visited May 7, 2012). Under this law, a garment can be protected under copyright if it is a work of artistic craftsmanship. Other garments receive shorter terms of protection under the design right. *Id.*

[18] At the time the European Union began to consider harmonization of design protection law, 11 member states had some kind of design registration system domestically, and seven member states adhered to the 1925 Hague Agreement on the International Deposit of Models and Designs. Some states had no domestic law on the subject. Commission of the European Communities, Green Paper on the Protection of Industrial Design at 2 (1991), *available at* http://aei.pitt.edu/1785/1/design_gp_1.pdf.

[19] European Parliament and Council, Directive 98/71/EC on the Legal Protection of Designs (Oct. 1998), *available at* http://eur-lex.europa.eu/LexUriServ.do?uri=CELEX:31998L0071:en:html. The initial Design Directive required that members permit registration of designs, including apparel, giving the owner exclusive rights for a minimum of five years, with renewals that could extend protection up to 25 years. Subsequently, in 2002, an additional change was made, allowing "new" designs with "individual character" to be protected without registration for three years. Council Regulation 6/2002, 2002 O.J. (L 3) 1 (EC).

outcome—not just designers and manufacturers, garment workers, and retailers but the ordinary clothing customer her- or himself, whose life is affected by access to status goods and look-alikes in ways that have simply gone unrecognized. This chapter will focus, therefore, on the concerns of those largely ignored fashion consumers of middling to modest means who have, for various reasons, barely been visible in the current debate. In section II, this chapter outlines a series of factors that help explain why the claims of these consumers have played such a minor role in the debate here and abroad on protecting fashion designers. Section III then turns to an examination of what is at stake for ordinary consumers from a political and psychosocial perspective. It discusses the expressive role of dress as well as its role in supporting basic beliefs in social egalitarianism. In the final section, the actual legislative regime proposed in the United States will be examined, and the reasons why this author remains convinced that fashion design protection is, on the whole, simply a bad idea.

II. She's Frivolous, She's Female, and She's Unliberated Besides

When the House of Representatives held hearings on proposed versions of bills to protect fashion design in 2006 and again in 2011, the witnesses were either representatives from various sectors of the fashion industry or academics who debated the wisdom of passing such laws based on economic theory and on disparate views of the need for new spurs to innovation.[20] No consumer representatives testified. In short, the consumer of fashion has remained largely underground and invisible in the design protection debate. This result is partly attributable to the workings of public choice theory, but I would argue that it is also fairly attributable to three quite different but inexorably linked beliefs: fashion is frivolous, fashion appeals mostly to women, and women who care about fashion simply are exhibiting their unfortunate tendencies toward consumerism and toward the embrace of their male-defined roles as sex symbols.

With such a trifecta of suspicious attributes, it can scarcely be surprising that the interest of the average consumer has played such a minor role in determining the desirability of fashion design protection. The only consumer who seems to count at all in discussions of legislative responses is the one whose means allow her to purchase the high-end

[20] In 2006, the witnesses were a fashion designer, Jeffrey Banks, Professor Christopher Sprigman (an opponent of the bill), Professor Susan Scafidi (an advocate for designers), and David Wolfe of the Doneger Group, a leading fashion forecasting group. H. R. Comm. on Jud., Hearing on H.R. 5055, 109th Cong., 2nd Sess., July 27, 2006, *available at* http://www.gpo.gov/fdsys/pkg/CHRG-109hhrg28908/html/CHRG-109hhrg28908.htm . In 2011, they were again Professor Sprigman, Professor Jeannie Suk of Harvard, Lazaro Hernandez (the designer for and co-founder of Proenza Schouler), and Kurt Courtney, representing the American Apparel and Footwear Assoc. *See* House of Rep. Comm. on Jud. Hearing Info. On H.R. 25ll, 112nd Cong., July 15, 2011. *See* http://judiciary.house.gov/index.cfm/hearings?ID=37AE0CA8-DDD2-A2C3-1583-835F17835ED6 (last visited April 6, 2015).

couture or ready-to-wear clothes and accessories produced by the would-be-protected class of designers. It is this consumer who acts as an advertisement for the skills of the designers and whose purchases reinforce their claims to exclusivity. This customer, too, is female, "frivolous," and "unliberated," but without her and the contents of her wallet, the creation of "fine design" in apparel would lack an economic point.

The presence of these elements clearly accounts for the defensive tone many academics feel compelled to take in explaining their interest in fashion as a discipline. As one such scholar remarked, "One who dares broach the topic [of fashion before a group of academics] will have confessed an interest in a subject that the group agrees bespeaks vanity or worse."[21] Another observed that "Much of what has been written on the subject of fashion by philosophers has been negative. . . ."[22] Even those who cared a great deal personally about their appearance could be dismissive of the desire in others to be fashionable. Immanuel Kant, one of the earliest modern thinkers to write about clothes, is described by Lars Svendsen as much given himself to silk shirts and silver shoe buckles,[23] but, nevertheless, he denigrated the practice of following fashion as belonging "to the style of courtiers, especially ladies."[24]

The evils attributed to an interest in clothing and physical appearance have been numerous. Centuries ago, the alleged harm was attempting to climb above one's station in a socially static society, and such effrontery was countered with sumptuary laws, laws (not coincidentally) largely enforced against women.[25]

Over time, arguments against paying attention to fashion have ranged from the accusation that fashion-consciousness creates an overemphasis on "change for its own sake, the body, imitation, superficiality," to charges that it results in "limiting of independence of women."[26] Add to this list such other ills as fostering of "depthless materialism," and encouragement of "perpetual dissatisfaction over one's current lifestyle and physical appearance,"[27] and it is easy to understand why any interest a consumer may

---

[21] Samantha Brennan, *Fashion and Sexual Identity, or Why Recognition Matters*, in FASHION: PHILOSOPHY FOR EVERYONE 121 (Jessica Wolfendale & Jeanette Kennett, eds., 2011) [hereinafter PHILOSOPHY].

[22] Marguerite La Caze, *A Taste for Fashion*, in PHILOSOPHY, *id.* at 200. John Harvey points out that, in Plato's Republic, Socrates expressed dismay at excessive attention to dress, directing his greatest ire toward matters having "to do with women's adornment." JOHN HARVEY, CLOTHES 8 (2008).

[23] SVENDSEN, *supra* note 4, at 18. Kant is quoted by Svendsen as having once said that "It is always better ... to be a fool in fashion than a fool out of fashion." *Id.*

[24] IMMANUEL KANT, ANTHROPOLOGY FROM A PRAGMATIC POINT OF VIEW 246 (Robert B. Louden trans., 2006). *See also* Dwight E. Robinson, *The Economics of Fashion Demand*, 75 QUARTERLY J. ECON. 376, 378 (1961) (noting that the study of fashion "has had a rather checkered career; after all, it bespeaks a side of life which rationally disposed men are bound to dismiss as sheer feminine caprice").

[25] ALAN HUNT, THE GOVERNANCE OF CONSUMING PASSIONS 214 (1996).

[26] La Caze, *supra* note 22, at 200.

[27] Craig J. Thompson & Diana L. Haytko, *Speaking of Fashion: Consumers' Uses of Fashion Discourses and the Appropriation of Countervailing Cultural Meaning*, 24 J. CONSUMER RES. 15, 16 (1997).

have in fashion and "looking good" has received less than comprehensive attention in the debate over protection of designers.

A claim that has particularly muddied the fashion waters is that assumption that women's interest in clothes is a trap designed by men to exploit hapless (or infantilized) females. Thorstein Veblen, in his much-celebrated book, *The Theory of the Leisure Class*, contended that clothes were not only a marker of social status. They were also a tool for turning the women in the families of prosperous men into display objects, embodying tangible evidence of the male's success by making clear that he could afford costly clothes for "his females," and perhaps even more important, that they need not lift a hand in common labor. Veblen called this phenomenon Conspicuous Leisure, and tartly noted, "The substantial reason for our tenacious attachment to the skirt is just that: it is expensive and it hampers the wearer at every turn and incapacitates her for all useful exertion."[28]

Although the times, as well as the lives of women, have changed greatly since Veblen's day, his take on fashion as a constraint on the freedom of women remains, expressed now in the writings of modern feminists who see women as bullied by cultural pressures to model themselves after some feminine ideal, and even as guilty of colluding with their own oppression. Simone de Beauvoir, in her famous work, *The Second Sex*, expressed early on what has become received wisdom about the sexist forces at work in promoting the interest women in clothes:

> A man's clothes, like his body, should indicate his transcendence and not attract attention; for him neither elegance nor good looks call for his setting himself up as object. Moreover, he does not normally consider his appearance as a reflection of his ego.
>
> Woman, on the contrary, is even required by society to make herself an erotic object. Fashion, to which she is enslaved, is not to reveal her as an independent individual, but rather to cut her off from her transcendence in order to offer her as prey to male desires. . . .[29]

---

[28] THORSTEIN VEBLEN, THE THEORY OF THE LEISURE CLASS 126 (Modern Library 2001) (1899).

[29] SIMONE DE BEAUVOIR, THE SECOND SEX 498 (trans. H.M. Parshley, Bantam 1961) (1949). A study done in the 1950s by a Columbia sociologist supported this claim. He said that, while women did dress for prestige and status, "The real basis of conformity [to fashion] seems to be the desire to be attractive to men, though this fact was not consciously recognized." W. Godfrey Cobliner, *Feminine Fashion as an Aspect of Group Psychology: Analysis of Written Replies Received by Means of a Questionnaire*, 31 J. SOC. PSYCHOLOGY 283, 289 (1950). To that, Charlotte Perkins Gilman, an early twentieth-century sociologist, would likely have replied, well, what would you expect them to dress for as long as they remain dependent on men for their economic well-being? CHARLOTTE PERKINS GILMAN, THE DRESS OF WOMEN: A CRITICAL INTRODUCTION TO THE SYMBOLISM AND SOCIOLOGY OF CLOTHING 95–96, 105 (eds. Michael R. Hill and Mary Jo Deagan, 2001) (collecting Gilman's 1915 essays).

It is certainly fair to state that women have been bullied by the expectation that they always look their best; but so, too, have they been accused when they try to meet that expectation of frivolousness, triviality, and conformity to stereotypes.[30] Particular styles and colors of clothes have also been imposed to mark off distinctions between males and females and to set standards for what is considered appropriate for each sex.[31] Deviations from those standards can carry with them considerable peril. Western women wear the color pink, skirts, panty hose, and high heels; men only rarely wear pink (shirts on occasion), and—with the exception of kilts—would be seen as engaging in seriously transgressive behavior if they were to appear in such "female" attire as a skirt. Women who wanted to wear pants, which are comfortable and afford greater ease of movement, had an uphill fight to do so, against stubborn social norms that took a long while to overcome. As an example, four members of the Women Air Force Service Pilots corps (WASPS) were arrested in a town in Georgia during World War II for wearing pants on the street during the evening.[32] I remember well, in the 1960s, Manhattan restaurants that would not seat a woman in a pantsuit, and, as well, law firms that continued almost until the twenty-first century to ban trousers in the office for female attorneys. What woman of a certain age, wearing pants, has not been chastised—only partly in jest—by a male who remarks, "Is something wrong with your legs?"

No matter which way one approaches the subject of fashion, one is likely to crash into a wall of sexism. Women's interest in their appearance is so commonly used to trivialize them that one is apt not to notice when it happens. Gail Collins, in her book *America's Women*, gives an excellent illustration. She tells the story of courageous military nurses who survived captivity during World War II in a Japanese prison camp in Manila. The women, who had already survived the Bataan death march, managed as a group to stay alive during their imprisonment while many others died of "malnutrition and tropical diseases."[33] But, Collins reports, after their release, it was not their heroism that reporters wrote about. Rather, she notes, "[T]he stories about them almost always focused on things like their eagerness to buy cosmetics and to investigate the newest hairstyles."[34]

While it is hoped that the stories would be written differently now, stereotypes remain. What is deemed important, and what is deemed insignificant or even morally deficient,

---

[30] Psychoanalytic interpretations exist as well. John Harvey reports that clothing, according to Neo-Freudians, permits a masquerade in which "the performance of womanly identity, including the priority given to clothes, is conditioned by anxiety about the absence of a phallus." HARVEY, *supra* note 22, at 8.

[31] "Dress demarcates and secures gender. Clothing is one of the basic mechanisms that provides for the legibility of sex and gender. If clothes convey and represent gender it follows that projects concerned with the regulation of dress must, whether intentionally or not, have an impact on the regulation of gender." HUNT, *supra* note 25, at 216.

[32] GAIL COLLINS, AMERICA'S WOMEN: FOUR HUNDRED YEARS OF DOLLS, DRUDGES, HELPMATES, AND HEROINES 368 (2003).

[33] *Id.* at 364.

[34] *Id.*

is all too often defined against a male norm.[35] As a woman lawyer and academic, I cannot imagine opening a discussion with female colleagues in the faculty lounge about clothes shopping—not because women in my position are uninterested in clothes but because we are more interested in being taken seriously by our peers. Having males overhear that particular conversation would not further the cause. On the other hand, lively discussions of sports or restaurants or the latest films are completely "appropriate" topics for discussion because they fall into familiar male or cross-gendered territory.

Enough has been said by now to alert interested readers and policymakers alike of the risk that under-explored assumptions may be masking the possibility that significant interests at stake in the fashion design protection debate are not being captured because attention is paid almost exclusively to the concerns of designers and their high-end clients.

III. What Do Women Want? Why We Shop

A. THE POLITICS OF CLOTHES

The subject of clothes and their importance to those who wear them is a matter of psychological, aesthetic, and creative significance. The choice of what to buy and what to wear also raises sociopolitical concerns, implicating issues of personal freedom, distributive justice, and power dynamics within a nation.

1. Clothes and Self-Creation: The Politics of Dressing

An observer once asked, "What does fashion have to do with politics? Many people take fashion to be private and trivial, while politics is public and important, yet from time to time, fashion's political importance is easier to see."[36] What he pointed out is both that clothes speak, and that people dress to say something. While the consumer's interest in having an extensive choice of styles to adopt does not ordinarily resonate with the casual observer as a serious liberty interest, it can actually raise such an issue if examined carefully.

The political significance of symbolic communication through dress can be subtle, but not always. One obvious example is the choice of Muslim women to adopt or reject the wearing of head scarves or veils. Clearly this is not merely personal. It tells us something about the nature of the women's religious beliefs, and also, in many countries,

---

[35] Note that this norm of male "indifference" to fashion is both overstated and also highly variable over time. Quentin Bell points out that men were often dandies in other periods of Western history, changing their dress to keep current with the times. QUENTIN BELL, ON HUMAN FINERY 91–92.

[36] Jonathan Miller, *Fashion and Democratic Relationships*, 37 POLITY 3 (2003). *See also* JENNIFER CRAIK, FASHION: THE KEY CONCEPTS (2009) 298 ("Very often, overt political action and ideology have been at the heart of clothing conventions").

how she relates to the will of the state and of authority figures.[37] When women in the Pacific Islands adopted the long, shapeless dress known as the Mother Hubbard, they were not making a charmingly frivolous fashion statement, but were responding to the pressure and shaming they experienced from Western missionaries who were appalled by the amount of flesh that indigenous forms of attire revealed.[38]

Dress is often a symbolic representation of a society's image of itself. In class-bound, hierarchical societies, norms of attire were enforced by sumptuary laws used to delineate people visually by class and occupation. The laws designated the appropriate costuming for various groups' stations in life.[39] Societies can also flip the use of dress and turn it into a device that ameliorates class and social markers. Uniform dress as a leveler was a favorite trope of utopian writers,[40] and marked out the Maoist period in China. The unadorned gray and blue Mao suits adopted by the Chinese for at least three decades not only blurred distinctions between the formerly wealthy and the proletariat, but ameliorated gender lines as well.[41] In a study of the relationship between women's status and attire, its author found that adoption of a unisex style of clothing in the People's Republic of China corresponded with the government's new policy of encouraging women to work outside the home. Women's labor at the time was seen as necessary to achieve increased economic productivity.[42] In the 1960s and 1970s in the United States, styles of dress were markers for social and political views as much as personal taste. Hippie-style attire, along with miniskirts for women and facial hair for men all spoke to

---

[37] In France, for example, Muslim women have been fired from jobs for wearing headscarves and fined for covering their faces. BBC News Europe, *French Veil Law: Muslim Woman's Challenge in Strasbourg,* November 27, 2013, *available at* http://www.bbc.uk/news/world-europe-25118160. Turkey once banned headscarves in government buildings entirely. Those restrictions are now being eroded. Associated Press, *Turkey's Female MPs Wear Headscarves in Parliament for the First Time,* THE GUARDIAN, Oct. 31, 2013, *available at* http://www.theguardian.com/world/2013/oct/31/turkey-female-mps-headscarves-parliament-end-ban.

[38] *See, e.g.*, Frédéric Angleviel, Marissa Dooris, Vikram Iyer, *Dress in New Caledonia*, in 7 BERG ENCYCLOPEDIA OF WORLD DRESS AND FASHION: AUSTRALIA, NEW ZEALAND, AND THE PACIFIC ISLANDS (2010), *available at* http://www.bergfashionlibrary.com/view/bewdf/BEWDF-v7/EDch7076.xml.

[39] *See generally* HUNT, *supra* note 25.

[40] *See, e.g.*, THOMAS MORE, UTOPIA, OF THEIR TRADES AND MANNER OF LIFE (Project Gutenberg 2005) (1516): "Throughout the island they wear the same sort of clothes, without any other distinction except what is necessary to distinguish the two sexes and the married and unmarried." *Available at* http://www.gutenberg.org/files/2130/2130-h/2130-h.htm.

[41] It should be noted, however, that distinctions were not totally erased. In a visit to China in the early 1980s, the author observed that people in positions of power or authority often wore Mao suits of distinctly better cut, fit, and fabric than ordinary people.

[42] Darlene Ora Standridge Ford, *Fashion Indicators of Women's Social Status* at 210–15 (UMI Dissertation Information Service 1986). As a visitor to large cities in China in the late 1980s, when uniformity of dress was in decline, it was fascinating to see people wearing whatever Western clothes they could get in their desire for modernity and sartorial freedom, even when the attire was arguably dangerous to the wearer. The author of this chapter, for example, observed a young woman repairing the tile on the roof of a temple, dressed in a flowered skirt and a pair of high-heeled sandals.

the sense of youthful rebellion against an unpopular war and an older (and presumably out-of-touch) generation.

That unorthodox choices of attire are transgressive is well understood, and societies do not need sumptuary laws or the imposition of formal dress codes to erect standards that one crosses at one's peril. The author Quentin Bell has observed that a sort of morality attaches to dress. When he was writing in the late 1970s, he pointed out that it would be viewed as a violation of an important social code to attend the theater unshaven, or to wear suspenders over otherwise impeccably correct evening clothes.[43] But he went on to add:

> In "good" society it is not however sheer lunatic eccentricity such as the absence of trousers or a wig worn back to front which excites the strongest censure; far worse are those subtler forms of incorrect attire: the "wrong" tie, the "bad" hat, the "loud" skirt, the "cheap" scent, or the flamboyant checks of the overdressed vulgarian. Here the censure excited is almost exactly comparable to that occasioned by dishonourable conduct.[44]

Efforts to ensure conformity to social norms in appearance can come perilously (if not always obviously) close to censorship. The effort of professional women entering the workplace in the 1970s and 1980s to overcome patriarchal assumptions about their capabilities was expressed through the perceived imperative to be very careful about what to wear.[45] A difficult balance had to be maintained among competing and sometimes inconsistent objectives: avoiding sexualized clothing while also avoiding overly masculine dress—and also selecting clothes that communicated "competence."[46] Schools' and employers' expectations of conformity to sartorial norms could also exert subtle racist pressure by demanding, for example, that African-Americans eschew Afro hairstyles or corn braids. Paulette Caldwell has written movingly on experiencing the reactions of non-blacks to such elements of appearance. She concluded:

> Hairstyle choices are an important mode of self-expression. For blacks, and particularly for black women, such choices also reflect the search for a survival mechanism in a culture where social, political, and economic choices of racialized individuals

---

[43] Bell, *supra* note 35–6, at 19.

[44] *Id.*

[45] Susan Faludi, Backlash: The Undeclared War against American Women (1991) 171, 176 (women dressing for work wanted suits; they did not want frills or clothes that made them look like young girls).

[46] Kate Gillan, *Choosing an Image: Exploring Women's Images through the Personal Shopper, in* Through The Wardrobe: Women's Relationships with Their Clothes 74 (Ali Guy, Maura Green, & Eileen Banim eds., 2001). Quentin Bell commented on the upside of this phenomenon. He noted that as women have become more and more emancipated, they have more freedom to choose more functional clothes because they are less and less forced into the role of symbolizing "conspicuous consumption." Bell, *supra* note 35, at 164.

> and groups are conditioned by the extent to which their physical characteristics, both mutable and immutable, approximate those of the dominant racial group. Hair becomes a proxy for legitimacy and determines the extent to which individual blacks can crossover from the private world of segregation and colonization (and historically, in the case of black women, service in another's home) into the mainstream of American life.[47]

William Keenan generalizes on this point, arguing that, "Dress is clearly neither culturally nor politically neutral. It is loaded with significance."[48] The ability to choose freely what to wear and how to look implicates, in his view, "freedom of expression and self-determination, individual liberty and human rights."[49]

I do not want to make too much of this argument or to imply that limiting variety in available dress through design legislation is ipso facto a free speech violation. But nonetheless it is important to remember that freedom to dress as one chooses is inextricably intertwined with self-expression and personal autonomy. This connection provides one hint that cutting off access to knockoffs of new designs implicates interests that go far deeper than mere vanity.

B. THE POLITICS OF CLOTHES: THE PSYCHOLOGY OF SELF-CREATION

On a psychological level, we dress not merely for warmth or to cover our nudity but to communicate about our personas to others. Modern writers on the sociology and psychology of clothing choice claim that today people dress to express their identities or to create them rather than to raise their apparent social status by emulating wealthier consumers (as they did in the late nineteenth century). As this article will show, the differences between the nineteenth century and today may well be overstated. But one change is clear: the wide availability at present of fashionable attire at a range of prices enables a large swath of the population in Western countries, and increasingly in non-Western ones as well, to experiment with dress for pleasure, to play with identities, and to affiliate with desirable groups or role models that may be, but often are not, defined by levels of affluence.

---

[47] Paulette M. Caldwell, *A Hair Piece: Perspectives on the Intersection of Race and Gender*, [1991] DUKE L. J. 365, 383. Anita Franklin agrees. She writes that the sexualization of hair braids in the movie *10* "cost many professional Black women time, money, and valuable energy in their subsequent fight for the right to be able to (continue to) wear braids on their job." Anita Franklin, *Black Women and Self-Presentation: Appearing in (Dis)guise, in* Guy, Green, & Banim, *supra* note 46, 155.

[48] William J. F. Keenan, *Dress Freedom, in* DRESSED TO IMPRESS: LOOKING THE PART 181 (William Keenan ed., 2001).

[49] *Id.* at 186.

The use of adornment as a source of pleasure and play may be innate across the universe of primates. Hurlock reports that when gestalt psychologist Wolfgang Kohler, who was famous for his studies of chimpanzees, gave the animals ribbons, they draped them around themselves and pranced around displaying their finery, giving every appearance of enjoying themselves enormously. "As Professor Kohler has said," she wrote, "'the objects hanging about the body serve the function of adornment in the widest sense. The trotting about of apes with objects hanging around them not only looks funny, it also seems to give them naive pleasure.'"[50]

That dress is a source of pleasure is beyond doubt. At least three sources of pleasure from clothing have been identified: touch—the feel of the fabric; bonding with others through sharing, discussing, or shopping for clothes; and enablement of fantasy.[51] And that pleasure is cross-cultural as well as cross-species. The authors of a study of the second-hand clothing market in Zambia, for instance, concluded that "There is genuine pleasure to be gained from being dressed well which in the view of local observers is a sign of well-being."[52]

Even though today no one "fashion" standard is dictated from on high and individuals who can gain access to contemporary styles happily put them together in their own ways,[53] the ability to be "in fashion" remains significant across economic and social lines. Being able to select from a wide range of interesting clothing facilitates the central human activity of identity creation because, as Svendsen pointed out, clothes are an extension of the person wearing them. Their role in establishing identity has become much more crucial in an era when the details of sartorial appearance are no longer imposed by tradition.[54]

One use of dress is to engage in the usually pleasurable process of self-enhancement, displaying our bodies in ways that, in our eyes, are attractive to ourselves and appealing to others.[55] In fact, it has often been said that we dress not so much for ourselves as for others. But what does the other-directedness of our choice of attire mean? That turns out to be a complex and meaty topic. Writers on fashion identify a number of motives for the interest in and choice of clothing, ranging from a desire to fit in to the hope of

---

[50] Elizabeth B. Hurlock, The Psychology of Dress: An Analysis of Fashion and Its Motive 22 (Ayer Co. 1984) (1929).

[51] La Caze, *supra* note 22, at 211. *See also* Stuart U. Rich & Subhash C. Jain, *Social Class and Life Cycle as Predictors of Shopping Behavior*, 5 J. Marketing Res. 41, 44 (1968) (women across social classes took pleasure from the "recreational and social aspects of shopping").

[52] Karen Tranberg Hansen, *Youth, Gender and Second-Hand Clothing in Lusaka, Zambia, in* Fabric of Cultures: Fashion, Identity and Globalization 131 (Eugenia Paulicelli & Hazel Clark eds., 2008).

[53] Diana Crane, Fashion and Its Social Agendas: Class, Gender, and Identity in Clothing 134–35 (2000).

[54] Svendsen, *supra* note 4, at 19. He adds that aesthetics is central to "the formation of identity." Svendsen, *supra* note 4, at 141–42.

[55] Jane Schneider, *From Potlatch to Wal-Mart: Courtly and Capitalist Hierarchies through Dress, in* Paulicelli & Clark, *supra* note 52-3, at 30; Susan B. Kaiser, Richard H. Nagasawa, & Sandra S. Hutton, *Fashion, Postmodernity and Personal Appearance*, 14 Symbolic Interaction 165, 172 (1991).

attracting members of the opposite sex to the desire to stand out from the crowd. But there is general agreement that, whatever else dress facilitates, it allows us to experiment with and project our preferred social identities.[56] Goffman has posited that when individuals interact with others, they strive to present an "idealized performance" of the identity they want others to see. "When an individual plays a part," Goffman wrote, "he implicitly requests his observers to take seriously the impression that is fostered before them. They are asked to believe that the character they see actually possesses the attributes he appears to possess. . . ."[57] Although this may sound as though people are seriously engaged in the perpetration of fraud by creating their preferred identity, Goffman denies that this is typically the case. Some image-making may indeed be in the service of illegal or anti-social behavior, but most falls within the limits of complete acceptability, such as dying one's hair to appear younger than one is.[58] In other instances, the image one wishes to present is one that will be congruent with the role one is playing at a particular moment. For example, a man who dresses carefully for business in a gray suit, white shirt, and conservative tie is not "lying" about his identity, even if, when he returns home, he relaxes in tattered shorts and tennis sneakers.

The management of one's public persona is facilitated by the use of what Goffman calls "sign vehicles"[59] associated with social class or with a particular group with which the individual wishes to affiliate. Prominent among such sign vehicles is attire. One example he gives, however, to illustrate the hazards associated with this use of sign vehicles to signify membership in a class or group is the shame the performer feels upon discovering that her slip is showing below the hem of her dress. "[W]e must be prepared to see that the impression of reality fostered by a performance is a delicate, fragile thing that can be shattered by very minor mishaps."[60] Not surprisingly, therefore, students of self-creation through fashion see the process as one "fraught with anxiety."[61] Although the risk of "wardrobe malfunctions" in our image-making partly explains that anxiety, another reason for it is that access to the appropriate sign equipment is not equally available to everyone.[62] Also, individuals, in creating their public identities, must negotiate complex balances between standing out, fitting in, establishing boundaries, making politicized

[56] In this eclectic age, that identification could be with Goth styles or with athletic ones or with "ethnic" dress, to give a few examples.

[57] ERVING GOFFMAN, THE PRESENTATION OF SELF IN EVERYDAY LIFE 28 (1959).

[58] *Id.* at 68.

[59] *Id.* at 13, 40.

[60] *Id.* at 63. Goffman notes that, to avoid such gaffes, people, even powerful ones, may submit themselves to "indignities ... to come off well." *Id.* at 219. Congressmen, for example, will "allow themselves to be made up and to be told what to wear." *Id.* at 219–20.

[61] Jennifer Smith Maguire & Kim Stanway, *Looking Good: Consumption and the Problems of Self-Production,* 11 EUROPEAN J. CULTURAL STUDIES 63, 66 (2008).

[62] *Id.* at 67. Crane estimated in 2000 that about 43 percent of the population had the attitudes and wherewithal to be what she terms "postmodernist consumers." CRANE, *supra* note 53, at 12. Adolescents are major consumers of high-fashion items. *Id.* at 14–15.

statements, and dealing with the other operations to which clothes are integral. As one commentator put it, "[I]mmense psychological work ... goes into the production of the social self, of which clothes are an indispensable part."[63]

Appearance can be an end itself, as it might be for a performance artist; it may involve the expression of a fantasy, as when one leaves behind everyday garments for a glamorous reincarnation in fancy dress. (One thinks, for example, of brides or of high school seniors dressing for their proms.) Feeling well dressed gives one the sense of validation, well-being, and empowerment.[64] But in all its various guises, "appearance management"[65] represents a search for meaning and for the appropriate tools to communicate that meaning.[66] Sometimes meaning comes from adopting visual cues that associate the individual with a particular group—sports lovers, or hip-hop fans. Whereas the upper classes were once a major source of inspiration for the clothes desired by the less well-to-do, today celebrities are more likely to influence which styles have the greatest cachet within a particular stratum.[67] In any event, how we dress " 'speaks' with enormous force and immediacy; dress can entirely 'capture' a social position, make a status claim and even secure the moral high-ground."[68] Clearly, those with little disposable income are likely to "speak" the language of constraint through their clothes, but as long as a wide range of clothing, including reasonable approximations of currently fashionable garb, remain available to as broad a group of income levels as possible, the opportunity to create identity and play with it will continue to offer substantial psychic rewards to large swathes of the population.

1. Money, Class and Power

> New Yorkers aren't better than anyone else. We just dress like it.[69]

> Important policies are obviously at stake. Should we encourage the artist and increase the compensation to the creative? Or should we allow cheap reproductions which will permit

[63] E. Wilson, Adorned in Dreams: Fashion and Modernity 246 (1985), quoted in Kaiser et al., *supra* note 55–6, at 173.

[64] Jane Schneider, *supra* note 55, at 30; Marilyn J. Horn & Louis M. Gurel, The Second Skin 147 (3d ed. 1981).

[65] This term comes from Kaiser et al., *supra* note 55, at 180.

[66] Clothes are sufficiently important to their owners as symbolic expression that many keep long-outdated, no-longer-worn outfits because "[T]hey are unwilling to let go of the images that the clothing had allowed them to achieve." Maura Banim & Ali Guy, *Dis/continued Selves: Why Do Women Keep Clothes They No Longer Wear?* in Guy, Green, & Banim, *supra* note 47, at 212.

[67] *See, e.g.*, Hansen, *supra* note 53, at 125 (young male street vendors in Zambia adopt the styles made fashionable by internationally known performers); Pamela Abbott & Francesca Sapsford, *Young Women and Their Wardrobes* in Guy, Green, & Banim, *supra* note 46, at 22 (young women like to imitate the clothes of pop music stars).

[68] Hunt, *supra* note 25, at 59.

[69] Advertising logo for Manhattan MiniStorage Company. A photograph of the advertisement can be found at http://adsonthesubway.files.wordpress.com/2012/02/photo11.jpg.

> our less affluent to afford beautiful artifacts? Appellant sold the original for $600.00 and up. Defendant's version went for one-fiftieth of that sum.[70]

The connection between money, class, power, and clothes is longstanding. In relatively static societies, distinctions based on dress were commonly relied on as markers of status.[71] Once a group lower in the social ranking, such as a commercial middle class, was able to control the economic resources to allow them to begin mimicking the dress of their betters, a common response was to enact sumptuary laws to reassert the invariability of the social order. Numerous examples of such laws from Europe as well as from Asia can be found, limiting who was entitled to wear certain fabrics or types of fur or colors, sometimes even using fabric type and color to make fine distinctions among people in the lower orders according to their occupations.[72] Generally speaking, however, those who could imitate the clothes of the nobility during the late Middle Ages and the early Modern period were few. Clothes and the fabrics from which they were made were hand-crafted; what the nobility wore was commonly distinguished by opulent fabrics, rare furs, and jewels, and were altogether too costly for many to attempt to copy them. According to historian Olwen Hufton, "Most people did not buy new clothes or did so only at very special periods in their lives."[73] Clothes, even of the most modest sort, she notes, were handed down to the next generation on the death of the owner and also were sold by secondhand dealers. So valuable were garments that they were "the most commonly stolen goods across the length and breadth of the [European] Continent."[74]

The Industrial Revolution brought about the mechanized mass production of fabrics and of garments, and the cost of clothing began to go down significantly, with the result that a demand for new clothes grew across the classes.[75] That change was sufficiently gradual that clothes, throughout the nineteenth century, remained a source of social demarcation, a point that was made vividly at the end of the century by Veblen. Veblen understood fashion as a symbol of "invidious distinction" because current styles in expensive fabrics and trims continued to be used by the wealthy in much the same way they had been used in earlier times to denote their favored position in the larger society.[76] He wrote, "In order to gain and hold the esteem of men it is not sufficient merely to possess wealth or power. The wealth or power must be put in evidence...."[77] One easy and

---

[70] Kieselstein-Cord v. Accessories by Pearl, Inc., 632 F.2d 989, 999 (2nd Cir. 1980) (Weinstein, J., dissenting).

[71] Today, that function, as Barton Beebe has trenchantly observed, is increasingly being performed by intellectual property laws. *See generally*, Barton Beebe, *Intellectual Property Law and the Sumptuary Code*, 123 HARV. L. REV. 809 (2010).

[72] *See generally* HUNT, *supra* note 25.

[73] OLWEN HUFTON, THE PROSPECT BEFORE HER 172 (Vintage Books 1998) (1995).

[74] *Id.* at 173.

[75] *See, e.g.*, HORN & GUREL, *supra* note 64, at 438 (relating the effect of industrialization on clothes and incomes).

[76] VEBLEN, *supra* note 28.

[77] VEBLEN, *supra* note 28 at 29.

difficult-to-miss tactic for such display was what Veblen characterized as the "waste" of resources on fashionable dress for rich men's wives and daughters.[78] But the effect was not to maintain a static differentiation among classes, as it might have been in earlier centuries. Those lower in the socioeconomic scale looked upward for their standards of respectability and reputability, and because they had some disposable income, they spent what they could to adopt the visible markers of elite society by emulating their styles and appearance.[79] In this way, according to Veblen's interpretation, fashion trickled down the socioeconomic ladder from above. Only those at the very bottom of society, who lacked even the means to meet the most basic needs, did not attempt, in Veblen's view, to use what he termed "conspicuous consumption" in an attempt to keep up with the Joneses.[80] Because this emulation in most cases depended on machine-made copies in less expensive fabrics rather than the custom-made attire of the rich, the charade was, of course, at best incompletely successful.[81]

This top-down understanding of fashion as a marker for the status and power to which the lower classes could only aspire was refined a bit further by sociologist Georg Simmel. Simmel explained what is known as the fashion cycle—the arrival of a style, followed by a rapid exhaustion of it as an object of desire and by its speedy replacement by something new—in slightly different terms. He wrote that the upper classes must abandon a style or fashion as soon as it is taken up by those below it on the social scale because it then loses its signaling capacity.[82] Once imitated, the visual cues that identified the top strata of society had to be replaced by a new set of markers.[83]

Because both Veblen and Simmel were writing at the end of the Gilded Age, income and class disparities in the society, though less than in previous centuries, remained huge. Furthermore, their conclusions may have been based on too narrow a range of observations. Diana Crane suggests that Veblen and Simmel's descriptions of how conspicuous consumption by the upper classes led to successive imitation by the classes below most likely applicable only to the behavior of the middle class vis-à-vis the upper, since the

---

[78] Edith Wharton's mother, a member of the New York City elite in the nineteenth century, is a good example. She is described as exhibiting "an advanced case of what Newland Archer, the male protagonist of *The Age of Innocence*, refers to as 'the religious reverence of American women for the social advantages of dress.'" KENNEDY FRASER, ORNAMENT AND SILENCE: ESSAYS ON WOMEN'S LIVES 66 (1996). Fraser notes that Wharton herself followed suit and "dressed in French couture to the end of her days." *Id.*

[79] VEBLEN, *supra* note 28, at 63.

[80] VEBLEN, *supra* note 28, at 64.

[81] VEBLEN, *supra* note 28, at 114–19. At a later point in the book, Veblen comments that "'Cheap and nasty' is recognized to hold true in dress with even less mitigation than in other lines of consumption." VEBLEN, *supra* note 28, at 124.

[82] *See generally* Georg Simmel, *Fashion*, reprinted in 62 AM. J. SOCIOLOGY 541 (1957). The article originally appeared in 10 INTERN'L QUARTERLY 130 (1904). Simmel was not the first to try to parse the reasons for the fashion cycle. See JOHN RAE, THE SOCIOLOGICAL THEORY OF CAPITAL 250–51 (McMillan 1905) (1834) (once fabric or color becomes available to the masses, it no longer serves "the purposes of vanity").

[83] Simmel, *supra* note 83, at 547.

incomes of the working class were typically too small to allow them to incorporate stylish clothes into their lives.[84]

Today, however, it has become fashionable, if I may so use the word, to treat the trickle-down, class-imitation/maintenance understanding of fashion cycles as outmoded, a creature of the time in which Veblen and Simmel wrote.[85] Many have suggested that, particularly since World War II, we have entered a post-modern period in which the increasing affluence of society at large has rendered social class distinctions blurred, or even largely obsolete.[86] Instead, scholars say that the use of fashion to mark social status has been replaced by its use as a way to express one's distinctiveness,[87] individuality,[88] and group affiliation.[89] Style, in this new world, trickles up from the street as well as down from the grand salons of high-fashion designers.

Clearly, one reason for the change in how appearance works as a marker is the development of the modern clothing industry, making up-to-date styles available across a range of price points. Even when Elizabeth Hurlock was writing in 1929, she was able, optimistically, to claim that commercial clothing designers and manufacturers understood how much less affluent women wanted to be in fashion and, in response, they "imitated in cheap materials the clothing of the fashion leaders. A hasty glance at any group of people gathered together in an American city would reveal scarcely any differences in wealth, social position or breeding, so completely are these hidden behind clothing of a uniform kind."[90] Or, as other, later commentators put it (with a substantial dose of irony),

---

[84] CRANE, *supra* note 53, at 7. By the late nineteenth century, however, young, unmarried working women in particular did spend money on "fashionable items." CRANE, *supra* note 53, at 4.

[85] *See, e.g.*, Kaiser et al., *supra* note 55, at 166 ("macro-based, class-structural explanations" cannot account for current multiplicity of fashionable styles and individualized personal appearances).

[86] Paul Blumberg, *The Decline and Fall of the Status Symbol: Some Thoughts on Status in a Post-Industrial Society*, 21 SOCIAL PROBS. 480, 483 (1974). See also HARVEY, *supra* note 22, at 25 (clothes not as differentiated by class as in Simmel and Veblen's day); CRANE, *supra* note 53, at 244 (we live in a "post-class" society). But see Wendy Bottero, *Class Identities and the Identity of Class*, 38 SOCIOLOGY 985, 994 (2004) (arguing that hierarchical relationships have replaced social class as markers of divisions in contemporary society).

[87] Bourdieu, for example, writes that taste, whether in art, food, or artifacts (including apparel) is what distinguishes groups and marks social status. He says that while the "very top bourgeoisie" and artists "are able to make their art of living one of the fine arts," whereas for the petite bourgeoisie, "the game of distinction is marked ... by the anxiety of exposing oneself to classification by offering to the taste of others such infallible indices of personal taste as clothes or furniture. . . ." PIERRE BOURDIEU, DISTINCTION: A SOCIAL CRITIQUE OF THE JUDGMENT OF TASTE 57 (trans. Richard Nice, 1984). Bourdieu suggests that high-status individuals desire distinctiveness, which is lost (and must therefore be reinvented) when those lower down the status ladder adopt their symbolic goods. *Id.* at 249–50. Once something becomes a marker of the "ordinary" or at least the less socially or culturally elevated person, it tends to be viewed by those in superior positions as vulgar and pretentious. *Id.* at 468.

[88] *Id.* at 5–6, 14–15. See also PETER CORRIGAN, THE DRESSED SOCIETY: CLOTHING, THE BODY AND SOME MEANINGS OF THE WORLD 5–6 (2008) (today clothes are used to create "status groups" that are not necessarily hierarchical).

[89] See HORN & GUREL, *supra* note 64, at 138–40.

[90] HURLOCK, *supra* note 50, at 40.

"The big push for copies of high-fashion merchandise has created an America with the best-dressed poverty the world has ever known."[91]

All of this suggested to students of dress that apparel had undergone democratization, and that this was a good thing. No longer was the choice of what to wear, particularly in the post–World War II, post-class society, solely an assertion of status or aspiration to it—everything was available to almost anyone at the price she chose to pay.[92] As one example, in the middle of the twentieth century a favorite activity of style-conscious New Yorkers was to flock to a department store, Ohrbach's, as soon as that season's line-for-line copies of the latest styles from the Paris and Milan runways were available. Ohrbach's sent buyers to the shows to buy the clothes they liked most and then had them reproduced under its own label in New York, held a fashion show attended by a crowd of celebrities, and watched the clothes walk out the door.[93] And they were not alone—competitors like Alexander's also rushed to make their own knockoffs.[94] The fashion press coverage was generally adoring. The prevailing view was, as far as one can tell from the news stories of the period, that the U.S. copyists were doing design houses a favor by giving them publicity, while selling clothes to fashion-conscious women who either could not or would not pay for the originals. This kind of imitation of the high-fashion houses ultimately fell away in the late 1960s and 1970s. Designer clothes and their clones lost status as more women went to work and also as they adopted a more casual style of dress.[95]

---

[91] HORN & GUREL, *supra* note 64, at 285. Blumberg, in a similar vein, writes that the modern mass-production fashion industry, which is quick to copy the latest "look," is "one of the great levelers of all times, diffusing class lines and permitting easy visual passage from one class to another." Blumberg, *supra* note 86, at 491.

[92] CRANE, *supra* note 53, at 11–12. She refers to modern society as "post-class." CRANE, *supra* note 53, at 244. See also Rich & Jain, *supra* note 51, at 47.

[93] Part of Ohrbach's success was its "editing"—focusing on the most wearable clothes. The initial copies might be in the original fabrics, but the prices could be cut further by using domestic fabrics. For example, the N.Y. TIMES reported in 1966 that a copy of a Balenciaga in the original fabric cost $300 whereas one in an American fabric was expected to cost $69. Bernadine Morris, *They're Curious About Ohrbach's Copies*, N.Y. TIMES, September 22, 1966, in ProQuest New York Times (1923–Current file) at 77. To illustrate the price differential between an original Balenciaga and a copy in the same fabric, the TIMES reported that a sari dress cost $3,000 if purchased from the designer, but was reproduced in "the original silver lamé" for $495. Marilyn Bender, *Ohrbach's Shows Its Picks of Paris*, N.Y. TIMES, March 16, 1965, ProQuest New York Times (1923–Current file) at 34.

[94] Enid Nemy, *Ohrbach's and Alexander's Battle to Hectic Draw in High-Fashion Clash: 34th Street Team is Sales Victor*, N.Y. TIMES, September 27, 1966, available in ProQuest Historical Newspapers: The New York Times (1851–2008).

[95] Author Susan Faludi documented the fall from grace of high fashion in her book, BACKLASH: THE UNDECLARED WAR AGAINST AMERICAN WOMEN. She wrote that, because women were attempting to establish themselves in the workplace, "Between 1980 and 1987, annual sales of suits rose by almost 6 million units, while dresses declined by 29 million units. The $600 million gain in suit sales in these years was nice–but it couldn't make up for the *billions* of dollars the fashion industry could have been getting in dress sales. Matters worsened when manufacturers raised their suit prices to make up for the shortfall—and women just started buying cheaper suits from foreign manufacturers." Susan Faludi, *supra* note 45, at 176. In a chapter she titles "Dressing Dolls," Faludi tells of the frustration felt by designer Christian Lacroix at the failure of his effort to get women back into "feminine" clothes, including his ill-fated bubble skirts. Susan Faludi, *supra* note 45, at 169–74.

Certainly, as outlined in the previous section of this chapter, contemporary women now have many reasons for the apparel they choose to wear, much of it related to statements about personal identity or group affiliation rather than to a desire to emulate the wealthier strata of the society. Nevertheless, even in a society that ostensibly values the absence of a rigid class system, clothes continue to "speak" about status.[96] As Alan Hunt, in his study on sumptuary laws, put it, "With regard to dress, women have long turned the burden of conspicuous consumption to their advantage by taking a close interest in clothing and their personal appearance. In an important and material sense it secures for women a claim on both capital and income, and beyond this it provides a socially important form of cultural capital."[97]

This observation is consistent with the conclusions of the late sociologist Erving Goffman. He pointed out that in stratified societies (that is to say, in most places), a desire for upward mobility is widely shared, partly from a desire for increased prestige and partly because the lifestyle, practices, tastes, and appearance of the well-off help set community norms. The use of status symbols not only serves to distinguish economic classes, but to allow those who aspire to those idealized strata to "embellish and illumine [their] daily performances with a favorable social style."[98]

A careful reading of the literature supports the claim that clothes, whatever else they may say, have continued to function as indicators of socioeconomic status. For many (although certainly not all)[99] wealthy people, consumption in the form of dress still conveys their success at a glance. Trademarks do some of that work, but much is also done by the apparent quality of materials, cut, fit, and contemporaneity of style. One student of the relationship between women and their attire conducted interviews of personal shoppers to get their take on how their customers make decisions about what to purchase. Wealthy women, she found, "knew that they had to be seen in designer outfits in order to preserve their own and others' image of them as rich and high-status individuals. . . ."[100]

Another study underlines how powerfully visual clues continue to convey information about status. Research subjects, drawn from a university community, were shown 17 bridal portraits taken from a newspaper in Syracuse, New York.[101] The portraits were

---

[96] Susan Faludi, *supra* note 45, at 111.

[97] HUNT, *supra* note 25, at 249.

[98] GOFFMAN, *supra* note 57, at 45–46. *See also* HARVEY, *supra* note 22, at 12 ("There is also the whole question of social status, and the work that clothes do as status symbols, which is not in itself attractive. Clothes may use their expensiveness like a weapon. Clothes perhaps converse between themselves, in the accents of an exclusive society. The smartness of smart clothes says, 'Respect me.' ").

[99] A recent news article, for example, indicated the kinds of status symbols that were and were not considered acceptable in Silicon Valley among its rich (often fabulously rich) entrepreneurs. Fancy cars and mansions: out; super-expensive bicycles: in. Certainly, if Mark Zuckerberg's trademark hoodies or the late Steve Jobs's black turtlenecks are any example, fancy clothes are out, too. Somini Sengupta, *Preferred Style: Don't Flaunt It in Silicon Valley*, N.Y. TIMES, May 18, 2012, at A1.

[100] Kate Gillan, *supra* note 46, at 74.

[101] Allan Mazur, *Signs of Status in Bridal Portraits*, 8 SOCIOLOGICAL FORUM 273 (1993).

all the same size, were all head shots, and all featured white women. In light of the occasion for which the pictures were taken, it is likely that all the women depicted had exercised considerable care and expense on their appearance. Nevertheless, subjects were able accurately to classify the brides by social class far more often than would have occurred by chance alone.[102]

Thus, research reports in recent years continue to support the idea that people who are not wealthy still use clothes to convey the appearance of higher status. It is not accidental that a stylist quoted in the *New York Times* business section advised both men and women anxious to convey competence in the workplace to buy clothes that at least look expensive, suggesting they search out stylish wear in such banes of the fashion industry as Forever 21.[103] While it is likely that many will be unsuccessful in creating the visual illusion of social equality because their cheap copies are detectable and because they may fail to capture some of the more subtle markers that contribute to the image of distinction, the importance of creating a visual semblance of equality continues to matter. Life experience and research have both shown that being marked out as "different" by virtue of one's inability to participate on a "level playing field" because one lacks the resources to acquire the basic markers of fashionability hurts emotionally. Children and young people are particularly vulnerable. The schoolgirl who does not own UGG boots or a reasonable facsimile when virtually all her classmates do can feel shut out of her peer group.[104] Sometimes the inability to afford to share in status markers can even spill over into violence. A dramatic recent example in New York was an attempted theft of an expensive "cult" parka that ended with one teenager paralyzed and the 20-year-old jacket owner injured.[105]

Researchers studying a group of older high school girls in Britain, for example, found that socioeconomic status was conveyed to others not only by what the young women were able to buy, but where they bought the items.[106] More significantly, they noted, "Those

---

[102] To test whether extraneous factors were influencing the judgment of the subjects, the researchers tested successive groups with the photographs grouped in different configurations and also, in one case with the brides' facial features obscured. *Id.* at 278.

[103] Eilene Zimmerman, *Career Couch: Mix, Match and Add a Layer of Confidence*, N.Y. TIMES, Nov. 18, 2012, *available at* http://www.nytimes.com/2012/11/18/jobs/in-a-work-wardrobe-the-best-accessory-may-be-confidence.html?_r=0.

[104] Catherine Pearlman, *The Power of Parents Who Say "No,"* Wall Street Journal Speakeasy, January 14, 2014, *available at* http://blogs.wsj.com/speakeasy/2014/01/14/the-power-of-parents-who-say-no/.

[105] Reuters, *Two Men Shot at Outdoor Skating Rink in Midtown Manhattan*, Chicago Tribune, Nov. 10, 2013, *available at* http://articles.chicagotribune.com/2013-11-10/news/sns-rt-uk-usa-newyork-skatingrink-20131110_1_outdoor-skating-rink-marmot-two-men. The jacket was reported to be a Marmot "Biggie," *id.*, valued at somewhere around $600. Leah Li, *Don't Jack My Jacket: Union Square Store Drops Orange Winter Coat Linked to Bryant Park Shooting*. THE NEW YORK OBSERVER, Nov. 11, 2013, at http://observer.com/2013/11/union-square-store-drops-orange-winter-coat-linked-to-bryant-park-shooting/.

[106] Abbott & Sapsford, *supra* note 67, at 24 (while the styles in the various stores catering to young women are similar, the prices are very different).

who are excluded from purchase by the poverty of their parents find it difficult to be part of the culture of young women."[107] In another study of 600 consumers, a compelling majority of subjects in ages ranging from the late teens through the 50s shared the conviction that women can improve their social position simply by improving their dress."[108] That looking well dressed can affect one's future and one's success in life is implicit in the widely recognized concept of "dress for success." Today, that concept resonates so powerfully that it has been taken on as the title of a nonprofit foundation dedicated to helping poor women get jobs.[109] Further underlining the point is the recent entry of high-fashion labels into children's wear. Parents aspiring to appear affluent may be unable to dress themselves in Burberry or Marc Jacobs, but with a bit of a stretch they can clothe their preschool daughters in a Gucci silk dress, if they are so inclined.[110]

Thus, rather than assume that the Veblen-esque desire to dress as though one were a success is simply an outdated idea, it would seem more accurate to say that one reason women who cannot afford expensive clothes continue to opt for copies or clones is that they are attempting to blur distinctions based on socioeconomic status. Were the world of Veblen and Simmel to be reproduced or even somewhat approximated, one might expect the emulation motive to increase in importance as well. And, in fact, their world does not, at the moment, actually seem all that remote.

The current awareness of growing inequality of wealth has caused public expressions of concern by economists, politicians, and the press, and has made headlines in the form of the Occupy Wall Street Movement. Berkeley economist Emmanuel Saez recently updated his and Thomas Picketty's report on income inequality.[111] He found that between the years 2002 and 2007, two-thirds of income growth was captured by the top 1% of Americans. For the bottom 99%, income growth rates fell from over 20% in the 1990s to under 7% in the 2002–07 time period.[112] In the two years following the major recession of 2007 to 2009, the income of the wealthiest rebounded, increasing by 11.6%; that of the rest rose on average a paltry 0.2%.[113] According to the Census Bureau, 8.7% of households in America had incomes of less than $15,000 in 2009.[114] The disparity is sometimes described

---

[107] Abbott & Sapsford, *supra* note 67, at 25.

[108] Tamar Horowitz, *Excitement vs. Economy: Fashion and Youth Culture in Britain*, 17 ADOLESCENCE 627, 634 (1982).

[109] Information about Dress for Success is *available at* http://www.dressforsuccess.org.

[110] Cathy Horyn, *That Dress Is So Preschool,* N.Y. TIMES, April 26, 2012, E 1, E7.

[111] The original report covered the period from 1913 to 1998. Thomas Picketty & Emmanuel Saez, *Income Inequality in the United States: 1913–1998*, 118 QUARTERLY J. ECON. 1 (2003).

[112] Emmanuel Saez, *Striking It Richer: The Evolution of Top Incomes in the United States (Updated with 2009 and 2010 Estimates)* at 3 (March 2, 2012), *available at* elsa.berkeley.edu/~Saez-UStopincomes-2010.pdf.

[113] *Id.* at 4.

[114] Table 696, from U.S. Census Bureau, *Income, Poverty and Health Insurance Coverage in the United States: 2009*, Current Population Reports, Sept. 2010, *available at* www.census.gov/compendia/statab/2012/tables/1250695/pdf.

as parallel to that which existed in the Gilded Age,[115] although today extreme wealth is generated more from salary and wages than from business income, dividends, and capital gains.[116] In practice, however, that difference probably does not much matter; the fact is that the purchasing power of most Americans is stalled at a time when jobs are tight. Furthermore, many homeowners in recent years found their houses, their major investment, were now, as the unfortunate expression goes, "underwater."

The growth in income inequality is not something that began in this century—it started in earnest in the 1970s[117] —and assuredly the average family in the first half of the twentieth century, despite significant wage compression, never came terribly close to the wealth of the top tier.[118] But what may make the current period a more sensitive one with regard to relative financial well-being is a the fact that more and more people no longer believe that their life style and expectations (for themselves and their children) are on a steady upward trajectory. During the early part of the last century, unionization helped pull up wages for manual laborers,[119] and increased educational opportunities resulted in a sharp rise in the percentage of people who graduated from high school.[120] After World War II, the G.I. Bill allowed many who could otherwise not have afforded it to attend college.[121] The belief in the possibility of upward mobility became a firmly embedded component of the American psyche. The erosion of that expectation, coupled with the gulf between the wealth of the upper 1% and that of the rest of the society suggests that one should be cautious about piling

---

[115] R. A., *Income Inequality: Growing Apart*, THE ECONOMIST, March 5, 2012, at www.economist.com/blogs/freeexchange/2012/03/income-inequality. Actual data for income disparities during the 1890s is difficult to cobble together because neither income tax nor detailed census data existed. It is interesting to note, however, that at late as 1925, many of the top 200 tax payers in the United States made their fortunes in the 1890s. Claudia Goldin & Lawrence F. Katz, *Decreasing (and then Increasing) Inequality in America: A Tale of Two Half-Centuries* at 22, *available at* http://scholar.harvard.edu/files/lkatz/files/decreasing_and_then_increasing_inequality_in_america_a_tale_of_two_half-centuries.pdf. The paper also appears in THE CAUSES AND CONSEQUENCES OF INCREASING INCOME INEQUALITY (Finis Welch ed., 2001) at 37–82.

[116] *Id.* This change took place quite a long time ago. *See* John E. Jacobi & S. George Walters, *Social Status and Consumer Choice*, 36 SOC. FORCES 209, 210 (1958) (noting that social status, except for a very small number of individuals, is now based on occupation rather than lineage).

[117] Picketty & Saez, *supra* note 111, at 3.

[118] Blumberg, writing in 1974, noted that "the distribution of income has not narrowed appreciably in recent decades, with the top fifth of the nation's families continuing to receive over 40 percent of total earnings, and the poorest fifth accounting for only about five percent." Blumberg, *supra* note 86, at 483.

[119] One example showing the diminishing gap between the incomes of blue collar workers and highly educated professionals in the earlier half of the twentieth century is provided by comparing the incomes of college professors with those employed in manufacturing. Professors earned on average 3.75 times more in 1910, but by the 1950s, their earnings were only double those of manufacturing workers. See Goldin & Katz, *supra* note 116, at 15.

[120] By early in the twentieth century, such vast numbers of students began to attend high school that the period of 1910–1940 has been called the "high school movement." Goldin & Katz, *supra* note 115, at 17.

[121] In 1890, only 15,539 bachelor's degrees were earned in the United States; that number increased to 186,500 in 1939–40, and then took a huge leap in 1949–50 (to nearly 400,000). Table 258, Degrees Conferred by Degree-Granting Institutions, by Level of Degree and Sex of Student, Selected Years, 1869–70 through 2016–17 (2007), at http://nces.ed.gov/programs/digest/d07/tables/dt07_258/asp.

extra layers of intellectual property protection on a basic need like apparel, lest it form what Barton Beebe has referred to as a new iteration of sumptuary law.[122] While preserving the appearance of an egalitarian society is not the same as achieving actual distributive justice, doing so clearly has psychic as well as economic significance. These realities make it difficult to assume that Veblen's theory of conspicuous consumption can safely be tossed into a bin labeled "ancient history" and that is cost-free to once more make high style the province of the well-to-do.

IV. Why Design Protection Is an Idea Whose Time Should Probably Not Be Now

Caution is always advisable when injecting new legal principles into complex existing markets because how those legal rules will impact those markets is inherently unpredictable. The apparel market is an important, indeed, huge market. Despite the downturn in consumer spending attributable to the 2007–2009 recession, the some 100,000 retail clothing stores in the United States have been estimated to bring in some $150 billion a year.[123] The manufacture of apparel worldwide is an industry worth more than $315 billion,[124] about $14 billion of which is earned by manufacturers in the United States.[125] About 85% of the domestic market for clothes, however, is served by foreign manufacturers, largely because they are cheaper.[126] Clearly, much of the massive production and sales are not of Louboutins and Armanis or even of up-and-coming young designers, but are mid- and lower-priced merchandise, including the kinds of inexpensive knockoffs that are the target of design protection.[127] It is important to understand that sanctioning the

---

122 Beebe, *supra* note 71, at 880.

123 Fulcrum Inquiry, Industry Guides: Retail Clothing Store (2010), at http://www.fulrum.com/clothing_appraisal.htm.

124 First Research, Apparel Manufacturing Industry Profile (Excerpt) (2012), at http://www.firstresearch.com/industry-research/Apparel-Manufacturing.html. The members of the European Union claim collectively to be the largest market in the world for textiles and clothing and to account for third place in clothing exports. Euratex, Annual Report: Activities of the Year 2010 at 54, *available at* www.euratex.org/content/annual-report-euratex-2010.

125 First Research, *supra* note 124.

126 China is by far the largest supplier of apparel both to the United States (*see* Fulcrum Inquiry, *supra* note 123) and to the European Union, Euratex, *supra* note 124, at 53 (chart showing Main Trading Partners in Textile-Clothing). Bangladesh is not far behind. As the recent tragic collapse of a clothing manufacturing plant in Bangladesh shows, the quest for the cheapest manufacturing carries costs of its own in the form of dangerous working conditions and worker exploitation. Jason Burke, *Bangladesh Factory Collapse Leaves Trail of Shattered Lives,* THE GUARDIAN, June 6, 2013, *available at* http://www.theguardian.com/world/2013/jun/06/bangladesh-factory-building-collapse-community. These costs raise serious issues that need to be addressed by the apparel industry. They are not problems, however, that passing design legislation will alleviate.

127 Bell made this point, writing that the best customer for fashionable clothes today is not "the rich elite, but ... the unmarried girl in a good job. It is she, if I understand the business correctly, who is now the best customer, for although as an individual she will not compete with the wives of oil magnates, collectively

manufacture and sales of knockoffs could have significant impacts on the welfare of consumers[128] and not just on the garment industry.[129] Clearly, the business implications of design protection do have an influence on legislators. For example, when fashion design protection legislation was reintroduced in the U.S. Senate in its most recent iteration, a section providing for secondary liability, which had been present in a previous version and could have ensnared retailers, was removed.[130] But taking account of business interests is not a perfect proxy for considering the interests of the consumers who drive this huge economic engine. This is a point that seems to get lost in the shuffle.

Design protection for fashion presents many problems that can have a negative impact on consumers. For example, understanding exactly what would be protected in the United States and what is protected in the European Union is problematic. It seems that when people advocate protecting designers by disrupting the market for cheaper copies, what they have in mind is the protection of the highly creative artists of the fashion world—the Alexander McQueens, not the designers and makers of "ordinary" (or what used to be called "dumb") attire. In itself, this desire runs counter to the deeply held belief, at least in American copyright doctrine, that the availability of intellectual property protection should not depend upon aesthetic judgments.[131] Translated into simple terms, consumer access to high-concept fashion should not be limited merely because such fashion is deemed aesthetically superior to other kinds. In any event, I suspect this

---

her purchasing power is enormous.... Such clientele cannot be interested in workmanship and is probably more concerned that the goods be pretty than that they should be durable." Bell, *supra* note 35, at 170.

128 A recent article points out that the benefits of intellectual property rights to consumers tend to skew "toward the interests of those with an ability to pay, who more often than not are the relatively rich. Using prices to allocate access to goods and services does not accurately reflect how relatively important that access is to different individuals because what a dollar is 'worth,' and therefore the value of what a dollar buys, sometimes depends on how many dollars one has." Michael W. Carroll, *One Size Does Not Fit All: A Framework for Tailoring Intellectual Property Rights*, 70 Ohio State L. J. 1361, 1377 (2009). Or, as a commentator on the 2006 version of the proposed design protection legislation put it: "Until the act is passed, ... the budget fashionista will continue to rejoice at the choices of affordable trend-setting styles available at her local department store." Olivera Nedenica, *Designers Seek to Prevent Cheaper Knockoffs*, National Law J., August 28, 2006, *available at* Lexis/Nexis, legal news tab.

129 Forever 21, the company designers love to hate because it specializes in inexpensive knockoffs, does a $3 billion a year in business, and employs 35,000 people at its 477 stores. Kay Tasker, *The Innovative Design Protection and Piracy Prevention Act: Litigation, Uncertainty, and Economic Harm*, Public Knowledge, July 15, 2011, at http://www.publicknowledge.org/print/5917. There seems to be considerable agreement that intellectual property rights will push manufacturers to avoid lawsuits by buying licenses, and that this will increase the cost of clothes. Lewis R. Clayton, *Fashion Design Protection Bill: The Right Balance?*, National L. J., Sept. 13, 2010 (*available at* Lexis/Nexis, legal news tab). *But see* Howard, *supra* note 7, at 355 (arguing that properly crafted legislation would enable copying of trends, while eliminating close replication).

130 S. 3728, Dec. 6, 2010, lllth Cong., 2d Sess. (Reported by Sen. Leahy, with amendment).

131 Bleistein v. Donaldson Lithographing Co., 188 U.S. 239, 251–52 (1903) ("It would be a dangerous undertaking for persons trained only to the law to constitute themselves final judges of the worth of pictorial illustrations, outside of the narrowest and most obvious limits.").

argument contains more than a little misleading romanticism because, today, many of the famous design houses are owned by huge corporations, and designers are employees who are hired and fired with sometimes startling frequency.[132] Hence the bulk of the benefit of design protection is more likely to flow to corporate management and shareholders than to individual artists.[133] Also, the assumption that pure creativity is what is being protected must be further modified to take account of the way in which designers recycle one another's work[134] and of the heavy reliance they place on so-called fashion bureaus to research and predict shifting consumer tastes and likely trends. This reliance is why, according to experts, there is often considerable coherence in the "looks" among many designers in a particular season.[135]

But, leaving these issues aside, creating a rule that successfully identifies a target class of established and rising designers of status apparel, without also sweeping in a broad swath of not-particularly-trendy companies, is clearly not easy to do. In the European Union, design protection by means of registration is supposedly available only to apparel[136] that embodies "novelty" in its design (in the sense that "no identical design has been made available to the public" before application for registration is filed).[137] Furthermore, the

---

132 Many examples have made press headlines. For example, when Tom Ford left Gucci, his successor, Alessandra Facchinetti, lasted through only two collections. Susie Rushton, *Catcalls on the Catwalk Drive Out Ford's Successor at Gucci*, The Independent, May 23, 2012, at http://www.independent.co.uk/news/world/europe/catcalls-on-the-catwalk-drive-out-fords-successor-at-gucci-6150812.html.

133 LVMH, PPR, and Richemont are three of the major players in the luxury apparel (and other luxury goods) market. *New York City Marketing, The Big 3 in the World of Luxury Brands—Infographic*, The Main Street Analyst, May 18, 2012, at http://themainstreetanalyst.com/2012/05/18/the-big-3-in-the-world-of-luxury-brands-infographic/. Each of them is publicly traded. Richemont owns Chloe, Azzedine Alaia, and Shanghai Tang, as well as makers of luxury watches and other goods. http://www.richemont.com/our-businesses.html. LVMH owns Louis Vuitton, Donna Karan, Emilio Pucci, and Marc Jacobs, to name a few. http://www.lvmh.com/the-group/lvmh-companies-and-brands. PPR owns Stella McCartney, men's clothing design house Brioni, Yves St. Laurent, and Alexander McQueen, among others. http://www.ppr.com/en/brands.

134 The phenomenon is widely discussed in the fashion press, and sometimes in courtrooms. Numerous examples of "borrowing" by one designer from another have been cited by fashion writer Venessa Lau. Venessa Lau, *Can I Borrow That? When Designer "Inspiration" Jumps the Fence to Full-on Derivation, the Critics' Claws Pop Out*, W Magazine, Feb. 2008, *available at* http://www.wmagazine.com/fashion/2008/02/fashion_derivations/. More recently, the Olsen twins were accused of copying their fashion line from other designers. Michele King, *Does the Row Copy Other Designers? This Stylist Sure Thinks So*, Bustle, July 2013, *available at* http://www.bustle.com/articles/1909-does-the-row-cop. Some instances of alleged copying end up in court. In 1994, for example, Yves St. Laurent successfully sued Ralph Lauren in France for copying his tuxedo dress. Amy M. Spindler, *COMPANY NEWS; A Ruling by French Court Finds Copyright in a Design*, N.Y. Times, May 19, 1994, *available at* http://www.nytimes.com/1994/0 5/19/business/company-news-a-ruling-by-french-court-finds-copyright-in-a-design.html.

135 According to Crane, "Fashion bureaus play a major role in predicting future trends and what types of clothing will sell." Crane, *supra* note 53, at 140.

136 The term "apparel" includes various accessories, including shoes and handbags.

137 Article 4, Directive 98/71/EC of the European Parliament and the Council of 13 October 1998 on the legal protection of designs, at http://eur-lex.europa.eu/LexUriServ/LexUriServ.do?uri+CELEX:31998l0071:en:HTML. Designs are deemed identical "if their features differ only in immaterial details." *Id.*

design in question must differ "from the overall impression produced on such a user by any design" made available before the date of applying for registration.[138] Such designs are given up to 25 years of protection (and unregistered designs can also be protected for 3 years from disclosure to the public[139]). But a random exploration of the registry reveals, for example, countless examples of athletic shoes and other pedestrian items with design elements that are certainly not in any obvious way unique. My impression that most of the registered designs are short on real distinctiveness is not idiosyncratic. Another commentator on fashion design protection reported that in 2006, Nike registered 471 designs in Europe. "One hundred of these designs are shirts that are remarkably similar in appearance with minimal variance. Differences between the shirts are as slight as fabric color, color of trim, color of accent fabric, presence of stripes, slightly longer length of the back of the shirt, slightly longer sleeves, or the presence of a patch on the front of the shirt."[140]

Various drafts of proposed United States design protection bills have stated the standard for eligibility in various ways. All are, to one degree or another, problematic. In 2006, the House bill was essentially silent on the requirement, presumably relying instead on the low-level originality test applied to copyrighted works generally.[141] In the 2010 Senate draft, protection was limited to designs that include original elements that "(i) are the result of a designer's own creative endeavor, and (ii) provide a unique, distinguishable, non-trivial variation over prior designs,"[142] standards which, if current interpretations of copyright are any guide, are unlikely to limit protection only to the most creative designs. In addition, actionable infringement is defined by the most recent bills to exclude "copies" that either are independently created (a sticky point since fashion designers not only are known to copy others' designs and present them as their own but may also come up with ideas by rummaging through secondhand clothes)[143] or "are not substantially identical in overall visual appearance to and as to the original elements of the protected design."[144] Although this language limits the right of action to some degree, it certainly does not confine coverage to "artistic" design, suggesting that makers

138 *Id.* at Article 5.

139 Office for Harmonization in the Internal Market (Trademarks and Designs), Unregistered Community Designs (April 24, 2008) at http://oami.europa.eu/ows/rw/pages/RCD/protection/UCD.en.do.

140 Lisa Hendrik, [Note] *Tearing Fashion Design Protection Apart at the Seams*, 65 WASH. & LEE L. REV. 215, 256–57 (2008).

141 H.R. 5055, 109th Cong., 2nd Sess., Mar. 20, 2006.

142 Section 2(b) (7)(B)(I), (ii), S 3728, 111th Cong., 2nd Sess., Dec. 6, 2010 (with amendment). The House version contained the same language. H.R. 2511, 112th Cong. 1st Sess., July 13, 2011. No vote was held. The bill was reintroduced in 2012 in the Senate, but again was not passed. S. 3523, 112th Cong., 2nd Sess., Sept. 20, 2012.

143 Victoria Elman, *From the Runway to the Courtroom: How Substantial Similarity Is Unfit for Fashion*, 30 CARDOZO L. REV. 683, 700–704 (2008); Margaret E. Wade, *The Sartorial Dilemma of Knockoffs: Protecting Moral Rights Without Disturbing the Fashion Dynamic*, 96 MINN. L. REV. 336, 361–62 (2011).

144 Section 2 (e)(3)(A),(B) in both bills.

of mass-market clothing are going to be inclined to license when in doubt and that consumers will have more expensive and fewer and not, as some have speculated,[145] more choices about what to buy, even if their tastes do not run to the fashion-forward. And, at the very least, the limiting language promises to be the source of some fairly vigorous litigation before the terms are satisfactorily defined.

In any event, none of the arguments about why fashion designers need protection explain why the European Union has found it desirable to offer up to two-and-a half decades of IP coverage to fashion designs of such motley sorts or for that matter, why three years is currently the presumed proper duration in the United States. Much of the expressed concern over "piracy" is over the speed with which copies make it into retail outlets, reducing or even eliminating the first-mover advantage of the original designer.[146] If that is the real problem, a month or two of protection would seem to cure the disease. The longer term seems designed either to cut less affluent consumers out of the fashion game entirely, or to assume that, with longer protection, the fashion cycle will slow down, giving designers a breather from pressure to innovate over and over. On that supposition, perhaps clothes styles would remain fashionable when the term expired, and those of us down the food chain could then partake in the party. Somehow, though, that seems unlikely. Styles change because designers get bored repeating themselves, and their customers are easily bored, too. It is hard to imagine devourers of *Vogue, Glamour*, and *W* getting excited about year three of wearing the same old style of gladiator-type platform and stiletto-heeled sandals.[147] Or, as one author puts it, the rapid turnover in styles "preserves us from what would otherwise be the Midas-like curse of durability."[148]

One possibility, of course, would be that design protection would encourage highly creative designers to appropriate more of the lower-price market for themselves. They do so to some degree now by means of so-called "bridge" lines, and some have even experimented with offering a limited number of garments to consumers at prices attractive to shoppers who frequent Target and H & M. This is not likely to cure the problem, however, because too much egalitarianism from the top would damage the very air of exclusivity and scarcity that gives luxury brands their true edge in the marketplace.[149] The other possibility is that designers and their owners will benefit because people who want

---

145 Howard, *supra* note 7, at 355.

146 *Id.* at 341–43 (what Howard terms "fast-fashion" retailing).

147 Howard argues that design protection has the advantage of forcing designers actually to design novel clothes rather than trying to be in synch of the current trend, thereby increasing consumer choice. *Id.* at 355–56. This could be an advantage, but it could also make the profession of clothing design far riskier; without input from advisors on what the most likely successful trends will be in a given season, the probability of guessing wrong and ending up with an unsaleable collection seems higher than it does under current conditions. While one might prefer the latter scenario from the perspective of innovation, being pushed to innovate things no one wants is not clearly a social benefit.

148 Dwight E. Robinson, supra note 25, at 392.

149 *See, e.g.*, Souiden et al., *supra* note 6, at 339 (urging luxury fashion houses not to dilute their brands).

to stay in style or experiment with new looks (and this includes men and children as well as women) will be pushed to funnel more money into luxury goods in the absence of cheaper alternatives. While consumerism is certainly a lifestyle many choose, encouraging proliferation of conspicuous consumption and economic waste by those who cannot actually afford it is not what most of us would consider the furtherance of an undeniably desirable public policy.[150] Adding irony to the mix, in an era when it is widely conceded that fashion trickles up as well as down, design protection could have the effect of limiting consumer access to styles that are largely attributable to appropriation of their own fashion sense.[151]

V. Conclusion

My conclusion, then, is that romanticism over great designers, passion for moral rights, a desire to shift more wealth from consumers to the higher tiers of the fashion industry, or even a firm conviction that innovation would be furthered by the move should not be the only considerations in deciding whether to adopt protection for the fashion industry or increase the protections it already has.[152] The interests of retailers, manufacturers, and workers in the apparel industry obviously must also be taken into account. But in the process, it is especially important not to leave out the majority of consumers who do not choose to, or cannot, buy Gucci and Vuitton. They have interests that broad access to a free-form and scrappy fashion domain has actually served quite well over the past hundred years. Messing with success is often a very bad idea.

[150] Social theorists have argued that ... glamorizing discourses [on high fashion] have facilitated the emergence of the consumer-driven capitalist economy by widely diffusing an image of "the good life" based on the attainment of material affluence.

Thompson & Haytko, *supra* note 27, at 17.

[151] Lars Svendsen points out that in the 1990s styles he refers to as "heroin chic" were adopted by designers and their wealthy clients from the street. "[C]onsiderable innovation has taken place in the lower classes ..., not least in the form of sometimes major modifications of upper-class fashions." SVENDSEN, *supra* note 4, at 46.

[152] Euratex, in its 2010 report, discussed its advocacy of stronger protections for textile and fashion designers, including new criminal sanctions against copyists, before the EU, and expressed disappointment that some of these measures had been blocked at the European Parliament the previous year. Euratex 2010 Report, *supra* note 125, at 32.

10 Shanzhai, Sumptuary Law, and Intellectual Property Law in Contemporary China

Barton Beebe*

I. Introduction

This chapter seeks to make sense of three related phenomena in contemporary China. The first is the Chinese central government's recent revival of direct, top-down sumptuary law. Up through at least the early-modern period, nearly every society in human history imposed some form of sumptuary law designed to regulate the consumption of distinctive goods, particularly luxury goods.[1] China was no exception. Indeed, Chinese sumptuary laws stood out as especially detailed and carried force well into the nineteenth century.[2] The purpose of such laws in China, as elsewhere, was two-fold: first, to

* John M. Desmarais Professor of Law, New York University School of Law.

[1] *See* JOHN HENRY GRAY, CHINA: A HISTORY OF THE LAWS, MANNERS, AND CUSTOMS OF THE PEOPLE 362 (William Gow Gregor ed., 1878) (noting with respect to sumptuary law that "[i]n almost all ages and nations there have been such laws"). *See generally* ALAN HUNT, GOVERNANCE OF THE CONSUMING PASSIONS: A HISTORY OF SUMPTUARY LAW (1996) (exploring the political, sociological, and historical linkages between sumptuary law and governance across various cultures).

[2] *See* GRAY, *supra* note 1, at 362–76; GEOFFREY MACCORMACK, THE SPIRIT OF TRADITIONAL CHINESE LAW 113–14 (1996); Wallace S. Johnson, *Sumptuary Laws in Chinese Law, in* 5 OXFORD INTERNATIONAL ENCYCLOPEDIA OF LEGAL HISTORY 409–10 (Stanley N. Katz ed., 2009). Even a brief excerpt from Gray's

prevent wasteful competitive consumption that might drain the nation's resources and through its extravagance incite social unrest, and second, to preserve the integrity of the society's sumptuary code, its system of consumption-based social differentiation.[3] The most recent example of Chinese sumptuary law comes to us from the Political Bureau of the Central Committee of the Communist Party of China, more commonly known as the Chinese Politburo. In December 2012, the Politburo issued its Eight Provisions meant to improve party member conduct.[4] Several of these provisions called for party members to curtail extravagant displays of wealth and privilege, which had begun to assume absurd proportions: "Officials have been known to compete over who could build the biggest offices and host the most extravagant parties."[5] As one report summarized the Politburo's December decrees: "Every official must adopt a more realistic approach and be on guard against pomp and circumstance; lighter luggage and fewer attendants should be favored, and reception simplified. Banners, red carpets and flowers together with dinner parties should be avoided at all costs."[6] Lest anyone believe these

---

discussion of the regulation of sedan chairs in late-nineteenth-century China may give some idea of the level of detail of such regulations:

> The state sedan-chair of an official, whether civil or military, of all ranks, must be covered with green cloth.... For the first three ranks, the ends of the poles or shafts may be tipped with brass moulded in the form of dragons' heads. For the fourth and fifth ranks, the ends of the poles may be tipped with brass moulded in the form of lions' heads. The ends of the poles of the sedan-chair of an official of any of the four remaining ranks, may be tipped with brass on which is engraven in relief representations of the clouds.... Blue cloth is to be used for the chair of a private gentleman, and the ends of the poles must be tipped with plain ferules of brass. Sedan-chairs, used by persons in the humbler walks of life, must be covered with cloth of a dark colour, and the ends of the poles or shafts perfectly plain.

GRAY, *supra* note 1, at 374. For an idiosyncratic interpretation of Chinese sumptuary law, see CHARLES DE SECONDAT, BARON DE MONTESQUIEU, THE SPIRIT OF LAWS bk. VII.6., at 119–20 (Thomas Nugent trans., Batoche Books rev. ed. 2001) (1748). *See, e.g.*, SUZANNE GREENE MARSHALL & MARY KEFGEN, INDIVIDUALITY IN CLOTHING SELECTION AND PERSONAL APPEARANCE 50 (2000) (equating the development of the "Mao suit" norm in Maoist China with twentieth-century forms of Chinese sumptuary law).

[3] *See* Barton Beebe, *Intellectual Property Law and the Sumptuary Code*, 123 HARV. L. REV. 809, 812–13 (2010) [hereinafter *Sumptuary Code*] (defining the "sumptuary code").

[4] *See Buzz-Words in China in First Half of 2013: Eight Provisions*, PEOPLE'S DAILY ONLINE (July 10, 2013), http://english.people.com.cn/90782/8318989.html. A summary of the Eight Provisions and of measures being taken by China's various provinces to implement them is available at *Party Bans Extravagance, Bureaucracy*, CHINA DAILY (Jan. 21, 2013), http://www.chinadaily.com.cn/china/2013-01/21/content_16150123.htm.

[5] *New Rules Tell Chinese Officials How to Behave*, NTD TELEVISION (Dec. 5, 2012), http://www.ntd.tv/en/news/china/20121205/76039-new-rules-tell-chinese-officials-how-to-behave.html.

[6] *The Eight Provisions*, CHINA WIKI, http://wiki.china.org.cn/wiki/index.php/The_ Eight_Provisions (last updated Feb. 5, 2013).

admonitions to be merely aspirational or too vague to carry force, officials have already been terminated for violating their terms.[7]

The Eight Provisions are consistent with other, stranger governmental efforts in China to restrain extravagance. For example, certain municipalities have condemned various forms of luxury goods advertising as "not conforming to the demands of socialist spiritual civilization" and, slightly more to the point, as "unhelpful for social harmony."[8] Beijing is reported to have banned the use of such words as "royal," "imperial," "supreme," "high class," and "luxury" in billboard advertising.[9] More ambitiously, Chongqing has banned the use of such terms as "best," "irreplaceable," and most interestingly, "unique."[10]

In contrast to, but nevertheless deeply consonant with, these top-down laws is a second, more grassroots development in contemporary China: the rapid and widespread emergence in the past decade of "shanzhai" (山寨, pronounced shan-chai).[11] Originally a term for a fortified mountain hamlet perhaps populated by virtuous bandits,[12] shanzhai

---

[7] *See* Laurie Burkett, *China's Frugality Fight Claims New Casualties*, WALL ST. J. (Feb. 6, 2013), http://blogs.wsj.com/chinarealtime/2013/02/06/local-figures-tv-ads-take-hit-from-corruption-push/; Chen Tian, *Officials Sacked for Breaking Xi's 8 Frugal Work Provisions*, GLOBAL TIMES (Mar. 20, 2013), http://www.globaltimes.cn/content/769229.shtml; *see also From the Chinese Press*, CHINA DAILY, Feb. 26, 2013, at 9, *available at* 2013 WLNR 9810355 ("Many officials were prone to hypertension or at risk of diabetes because of the frequent social activities and banquets they enjoyed. Such a 'wine culture' also gave rise to power-for-money deals under the table. Fortunately, the eight measures to reduce official extravagance and waste have bunged a cork in the traditional alcohol-lubricated activities prior to the Spring Festival and officials had the time and energy to concentrate on their duties."); *Pursuing a Dream for 1.3 Billion Chinese*, CHINA DAILY, Mar. 18, 2013, at 5, *available at* 2013 WLNR 9821437 (reporting positive impact of Eight Provisions, including on the conduct of President Xi himself, who "turned down suggestions for him to stay at a better hotel when he inspected Fuping county in Hebei province in late December. 'Do not make a fuss over where to stay,' he said. 'It's alright.' ").

[8] *Beijing Targets Luxury Housing Billboards*, CHINA DAILY (May 20, 2007), http://www.chinadaily.com.cn/2008/2007-05/20/content_876319.htm; *see also* Wang Wen, *Ads Promoting Wealthy Goods, Lifestyles Banned*, CHINA DAILY (Mar. 21, 2011), http://www.chinadaily.com.cn/cndy/2011-03/21/content_12199764.htm.

[9] *See* Malcolm Moore, *China Bans Luxury Advertising in Beijing*, TELEGRAPH (Mar. 22, 2011), http://www.telegraph.co.uk/news/worldnews/asia/china/8398097/China-bans-luxury-advertising-in-Beijing.html; Dexter Roberts, *China's Ad Business Faces a Crackdown*, BLOOMBERG BUSINESSWEEK (Apr. 7, 2011), http://www.businessweek.com/magazine/content/11_16/b4224011340471.htm.

[10] *See* Moore, *supra* note 9.

[11] *See generally* William Hennessey, *Deconstructing Shanzhai—China's Copycat Counterculture: Catch Me If You Can*, 34 CAMPBELL L. REV. 609 (2012) (discussing the emergence and meaning of shanzhai practices in China); Haochen Sun, *Can Louis Vuitton Dance with HiPhone?: Rethinking the Idea of Social Justice in Intellectual Property Law*, 15 U. PA. J.L. & SOC. CHANGE 389 (2012) (discussing the conflict between shanzhai practices and luxury consumption in China).

[12] YU HUA, CHINA IN TEN WORDS 181 (Allan H. Barr trans., 2012) ("The word rendered here as 'copycat' [shanzhai] originally denoted a mountain hamlet protected by a stockade or other fortifications; later it acquired an extended meaning as a hinterland area, home to the poor. It was also a name once given to the lairs of outlaws and bandits, and the word has continued to have connotations of freedom from official control").

is now the term given to a wide array of sometimes licit but usually illicit copying and appropriationist practices in China. Shanzhai is often commercial in nature: for example, the "HiPhone"[13] or the "BlockBerry" phone advertised by President Obama;[14] shoes bearing something resembling the Nike swoosh and the word marks "Like,"[15] "Hike,"[16] or "Dike";[17] apparel bearing a "Kuma"[18] mark with a leaping bear or the mark "Dolce & Banana";[19] a belt labeled with a kind of "Gucci" word mark as well as a logo in the form of interlocking G's outfacing in the manner of Chanel.[20] Instead of "Tide" laundry detergent, there is "Tids";[21] instead of "Oil of Olay" shampoo there is "Okay" shampoo in a similar trade dress;[22] instead of "Starbucks" there is "Sunbucks."[23] Sometimes shanzhai is noncommercial and takes the form of deliberate culture jamming, as in Hong Huang's brilliant appropriations of fashion magazine covers.[24] Shanzhai may also be overtly political in intent, as with the Shanzhai Olympic Torch Relay[25] or the Shanzhai National Spring Gala.[26] Sometimes it is vaguely Rabelaisian, as in automobile mud mats featuring the repeating-monogram pattern of Louis Vuitton[27] or toilet seat covers featuring the bitten-apple logo of Apple[28] or pigs

---

[13] *See* Tim Stevens, *HiPhone 5 Is Just a Few Curves Away from KIRF*, ENGADGET (Mar. 16, 2011), http://www.engadget.com/2011/03/16/hiphone-5-is-just-a-few-curves-away-from-kirf-video.

[14] *See* Brendon Chase, *Shanzhai Ji: All You Need to Know About Fake Phones*, CNET AUSTRALIA (July 10, 2009), http://www.cnet.com.au/shanzhai-ji-all-you-need-to-know-about-fake-phones-339297258.htm.

[15] *See* Alvin Tsang, *Fake Friday: Like*, CHINALERT (Feb. 25, 2011), http://chinalert. com/category/fake-stuff/page/2/.

[16] *See* Olivia, *Photo Hunt Game of Chinese Shanzhai Products*, CHINAHUSH (July 31, 2011), http://www.chinahush.com/2011/07/31/photo-hunt-game-of-chinese-shanzhai-products/.

[17] *See Shanzhai Eye: Dike Shoes*, SHANGHAI GINGER GUY (Jan. 19, 2009), http://shanghaigingerguy.com/2009/01/19/shanzhai-eye-dike-shoes/.

[18] *See* Olivia, *supra* note 16.

[19] *See* Kunal Sinha, *Shanzhai: China's Brand Copycats*, SPARKSHEET (Feb. 7, 2012), http://sparksheet.com/shanzhai-chinas-brand-copycats/.

[20] *See* Olivia, *supra* note 16.

[21] *See* Joe, *Funny and Clever Chinese "Shanzhai" Brands*, CHINASMACK (Nov. 4, 2008), http://www.chinasmack.com/2008/pictures/funny-clever-chinese-shanzhai-brands.html.

[22] *See* Olivia, *supra* note 16.

[23] *See* Peter, *Funny Fake Chinese Brands Play Word Games*, CHINA WHISPER (Dec. 11, 2010), http://www.chinawhisper.com/funny-fake-chinese-brands-play-word-games/; *see also* Paul Ertel, *Shanzhai: Kopierkultur in China*, PAPERBLOG (June 7, 2012), http://de.paperblog.com/shanzai-kopierkultur-in-china-von-paul-ertel-374259/(displaying photo of "Star Fucks Coffe" store sign); Sinha, *supra* note 19 (displaying photo of "Buckstar Coffee" store sign).

[24] *See Hong Huang Interprets Shanzhai in Her Own Way*, CHINA DAILY (Apr. 29, 2009), http://www.chinadaily.com.cn/showbiz/2009-04/29/content_7730403.htm.

[25] *See* Sun, *supra* note 11, at 416–17 (describing the "Shanzhai Olympic Torch Relay" in Henan Province, which rural villagers organized to protest the degree to which the official Olympic Torch Relay excluded ordinary Chinese); *see also* HUA, *supra* note 12, at 189–90.

[26] *See* Sun, *supra* note 11, at 421–22 (describing the Shanzhai Spring Festival Gala, which was organized to protest the official Spring Festival Gala, an annual televised variety program designed to pay tribute to the Communist Party); *see also* HUA, *supra* note 12, at 187–88.

[27] *See Does This Chinese Cabbie Love Louis Vuitton? Or Hate Them?*, THE KNOCKOFF ECON. (Aug. 29. 2012), http://www.theknockoffeconomy.com/does-this-chinese-cabbie-love-louis-vuitton-or-hate-them/.

[28] *See* Jin Ge, *Shanzhai State of Mind*, 88 BAR (May 15, 2012), http://www.88-bar.com/2012/05/shanzhai-state-of-mind/.

inexplicably tattooed with the Louis Vuitton pattern.[29] And sometimes shanzhai is, at its grandest, simply unfathomable, as in the many simulated European monuments and towns in China, like the "Mediterranean Shopping Village" recently built within the world's largest building in Chengdu.[30] Whatever form it takes, shanzhai is pervasive in contemporary China. As Yu Hua observes, "The force and scale of copycatting demonstrate that the whole nation has taken to it as a form of performance art."[31]

A third recent development in China is the increasing number and effectiveness of intellectual property lawsuits and administrative enforcement actions brought by foreign luxury goods producers against Chinese defendants. Luxury brand owners have been especially aggressive in seeking to suppress counterfeiting activity, and for good reason, since the Chinese now constitute the largest luxury goods market in the world.[32] But luxury brands have also aggressively sought to suppress shanzhai practices directed toward them, which often fail to rise to the level of outright identical-mark-on-identical-goods counterfeiting but can still significantly damage the targeted brand. These efforts seem to be paying off. Hermès, Burberry, Cartier, and Coach have each recently won significant cases against infringers, with Coach making headlines for its award of $257 million in damages.[33] Meanwhile, in a first for the two countries, the United States and China recently collaborated to shut down a massive counterfeiting operation in Guangdong province valued at $802 million.[34] Authoritative media reports even suggest that "[t]he tide may be turning against forgers of fakes operating in China."[35]

I present together these three developments—the Politburo's Eight Provisions, the rapid emergence of shanzhai, and the somewhat less rapid emergence of intellectual property law actions directed against shanzhai status goods—because of the strange

---

[29] *See Louis Vuitton Tattoos for Chinese Pigs*, CINA PIG (June 29, 2011), http://cinapig.com/2009/06/29/louis-vuitton-tattoos-for-chinese-pigs/; *see also* David Burn, *Pigs Endure Logo Treatment*, ADPULP (July 22, 2005), http://www.adpulp.com/pigs_endure_log/ ("The pigs are owned by Belgian artist Wim Delvoye, who has a staff of local farmers and tattoo artists raising sows to use them as canvases for skin art."). For a Bahktinian reading of shanzhai, see Anqi Hu, *Copycatting Culture Study: A Perspective of Bakhtin's Carnival Theory*, 7 J. CAMBRIDGE STUD. 120 (2012).

[30] *See* Oliver Wainwright, *Largest Building in the World Opens in China—Complete with Indoor Seaside*, GUARDIAN (July 9, 2013), http://www.guardian.co.uk/artanddesign/architecture-design-blog/2013/jul/09/largest-building-world-china-seaside; Oliver Wainwright, *Seeing Double: What China's Copycat Culture Means for Architecture*, GUARDIAN (Jan. 7, 2013), http://www.guardian.co.uk/artanddesign/architecture-design-blog/2013/jan/07/china-copycat-architecture-seeing-double. *See generally* YI-CHIEH JESSICA LIN, FAKE STUFF: CHINA AND THE RISE OF COUNTERFEIT GOODS 66–70 (2011) (discussing the production and consumption of counterfeit status goods in China).

[31] HUA, *supra* note 12, at 188.

[32] *See* discussion *infra* section II. A.

[33] *See* Casey Hall, *Cartier Wins Case in Shanghai*, WOMEN'S WEAR DAILY, Apr. 11, 2013, at 17 [hereinafter *Cartier Wins*]; Alexandra Steigrad, *Coach Wins $257M Counterfeit Case*, WOMEN'S WEAR DAILY (Nov. 2, 2012), http://www.wwd.com/business-news/legal/coach-wins-cybersquatting-suit-6467590?module=hp-business.

[34] Casey Hall & Kristi Ellis, *China and U.S. Team for Counterfeit Sting*, WOMEN'S WEAR DAILY, Nov. 20, 2012, at 11.

[35] *Id.*

similarities and differences that run among them. The Eight Provisions and shanzhai status goods are similar in that they are both reactions against competitive consumption. The important difference, of course, is that the Eight Provisions are a reaction by social elites seeking to preserve social stability, while shanzhai status goods are a reaction primarily by the non-elite that is at least symptomatic of, if not an incitement to, social instability. The former attacks competitive consumption through top-down controls on consumption; the latter attacks competitive consumption through bottom-up appropriation and recoding. But more interesting is the similarity between the Eight Provisions and intellectual property laws directed against shanzhai—more interesting because of what this similarity reveals about contemporary intellectual property law not simply in China but around the world. Both, in short, are forms of sumptuary law, and both seek to preserve social stability. The difference is that while the Eight Provisions seek to preserve social stability by limiting socially destabilizing forms of competitive consumption, intellectual property law directed against counterfeit and shanzhai status goods seeks to preserve social stability by defending the internal integrity of the society's system of consumption-based social differentiation. The former seeks to limit the system's excesses; the latter seeks to ensure its smooth functioning.

In what follows, I will further consider the degree to which Chinese intellectual property law, like intellectual property law elsewhere, has come to take on, among its many functions, the function of sumptuary law. I will also consider, more speculatively, whether Chinese intellectual property law can hope to succeed in this new role and what the implications of its success or failure might be. To do so, I will draw upon previous work[36] to propose two images of the future of shanzhai and its impact on Chinese and even global consumer culture. One image of the future of shanzhai, which I take to be the pessimistic and perhaps more probable future, is that intellectual property law will succeed in suppressing shanzhai, or in any case, that shanzhai will fail to disrupt the new system of consumption-based social differentiation taking root in China. The other, more optimistic and improbable image of the future is that intellectual property law will fail to suppress shanzhai practices and the damage they inflict on China's new sumptuary code. Part I reviews the rise of status consumption and the emergence of shanzhai practices in China. Part II considers in more detail the two images of the future of shanzhai.

II. Status Goods and Shanzhai in China

A. THE RISE IN CHINESE LUXURY GOODS CONSUMPTION

Chinese luxury goods consumption has exploded in the past decade, which goes far toward explaining China's recent turn to sumptuary law, be it in the form of the Eight Provisions or enhanced intellectual property enforcement. The statistics are

---

[36] *See* Beebe, *Sumptuary Code, supra* note 3. *See also* Barton Beebe, *Fair Use and Legal Futurism*, 25 LAW & LITERATURE 10 (2013) (discussing legal "images of the future").

remarkable.[37] Only in 2003 did Chinese consumers first begin to account for more than 1 percent of global luxury purchases, but from 2003 through 2011, Chinese luxury good consumption grew at annual rates above, by some estimates well-above, 30 percent.[38] As of 2012, one-in-four luxury goods consumers in the world are Chinese, which means that Chinese luxury goods purchasers have now edged out their European and American counterparts to become the world's largest population by nationality (or region) of luxury goods consumers.[39] Because as much as 60 percent of Chinese luxury purchases occur outside of mainland China and its regime of high duties and taxes on luxury goods,[40] luxury shops around the world have had to adjust quickly, with the hiring of Mandarin speakers, the expansion of VIP rooms to accommodate large tour groups, and the deployment of payment systems that can process Chinese credit cards.[41] This has especially been the case in Europe, where Chinese tourists make nearly one-third of luxury purchases.[42] Even with significantly lower growth rates (of about 6 to 8 percent) predicted for Chinese luxury consumption in 2013, Greater China (including Taiwan, Hong Kong, and Macau) is expected to account for $35 billion in luxury sales this year, making it the second-largest market for luxury goods in the world, behind only the United States.[43]

The scale of this expansion in Chinese luxury spending may be especially surprising given that Chinese per capita GDP ranked 93rd in the world in 2011, at $5,447, just behind Iraq,

---

[37] They are also quite varied and ambiguous. News reports may use the term "China" to refer to the Chinese, who make a significant proportion of their luxury purchases outside of China. *See, e.g., Beyond Bling*, ECONOMIST (June 8, 2013), http://www.economist.com/news/business/21579015-life-getting-harder-purveyors-luxury-china-growth-prospects-are-still ("Measured by the nationality of the buyer, China is now the world's biggest luxury market, and growing fast."). News reports may also use the term "China" to refer only to mainland China or to a greater China that includes Hong Kong, Macau, and even Taiwan. *See, e.g., id.* (arguing that the new round of sumptuary law–making globally taking place is driven by intellectual property concerns).

[38] *See* HSBC, GLOBAL LUXURY GOODS 7 (2011) ("[S]ince the Chinese luxury market became relevant ([i.e.,] in 2003 when China started to account for more than 1% of luxury groups' sales), it has grown at rates above 30% without interruption . . . .").

[39] *See* BAIN & CO. & FONDAZIONE ALTAGAMMA, 2012 LUXURY GOODS WORLDWIDE MARKET STUDY 2 (11th ed. 2012) [hereinafter LUXURY GOODS WORLDWIDE], *available at* www.ipmark.com/pdf/lujo_2012.pdf.

[40] *See* BAIN & CO., BAIN POINT OF VIEW, 2012 CHINA LUXURY STUDY 2 (2012), *available at* http://www.fccihk.com/files/dpt_image/5_committees/Luxury%20Committee/121212-2012%20Luxury%20study_Media%20release.pdf; *see also Luxury Market Takes Hit*, WORLD FIN. (Nov. 7, 2012), http://www.worldfinance.com/home/special-reports-home/luxury-market-takes-hit ("Every luxury item imported into China is subject to customs tariffs that range between 4.4 percent and 60 percent, in addition to standard value added tax (VAT) of 17 percent, and a one off consumption tax of 30 percent"). Luxury producers have also simply been charging higher prices in China. *See* Wei Gu, *Luxury-Goods Firms' Little China Secret*, WALL ST. J. (Apr. 25, 2013), http://online.wsj.com/article/SB10001424127887324474004578444090260265834.html.

[41] *See Beyond Bling*, *supra* note 37.

[42] *See* BAIN & CO., LUXURY GOODS WORLDWIDE, *supra* note 39, at 2.

[43] *See Beyond Bling*, *supra* note 37.

Namibia, Turkmenistan, and the Dominican Republic.[44] It becomes less surprising—and shanzhai practices directed at status goods become more understandable—when one considers the extent of the wealth-gap in present-day China. Recent estimates suggest that there are approximately 700,000 households in China with assets greater than $1 million, and at 0.2 percent of the population, they control 48 percent of China's wealth.[45] In January 2013, the Chinese government released for the first time in twelve years an official estimate of China's Gini coefficient,[46] which it pegged at 0.474 in 2012.[47] Many believe the true figure to be significantly higher, however, possibly as high as 0.61 or more,[48] which would put China near the top of the list of the most unequal countries in the world.[49] Such concentrations of wealth and extremes of inequality drive the global luxury goods industry generally. In China more specifically, they help to explain how a country where 68 percent of the population lives on less than $5 a day[50] can outpace North America and Europe in total luxury goods purchasing.

Other factors have also contributed to China's extraordinary increase in luxury consumption. Commentators frequently point to Chinese culture's emphasis on maintaining face and on projecting respectability—or in Weberian terms, on maintaining and projecting "status honor"[51]—to explain why the newly rich have begun to engage so

---

[44] World Bank, Data Catalog, GDP Per Capita (Current US$), *available at* http://data.worldbank.org/indicator/NY.GDP.PCAP.CD?order=wbapi_data_value_2011+wbapi_data_value&sort=desc (last visited Sept. 21, 2013).

[45] *See* Kenneth Rapoza, *For China's Wealthy, A New "Post-Luxury" Luxury*, Forbes (Apr. 24, 2013), http://www.forbes.com/sites/kenrapoza/2013/04/24/for-chinas-wealthy-a-new-post-luxury-luxury/ ("In China, Boston Consulting Group (BCG) estimates that there are around 700,000 households with assets greater than $1 million. They make up China's 0.2 percenters. And they control 48% of China's wealth").

[46] The Gini coefficient, named after its creator Corrado Gini, measures inequality in a society. A coefficient of 1.00 describes a society of extreme wealth inequality, where, for example, one person possesses all of the wealth of that society. A coefficient of 0.00 describes a society of perfectly equal wealth distribution, where, for example, each member possesses the same amount of wealth. Countries with a Gini coefficient over 0.4 are generally considered to be countries with a high—and destabilizing—degree of economic inequality.

[47] *Gini Out of the Bottle*, Economist (Jan. 26, 2013), http://www.economist.com/news/china/21570749-gini-out-bottle.

[48] Jennifer Duggan, *Income Inequality on the Rise in China*, Al Jazeera (Jan. 12, 2003), http://www.aljazeera.com/indepth/features/2012/12/2012122311167503363.html. The Chinese Bureau of Labor Statistics recently estimated China's Gini coefficient to be 0.474 in 2012, but few apparently believe this statistic. *See* Didi Kirsten Tatlow, *China's Lamborghini Coefficient: Who's Getting Richer and Who Poorer?*, Int'l Herald Trib. (Jan. 20, 2013), http://rendezvous.blogs.nytimes.com/2013/01/20/chinas-lamborghini-coefficient-whos-getting-richer-who-poorer/.

[49] *See* World Bank, Gini Index, http://data.worldbank.org/indicator/SI.POV.GINI? page=1 (last visited Oct. 20, 2013). Chinese inequality is characterized above all by an extreme rural-urban wealth gap. *See* Damian Tobin, *Inequality in China: Rural Poverty Persists as Urban Wealth Balloons*, BBC News (June 29, 2011), http://www.bbc.co.uk/news/business-13945072. *See generally* One Country, Two Societies: Rural-Urban Inequality in Contemporary China (Martin King Whyte ed., 2010) (discussing different facets and theories of the rural-urban income gap in China).

[50] World Bank, China, Poverty & Equity Country Dashboard, http://povertydata.worldbank.org/poverty/country/CHN (last visited July 17, 2013). The 68 percent figure is for 2009.

[51] *See* Michael Pinches, *Cultural Relations, Class, and the New Rich of Asia, in* Culture and Privilege in Capitalist Asia 1, 8 (Michael Pinches ed., 1999) [hereinafter Culture and Privilege].

aggressively in luxury consumption,[52] particularly in the consumption of merchandise bearing large and easily legible logos.[53] Chinese culture also relies heavily on gift-giving to develop and maintain "social reciprocity,"[54] with business interests routinely engaging in gift-giving to government bureaucrats to obtain favorable treatment—a practice which was another target of the Eight Provisions.[55] The strange result is that China remains the only male-dominated luxury market in the world.[56] Finally, members of China's newly enriched class, particularly its "princelings,"[57] tend to be relatively young and thus apparently "more knowledgeable about global brands, and less value-for-money driven than their elders."[58] As for why Chinese consumers purchase foreign rather than local luxury brands, the general explanation is that there are not yet any Chinese luxury brands that can compete against well-established brands from Europe (e.g., Chanel, Louis Vuitton, Rolex) and even

---

[52] *See, e.g.*, Julie Juan Li & Chenting Su, *How Face Influences Consumption: A Comparative Study of American and Chinese Consumers*, 49 INT'L J. MARKETING RES. 237 (2007) (explaining the concept of "face" as distinguished from "prestige" and showing how face impacts East Asian consumption practices); Pinches, *supra* note 51 (discussing cultural representations and interpretations of the newly rich in Asia); Nancy Y. Wong & Aaron C. Ahuvia, *Personal Taste and Family Face: Luxury Consumption in Confucian and Western Societies*, 15 PSYCH. & MARKETING 423 (1998) (using self-concept theory to explain the cultural factors that motivate East Asian luxury consumption); Nan Zhou & Russell W. Belk, *Chinese Consumer Readings of Global and Local Advertising Appeals*, 33 J. ADVERT. 63 (2004) (using a reader-response approach to analyze upscale Chinese consumers' understanding of advertising); *see also* Sun, *supra* note 11, at 401.

[53] *See* Xavier Dréze, Young Jee Han, & Joseph C. Nunes, *First Impressions: Status Signaling Using Brand Prominence* 21–22 (Marshall Sch. of Bus., Working Paper No. MKT 15-09, 2009), *available at* http://papers.ssrn.com/sol3/papers.cfm?abstract_id=1262479; *see also* KPMG, CONSUMER MARKETS, LUXURY EXPERIENCES IN CHINA 7 (2011), *available at* http://www.kpmg.com/DK/da/nyheder-og-indsigt/nyhedsbreve-og-publikationer/publikationer/brancher/consumer-markets/Documents/luxury-expierence-China.pdf ("[L]uxury consumption continues to fulfill a strong status and social function need. Luxury executives may be reluctant to admit it openly, but many conceded that products with visible logos often sell more strongly, we believe for this reason"); Lingjing Zhan & Yanqun He, *Understanding Luxury Consumption in China: Consumer Perceptions of Best-Known Brands*, 65 J. BUS. RES. 1452, 1455 (2012). Chinese consumers' preference for prominent logos is apparently evolving, however, with more experienced consumers opting for more subtle displays of distinction. *See* BAIN & CO., LUXURY GOODS WORLDWIDE, *supra* note 39, at 17.

[54] *See* Christopher Buckley, *How a Revolution Becomes a Dinner Party: Stratification, Mobility and the New Rich in Urban China, in* CULTURE AND PRIVILEGE, *supra* note 51, at 208, 225.

[55] *See* Casey Hall, *China Crackdown Could Hit Men's*, WOMEN'S WEAR DAILY, Feb. 14, 2013, at 10b [hereinafter *China Crackdown*].

[56] *See* HSBC, *supra* note 38, at 15; *see also* Hall, *China Crackdown*, *supra* note 55, at 10b ("According to research from brokerage CLSA, men account for about 55 percent of China's luxury goods market, well above the global average of 40 percent").

[57] *See* David Barboza & Sharon LaFraniere, *"Princelings" in China Use Family Ties to Gain Riches*, N.Y. TIMES, May 17, 2012, at A1, *available at* http://www.nytimes.com/2012/05/18/world/asia/china-princelings-using-family-ties-to-gain-riches.html?pagewanted=all&_r=0 (reporting examples of sons and daughters of party officials profiting from nepotism).

[58] *See* HSBC, *supra* note 38, at 7.

the United States (e.g., Tiffany, Coach, Ralph Lauren). Relatedly, Chinese consumers also remain heavily biased against the "Made in China" label,[59] especially for luxury goods.[60]

B. THE RISE OF SHANZHAI

The conventional history of shanzhai traces its emergence to Shenzhen, Zhejiang, and Jiangsu provinces, where in the mid-2000s small factories took advantage of the availability of low-cost chip sets to produce inexpensive knockoffs of well-known high-technology products, particularly cell phones.[61] Shanzhai cell phone manufacturers could also keep costs and prices low because they ignored the requirement that they purchase a cell phone-manufacturing license (a requirement which the Chinese government abandoned in 2007 largely because it had become unenforceable).[62] Much to the chagrin of other, legitimate cell phone manufacturers in China and around the world, shanzhai cell phone sales skyrocketed. In 2008, for example, it is estimated that 150 million, or 20 percent, of the 750 million cell phones produced in China were shanzhai phones, and almost 100 million of these were shipped abroad.[63] Shanzhai cell phone producers were highly innovative in the features they built into their phones (e.g., a cell phone with a built-in electric razor, advertised with a picture of David Beckham using it to shave,[64] or a Louis Vuitton cell phone belt buckle)[65] and in the degree to which they customized their phones for particular consumer populations (e.g., a cell phone with a built-in flashlight for use by consumers in rural areas without reliable electricity,[66] or a cell phone with four SIM card slots).[67]) They were also innovative, in a way, in how they branded their phones. Some producers modified the famous brand names they were copying, so that "Nokia" became "Nokir" or "Nckia,"

---

[59] *See* Daniel Gross, *Consumers Love the Made in the U.S.A. Brand*, DAILY BEAST (Nov. 20, 2012), http://www.thedailybeast.com/articles/2012/11/20/consumers-love-the-made-in-the-u-s-a-brand.html.

[60] *See* Bruno Godey et al., *Brand and Country-of-Origin Effect on Consumers' Decision to Purchase Luxury Products*, 65 J. BUS. RES. 1461, 1468 (2012).

[61] *See generally* LIN, *supra* note 30, at 13–14, 17 (discussing "shanzhai" copycat cell phones, cars, and a variety of other products); LI WUWEI, HOW CREATIVITY IS CHANGING CHINA 33 (2011) (exploring the origin of shanzhai).

[62] *See* Zhimin Liao & Xiaofang Chen, *Why the Entry Regulation of Mobile Phone Manufacturing in China Collapsed: The Impact of Technological Innovation*, 54 J. LAW & ECON. S207, S208 (2011).

[63] Lara Farrar, *China's "Bandit Phones" Making Big Scores*, CNN (Aug. 3, 2009), http://www.cnn.com/2009/TECH/07/29/china.fake.phones/.

[64] *See Shanzhai State of Mind*, CYBER LABOR (May 15, 2012), http://cyber-labor.org/?p=65.

[65] *See Ostentatious Louis Vuitton Belt Buckle Phone w/Built in Fashion Police Alarm*, GIZCHINA.COM (Jan. 9, 2011), http://www.gizchina.com/2011/01/09/ostentatious-louis-vuitton-belt-buckle-phone-wbuilt-fashion-police-alarm/.

[66] *See, e.g.*, LIN, *supra* note 30, at 18, 20 (discussing various shanzhai cell phone designs); *see also* Steven Millward, *Chinese Shanzhai Phone Sales in India Are Nose-Diving*, TECHINASIA (Mar. 6, 2012), http://www.techinasia.com/chinese-shanzhai-phones-india/ (discussing "gimmick-packed" shanzhai cell phone sales in India).

[67] *See* Ge, *supra* note 28.

"Samsung" became "Samsing," "Sony" became "Scny," and "Sony-Ericsson" became "Suny-Ericcson."[68] (As for the iPhone, it continues to attract numerous copiers, who have used marks like "HiPhone," which is currently a registered mark at the Chinese Trademark Office,[69] as well as "Mini iPhone," "iPhone Air," and "APhone").[70] Shanzhai cell phone producers also appropriated brand names from very different industries, as with the "Ferrari" and "Porsche" cell phones vaguely shaped like sports cars.[71] And one producer famously developed the "Obama"-branded cell phone, with the phrase "Yes We Can" printed on its back, and included radio and flashlight functions, for sale in 2008 in Kenya.[72]

Shanzhai practices soon spread beyond cell phones to encompass, as they do now, a wide array of shanzhai products, including all manner of goods bearing marks appropriated from luxury and other status goods producers. One finds "iPhone" gas burners featuring Apple's bitten-apple mark,[73] "iPhone 5" ice cream,[74] "Lexus" children's bicycles,[75] "Ferrari" athletic shoes,[76] "BMW" plastic slippers,[77] a "Gucci" watch whose face consists of something resembling the familiar outline of Mickey Mouse,[78] the "Hiyatt Boutique Hotel" still operating in Shenyang,[79] or a vehicle resembling a Lamborghini Countach built by a truck driver from Hunan Province.[80]

Indeed, as many have noted, foreign status brands appear to attract the special attention of shanzhai producers. The explanations for this are quite varied and go directly to the difficult question of the broader cultural meanings of shanzhai, a question made all the more difficult because so many different practices have come to be given the shanzhai

---

68 *See* LIN, *supra* note 30, at 33, 14–25; Bai Gao, *The Informal Economy in the Era of Information Revolution and Globalization: The Shanzhai Cell Phone Industry in China*, 31 CHINESE J. SOC. 1, 8 (2011) (cited by Sun, *supra* note 11, at 396 n.39).

69 *Top 10 Shanzhai Phenomena in 2009*, CHINA DAILY (Jan. 11, 2010), www.chinadaily.com.cn/china/09tentopnews/2010-01/11/content_9301764.htm.

70 *See* Sun, *supra* note 11, at 406; Justin Bergman, *Top 10 Chinese Knockoffs*, TIME (June 22, 2010), http://www.time.com/time/specials/packages/article/0,28804,1998580_ 1998579_1998575,00.html.

71 *See* LIN, *supra* note 30, at 16, 20.

72 LIN, *supra* note 30, at 20–21. Lin notes that the producer sold as many as a thousand such phones in a single week.

73 *See Pictures of the Day: 24 February 2012*, TELEGRAPH (Feb. 24, 2012), http://www.telegraph.co.uk/news/picturegalleries/picturesoftheday/9103319/Pictures-of-the-day-24-February-2012.html?image=11.

74 *See* Michael Santo, *iPhone 5 Already a Smash in China: Ice Cream That Is*, EXAMINER (Aug. 19, 2012), http://www.examiner.com/article/iphone-5-already-a-smash-china-ice-cream-that-is.

75 *See* Sinha, *supra* note 19.

76 *See* Sinha, *supra* note 19.

77 Brad Kuhl, *Shanzhai*, KUHL & LEYTON, http://www.bradkuhl.com/shanzhai/shanzhai.html# (last visited Sept. 22, 2013).

78 Victoria Camblin, *Shanzhai Anxiety*, DIS, http://dismagazine.com/discussion/14213/shanzhai-anxiety/ (last visited Sept. 22, 2013).

79 *See Hiyatt Boutique Hotel Shenyang*, 51766.COM, http://english.51766.com/detail/hotel_custdetail.jsp?ent_id=syjunyue (last visited Sept. 22, 2013).

80 Annie Lee, *Shanzhai Lamborghini by a Post-80s Chinese*, CHINAHUSH (Apr. 27, 2010), http://www.chinahush.com/2010/04/27/shanzhai-lamborghini-by-a-post-80s-chinese/.

honorific—so that *China Daily* listed Michaele and Tareq Salahi's crashing of a White House State Dinner as among the top ten shanzhai phenomena of 2009.[81] Undoubtedly, shanzhai producers are attracted to foreign status brands largely because the copying of such brands is simply more profitable. But regardless of what may motivate shanzhai producers, the cultural meaning of their conduct is essentially oppositional and anti-elitist in nature. Arising out of the "displacements of exile" from mainstream, establishment culture,[82] shanzhai openly challenges the inequalities in power and wealth that establishment culture perpetuates. Yu Hua, for example, asserts that shanzhai "represents a challenge of the grassroots to the elite, of the popular to the official, of the weak to the strong."[83] He continues:

> Over the past twenty years our development has been uneven rather than comprehensive, and this lopsided development is compromising the health of our society. It seems to me that the emergence—and the unstoppable momentum—of the copycat phenomenon is an inevitable consequence of this lopsided development. The ubiquity and sharpness of social contradictions have provoked a confusion in people's value systems and worldview, thus giving birth to the copycat effect, when all kinds of social emotions accumulate over time and find only limited channels of release, transmuted constantly into seemingly farcical acts of rebellion that have certain anti-authoritarian, anti-mainstream, and anti-monopoly elements.[84]

It makes sense, then, that status goods would be among the primary targets of shanzhai practices, particularly those that are commercial in nature. Such goods embody and even celebrate (or, more precisely, aestheticize) the inequalities that shanzhai seeks to attack (and de-aestheticize). To their purchasers, shanzhai status goods offer a different kind of status: "[W]hile big brands may embody a 'status' in a conventional way, shanzhai phones may imply a 'status' of rebellion."[85] At its core, this is at least in part a "rebellion" against China's newly emerging sumptuary code, its new system of consumption-based social differentiation based on the consumption of global status brands.

There is nevertheless a competing and admittedly plausible interpretation of the phenomenon of shanzhai status goods, one that distinguishes the cultural meaning or

---

81 *See Top 10 Shanzhai Phenomena in 2009*, *supra* note 69.

82 Stephanie Hemelryk Donald, *Introduction: Why Mobility Matters: Young People and Media Competency in the Asia-Pacific*, *in* Youth, Society, and Mobile Media in Asia 3, 5–6 (Stephanie Hemelryk Donald, Theresa Dirndorfer Anderson, & Damien Spry eds., 2010) (discussing the common themes of *Outlaws of the Marsh* and contemporary shanzhai).

83 Hua, *supra* note 12, at 188.

84 Hua, *supra* note 12, at 189.

85 Donald, *supra* note 82, at 5 (emphasis omitted) (citing Chandy Yang & Lisa Li, *Decoding Shan Zhai Ji (Bandit Cell Phone)—The Opposite Side of Brand Chasing*, China Youthology (Nov. 17, 2008), http://chinayouthology.com/insights/27).

effect of such goods from that of other shanzhai practices. This view holds that while the Shanzhai Olympic Torch Relay or the Shanzhai National Spring Gala may well be anti-establishment in nature, shanzhai status goods are not. In fact, they work to reinforce established hierarchies. The argument is that the widespread propagation of, for example, inauthentic Louis Vuitton bags creates widespread desire for the authentic. In this way, shanzhai status goods simply promulgate the new sumptuary code, and as Chinese consumers grow wealthier, they will shift their consumption from the simulation to the real.[86] Attacks on the code, in other words, only make it stronger. In a recent blog entry, Rob Horning formulates this "free advertising" argument especially incisively:

> It would be great if counterfeit chic damaged the integrity of the brands it copied—if IP piracy and détournement worked as an attack on consumer capitalism—but it doesn't. It just strengthens the hold of chic over the consumer imagination. You can't travesty your way to revolution.... Shanzhai strengthens the status hierarchies articulated by possession of "real" luxury goods and makes those goods more desirable. It makes "the genuine" seem even more rarefied by comparison.[87]

Kal Raustiala and Chris Sprigman point to a good example of this thinking in practice. They note that the U.S. fast food chain Subway is the target of several copyists in China, but "Subway's executives, wisely, are not overreacting. Alexander Moody-Stuart, the managing director of the chain, recently told *The Wall Street Journal* that for a Western brand like Subway, which is trying to build awareness for a type of food that Chinese don't usually eat, 'mimicking isn't exactly a bad thing.'"[88]

Though the argument is certainly plausible with respect to many goods and services, I do not think it is persuasive in the context of status goods—and if the luxury goods industry's persistent calls for more effective enforcement of their intellectual property rights in China are any indication, the luxury goods industry does not find it persuasive either. To succeed,

---

[86] *See, e.g.*, Radha Chadha & Paul Husband, The Cult of the Luxury Brand: Inside Asia's Love Affair with Luxury 281 (2006) ("Evil as they are, fakes have played a role in spreading the luxury brand cult in Asia. They have acted as a 'trial pack,' giving a taste of these brands to millions, who slowly but surely over time seek out the real thing"); Kal Raustiala & Chris Sprigman, *Fake It Till You Make It: The Good News About China's Knockoff Economy*, Foreign Aff., July–Aug. 2013, at 25, 28, *available at* http://www.foreignaffairs.com/articles/139452/kal-raustiala-and-christopher-sprigman/fake-it-till-you-make-it (arguing that copies of Western products "often serve as effective advertisements for the originals: gateway products that, in the long run, might spur demand for the real thing as China's burgeoning middle class grows"); *see also* Jonathan Barnett, *Shopping for Gucci on Canal Street: Reflections on Status Consumption, Intellectual Property, and the Inventive Thesis*, 91 Va. L. Rev. 1381, 1385 (2005).

[87] Rob Horning, *Shanzhai*, Marginal Util. Annex (June 23, 2013), http://marginalutilityannex.wordpress.com/2013/06/25/shanzhai/.

[88] Raustiala & Sprigman, *supra* note 86, at 28 (quoting from Laurie Burkett & Loretta Chao, *Made in China: Fake Stores*, Wall St. J. (Aug. 3, 2011), http://online.wsj.com/article/SB10001424053111904292504576484080863377102.html).

status goods must project an aura of exclusivity, and in the extremely competitive luxury goods sector, the slightest tarnishment of this aura, even by counterfeit goods, can be devastating. Burberry learned this to its dismay a decade ago. As *The Economist* tells the story:

> By the early 2000s the company's distinctive camel-coloured check had become the uniform of the "chav," the stereotypical white working-class delinquent looking for trouble. Bouncers and taxi drivers learned to turn away young men sporting Burberry baseball caps and jackets. When Daniella Westbrook, a soap actress, was photographed with the Burberry check adorning herself, her daughter and her pushchair, the brand's elite reputation seemed to be lost.[89]

Indeed, one of the most interesting problems facing status goods producers in the Chinese market is how to overcome the paradox of mass-produced rarity. Their challenge is how to project an aura of uniqueness while at the same time selling tens of thousands of items of merchandise bearing their marks. Research by Lingjing Zhan and Yanqun He suggests that this is already a serious problem for the most well-known brands: "As consumers learn more about different luxury brands, they evaluate the best-known brands more negatively as uniqueness-seeking becomes a more important goal."[90] This helps to explain why Louis Vuitton has recently announced plans to de-emphasize its monogrammed products to reduce the risk—or to repair the damage—of overexposure.[91] For Louis Vuitton, as for other "Veblen brands,"[92] the pervasiveness of shanzhai goods can only exacerbate this fundamental problem.

III. Two Possible Futures of Shanzhai

Consider a party that Louis Vuitton held in Taipei several years ago, as described by Yi-Chieh Jessica Lin:

> On April 26, 2006, the world's largest Louis Vuitton party was held in the Chiang Kai-Shek Memorial Hall in Taipei. Said to be an ambitious attempt by Louis Vuitton in expanding its business in East Asia, Louis Vuitton purposely organized the event

---

[89] *Burberry and Globalisation: A Checkered Story*, Economist (Jan. 20, 2011), http://www.economist.com/node/17963363.

[90] Zhan & He, *supra* note 53, at 1452; *see also* Casey Hall, *Changing China Forces Shift in Strategies*, Women's Wear Daily, Mar. 25, 2013, at 11 (quoting luxury consultant Charles de Brabant that: "[O]verexposure of some early-moving brands means opportunities for newer brands to enter the market. There is a real desire for newness").

[91] *See* Roberto A. Ferdman, *The Classic Louis Vuitton Logo May Be Killing the Company's Handbag Sales*, Quartz (Oct. 16, 2013), http://qz.com/135639/the-classic-louis-vuitton-logo-may-be-killing-the-companys-handbag-sales/.

[92] *See* Jeremy Sheff, *Veblen Brands*, 96 Minn. L. Rev. 769, 772–76 (2012).

> by social status. Guests were categorized into three groups designated to enter the venue at 9 pm, 10 pm, and 11 pm respectively. At the designated time, most guests took golf carts from the main gate of Chiang Kai-Shek Hall to their seats. Only the most famous celebrity guests were invited to enter the "VIP Boxes." The celebrities then carried their collection of brand name accessories for photographers to take glamorous shots to be reported in the newspapers the next day. In the months that followed, fashion critics commented that the party was key to Louis Vuitton's successful brand marketing.[93]

In its own modest way, whether consciously or not, Louis Vuitton was here partaking of the finest traditions of Western imperialism. Generally speaking, upon entering a new area to be exploited, Western imperialist powers did not seek to upset the social hierarchies it found there. On the contrary, it offered new means to reinforce those hierarchies provided that all recognized who was now at the top of whatever hierarchy already existed. Of course, there are fundamental differences between how, for example, the British opened up China and how Louis Vuitton has done so, not least in the nature of the goods being sold. But in this limited respect, in the status goods industry's readiness to reinforce—and exploit—local hierarchies, the general spirit remains the same. The industry offers new forms of power—in this case, cultural power—by which the local elite can assert their local supremacy. Ultimately, the local elite can entertain ambitions of broader supremacy. As Radha Chadha and Paul Husband record the sentiment, "If I buy you, then I am superior."[94] They go on: "If a lovely French saleswoman plying a French brand is showering you with sweet attention, then who's boss?"[95] Such are the workings of the luxury goods industry.

It should thus not be surprising how quickly the Chinese have fallen. Chinese elites may resent many kinds of foreign influence, but when that influence works to reinforce their status in a newly emerging consumer culture, an exception can apparently be made. Radha Chadha and Paul Husband may not be exaggerating when they write: "Air meets vacuum. Knife meets butter. Gucci meets tai-tai."[96] Extremes of inequality, a gifting culture, and an emphasis on maintaining face have all no doubt played an important role, but at bottom, what is driving the luxury goods boom in China, as once in Japan, is the extraordinary skill, developed over centuries in the West, of the luxury goods industry itself in exploiting these local characteristics of a new territory. And the industry is carried forward by the universal adaptability of its message: it offers a new, more powerful sumptuary order, a new system of consumption-based social differentiation, that promises to preserve and even intensify established hierarchies.

---

[93] LIN, *supra* note 30, at 31.

[94] CHADHA & HUSBAND, *supra* note 86, at 172.

[95] CHADHA & HUSBAND, *supra* note 86, at 172–73.

[96] CHADHA & HUSBAND, *supra* note 86, at 67.

This new sumptuary code is what shanzhai status goods threaten and what intellectual property controls on such goods seek to defend. The question to which I now turn is how we can expect, or hope, this struggle to play out.

A. A PESSIMISTIC VIEW: INTELLECTUAL PROPERTY LAW AS SUMPTUARY LAW

Intellectual property owners around the world have long complained about the inefficacy of intellectual property protection in China and have gone so far as to accuse the Chinese government, as the bipartisan Congressional *Commission on the Theft of American Intellectual Property* recently did, of deliberately encouraging intellectual property "theft."[97] Nevertheless, Chinese intellectual property protection has improved dramatically in the past decade, particularly with respect to trademark infringement and counterfeiting. Admittedly, it has not approached anything near satisfactory levels, but the momentum is in the right direction. In its 2013 Special 301 Report, the U.S. Trade Representative noted that: "Rights holders report a significant increase in administrative and criminal enforcement against trademark counterfeiting in China. They indicate that the number of administrative enforcement actions more than doubled in 2012 compared to the prior year, and that the number of criminal convictions appears to have doubled as well."[98] Chinese trademark case law is also improving,[99] and the Third Amendment to the Trade Mark Law, which the National People's Congress adopted this year,[100] is expected to improve the position of foreign trademark owners seeking to cancel bad faith registrations by trademark squatters.[101]

---

[97] Comm'n on the Theft of Am. Intellectual Prop., The IP Commission Report 3 (Nat'l Bureau of Asian Research 2013) ("National industrial policy goals in China encourage IP theft, and an extraordinary number of Chinese in business and government entities are engaged in this practice"). *See generally* Merrill Goozner, *Report: Time to Confront China over Tech Thievery*, Fiscal Times (Feb. 29, 2012), http://www.thefiscaltimes.com/Articles/2012/02/29/Report-Time-to-Confront-China-over-Tech-Thievery (discussing the Information Technology and Innovation Foundation's report Robert D. Atkinson, Info. Tech. & Innovation Found., Enough Is Enough: Confronting Chinese Innovation Mercantilism (2012), *available at* http://www2.itif.org/2012-enough-enough-chinese-mercantilism.pdf).

[98] Demetrios Marantis, U.S. Trade Rep., 2013 Special 301 Report 32–33 (2013), *available at* http://www.ustr.gov/sites/default/files/05012013%202013%20Special% 20301%20Report.pdf.

[99] *See, e.g.*, Linda Chang, *How to Tackle Chinese Trade Mark Squatters*, Managing Intell. Prop. (Dec. 7, 2012), http://www.managingip.com/Article/3128602/How-to-tackle-Chinese-trade-mark-squatters.html (discussing *Landrover Co. v. Geeley Grp.*, in which the Beijing Intermediate and High Courts found that Geeley had registered in bad faith the Chinese equivalent of Land Rover); Hall, *Cartier Wins, supra* note 33, at 17 (discussing Cartier's successful trademark infringement lawsuit against two Beijing-based jewelry companies and the online marketplace Yihaodin.com).

[100] *See China Adopts New Trademark Law*, China Briefing (Sept. 11, 2013), http://www.china-briefing.com/news/2013/09/11/china-adopts-new-trademark-law.html.

[101] *See* Jinchen Song & Jiayan Xie, *How China's New Trademark Law Will Improve Protection*, Managing Intell. Prop. (Mar. 1, 2013), http://www.managingip.com/Article/3181496/How-Chinas-new-trade-mark-law-will-improve-protection.html.

These are all salutary trends, but they raise the question of what the next stage of Chinese trademark law will look like and how it will address not counterfeiting, but shanzhai. Though they rarely qualify as line-for-line counterfeits, there can be no question that most of the shanzhai goods identified above are infringing on foreign firms' trademark rights, and that in a world of perfect enforcement nearly all shanzhai status goods would be suppressed. And yet there can also be no question that such goods carry political content, even when their producers are motivated entirely by profit and their consumers are motivated entirely by the desire simply to deceive. In their mere existence, such goods embody a form of "rebellion" against China's newly imported sumptuary code and the inequalities that undergird it. Just as nearly every society in history has instituted sumptuary law, so nearly every society has seen its sumptuary law defied,[102] and contemporary China is no exception.

This is not to suggest that shanzhai status goods should be allowed, for most of them are indeed a form of "theft" of intellectual property. But it is to suggest that we recognize what social function we are calling upon Chinese intellectual property law to perform with respect to such goods, and what the normative contours of this social function are. Intellectual property law is in many ways economically and technologically progressive, but in its peculiar role as sumptuary law, it is socially and culturally reactionary.[103] Intellectual property law may perhaps claim some degree of responsibility for the technological progress that has enabled shanzhai producers so quickly and inexpensively to produce their goods, but now in the context of shanzhai status goods we are calling upon intellectual property law to defend our established system of consumption-based social distinction against that very technology.[104] Now in China, as it has for many years in the West, intellectual property law will perform a conflicted, dual role. It will help to create technological progress certain social implications of which it will also seek to suppress. As enforcement efforts continue to improve, the production and consumption of shanzhai status goods, meanwhile, will likely slowly be reduced to manageable and non-threatening levels.

I have called this a pessimistic image of the future of shanzhai, or at least of shanzhai status goods, which is a characterization that many readers may find odd. After all, in this possible (and in my view, probable) future, China will finally satisfactorily enforce intellectual property rights against practices that are clearly infringing on those rights. More specifically, the purchaser of, for example, a Louis Vuitton tchotchke will finally be reasonably confident not only that he is purchasing (or receiving as a gift) an authentic, but more importantly, that the Louis Vuitton brand (and his own status) will not be diluted or tarnished by the widespread existence of counterfeits or shanzhai parodies.

---

102 *See generally* HUNT, *supra* note 1 (discussing sumptuary law and its demise).

103 *See generally* Beebe, *Sumptuary Code, supra* note 3 (discussing the juncture and possible conflicting goals of intellectual property law and sumptuary law).

104 Beebe, *Sumptuary Code, supra* note 3, at 814.

But it is a pessimistic prediction because of the implications of this state of affairs for Chinese consumers' consumption practices, particularly in a country that is now trying to orient its economy toward consumption as a matter of national policy.[105] It has long been recognized that status consumption is zero-sum. The possession of a status good yields primarily "relative utility," which can be extinguished by a competitor's purchase of the same or a hierarchically superior good. To be sure, status consumption may yield membership in a status group, but given the ever-changing cycles of fashion and the underlying competitiveness of the game, even this reward is likely transitory, offering not lasting solidarity, but momentary cliquism. In time, the possession of certain positional goods, as with the possession of Louis Vuitton in Tokyo, just gets the possessor to normal, and she, like everyone else, must move on to other goods to excel. Status consumption is, in short, profoundly wasteful and, in a severely unequal society, socially destabilizing—as the Politburo has recognized with respect to its own party members but has lacked the will to recognize with respect to the rest of Chinese society.

Of course, luxury industry apologists dismiss this common critique as born from the paternalism of "moralistic scolds"[106] or perhaps as insensitive to the recent history of men who by dint of extraordinary hard work and ambition (and cunning) "have gone from surviving in one Mao suit, often without the means to wash it clean, to wearing only the finest Italian suits with a thread count of 120+."[107] Coming from the luxury goods industry, these objections ring hollow, however. It is always strange to hear the charge of paternalism directed against critics of consumerism who seek through persuasion to alter the consumption preferences of others when that charge is coming from an industry that spends hundreds of millions of dollars each year seeking to do exactly the same thing.

B. AN OPTIMISTIC VIEW: THE "SHANZHAI ATTITUDE"

Among the various images of shanzhai goods that populate the Internet, two are especially interesting. One portrays a children's backpack bearing, in bold multicolored capital letters, the word "Obama" next to a cartoon image of a kind of superhero mouse with the number "10" on his chest. Above this on the backpack is imprinted in highlighted red script the words "Harry Potter."[108] The other image portrays plastic slippers branded on the upper with the Adidas word mark and three-stripe logo and on the insole with the Nike word mark and swoosh logo, apparently on the assumption that two status symbols are better

---

[105] *See* Victoria Ruan, *China's Slower Growth Raises Rebalancing Stakes*, S. CHINA MORNING POST (July 23, 2013), http://www.scmp.com/business/economy/article/1283509/slower-growth-raises-rebalancing-stakes.

[106] CHADHA & HUSBAND, *supra* note 86, at 178.

[107] CHADHA & HUSBAND, *supra* note 86, at 155.

[108] *See* Jiashan Wu, *Nothing New in Shanzhai: More than Fake Apple Stores and Knock-off Nikes*, CREATORS PROJECT (Aug. 3, 2011), http://thecreatorsproject.vice.com/blog/nothing-new-in-shanzhai-more-than-fake-apple-stores-and-knock-off-nikes.

than one.[109] What these two shanzhai goods convey especially clearly is the strange sensibility of shanzhai, which seems to take all the intellectual properties of global consumerism as so many random "floating signifiers"[110] available for free appropriation. To those already assimilated to this global system, such products, apparently completely innocent of knowing art world irony, are absurd. At best, they are the subject of countless blog posts and magazine articles recounting the silliness bordering on infantilism of the not-yet-assimilated Chinese. But to their producers and consumers, such products are no doubt quite meaningful. They are initial forms of participation, however rudimentary, in the language of global consumerism.

Though such goods will likely eventually be suppressed in China as effectively as their equivalents have been suppressed in the United States, one hopes that their example and the sensibility that brought them forth may at least be remembered. Appropriationist practices have long been commonplace in the United States and elsewhere, but shanzhai is different, and not just because of its grassroots spontaneity and pervasiveness. Shanzhai is also distinctive for the peculiar quality of its irreverence. Georg Simmel spoke a century ago of the "blasé attitude" of the modern metropolitan, an attitude that "consists in the blunting of discrimination,"[111] an "affectation of cold indifference,"[112] in which "the meaning and differing value of things, and thereby the things themselves, are experienced as insubstantial. They appear to the blasé person in an evenly flat and gray tone; no one object deserves preference over any other."[113] Shanzhai practices, by contrast, may be symptomatic of an entirely different mentality; rather than the "blasé attitude," we have what might be called the "shanzhai attitude." Far from being cool, ironic, and dismissive, this attitude is marked by a fervid, even carnivalesque engagement with and irreverence toward the norms and hierarchies of global consumerism.[114] At times, it seeks illicitly to partake of these hierarchies; at other times, it seeks to ridicule them; at other times still, it is not at all clear what its point, if any, is. But at its best, it reduces this system of consumption-based distinction to so much

---

[109] *See* Tsang, *supra* note 15.

[110] *See* Barton Beebe, *The Semiotic Analysis of Trademark Law*, 51 UCLA L. REV. 621, 667–69 (2004).

[111] GEORG SIMMEL, *The Metropolis and Mental Life, in* THE SOCIOLOGY OF GEORG SIMMEL 413–14 (Kurt H. Wolff ed. & trans., 1950) (quoted in Beebe, *Sumptuary Code, supra* note 3, at 828).

[112] RENÉ GIRARD, DECEIT, DESIRE, AND THE NOVEL: SELF AND OTHER IN LITERARY STRUCTURE 162 (Yvonne Freccero trans., Johns Hopkins Univ. Press ed. 1965) (quoted in Beebe, *Sumptuary Code, supra* note 3, at 883).

[113] SIMMEL, *supra* note 111, at 414 (quoted in Beebe, *Sumptuary Code, supra* note 3, at 883).

[114] *Cf.* Winnie Wong, *The Panda Man and the Anti-Counterfeiting Hero*, 11 J. VISUAL CULTURE 20 (2012) (discussing the rebellion against trademark hierarchy). Wong educes the examples of the appropriationist artist Zhao Bandi and the social activist Wang Hai to question the conventional account of shanzhai practices as somehow oppositional or rebellious. She explains:

> Remembering the heroism of the anti-counterfeiting vigilante [Wang Hai] and the panda doll celebrity [Zhao Bandi], we might see how the distinctly Chinese alternative of *shanzhai* became safe and cute, socially creative, and effectual through figures like Zhao and Wang, who redrew the

unintelligible noise, overloading it with hybridized re-codings, mounting an argument ad absurdum against its claims of distinction.

This may help to explain why shanzhai phenomena remain such an object of fascination outside of China. The same innumerable blog posts that seem to make fun of shanzhai also typically betray a degree of admiration for the audacity and eccentricity of the conduct, as if far from being clueless wannabes, Chinese shanzhai producers and consumers have seen the West's sumptuary code for the hollow language that we ultimately know it to be. The modern's laughter that invariably attends exposure to the bizarre world of shanzhai merchandise is akin, to borrow from a commentator writing of a much grander subject, to "the laughter that shattered ... all the familiar landmarks of thought—our thought, the thought that bears the stamp of our age and our geography—breaking up all the ordered surfaces and all the planes with which we are accustomed to tame the wild profusion of existing things."[115] Shanzhai is akin to "another system of thought," in which we see "the limitation of our own, the stark impossibility of thinking *that*."[116] And yet it is this possibility of seeing the sumptuary code as the shanzhai producer and consumer sees it that represents the most profound challenge to our system of consumption-based distinction, whose intelligibility and coherence—and imperatives—we otherwise typically take for granted.[117] In its daily acts of enforcement and reinforcement, wherever they may occur now around the world, sumptuary intellectual property law functions to suppress this challenge and discipline our thinking. The optimistic hope is that it will somehow fail.

IV. Conclusion

I have focused in this chapter on what are among the easiest forms of shanzhai to celebrate. But there is another side, of course, to China's copying culture, the side to which the luxury goods industry typically tries to shift attention when it seeks to emphasize the harms of counterfeiting. This is the side in which we find counterfeit pharmaceuticals, counterfeit aerospace spare parts, and counterfeit food. No one can seriously applaud

---

> boundaries of consumption and citizenship in ways that were appropriationist, but far from oppositional or antagonistic. Rather, after their art and activism, we might say that this newly nationalistic term for "appropriation" in the Chinese homeland is rooted in that gradual awareness of the performativity of consumption and citizenship ....

Id. at 35.

[115] MICHEL FOUCAULT, THE ORDER OF THINGS: AN ARCHAEOLOGY OF THE HUMAN SCIENCES, at xv (1994).

[116] *Id.* (emphasis added).

[117] *See* Camblin, *supra* note 78 ("Counterfeits and hybrids are surreally aware of the symbolic terms of the game of snakes and ladders we play as inhabitants of a Western democracy—a game in which we are as upwardly mobile as we are prone to social slide. Objects that register and embrace the dizziness of that freedom, though, may make for a fortunate fall").

these forms of copying as somehow liberatory or socially progressive, and all must agree that intellectual property law should be used to its fullest extent to suppress these practices. The problem is that the law we use to prevent counterfeit pharmaceuticals is the same law we use to prevent counterfeit and shanzhai status goods. There is no coherent way to use intellectual property law to prevent the one without also enabling its prevention of the other.[118]

This is why one may reasonably expect that China's latest form of sumptuary law will likely succeed. Henry Gray, in his account of nineteenth-century China mentioned above, noted that the Chinese sumptuary laws of his time were as ineffective as such laws had always proven to be:

> The sumptuary laws of China, however, like its civil and common laws, are very badly executed. This is, doubtless, due not to maladministration only, but in part to the reason which [Henry] Hallam assigns for the desuetude of sumptuary laws among western nations—that they are attempts to restrain what cannot be restrained.[119]

But Gray could not have anticipated the strange form that Chinese sumptuary law would eventually take in the twenty-first century, and that it would be a subject of discussion at the very highest levels between the major trading blocks of the world. Perhaps this new attention to sumptuary law is a side effect of how important intellectual property law more generally has become. But perhaps it is also a measure of how important the maintenance of a clear and coherent system of consumption-based social differentiation, with all of its attendant waste and irrationality, is to the continued viability of global capitalism in its current form. Under the rubric of "rebalancing," the latest news from China is that, in essence, it needs its own people to consume more so that their consumer demand will create more opportunities for them to work more.[120] Sumptuary intellectual property law will no doubt help to create the conditions for more consumption and more work.

---

[118] In the United States, we sometimes rely on our broad tradition of freedom of expression to allow products that parody status goods. *See, e.g.*, Louis Vuitton Malletier S.A. v. Haute Diggity Dog, LLC, 507 F.3d 252 (4th Cir. 2007) (finding that the defendant's parodies of the plaintiff's luxury goods do not infringe the plaintiff's trademarks). But our First Amendment tradition has proven to be an unreliable filtering device and, in any case, we cannot expect China to follow this example anytime soon.

[119] GRAY, *supra* note 1, at 362.

[120] *See* Nick Edwards, *Rebalancing Reforms May Close China's Wealth Gap*, S. CHINA MORNING POST (Sept. 2, 2013), http://www.scmp.com/business/economy/article/1301479/rebalancing-reforms-may-close-chinas-wealth-gap.

Luxury is a word of an uncertain signification, and may be taken in a good as well as in a bad sense.
DAVID HUME[1]

[T]he Beijing government appears to have decided that the outdoor [luxury goods] advertisements are too ostentatious and a painful reminder to the city's more downtrodden residents of the growing gap between rich and poor.
THE TELEGRAPH[2]

11 The Ethical Responsibilities of Luxury Companies and Consumers

Haochen Sun*

I. Introduction

Imagine a day shopping in Hong Kong, an international hub of luxury goods where there are more Louis Vuitton stores than in any other city in the world. You enjoy the hustle and bustle of luxury stores there: fancy luxury goods, grand luxury stores, and long lines of luxury consumers anxiously waiting outside. But you may not be aware that hidden behind the facade of luxury stores is another world of absolute poverty. There, staggering poverty has brutally reduced tens of thousands of Hong Kong residents to live as so-called "cage dogs." Sadly, their private living spaces are actually tiny iron cages.

---

* Haochen Sun. Assistant Professor of Law, University of Hong Kong. For helpful conversations or generous comments on previous drafts, or both, I would like to thank: Ann Bartow, Barton Beebe, James Boyle, Oren Bracha, Irene Calboli, Anupam Chander, Graeme Dinwoodie, Lusina Ho, Sonia Katyal, Peter Lee, Mark Lemley, Jed Purdy, Kal Raustiala, Susan Scafidi, Jeremy Sheff, Christopher Sprigman, Madhavi Sunder, Talha Syed, Rebecca Tushnet, Peter Yu, and Diane Zimmerman. Any errors or oversights are mine alone.

[1] DAVID HUME, HUME: POLITICAL ESSAYS 105 (Knud Haakonssen ed., 1994).

[2] Malcolm Moore, *China Bans Luxury Advertising in Beijing*, TELEGRAPH (Mar. 22, 2011, 1:34 PM), www.telegraph.co.uk/news/worldnews/asia/china/8398097/China-bans-luxury-advertising-in-Beijing.html.

Hong Kong is a city where the luxury market has rapidly expanded hand in hand with the rising poverty rate. This Oriental Pearl city of luxury marketing had approximately 1.2 million people living in poverty in 2012, which is nearly 20% of the city population.[3]

This stark contrast between the rich and the poor, in fact, exists in many other major cities in the world where luxury stores shine through the city centers. Long-established luxury capitals like London and New York flaunt the co-existence of slums and luxury stores, a rising poverty rate, and luxury spending. More staggering is the growing luxury market in developing countries where the poverty rate is on the rise. It took just a few years for China to become the world's largest luxury market.[4] In Nigeria, the luxury market has been booming in this country still riddled with poverty and violence.[5]

This chapter presents the stark contrast between the different worlds of luxury and poverty as a lens through which we can see the existence of an ethical crisis in our society. It offers a proposal to tackle this crisis, arguing for the creation of an "Ethical Responsibility Initiative" that requires luxury companies to take on an ethical responsibility to actively disseminate information about the plight of human life under absolute poverty. It further examines how trademark law should be reformed to foster and promote the ethical responsibilities of luxury companies and consumers. Based on this proposal, the chapter shows how trademark law can play a better social role from the ethical responsibility perspective.[6]

II. The Ethical Crisis in the Luxury Market

The past two decades have witnessed an unprecedented growth of the luxury goods industry. Globalization has prompted trade liberalization by lowering customs tariffs and other trade barriers, and luxury companies have vastly expanded their businesses

---

[3] Jennifer Ngo, *One in Three Old People in Hong Kong Are Living Below the Poverty Line*, S. CHINA MORNING POST (Jan. 27, 2013, 9:38 AM), http://www.scmp.com/news/hong-kong/article/1136870/one-three-old-people-hong-kong-are-living-below-poverty-line.

[4] *See Luxury Goods in China: Beyond Bling*, ECONOMIST (June 8, 2013), www.economist.com/news/business/21579015-life-getting-harder-purveyors-luxury-china-growth-prospects-are-still ("Measured by the nationality of the buyer, China is now the world's biggest luxury market, and growing fast").

[5] *See Amid Poverty and Fuel Riots, A Booming Luxury Market Has Opened in Nigeria*, BUS. INSIDER (Mar. 22, 2012, 6:51 AM), http://articles.businessinsider.com/2012-03-22/news/31223053_1_nigeria-luxury-brands-commercial-capital#ixzz2PxyiiLJf.

[6] For general discussion about the social role of intellectual property, see, for example, MADHAVI SUNDER, FROM GOODS TO A GOOD LIFE: INTELLECTUAL PROPERTY AND GLOBAL JUSTICE 31 (2012) (suggesting that "intellectual property law must adopt broader social and cultural analysis"); Barton Beebe, *Intellectual Property and the Sumptuary Code*, 123 HARV. L. REV. 809, 810 (2010) [hereinafter *Sumptuary Code*] (arguing that intellectual property should "play a crucial—and progressive—social role"); William Fisher, *Theories of Intellectual Property, in* NEW ESSAYS IN THE LEGAL AND POLITICAL THEORY OF PROPERTY 168, 172–75 (Stephen R. Munzer ed., 2001) (advocating a "social planning" theory of intellectual property and discussing the social planning role of intellectual property).

across the globe. Rapid economic development in developing countries, especially in Asia, has made an exponentially increasing number of people in these regions able to afford luxury goods and pursue luxury lifestyles.

It is estimated that global luxury goods sales in 2013 reached around $ 296 billion.[7] Leading luxury brands were highlighted in the 2012 Top 100 Brands ranking. Chief among them were Mercedes-Benz, BMW, Louis Vuitton, Gucci, Cartier, Tiffany & Co., Porsche, Burberry, Ralph Lauren, Prada, and Ferrari. The worth of these brands ranged from $3 to 0.377 billion. The 2012 stock values of major luxury companies such as LVMH Moët Hennessy–Louis Vuitton S.A. (LVMH), Richemont S.A., Hermès, Coach, and Prada were estimated to be above $10 billion.[8] Prada's initial public offering in Hong Kong in 2012 was "five times oversubscribed," which exhibited its enormous global market influence.[9]

Yet the splendor of the luxury industry has, in fact, overshadowed the enormous social injustice that still exists abundantly in society. As noted above, luxury capitals, such as Hong Kong, London, and New York, exemplify the harsh reality of massive social injustices reflected by two dividing worlds of luxury and poverty. Why can the rich afford a wide range of products and services whose prices are astronomical for the poor? The roots of social injustice are very complicated. On the surface of the problem, as many people can easily tell, is the maldistribution of economic resources among citizens. As Thorstein Veblen pointed out, luxury spending is made possible "indirectly through [the] system of unequal distribution of wealth and sustenance on which the institution itself rests."[10]

Beneath economic inequality, however, lies an ethical crisis. This crisis evinces rich people's indifference to the sufferings of poor people while the rich enjoy expensive luxury goods. As I pointed out in a recent article, central to the social injustice is a fundamental ethical issue. There is a stark contrast between those who are rich enough to shop happily in luxury stores without regard for those who die of hunger. This very contrast questions whether luxury consumers are civilized enough to call themselves human beings or are too insensitive to feel the pain of their peers.[11]

---

[7] *Global Luxury Goods Market - Industry Analysis, Size, Share, Growth, Trends, and Forecast, 2014–2020*, www.researchandmarkets.com/research/3mqplj/global_luxury [hereinafter *Global Luxury Goods Market*].

[8] *Prada IPO Hits Bargain Bin*, WALL ST. J. (June 18, 2011), http://online.wsj.com/article/SB10001424052702304186404576390350685422420.html.

[9] Garry White, *Prada's Hong Kong IPO is "Five Times Oversubscribed,"* TELEGRAPH (June 12, 2011), http://www.telegraph.co.uk/finance/newsbysector/retailandconsumer/8571143/Pradas-Hong-Kong-IPO-is-five-times-oversubscribed.html.

[10] THORSTEIN VEBLEN, THE THEORY OF THE LEISURE CLASS 150 (2007).

[11] Haochen Sun, *Can Louis Vuitton Dance with HiPhone?: Rethinking the Idea of Social Justice in Intellectual Property Law*, 15 U. PA. J.L. & SOC. CHANGE 389, 434 (2012).

Why are luxury consumers so indifferent to the sufferings of the poor? After all, luxury goods are not necessary goods for survival.[12] A luxury consumer would not die or suffer physically if he or she did not buy more jewelry or handbags. But the money that might be spent on these luxury goods could actually save starving people from dying of hunger. In 2013, rich people spent $296 billion in total on luxury goods,[13] while approximately 1.5 million children died from hunger in the same year.[14]

What is wrong with luxury goods? Why on earth cannot a tiny portion of the $250 billion luxury spending be diverted to save the lives of starving children? The obstacle is, in fact, the egoism growing in the wonderlands of self-indulgence bred by the luxury industry; I examine two types of such egoism below.

First, luxury companies have created a private wonderland of goods or services in which people are induced to relentlessly pursue the bubbles of self-perfection and self-comfort. The marketing strategies of the luxury industry open the door for their consumers to the wonderland of luxury spending and consumption. These strategies are meticulously designed to highlight high quality, exclusivity, craftsmanship, precision, and innovation that luxury goods can deliver to their customers. Perfect-looking celebrities or models are featured in their advertisements, fashion shows,[15] magazines, TV programs, and social media like YouTube.[16] Many luxury stores are designed to look like modern urban palaces. They function to impress luxury consumers with an aura of prestige, elegance, and comfort. The combination of luxury advertising and merchandizing strategies arouses luxury consumers' desire to possess more luxury goods, making them fantasize about the perfection of personal outlooks and goods quality.[17] Luxury goods lead people to experience the comfort of achieving perfection as they imagine it. As Coco Chanel pointed out, "Some people think luxury is the opposite of poverty. It is not. It is the opposite of vulgarity. Luxury must be comfortable, otherwise it is not luxury."[18]

---

[12] Pierre Bourdieu divides consumption of goods into two kinds of tastes: "the tastes of luxury" and "the tastes of necessity." PIERRE BOURDIEU, DISTINCTION: A SOCIAL CRITIQUE OF THE JUDGEMENT OF TASTE 175 (1984). Bourdieu also observes that the working-class lifestyle is characterized by both "the absence of luxury goods, whisky or paintings, champagne or concerts, cruises or art exhibitions, caviar or antiques" and "the presence of numerous cheap substitutes for these rare goods...." *Id.* at 386.

[13] *Global Luxury Goods Market, supra* note 7.

[14] *World Hunger Statistics*, STAT. BRAIN (May 7, 2013), http://www.statisticbrain.com/world-hunger-statistics/.

[15] Here I take many fashion shows as a means of advertising for luxury goods copmanies.

[16] *See* JEAN-NOËL KAPFERER & VINCENT BASTIEN, THE LUXURY STRATEGY: BREAK THE RULES OF MARKETING TO BUILD LUXURY BRANDS 262–63 (2012) (discussing the importance of brand ambassador strategy for merchandizing luxury goods).

[17] *See* Antoine Danchin, *The Biology of Luxury*, PROJECT SYNDICATE (Oct. 16, 2012), http://www.project-syndicate.org/commentary/why-we-buy-luxury-goods-by-antoine-danchin (arguing that luxury products "signal[] a lifestyle that values the preservation of beauty and youth. Cosmetics, like all luxury products, gain influence not from their production, or even their purchase, but from their visibility").

[18] Paulo Coelho, *Coco Chanel and Elegance*, PAULO COELHO'S BLOG (Feb. 22, 2012), http://paulocoelhoblog.com/2012/02/22/coco-chanel/.

Upon entering the luxury wonderland created by luxury companies, most people become willing to indulge themselves with the egoistic pursuit of perfection and comfort. They look at fashion shows, advertisements, luxury stores, or their peer consumers to figure out the next item they need to buy to make themselves look and behave better. The more they buy luxury goods, the more they think that they look and behave better. The more they buy luxury goods, the more they become egoistical in caring only about the perfection and comfort of their own lives.[19]

Second, luxury companies have created a public wonderland of goods or services in which people spend for the purpose of showing off their wealth and social status. Conspicuous consumption is a major element in luxury spending. More than a century ago, Thorstein Veblen explained the relationship between luxury goods and conspicuous consumption. He noted that "[t]he basis on which good repute in any highly organized industrial community ultimately rests is pecuniary strength; and the means of showing pecuniary strength and so of gaining or retaining a good name are leisure and a conspicuous consumption of goods."[20]

As positional goods, luxury goods are priced much higher than their non-luxury equivalents. Prices signal the quality, craftsmanship, and design of luxury goods. With high prices, luxury goods are supposed to belong exclusively to a tiny group of people who can afford them. The price-based exclusivity of luxury goods, therefore, enables people to publicly signal their status in society and therefore to gain the esteem of others.[21]

The status recognition is achieved publicly, whether directly or indirectly. The consumption of luxury goods may be photographed, videotaped, or verbally described in media reports even if consumption occurs in private gatherings or events. Luxury consumers can also use luxury items in public spaces like squares, shopping malls, parks, and airports, attracting the attention of passersby. In these processes, recognition of wealth status is essentially achieved for luxury consumers. The conspicuous consumption of luxury goods, therefore, caters to the egoistic quest for "self-perceived 'position' in society."[22]

Professor Peter Singer highlighted a very important observation in his influential essay published in 1972. This observation is still timely enough to capture the nature of the ethical crisis simmering in the luxury market:

> People do not feel in any way ashamed or guilty about spending money on new [luxury] clothes or a new [luxury] car instead of giving it to famine relief. (Indeed,

---

[19] *See, e.g.*, JAMES RACHELS, THE ELEMENTS OF MORAL PHILOSOPHY (4th ed. 2002) ("We spend money on ourselves, not only on necessities but on luxuries-DVDs, jewelry, concert tickets, iPods, and so on. In America, even people with modest incomes enjoy such things. But we could forgo our luxuries and give the money for famine relief instead. The fact that we don't suggests that we regard our luxuries as more important than the lives of the starving").

[20] VEBLEN, *supra* note 10, at 63–64.

[21] *See* Young Jee Han, Joseph C. Nunes, & Xavier Drèze, *Signaling Status with Luxury Goods: The Role of Brand Prominence*, J. MARKETING, July 2010, at 15, 15.

[22] *See* CHRISTOPHER J. BERRY, THE IDEA OF LUXURY: A CONCEPTUAL AND HISTORICAL INVESTIGATION 31 (1994).

> the alternative does not occur to them.) This way of looking at the matter cannot be justified. When we buy new clothes not to keep ourselves warm but to look "well-dressed" we are not providing for any important need.[23]

The interplay of private and public wonderlands, as I described earlier, explains why many luxury consumers are almost "unjustifiably" indifferent to the poor. The process of purchasing and consuming luxury goods, in fact, has locked them in the egoistic pursuit of self-indulgence without due regard to the suffering of the poor.

III. A Proposal to Combat the Injustice of the Ethical Crisis

A. THE ETHICAL RESPONSIBILITY INITIATIVE

How can we deal with the ethical crisis brought about by the luxury industry? I argue that we should reconsider the nature of the ethical responsibilities of luxury companies and consumers. To this end, I put forward that luxury companies should take on an ethical responsibility that would require them to actively disseminate information about the plight of human life under absolute poverty. For example, each luxury company would be required to hand out a brochure containing information about a poor child and how people can help poor children. The following steps should be taken to carry out the Ethical Responsibility Initiative.

First, a non-governmental or governmental organization should take charge of collecting information about poor children. The organization could first select one hundred children and design a brochure for each of them. Each brochure would contain pictures of a poor child, the child's story, and information about how people can help him or her. The costs for running this program can be covered by a special fund to be created by the government or a charitable organization.

Second, the organization should distribute copies of the brochures to luxury companies. After receiving the brochures, luxury companies should distribute them to their stores and ask their sales associates to give a brochure to each of their customers when they check out items. Sales associates should also explain to customers the background and purpose of the brochures. The initial targets should be companies that are widely recognized as luxury companies: Chanel, Dior, Hermès, Louis Vuitton, and Prada, just to name a few. To select an initial subset of luxury companies, easy targets are luxury companies that have opened flagship stores in central shopping districts in cities like Hong Kong (Canton Road), London (Bond Street), New York (Fifth Avenue), Milan (Via Montenapoleone), and Paris (Avenue Montaigne).[24]

---

[23] Peter Singer, *Famine, Affluence, and Morality*, 1 PHIL. & PUB. AFF. 229, 235 (1972).

[24] *See The Top European Streets for Luxury Retail*, LUXURY SOC'Y (Aug. 31, 2011), http://luxurysociety.com/articles/2011/08/the-top-european-streets-for-luxury-retail.

Third, this brochure distribution initiative should have a review program that would take place every other year. The program could organize an international conference open to the representatives of luxury companies and their customers. Before the conference, interested parties such as luxury companies and relevant fashion and luxury associations could submit reports. They could make suggestions on how the initiative could better be carried out and any additional companies that should be included in the initiative.[25] At the conference, the organization in charge should submit a report about how poor children have been helped and also highlight any major donations from luxury customers. Anonymity could be strictly preserved if particular luxury customers prefer.

This review program would function as a venue for conducting "democratic" deliberation about the progress of the Ethical Responsibility Initiative. This open-ended program would not only make the operation of the initiative transparent, but also engage more companies and individuals to consider the ethical dimensions of luxury merchandizing, spending, and consumption. With years of meticulous planning and devoted organization, this program has the potential of expanding to a global event called World Ethics Forum. It would function to engage representatives from different regions, countries, and industries to deliberate on major ethical issues associated with luxury goods and services. In section IV of this chapter, I will discuss how legislators and judges can utilize trademark law to incentivize luxury companies to become part of this initiative.

B. PROBLEMS WITH TAXATION AND CHARITY

The Ethical Responsibility Initiative is proposed to deal with the problems created by previous measures that have been adopted to address social injustice related to the luxury industry. As this section will show, these previous voluntary and involuntary measures lack the dynamics to ignite ethical sentiments among the rich to confront not only the social roots of injustice but also their responsibility to tackle it. To some extent, they even help to obscure the enormous social inequalities that still exist in our society. In the following, I will discuss why taxation and charity exemplify such measures.

1. Taxation

Taxation is a policy tool that can function to alleviate economic inequality. The government imposes heavier pecuniary burdens on the rich and then utilizes social welfare schemes to transfer appropriate benefits to the poor. Under this redistributive scheme, the rich, to a certain extent, bear a burden to financially aid the poor.[26]

---

[25] The scope of luxury brands is controversial. Therefore, the conference would serve as an opportunity for people to deliberate the scope of luxury brands. This element reflects that luxury is still a controversial idea. Different people have different visions of luxury. *See* KAPFERER & BASTIEN, *supra* note 16, at 45 ("Luxury is an elusive concept. There are as many definitions as there are authors").

[26] *See* LIAM MURPHY & THOMAS NAGEL, THE MYTH OF OWNERSHIP: TAXES AND JUSTICE 76 (2002) (discussing the distributive function of taxation).

Luxury companies are required to pay corporate taxes. Luxury customers are required to pay sales taxes in countries such as the United States. While these taxation schemes imposed on luxury companies and consumers have been instrumental in ameliorating social injustices, they have failed to require luxury companies and consumers to fulfill their ethical responsibilities. First, many luxury companies and consumers have made every effort to avoid paying taxes. For example, the head of LVMH, the largest luxury conglomerate, Bernard Arnault, applied for Belgian nationality because the president of France proposed a new tax rate of 75% on earnings over 1 million euros.[27] Recently, the Italian tax authority fined Dolce & Gabbana 343.4 million euros for tax evasion.[28]

Second, taxation schemes do not encourage luxury companies and consumers to think seriously about their ethical responsibilities. Often they just take it for granted that they are forced to pay taxes, or even hate paying taxes. Take luxury taxes as an example. The levy of luxury taxes would increase government revenues to finance programs that benefit the entire society. Luxury taxes, therefore, can be seen as a redistributive tax regime. When higher taxes are levied, the luxury industry, however, often launches severe protests against them. In November 1990, the U.S. government decided to levy a 10% luxury tax on private yachts priced above $100,000 and luxury cars above $30,000.[29] The luxury boating industry ferociously opposed this. They argued that it had significantly decreased their sales volume[30] and caused the loss of over 7,600 jobs.[31] Due to severe protests against the luxury tax on such economic grounds, almost all of the luxury taxes were subsequently repealed by the Budget Reconciliation Act of 1993. Generally there is no luxury tax in the United States, although President Obama recently proposed a luxury tax on corporate jets.[32]

2. Charity

Compared with taxation that is imposed by the government, charity activities are voluntarily organized by individuals and organizations for the purpose of benefiting the poor. Many luxury companies have organized charity activities that attract their consumers.

---

[27] *See* Devorah Lauter, *Bernard Arnault Applies for Belgian Citizenship as Francois Hollande Plans New Taxes*, TELEGRAPH (Sept. 9, 2012), http://www.telegraph.co.uk/news/worldnews/francois-hollande/9532131/Bernard-Arnault-applies-for-Belgian-citizenship-as-Francois-Hollande-plans-new-taxes.html.

[28] *See* Kelly Phillips Erb, *Dolce & Gabbana Fined Millions for Tax Evasion*, FORBES (Apr. 3, 2013), http://www.forbes.com/sites/kellyphillipserb/2013/04/03/dolce-gabbana-fined-millions-for-tax-evasion/.

[29] *See* Omnibus Budget Reconciliation Act of 1990, Pub. L. No. 101-508, §§ 4001-4007, 104 Stat. 1388, 439–42.

[30] *See* Joe Meglen, Letter to the Editor, *Boat Luxury Tax Drives an Industry Aground*, N.Y. TIMES (Dec. 27, 1990), http://www.nytimes.com/1991/01/03/opinion/l-boat-luxury-tax-drives-an-industry-aground-926091.html.

[31] *See* ROBERT H. FRANK & BEN S. BERNANKE, PRINCIPLES OF ECONOMICS 96 (2d. ed. 2004).

[32] *See* Walter Williams, *Luxury Tax Idea Reveals Poor Thinking*, COLUMBIA DAILY TRIB. (Aug. 16, 2011), http://www.columbiatribune.com/opinion/luxury-tax-idea-reveals-poor-thinking/article_a71f6124-2e5a-5745-936d-15467a93e053.html.

For example, Montblanc has initiated a charity program called "Signature for Good." It supports UNICEF's educational projects that benefit children around the globe. To date Montblanc has raised over $5 million for this charity program.[33]

However, charity programs have very limited power in making rich individuals and luxury company shareholders think ethically about social injustice. A recent study has revealed that rich people are on average more reluctant to donate for charity purposes than middle- or low-income people are.[34] Despite the fact that charity programs may be initiated for tax break[35] or personal fame[36] purposes, statistics showed that Americans with earnings in the top 20% contributed on average 1.3% of their income to charity, while those in the bottom 20% donated 3.2% of their income.[37]

Large companies commonly promote corporate social responsibility (CSR) and organize charitable activities. They often claim that their aim is not solely for profits, but also to serve the greater purposes of the society. While it is certainly encouraging to see large corporations acting to benefit society and to ease the burden of normal citizens, the truth is that most of these corporations do so in order to further their commercial interests. Through CSR and charity, they can raise their reputation with the public or with the government[38] or avoid their share of tax contribution. Companies, especially large corporations, exist as legal entities to generate income for the shareholders. A recent study shows that the primary role of companies to generate profit is inherently in conflict with CSR and charity activities because the executives' decisions must answer to the shareholders.[39]

Similarly, many luxury companies host charity activities primarily for the purpose of promoting their businesses rather than promoting social justice. Luxury companies thrive on the creation of public images that communicate brand associations to their

---

[33] *See The Montblanc "Signature for Good" Initiative*, MONTBLANC (Feb. 26, 2013), http://stories.montblanc.com/2013/02/the-montblanc-signature-for-good-initiative/#.UYdoAIKaS5I.

[34] *See* Ken Stern, *Why the Rich Don't Give to Charity*, THE ATLANTIC (Mar. 20, 2013), http://www.theatlantic.com/magazine/archive/2013/04/why-the-rich-dont-give/309254/.

[35] Many donate money in order to use tax reliefs, but some even go as far as to "exploit" the system to pay less in tax than the average family. *See* Robert Winnett, James Kirkup, & Christopher Hope, *Wealthiest People "Abusing Tax System with Donations to Charities That Don't Do Charitable Work,"* TELEGRAPH (Apr. 10, 2012), http://www.telegraph.co.uk/news/politics/georgeosborne/9195571/Wealthiest-people-abusing-tax-system-with-donations-to-charities-that-dont-do-charitable-work.html.

[36] KEN STERN, WITH CHARITY FOR ALL: WHY CHARITIES ARE FAILING AND A BETTER WAY TO GIVE 131 (2013) (pointing out that sometimes people donate for "public acclaim through naming rights").

[37] Stern, *supra* note 34.

[38] PETER SINGER, THE LIFE YOU CAN SAVE: ACTING NOW TO END WORLD POVERTY 65 (2009) (pointing out that "many of us believe that if people are motivated only by a desire to 'be honored by men' or to improve their reputations for generosity, they are not really being generous, and will not be generous when no one is looking").

[39] *See* Aneel Karnani, *The Case Against Corporate Social Responsibility*, WALL ST. J. (June 14, 2012), http://online.wsj.com/article/SB10001424052748703338004575230 112664504890.html.

customers.[40] While they may choose to accept diminished profits to enhance social welfare, luxury companies—like most public companies—must also answer to their investors. Realistically, they may only engage in charitable activities that are in line with the interests of the company, and this is not often the case. When private profits conflict with the public interest–related CSR/charitable activities, luxury companies will have to opt for protecting their private interests for shareholders. For instance, the decline in the sales of luxury goods in the Chinese market has prompted some luxury companies to eschew their anti-corruption CSR in exchange for the boost to their retail business. It has been reported that many luxury stores deliberately aided corruption in China by following their clients' requests to invoice their luxury goods as "gift[s] or expenses for work."[41] The invoices can later be used by their clients as documents for obtaining reimbursements from public funds.

C. INDUCING ETHICAL DELIBERATION ABOUT INJUSTICE

The core problem with the above two conventional ways is that they still leave many luxury consumers with little direct access to information about the plight of the poor people's lives. Instead, the purchase and consumption experience of luxury goods only makes many luxury consumers confined in the self-oriented world of perfection, comfort, and status. Research has shown that the lack of generosity from the rich people may be attributed to their isolation from people in need.[42] Consequently, it has become much more difficult for most rich people to care about social injustice.

A recent study conducted by the *Chronicle of Philanthropy* affirms this propensity of luxury consumers. The researchers analyzed giving habits across all zip codes in the United States. They found out that the differences in behavior among wealthy households depended on the type of neighborhood they lived in. Wealthy people who lived in homogeneously affluent areas were less generous than wealthy people who lived in more socioeconomically diverse surroundings. The research suggests that greater exposure to the challenges of meeting basic needs may create higher empathy and willingness to give.[43]

---

[40] UCHE OKONKWO, LUXURY FASHION BRANDING: TRENDS, TACTICS, TECHNIQUES 122 (2007) (emphasizing that the value of luxury brands is sustained by "the enhancement of the brand associations in the consumers' minds").

[41] *See Why the Luxury Market in China Has Taken a Sudden Dive*, WORLDCRUNCH (May 7, 2013, 12:47 PM), http://www.worldcrunch.com/business-finance/why-the-luxury-market-in-china-has-taken-a-sudden-dive/luxury-officials-china-public-money-corruption/c2s11711/#.UYn6k8u9KSM.

[42] ANEEL KARNANI, FIGHTING POVERTY TOGETHER: RETHINKING STRATEGIES FOR BUSINESS, GOVERNMENTS, AND CIVIL SOCIETY TO REDUCE POVERTY 85 (2011) ("The affluent can actually visit poor neighbourhoods and photograph or film the poor in their 'natural habitat,' either sanitizing or romanticizing their lives").

[43] Stern, *supra* note 34.

As a response to the lack-of-information problem, the Ethical Responsibility Initiative directly exposes luxury consumers to information about the enormous social injustice that still exists in society. It seeks to open the possibility that the dissemination of information about poor children through luxury stores would encourage luxury merchandisers and consumers to engage in ethical deliberation about the stark contrast between the rich and the poor and the roots of social injustice. The moral deliberation could further play a role in inducing them to adopt more ethical merchandising, purchasing, or consuming behaviors. The Ethical Responsibility Initiative, therefore, responds directly to the problems that have significantly weakened the conventional practices to grapple with social injustice in the context of the luxury market. It is a proposal to steer away from the direct use of money as a tool to deal with social injustice, because the primary function of the initiative is to induce ethical deliberation about social injustice among luxury consumers.

Empathy has been hailed as "the most essential quality of civilization."[44] By nature, the initiative celebrates empathy as an ethical power that a human being can acquire and strengthen through proper ethical deliberation to deal with poverty and hardships that have deteriorated other human beings' lives. To nurture empathy, the initiative takes the following two steps.

The first step involves the process that one can only nurture empathy in him- or herself through his exposure to information about people who need empathy.[45] Psychologists have conducted a controlled experiment with low-income and upper-class participants. Initially, the low-income group exhibited a higher willingness to help others. However, when both groups were exposed to a sympathy-eliciting video on child poverty, the compassion of the wealthier group began to rise. Later on, the two groups' willingness to help others became almost identical.[46]

After disseminating information that may arouse empathy, the second step of the initiative requires a luxury consumer to engage in deliberation about his or her individual responsibility toward others whose situations call for empathy. In this process, a luxury consumer is supposed to treat him- or herself as a responsible member of a just society that requires proper division of responsibilities among its members.[47]

---

[44] *See 11th Hour "Roger Ebert"* (Colorado Public Television 12 broadcast Apr. 4, 2013), *available at* video.cpt12.org/video/2364991008. For a comprehensive discussion about empathy, see Karsten Stueber, *Empathy*, STAN. ENCYCLOPEDIA PHIL. (June 21, 2013), http://plato.stanford.edu/archives/sum2013/entries/empathy/.

[45] *See* PETER UNGER, LIVING HIGH AND LETTING DIE: OUR ILLUSION OF INNOCENCE 35–36 (1996) (pointing out that social distance and informative directness play important roles in people's ethical deliberations).

[46] Stern, *supra* note 34.

[47] *See* JOHN RAWLS, *Social Unity and Primary Goods, in* COLLECTED PAPERS 359, 371 (Samuel Freeman ed., 1999) (arguing that "[t]he conception [of justice] includes what we may call a *social division of responsibility*").

The Ethical Responsibility Initiative seeks to strengthen empathy by encouraging luxury consumers to consider how they can take on individual responsibility to help poor people, with a focus on children.[48] The brochures contain information about how the rich can help poor children. When luxury consumers see it, they may empathize with poor children and think about how they should help them. Therefore, the most important feature of the Ethical Responsibility Initiative is its potential to induce luxury consumers to think about their individual responsibilities in the social justice setting. This echoes a principle of ethical conduct that Professor Peter Singer proposed as a path to alleviate economic inequality.[49] By highlighting the importance of responsibility, the principle dictates that "if it is in our power to prevent something very bad from happening, without thereby sacrificing anything else morally significant, we ought, morally, to do it."[50]

Moreover, the initiative encourages shareholders and managerial personnel of luxury companies to engage in ethical deliberation about their companies' responsibilities in addition to distributing brochures. First, luxury consumers who have conducted ethical deliberations may publicly urge luxury companies to take further responsibilities. Second, as luxury consumers, many of those shareholders or managerial personnel will receive brochures as well. This opportunity may induce them to deliberate about their individual responsibilities as well as any further responsibilities that their companies should fulfill. For example, they may consider any additional charity programs their companies should create.[51]

IV. Reforming Trademark Law

Trademark law could play an important role in implementing the Ethical Responsibility Initiative. To this end, trademark law should be reformed in a manner conducive to promoting ethical responsibility. Courts have ruled that "a mark with extensive public recognition and renown deserves and receives more legal protection than an obscure or weak mark."[52] Therefore, if luxury companies endeavor to fulfill ethical responsibilities, their brands will be entitled to stronger anti-confusion as well as anti-dilution

[48] *See, e.g.*, Iris Marion Young, Responsibility for Justice 40–41 (2011) (highlighting the importance of "a more active relation between individuals, social-structural processes, and responsibility").

[49] Singer, *supra* note 23, at 235.

[50] Singer, *supra* note 23, at 235.

[51] For example, Kate Spade has been helping Women for Women International create meaningful employment opportunities for women in Bosnia and Herzegovina, Kosovo, Rwanda, and Afghanistan. *See Hand in Hand: Kate Spade New York and Women for Women International Expand Partnership*, Women for Women Int'l, http://www.womenforwomen.org/help-women/kate-spade-hand-in-hand.php (last visited Oct. 13, 2013).

[52] Kenner Parker Toys Inc. v. Rose Art Indus., Inc., 963 F.2d 350, 353 (Fed. Cir. 1992).

protection of their brands. This section will discuss why this reform of trademark law in the United States would encourage luxury companies to take proactive measures to fulfill their ethical responsibilities. It will show that the international intellectual property system can embrace this reform without amending relevant treaty rules, making it possible to further reform in other countries.

A. ADDITIONAL FACTORS FOR RECOGNIZING FAMOUS TRADEMARKS

First, factors for determining the famous mark status should include a factor involving whether and how luxury companies fulfill their ethical responsibilities. The fame of the registered mark plays a "dominant" role in the likelihood of confusion analysis.[53] Famous marks, according to judicial decisions, should "enjoy a wide latitude of legal protection."[54] A famous mark is one that has "extensive public recognition and renown."[55] Thus, anti-confusion protection under the Lanham Act usually favors famous marks.[56] As a senior mark's fame increases, the Act's tolerance for similarities in competing senior and junior marks falls, leading to stronger anti-confusion protection for the senior mark. This may be a disputable standard of protection. But courts have at least cautioned that a third party intending to use marks that may be similar to famous marks must take vigilant measures to avoid causing confusion.[57] Although proof of fame alone is insufficient to establish likelihood of confusion, fame deserves its full measure of weight in assessing likelihood of confusion.[58] Article 16.3 of the Agreement on Trade-Related Aspects of Intellectual Property Rights (the TRIPS Agreement) mandates that member states should extend protection of well-known trademarks against unlawful uses in dissimilar classes of goods or services.

Currently, factors for determining the fame of a mark for anti-confusion analysis focus heavily on brand owners' promotional activities that increase the popularity of brands.

---

[53] *Kenner Parker*, 963 F.2d at 352 (ruling that "fame of the prior mark ... plays a dominant role in cases featuring a famous or strong mark. Famous or strong marks enjoy a wide latitude of legal protection").

[54] *See* Recot, Inc. v. M.C. Becton, 214 F.3d 1322, 1327 (Fed. Cir. 2000); *see also* Palm Bay Imps., Inc. v. Veuve Clicquot Ponsardin Maison Fondee En 1772, 396 F.3d 1369, 1374 (Fed. Cir. 2005) ("[A] strong mark ... casts a long shadow which competitors must avoid" (citation omitted)).

[55] *See Kenner Parker*, 963 F.2d at 353.

[56] *See, e.g.*, Louis Vuitton Malletier S.A. v. Haute Diggity Dog, LLC, 507 F.3d 252 (4th Cir. 2007) ("[F]inding a mark to be strong and famous usually favors the plaintiff in a trademark infringement case ....").

[57] *See, e.g., Kenner Parker*, 963 F.2d at 353 (noting that when a famous mark is at issue, a competitor must pause to consider carefully whether the fame of the mark, accorded its full weight, casts a "long shadow which competitors must avoid"); *see also* Nina Ricci, S.A.R.L. v. E.T.F. Enters., Inc., 889 F.2d 1070, 1074 (Fed. Cir. 1989) ("[T]here is no excuse for even approaching the well-known trademark of a competitor" (internal quotation omitted)).

[58] *See, e.g.*, Coach Servs., Inc. v. Triumph Learning LLC, 668 F.3d 1356, 1367 (Fed. Cir. 2012) (ruling that a mark's fame "'deserves its full measure of weight in assessing likelihood of confusion'" (quoting Recot, Inc. v. M.C. Becton, 214 F.3d 1322 (Fed. Cir. 2000))).

The TRIPS Agreement directs member states to include public recognition "obtained as a result of the promotion of the trademark" as a factor determining fame.[59] Similarly, additional factors adopted by the World Intellectual Property Organization (WIPO) Joint Recommendation Concerning Provisions on the Protection of Well-Known Marks center on the promotional efforts made by well-known trademark owners.[60] The *DuPont* factors adopted by U.S. courts in determining whether the registration of a mark would cause likelihood of confusion examine a factor about "[t]he fame of the prior mark."[61] Courts have clearly pointed out that this factor should be examined by considering sales, advertising, and length of use of the prior mark.[62] More specifically, courts held that "statistics of sales and advertising"[63] should be accepted as a primary indicator of fame. With regard to luxury brands, courts have ruled that factors for measuring the fame of a mark include "sales, advertising, length of use of the mark, market share, brand awareness, licensing activities, and variety of goods bearing the mark."[64]

If we integrate the ethical responsibility consideration into trademark law, the determination of the fame of a mark should include one additional factor. Different from the economic calculation-based factors as discussed above, this factor inquires into how luxury companies have taken measures to fulfill their ethical responsibilities. It is true that promotional efforts made by a brand owner can anchor its unique image (e.g., a certain level of quality of goods) in the minds of the relevant sector of consumers. Therefore, promotional efforts should be a significant factor in determining the fame of a brand. Meanwhile, how luxury companies fulfill their ethical responsibilities can also strengthen the unique identity of a brand and thereby increase the fame of the brands in the minds of the consumers. Luxury companies would distribute brochures together with goods merchandized with their brands. When consumers take a closer look at a brochure, they can always recall where they acquired it. Luxury companies can also request to put their brands directly on the brochures. Media coverage also helps luxury companies raise the fame of their brands, and media reports about the ethical responsibility–related activities of luxury companies convey these stories to their audiences. Therefore, whether a brand owner has taken measures to fulfill its ethical

---

[59] *See* TRIPS Agreement, art. 16.2 ("Members shall take account of the knowledge of the trademark in the relevant sector of the public, including knowledge in the Member concerned which has been obtained as a result of the promotion of the trademark.").

[60] *See* WIPO Well-Known Trademark Recommendation, art. 2(1)(b).

[61] *In re* E. I. DuPont DeNemours & Co., 476 F.2d 1357, 1361 (C.C.P.A. 1973).

[62] *See, e.g.*, Citigroup Inc. v. Capital City Bank Grp., Inc., 637 F.3d 1344, 1355 (Fed. Cir. 2011) ("The 'fame of a mark may be measured indirectly, among other things, by the volume of sales and advertising expenditures of the goods traveling under the mark, and by the length of time those indicia of commercial awareness have been evident'") (citing Bose Corp. v. QSC Audio Products, Inc., 293 F.3d 1367, 1371 (Fed. Cir. 2002)).

[63] Bose Corp. v. QSC Audio Prods., Inc., 293 F.3d 1367, 1371 (Fed. Cir. 2002) (noting that "when the numbers are large, [the Court has] tended to accept them without any further supporting proof").

[64] Coach Servs., Inc. v. Triumph Learning LLC, 668 F.3d 1356, 1367 (Fed. Cir. 2012).

responsibility can be added as a factor for determining the fame of luxury brands not only in economic terms but also in ethical terms.

Not all luxury brands have been recognized as well-known trademarks. The additional factor should be very helpful for luxury brands that have adopted low-profile marketing strategies. For example, Bottega Veneta is known for not using logos on the surfaces of their products for the purpose of increasing brand exclusivity.[65] Hermès has been marketing their products without much promotion.[66] But these low-profile marketing strategies could make it difficult for the relevant luxury companies to prove the well-known status of their trademarks. Recently, a Chinese court ruled that the Chinese name of Hermès was not a well-known trademark in China on the grounds that Hermès lacked promotional activities to increase its fame in China.[67] If Hermès participated in the Ethical Responsibility Initiative, then the additional factor would help its Chinese version win recognition as a well-known trademark.

B. RAISING THE BAR FOR ANTI-DILUTION PROTECTION

Second, legislators should revise trademark law to provide anti-dilution protection only to luxury brands that adequately fulfill their responsibilities within the ambit of the Ethical Responsibility Initiative. Anti-dilution is a form of trademark protection that guards against blurring the distinctiveness of brands and tarnishing the reputation of brands.[68] It plays an important role in protecting the exclusivity of brands, which is crucial for luxury companies.[69] For example, in *Cartier, Inc. v. Deziner Wholesale, LLC*,[70] the court pointed out that Cartier consumers were sophisticated enough to tell the difference between the sunglasses produced by Cartier and Deziner.[71] However, the court enjoined the defendant Deziner from using the CARTIER mark on its sunglass box label, because Cartier's distinctive reputation in the marketplace may still be harmed by the defendant's use of the CARTIER mark.[72] The court reasoned that "it is also likely that these sophisticated, brand conscious consumers will lose interest in the Cartier name as they see the number of inferior products in the market bearing the Cartier

---

[65] *See* Kate Betts, *Fashion: The Height of Luxury*, TIME (Apr. 23, 2006), http://www.time.com/time/magazine/article/0,9171,1186563,00.html (describing Bottega Veneta's strategy of not using logos with the concept that "the consumer can recognize a brand by the design and quality of the product instead of by a logo").

[66] *See* Jing Jing, *Fashion Forward*, CHINADAILY (June 30, 2007), http://www.chinadaily.com.cn/bw/2007-07/02/content_907229.htm (noting that Hermès "usually takes a low-profile marketing approach").

[67] *See France's Hermès Loses China Trademark Fight*, REUTERS (Feb. 26, 2012), http://www.reuters.com/article/2012/02/27/hermes-china-idUSL4E8DR01820120227.

[68] 15 U.S.C. § 1125(c)(1) (2012).

[69] Sun, *supra* note 11, at 404–5.

[70] No. 98 Civ. 4947 (RLC), 2000 U.S. Dist. LEXIS 4157 (S.D.N.Y. Apr. 3, 2000).

[71] *Id.* at *6.

[72] *Id.*

name grow."[73] Implied in this line of reasoning is that the exclusivity of Cartier products would be diminished when Cartier consumers are alerted to the availability of inferior Deziner sunglasses in the mass market. Therefore, trademark protection shields Cartier against the dilutive use of its brand that would harm the exclusiveness of its brand.

While anti-confusion protection only treats the fame of a mark as one factor among others to be weighed by courts, proving the fame of a mark is the prerequisite for seeking anti-dilution protection. A trademark owner alleging fame must establish that its mark "is widely recognized by the general consuming public of the United States."[74] The Trademark Dilution Revision Act of 2006 (TDRA) provides a non-exhaustive list of factors that a court may consider in determining the famous trademark status:

(i) The duration, extent, and geographic reach of advertising and publicity of the mark, whether advertised or publicized by the owner or third parties.
(ii) The amount, volume, and geographic extent of sales of goods or services offered under the mark.
(iii) The extent of actual recognition of the mark.
(iv) Whether the mark was registered under the Act of March 3, 1881, or the Act of February 20, 1905, or on the principal register.[75]

The first three are the main factors. Ostensibly, they focus on the promotional efforts made by brand owners. Some luxury companies have relied on their promotional activities to successfully claim the famous mark status. In *Rolex Watch U.S.A., Inc. v. AFP Imaging Corp.*,[76] Rolex opposed the registration of the mark "Roll-X" for medical and dental X-ray tables based upon a likelihood of dilution by blurring of its ROLEX mark for timepieces. The main pieces of evidence Rolex submitted included extensive sales figures in the hundreds of millions of dollars over the course of 25 years; extensive sales presence in the United States through the operation of 700 official branded jewelers; $10 million or more in annual advertising expenditures for promoting the mark in the United States since 1985; and continuous and prominent advertisements in nationally circulated publications reaching the general public.[77] In *Audi AG v. Shokan Coachworks, Inc.*,[78] the court recognized AUDI as a famous mark entitled to anti-dilution protection because plaintiffs submitted evidence of their multi-million dollar international advertising and sales of their products, as well as the length of time of the registration of the AUDI mark.[79]

[73] *Id.*
[74] 15 U.S.C. § 1125(c)(2)(A) (2012).
[75] *Id.*
[76] 101 U.S.P.Q.2d (BNA) 1188 (T.T.A.B. 2011).
[77] *Id.* at *11.
[78] 592 F. Supp. 2d 246 (N.D.N.Y. 2008).
[79] *Id.* at 280 (ruling that Audi successfully established famousness element of its dilution claim under Federal Trademark Dilution Act (FTDA), based on the length of time of its trademark registration, its multi-million

Although some luxury brands have already been recognized by courts as famous marks,[80] the inclusion of the ethical responsibility factor would help luxury companies that have taken on this responsibility achieve sufficiently high fame for anti-dilution protection. It is well established that such fame is "difficult to prove"[81] and that courts apply "a rigorous standard."[82] Fame for dilution protection "requires widespread recognition by the general public"[83] and a mark owner "must show that, when the general public encounters the mark 'in almost any context, it associates the term, at least initially, with the mark's owner.'"[84] The reference to the general public eliminates any possibility that a brand owner can rely on a brand's niche fame in a limited geographic area or a specialized market segment to claim anti-dilution protection.[85] The stakes in alleging dilution and setting out to prove fame, therefore, are high. If a plaintiff fails to provide sufficient evidence of fame as defined in Lanham Act § 43(c)(2)(A), then its dilution claim completely fails.

The Federal Circuit's recent decision in *Coach Services, Inc. v. Triumph Learning LLC*[86] demonstrates significant evidentiary pitfalls that even the owner of a very familiar brand may face for satisfying the fame precondition for anti-dilution protection. In this case, Coach opposed the registration of the defendant's mark COACH for educational materials used to prepare students for standardized tests. It asserted that the defendant's trademark registration had caused consumer confusion and diluted the COACH mark for luxury goods.[87] Coach successfully proved the famous mark status of COACH for its anti-confusion claim.[88] But it failed to prove that the fame of COACH is high enough to deserve anti-dilution protection.[89] In this respect, the court ruled that Coach failed to submit sufficient evidence to prove the following three points regarding the fame of COACH: (1) media coverage showing its "widespread recognition" in

---

dollar international marketing campaign, and the large amount, volume, and geographic extent of sales); *see also* Audi AG v. D'Amato, 469 F.3d 534, 543 (6th Cir. 2006) (ruling that Audi trademarks are famous because they are recognizable and widely known).

[80] In addition to Rolex and Audi, courts have recognized a few other luxury brands as famous marks entitled to anti-dilution protection. These brands include Louis Vuitton, Victoria's Secret, and Tiffany.

[81] Coach Servs., Inc. v. Triumph Learning LLC, 668 F.3d 1356, 1373 (Fed. Cir. 2012) (citing Toro Co. v. ToroHead Inc., 61 U.S.P.Q.2d (BNA) 1164, 1180 (T.T.A.B. 2001) ("Fame for dilution purposes is difficult to prove")).

[82] Everest Capital, Ltd. v. Everest Funds Mgmt., LLC, 393 F.3d 755, 763 (8th Cir. 2005) ("The judicial consensus is that 'famous' is a rigorous standard [for anti-dilution protection]").

[83] *Coach Servs.*, 668 F.3d at 1373.

[84] *Id.*

[85] Top Tobacco, LP v. N. Atl. Operating Co., 509 F.3d 380, 384 (7th Cir. 2007) (noting that the general public requirement "eliminated any possibility of 'niche fame,' which some courts had recognized before the amendment").

[86] *Coach Servs.*, 668 F.3d 1356.

[87] *Id.* at 1362.

[88] *Id.* at 1365–71.

[89] *Id.* at 1376 (ruling that Coach "failed to provide sufficient evidence of fame for dilution purposes").

the market;[90] (2) success of joint marketing efforts with LEXUS and CANON and the effect of these efforts in promoting the COACH mark in these partners' products;[91] and (3) a high level of brand awareness among women or men generally.[92]

The inclusion of the ethical responsibility factor would help Coach to achieve the famous mark status for anti-dilution protection by increasing its fame not only within a narrow consumer segment but also in the general marketplace. The *Coach Services* decision shows that in order to prove fame for anti-dilution protection, trademark owners should submit consumer surveys or recognition studies that are broad enough to satisfy the general public requirement.[93] If Coach carries out the ethical responsibility to disseminate brochures as required, it would be able to reach out to the wider public. The segment of the public would not just be confined to consumers of luxury goods. Instead, it would expand to the general public as media reports become abundant. Evidence of advertising alone may not satisfy the court. Rather, trademark owners should endeavor to prove the fruits of their marketing, either through timely brand awareness surveys or by other means such as media coverage. Again, the ethical responsibility activities would help Coach. The company may rely on the consumers' response to media reports on its efforts to carry out its ethical responsibilities to prove its fame. There would be news reports about Coach's efforts that would appear on different kinds of social media and public discussions about the effects of those efforts. With the increased flurry of media exposure, the public recognition of Coach's brand will significantly increase. The same applies to other luxury brands.

The inclusion of the ethical responsibility factor would not be a problem. First, the 2006 TDRA makes it clear that the factors listed therein for measuring fame are non-exhaustive.[94] Therefore, courts have the liberty to consider more factors that are appropriate for measuring the fame of a mark. So far luxury brands such as Louis Vuitton,[95] Victoria's Secret,[96] and Tiffany[97] have been recognized by courts as having adequate fame for anti-dilution protection. The additional ethical responsibility factor would help other luxury brands to achieve the famous mark status for anti-dilution protection.

---

90 *Coach Servs.*, 668 F.3d at 1375.

91 Coach "argued that other popular brands, including LEXUS and CANON, have used the COACH mark in connection with their products." *Id.*

92 The court agreed that "although the study [conducted by Coach] showed a high level of brand awareness among women ages 13–24, it provided no evidence of brand awareness among women generally, or among men." *Id.*

93 *Id.*

94 15 U.S.C. § 1125(c)(2)(A) (2012) (providing that "[i]n determining whether a mark possesses the requisite degree of recognition, the court may consider all relevant factors," including the four factors listed in *supra* note 75).

95 Louis Vuitton Malletier S.A. v. Haute Diggity Dog, LLC, 507 F.3d 252, 265 (4th Cir. 2007).

96 V Secret Catalogue, Inc. v. Moseley, 558 F. Supp. 2d. 734, 743–44 (W.D. Ky. 2008).

97 Tiffany (NJ) Inc. v. eBay, Inc., 576 F. Supp. 2d 463, 523 (S.D.N.Y. 2008), *aff'd in part, rev'd in part*, 600 F.3d 93 (2d Cir. 2010).

Moreover, the ethical responsibility factor would help luxury companies to prove whether the distinctiveness of their brands has been blurred or the reputation of their brands has been tarnished. Take the dilution by blurring, for example. Under the 2006 TDRA, dilution by blurring is defined as "association arising from the similarity between a mark or trade name and a famous mark that impairs the distinctiveness of the famous mark."[98] The TDRA also identifies a non-exhaustive list of six factors that courts "may consider" when determining whether a mark is likely to cause dilution by blurring.[99] In *Tiffany (NJ) Inc. v. eBay Inc.*,[100] Tiffany sued eBay for offering venues for selling counterfeit Tiffany products. The circuit court rejected Tiffany's dilution by blurring claim, because Tiffany failed to demonstrate that eBay's promotional efforts were likely to dilute the distinctiveness of the TIFFANY mark.[101] Agreeing with the district court, it reasoned that while eBay had certainly used the TIFFANY mark to describe products available on the eBay website, eBay had not used it to identify its own goods and services.[102] Therefore, eBay never used the TIFFANY mark in an effort to create an association with its own products. Instead, it used the mark directly to advertise and identify the availability of authentic Tiffany merchandise on the eBay website.

The ethical responsibility factor would help Tiffany convince court to uphold its dilution by blurring claim if a similar dispute arises in the future. Courts have ruled that not every factor listed by the TDRA will be relevant in every case, and not every blurring claim will require extensive discussion of the factors.[103] As the list of factors is non-exhaustive, when dealing with the Tiffany case, courts should have the liberty to apply the ethical responsibility factor to weigh whether eBay's use of its mark blurs the distinctiveness of the TIFFANY marks. Central to proving dilution by blurring is "the whittling away of [the] established trademark's selling power and value through its unauthorized use by others."[104] According to Professor Barton Beebe, if the plaintiff just proves a loss of uniqueness in the marketplace in general, the court would not uphold its dilution claim.[105] Instead, plaintiff must show that "consumers who are exposed to both the plaintiff's and

---

[98] § 1125(c)(2)(B).

[99] These six factors are: (1) "[t]he degree of similarity between the mark or trade name and the famous mark"; (2) "[t]he degree of inherent or acquired distinctiveness of the famous mark"; (3) "[t]he extent to which the owner of the famous mark is engaging in substantially exclusive use of the mark"; (4) "[t]he degree of recognition of the famous mark"; (5) "[w]hether the user of the mark or trade name intended to create an association with the famous mark"; and (6) "[a]ny actual association between the mark or trade name and the famous mark." § 1125(c)(2)(B)(i-vi).

[100] 600 F.3d 93, 101 (2d Cir. 2010).

[101] *Id.* at 112.

[102] *Id.* at 111–12.

[103] Louis Vuitton Malletier S.A. v. Haute Diggity Dog, LLC, 507 F.3d 252, 266 (4th Cir. 2007).

[104] Starbucks Corp. v. Wolfe's Borough Coffee, Inc., 588 F.3d 97, 105 (2d Cir. 2009).

[105] Barton Beebe, *A Defense of the New Federal Trademark Antidilution Law*, 16 Fordham Intell. Prop. Media & Ent. L.J. 1143, 1169–70 (2006).

the defendant's marks are less competent to make a 'mental connection' between the plaintiff's mark and the plaintiff's source ...."[106] Following this approach, the court can rule that eBay's use of the TIFFANY mark may blur the mental connection between the marks and Tiffany's responsibility fame. Because Tiffany only sells new products in their own retail stores,[107] the company can accumulate adequate fame for fulfilling the ethical responsibility to distribute brochures. By contrast, the first sales of both genuine and counterfeit Tiffany products on the eBay sites did not distribute the brochures from the Ethical Responsibility Initiative. The absence of this process would lead luxury consumers to think that Tiffany does not distribute the brochures through online sales, resulting in a likelihood of blurring Tiffany's ethical responsibility fame. However, for genuine Tiffany products, this decision only applies to the situations in which eBay is used as the venue to start the first sale of genuine products. Because of the first-sale doctrine,[108] it does not apply to the situations in which the subsequent sales of genuine, unaltered Tiffany products are made on eBay after they are first sold to consumers by Tiffany.

C. THE POWER OF TRADEMARK LAW IN INDUCING ETHICAL DELIBERATION

The new ethical responsibility as discussed in the preceding section presents a call to alter the common understanding of the function of trademark law. Trademark law has long been shaped by the economic efficiency policy.[109] Following this policy, trademark law serves the economic need to incentivize enterprises to offer high-quality goods and to protect the consumer interest in obtaining correct information about the source of goods.[110]

---

106 *Id.* Regarding this point, the recent Rolex Watch decision must prove a likelihood of blurring in the minds of consumers after proving fame of a mark for a dilution claim. Rolex Watch U.S.A., Inc. v. AFP Imaging Corp., 101 U.S.P.Q.2d (BNA) 1188 (T.T.A.B. 2011).

107 *See* Complaint at 6, Tiffany & Co. v. Costco Wholesale Corp., No. 13-CV-1041 (S.D.N.Y. Feb. 14, 2013), *available at* http://www.ipwatchdog.com/blog/Tiffany-Costco-Complaint.pdf ("To protect the brand, Tiffany fine jewelry is only sold in Tiffany retail stores in the United States by trained sales professionals, and is not distributed or sold at discount through off-price retail establishments anywhere in the world").

108 *See* Tumblebus Inc. v. Cranmer, 399 F.3d 754, 767 (6th Cir. 2005); Sebastian Int'l, Inc. v. Longs Drug Stores Corp., 53 F.3d 1073, 1076 (9th Cir. 1995).

109 *See* SUNDER, *supra* note 6, at 31 (pointing out that "intellectual property is understood almost exclusively as being about *incentives*" (emphasis in original)); Barton Beebe, *The Semiotic Analysis of Trademark Law*, 51 UCLA L. REV. 621, 624 (2004) [hereinafter *Semiotic Analysis*] (observing that the economic efficiency-based theory "has been adopted at the highest levels of American law. No alternative account of trademark doctrine currently exists" (citation omitted)); Mark P. McKenna, *The Normative Foundations of Trademark Law*, 82 NOTRE DAME L. REV. 1839, 1844 (2007) (concluding that the conventional wisdom about "the goal of trademark law is—and always has been—to improve the quality of information in the marketplace and thereby reduce consumer search costs").

110 Beebe, *Semiotic Analysis, supra* note 109, at 623 ("The Chicago School asserts that trademarks serve two efficiency-enhancing functions: First, trademarks lessen consumer search costs by making products and

The infusion of the ethical responsibility–based reform shows that trademark law can also perform an ethical function. Following the ethical responsibility proposal, trademark law would function to shape socially beneficial behaviors of producers and consumers.[111] Trademarked signs signify social and cultural information.[112] Trademark law should be empowered to inform both producers and consumers of the importance of ethical consumerism through the signs it protects. This informing power facilitates both producers' and consumers' acquisition and appreciation of information about humanistic values such as justice and dignity for combating social inequality and promoting environmental protection.

It would also change our vision about brands, leading us to highlight the ethical value of brands. Underpinning the conventional wisdom about the function of trademark law is the notion that brands are symbols that have only economic values. We hail the top 100 brands, each of which is worth billions of dollars.[113] Standards for recognition of well-known trademarks closely follow this pattern of evaluation by focusing on the economic value that promotional efforts inject into brands.[114]

The proposed change to trademark law channels in the ethical value of brands. Brands would no longer be valued only in economic terms. Instead, brands would also play a role in shaping the ethical sentiments of consumers. When consumers purchase and consume goods, they would be encouraged to consider whether companies that produce branded goods or services fulfill the ethical responsibility to distribute information about poor children. Increasingly, consumers would think more about other ethical issues. For instance, consumers would make purchase decisions by associating branded goods or services with an extra consideration on whether they have established the reputation for being environmentally friendly.[115] From this perspective, trademark law would

producers easier to identify in the marketplace, and second, trademarks encourage producers to invest in quality by ensuring that they, and not their competitors, reap the reputation-related rewards of that investment." (citation omitted)).

111 *See generally* Seana Valentine Shiffrin, *Inducing Moral Deliberation: On the Occasional Virtues of Fog*, 123 HARV. L. REV. 1214 (2010) (discussing the role of law in inducing ethical/moral deliberation).

112 *See* Beebe, *Semiotic Analysis*, *supra* note 109, at 648 ("The trademark … is not an irreducible, indivisible thing, but rather a set of relations, specifically, of semiotic relations of reference."); Rochelle Cooper Dreyfuss, *Expressive Genericity: Trademarks as Language in the Pepsi Generation*, 65 NOTRE DAME L. REV. 397, 397 (1990) (arguing that trademarks should be seen as "indicators of the status, preferences, and aspirations of those who use them" and "bases for vibrant, evocative metaphors"); Sonia K. Katyal, *Trademark Intersectionality*, 57 UCLA L. REV. 1601, 1612 (2010) ("Both views—trademark as commodity and trademark as social symbol—are deeply suffused with notions of culture and identity.").

113 *The World's Most Valuable Brands*, www.forbes.com/powerful-brands/list/.

114 *See* section IV.A.

115 *See* Annamma Joy et al., *Fast Fashion, Sustainability, and the Ethical Appeal of Luxury Brands*, 16 FASHION THEORY 273, 291 (2012) (arguing that "luxury brands can become the leaders in sustainability").

function to design "rules that will encourage the production of reputation but not its consumption."[116] Similarly, the implementation of the Ethical Responsibility Initiative would encourage luxury consumers and companies to increasingly care about their reputations with regard to ethical behaviors. Meanwhile, what they increasingly would care less about is the social distinction that traditionally was derived from consumption of luxury goods or services.

Measuring the value of brands from the ethical viewpoint is important for the success of the Ethical Responsibility Initiative. Luxury companies may oppose the initiative by arguing that it may associate their products, services, and brands with undesirable images of poverty, resulting in the reduction of their popularity among their consumers. When they have direct access to information about poverty, luxury consumers may feel guilty. As a result, they may purchase less or stop purchasing luxury goods. This might lead to a negative impact on the business of luxury companies and the value of their luxury brands.

However, if we measure the value of brands not only in economic terms but also in ethical terms, then the above concern would not arise. This is because ethical considerations would lead us to ponder whether luxury companies have fulfilled their responsibilities. By being proactive in their social responsibilities in their business operations, an organization can build a good reputation and image that helps the organization in the long run. For example, sections A and B of this section have shown that the use of the ethical responsibility factor in trademark law would benefit luxury companies, as they would receive enhanced anti-confusion and anti-dilution protection. Therefore, the efforts that luxury companies would make to fulfill their responsibilities would increase the ethical value and thus the total value of their brands.

V. Conclusion

The future of our society depends on how we can care about the pains suffered by our fellow human beings. Anyone or any society that is obsessed with the luxury of perfection, comfort, or status recognition will have no claim to be regarded as an ethical person or community.

Nobody is born as an ethical being from the outset of his or her lifelong journey into the world of civilization. The same applies to every luxury company and consumer from the outset of their fanciful journey into the world of luxury. All need to undergo a learning process to cultivate ethical impulses. The Ethical Responsibility Initiative I propose opens up this learning process. It highlights the need for luxury consumers to deliberate on ethical issues relating to their luxury spending and consumption. The ultimate goal of the Ethical Responsibility Initiative is to raise an ethical question about how

[116] Beebe, *Sumptuary Code, supra* note 6, at 886.

luxury consumers should react appropriately to the two worlds of luxury and poverty that co-existed in 2013: $296 billion was spent on luxury goods while 1.5 million children died from hunger.[117]

This question carries significant ethical consequences. Today, luxury consumers control much of society's wealth and political power.[118] If they cannot take part in the ethical learning process, the future of human civilization will not bear the sparks of ethics but will sink into the abyss of luxury.

---

[117] For the data about the amount of luxury spending and death of children resulting from hunger in 2013, see *supra* text accompanying notes 13 and 14.

[118] Professor Peter Singer reports that governmental officials in various countries are luxury consumers obsessed with the conspicuous consumption of luxury goods. *See* Peter Singer, *Why Pay More?*, PROJECT SYNDICATE (May 9, 2013), http://www.project-syndicate.org/commentary/the-moral-shortcomings-of-conspicuous-consumption-by-peter-singer (lamenting that "[w]earing a ridiculously expensive watch to proclaim that one has achieved an elevated social standing seems especially immoral for a public official in a country where a significant portion of the population still lives in real poverty").

12 The Scholarship of Envy

HOW THE FRAMING OF FASHION LEAVES A LEGAL LACUNA

Susan Scafidi*

LEGAL ACADEMIA ADORES status. From our educational pedigrees to our clerkships, and from the relative rankings of the law schools where we teach to those of the journals in which we publish, our preoccupation with positioning has become so conspicuous that even the American Bar Association has called upon faculty to "reduce the role of status" as a measure of success,[1] a recommendation that some have dismissed as unrealistic, if not incomprehensible.[2] Law often takes the form of a luxury good, and elite legal education still more so, but the legal academy is largely uncritical of its own love of labels.

While denizens of the faculty lounge may be reluctant to eschew intellectual insignia and professorial plumage, academics tend to show no such indulgence when it comes

---

* Professor, Founder, and Academic Director, Fashion Law Institute, at Fordham Law School. Thanks to the editors, the University of Hong Kong, and the many collaborators and friends across three industries—fashion, law, and academia—who have generously contributed to this discussion, in particular my esteemed colleague Jeff Trexler.

[1] Task Force on the Future of Legal Education, American Bar Association, Working Paper 32 (August 1, 2013).

[2] Lawrence Cunningham, *ABA Task Force on Legal Education: Down With Status*, Concurring Opinions, August 7, 2013, http://www.concurringopinions.com/archives/2013/08/aba-task-force-on-legal-education-down-with-status.html.

to criticizing the collectors and even creators of traditional luxury goods. This is especially true in regard to the world of fashion, which, as this volume illustrates via its focus on clothing and accessories to the virtual exclusion of categories such as automobiles, homes, cuisine, wine, artworks, and travel, tends to be conflated with luxury. Even as scholars from other disciplines have developed a rich panoply of theoretical models for understanding the full range of human personal adornment, legal scholarship has barely moved beyond the century-old critique in Thorstein Veblen's *Theory of the Leisure Class*, which famously explained changes in style as "conspicuous consumption" designed to display "prima facie evidence of social worth."[3] In other words, legal academics as a whole are both acutely conscious of status and dismissive of perceived status markers that exist outside of law schools, particularly in the sartorial realm.

The persistent attempts to reduce fashion to a fundamentally uncreative means of signaling status and utility is a telling opportunity for analytical omphaloskepsis, revealing more about the culture giving rise to the inquiry than about the significance of luxury itself in the legal arena. I have frequently explored the broad cultural factors that contribute to the perception of fashion as frivolous and unworthy of protection as intellectual property, much less the attention of an entire new field of law,[4] but in this chapter I focus on a single phenomenon that has particular relevance to legal scholarship: envy.

Like fashion, envy has in recent years been the subject of extensive study outside of the legal academy, which, following the precedent set by neoclassical economics and Rawlsian political theory, has continued to treat it as an irrational externality of little relevance to the dynamics of social competition.[5] Nevertheless, the scholarly assessment of envy offers a provocative framework for understanding why arguments that deny fashion the protection afforded other creative works have formed a trend among legal academics—and how fashion responds to this unflattering light.

I. Understanding Envy

Envy is an unpleasant word. First defined by Aristotle as "pain at the good fortune of others,"[6] envy summons the image of a green-eyed monster[7] and scenes of petty resentment at someone else's success, a feeling far beneath the lofty aspirations of the scholarly mind.

---

[3] Thorstein Veblen, The Theory of the Leisure Class: An Economic Study of Institutions 112 (Oxford University Press 2007) (1899).

[4] Susan Scafidi, *Fiat Fashion Law! The Launch of a Label—and a New Branch of Law, in* Navigating Fashion Law 7 (2012).

[5] Young Back Choi, Paradigms and Conventions: Uncertainty, Decision Making and Entrepreneurship vii, 3 (1993); John Rawls, A Theory of Justice: Revised Edition 123–25 (1999); Richard H. McAdams, *Relative Preferences*, 102 Yale Law Journal 1, 7 (1992).

[6] Aristotle, Rhetoric, bk. 2, ch. 10.

[7] William Shakespeare, Othello, act 3, sc. 3 (describing the related emotion of jealousy).

As Princeton social neuroscientist Susan Fiske observes, however, envy is a pervasive phenomenon that transcends social boundaries.[8] The abundant experimental evidence for the subconscious emergence of envious thoughts has given rise to an envy theory of the mind, in which the innate drive toward social comparison plays a primary role in defining personal identity.[9]

Yale psychiatrist Frank John Ninivaggi aptly summarizes the current understanding of envy when he describes it as a "sensation and conflated feeling of privation, powerlessness, inferiority, and hostile distress coupled with the urge to rob and spoil in the face of advantages and their enjoyment existing elsewhere."[10] Variations can be found across interpretive models, but the two main elements of this definition—the sense of relative deprivation and the urge to destroy others' perceived advantages—recur in theories of envy across academic disciplines, from philosophical debates over the role of envy in a democratic polity to studies in cognitive science that pinpoint the stimulation of neurons when individuals react to images of people who appear better off.

Grounded in a tradition extending back through the Enlightenment to classical Greece and sacred texts, this approach to envy views it as something more than just a petty emotion unworthy of serious academic study. An organic response to perceived difference, envy is a way of seeing oneself and others that can spawn a range of destructive effects, such as the development of reductionistic stereotypes, that have nothing to do with wasteful status displays.[11] For example, Fiske notes that the perception of superiority can be triggered almost instantaneously by an individual's good posture and the absence of what cultural critic Paul Fussell has called the "prole jacket-gape," a separation between the shirt and jacket collars that can occur when a suit fits poorly.[12] Even if factors such as good posture and an eye for flattering off-the-rack clothes rather than the purchase of luxury apparel led to the envied individual's sartorial superiority, an apparent indicator of success displayed directly on one's person can recast the unwitting target of envy as an indulgent self-promoter who does not deserve what he enjoys.

Although the price of expensive designer apparel that enhances the wearer's appearance may contribute to the viewer's response, economic disparity is but one easily cited potential source of envy and concomitant social friction. In contrast to Veblen and other industrial-age social theorists who saw the signaling of leisure and excess as core values associated with luxury goods, Ninivaggi notes that the main target of envy is not wealth

---

[8] Susan T. Fiske, Envy Up, Scorn Down: How Status Divides Us 15 (2011).

[9] Frank John Ninivaggi, Envy Theory: Perspectives on the Psychology of Envy (2010).

[10] *Id.* at 2.

[11] For discussions of the current state of research on envy and its effects, *see, e.g.,* Fiske note 8; Ninivaggi, *supra* note 9; Joseph Epstein, Envy: The Seven Deadly Sins (2003); Richard H. Smith, The Joy of Pain (2013)

[12] Fiske, *supra* note 8, at 53 (quoting Paul Fussell, Class: A Guide Through the American Status System 63 (1983)).

but creativity.[13] Productivity, innovation, and other evidence of adeptness at generating value can create in the observer a sense of inadequacy and impotence, which in turn can fuel active attempts to establish personal worth by "nullify[ing] any semblance of goodness" in the envied other.[14]

Fashion, as both an immediate and inevitable expression of personal identity and an indicator of creativity, arguably has greater potential to provoke envy than any other luxury good. Few people spend their whole lives in their homes or cars, and fine dining experiences and luxury vacations take place out of view of our co-workers and neighbors, but clothing is an almost omnipresent part of our individual appearances. In the words of Marshall McLuhan, "clothing is an extension of our skin."[15] What individuals choose to wear conveys information about personal identity and creates an immediate impression available for personal comparison, with envy a common result. As I have noted elsewhere, the intimate connection between apparel and identity has been a contributing factor to the reduced level of intellectual property protection provided for clothing design under U.S. law,[16] a state of affairs reinforced by the complicating impulse of envy.

Since most contemporary clothing is not designed and made entirely by the wearer, moreover, the creative force that is the object of envy and the target of desire or destruction typically flows through the consumer from the designer—at all price points and levels of production. Established and well-capitalized fashion houses may in some cases be able to respond by expending resources to secure protection of their creative designs to the limited extent legally possible, but both famous and unknown designers remain subject to the effects of envy-fueled behavior.

II. Envy and Equality

At the heart of the scholarly understanding of envy lie comparison and a resulting resentment of perceived inequality. In the fashion context, attempts to secure fashion design protection from the early decades of the twentieth century onward have been met with arguments decrying the injustice of enabling wealthy individuals to have clothes that ordinary people could not afford. What is presented rhetorically as a clear matter of economic fairness and sartorial democracy, however, is actually an argument rife with ethical complexity. Reducing the issue to a stereotyped conflict between undeserved privilege and absolute right not only defines away all other values associated with the purchaser's expression and creation of identity through clothes, but it also nullifies the interests of designers, manufacturers, distributors, retailers, and employees throughout fashion and related industries—few of whom are particularly affluent.

---

[13] NINIVAGGI, *supra* note 9, at 250.

[14] NINIVAGGI, *supra* note 9, at 88.

[15] MARSHALL MCLUHAN, UNDERSTANDING MEDIA (MIT Press 1994) (1964).

[16] Susan Scafidi, *FIT: Fashion as Information Technology*, 59 SYRACUSE L. REV. 69 (2008).

Even if this reductionist characterization were accurate and fashion were to serve merely as an instrument of the privileged for displaying high status, the distributive impulse is not without its own difficulties. In the oft-cited lament of Immanuel Kant, envy is an "abominable vice of a sullen passion" that arises when "the standard we use to see how well-off we are is not the intrinsic worth of our own well-being but how it compares with that of others."[17] Social justice may be an overt motivator for redistribution, or at least invoked as a motivating force, but responses to difference in position that seek to deprive others of their advantages have been the subject of extensive debate as to the less-compelling interests evidently at play.

At one end of the spectrum of attempts to address the place of envy within the public realm is the philosophy of Plato, who cites the civil strife resulting in part from envy as a reason for eliminating all private property.[18] A more contemporary line of argument takes Plato's reasoning to its polar opposite, challenging the validity of egalitarian distribution precisely because it is an institutional response to envious desire. Within jurisprudential circles the most familiar proponent of this position is Robert Nozick, who grounds the link between equality and envy in self-esteem. According to Nozick, the desire to deprive others of their advantages does not stem from the conviction that the envied individuals do not deserve what they have, but rather reflects an implicit judgment on one's own lack of merit.[19]

Insofar as Nozick recognizes state-enforced copyright as legitimate, we can infer that he would not have been sympathetic to arguments against intellectual property protection aimed at preventing the rich from enjoying a relative superiority in apparel. Instead, his model calls for the cultivation of a diverse range of forms perceived as advantageous, such that an individual who, say, lacked the means to buy an Hermès Birkin bag could nevertheless signal her creative value in a less expensive but more personally expressive manner. A popular expression of this very impulse can be heard in the hit rap video "Thrift Shop," in which Macklemore & Ryan Lewis sing the praises of buying "your granddad's clothes" at Goodwill instead of an expensive new designer T-shirt likely to be seen on six other people in the same club.[20]

Intermediate strategies for addressing envy can be found in the works of scholars such as John Rawls and Ronald Dworkin, each of whom has offered what purport to be schema optimally resulting in envy-free distribution.[21] For example, Rawls concedes that a certain degree of envy is indeed inevitable in human society in light of evident

---

[17] Immanuel Kant, *The Metaphysics of Morals* 252 (Mary Gregor ed., Cambridge University Press 1991) (1797).

[18] Jeremy Waldron, *Property and Ownership*, Stanford Encyclopedia of Philosophy, http://plato.stanford.edu/entries/property/.

[19] Robert Nozick, Anarchy, State, and Utopia 239–46 (1974).

[20] Macklemore and Ryan Lewis, *Thrift Shop, on* The Heist (Macklemore LLC 2012), official video available at http://www.youtube.com/watch?v=QK8mJJJvaes.

[21] See Rawls, *supra* note 5, at 124–25; Ronald Dworkin, Sovereign Virtue: The Theory and Practice of Equality 67 (2002).

differences in what we each possess and distances himself from an absolutist approach to egalitarianism that would appear to grounded in envious desire.[22] Nevertheless, in terms of equitable distribution envy can be circumvented through principles of justice rooted in Rawls's concept of the original position, in which principles of fairness are established in a "veil of ignorance" as to individuals' particular personal advantages.[23]

In the realm of fashion, however, the Rawlsian thought experiment and other attempts to balance equality and envy are frustrated by the quality that Cambridge philosopher of science John Forrester has described as the locus of envy's destructiveness: its "visuality."[24] Social comparison of stylistic differences is a stubborn fact in a world where the emperor's new clothes are just a fairy tale, and, as recent cognitive studies confirm, feelings later expressed in envious terms can be instantaneously triggered at first sight. Guido Calabresi draws on this reality in citing envy as a sentiment whose existence renders Pareto optimality a "pointless" abstraction,[25] an argument that is just one of several instances in which Calabresi anticipated the rise of behavioral economics.[26] Ultimately, neither the true multivalence of human adornment nor the varied analyses of and prescriptions regarding envy allow for a simple response based on the rhetoric of equality.

III. Fashion and Envy in the Legal Academy

Fashion would thus appear to be a rich avenue through which to explore envy's implications for distributive justice, but in the legal academy at least this discussion has been absent. Instead, the tension between desire and perceived deprivation frequently continues to be simplified and cloaked by Veblen's hoary mantle, and fashion cast merely as an instrument of the privileged for displaying high status—the antithesis of the egalitarian values and democratic ideals publicly endorsed by the academy—rather than as a medium of varied and complex expression.

A representative example of this limited perspective is the treatment of fashion in an article by University of Chicago law professor Richard McAdams, in which he attempts to eliminate the problem of envy in analytical terms by recasting the debate in the rationalized language of neoclassical economic theory.[27] After dismissing envy as an all but irrelevant irrational feeling discouraged by social norms, McAdams's model cites fashion as an area in which understanding social comparison in terms of relative preferences

---

[22] *See* John Forrester, *Psychoanalysis and the History of the Passions: The Strange Destiny of Envy, in* FREUD AND THE PASSIONS 127, 138 (John O'Neill ed., 2010) (quoting JOHN RAWLS, A THEORY OF JUSTICE 537 (1971)).

[23] *See* RAWLS, *supra* note 5, at 124–25.

[24] Forrester, *supra* note 22, at 137.

[25] Guido Calabresi, *The Pointlessness of Pareto: Carrying Coase Further*, 100 YALE L.J. 1211, 1217 (1991).

[26] Michael G. Faure, *Calabresi and Behavioural Tort Law and Economics*, 1 ERASMUS L. REV. 75 (2008).

[27] See McAdams, *supra* note 5, at 7–10.

can provide a solid basis for egalitarian public policy. In what amounts to a terminological update of Veblen's critique of conspicuous consumption and Pierre Bourdieu's concept of cultural capital, McAdams describes fashion exclusively in terms of status display: even when people think that they want clothing because it is attractive or well made, their expression of this particular relative preference indicates that they are subconsciously seeking to engage in status competition by showing their wealth and good taste. Because the pursuit of the latest status symbols in fashion is an intrinsically wasteful market enterprise, he concludes, the government should enact legal reforms designed to undercut competitive consumption.

What then of aesthetic appeal, designers' creativity, or the many facets of innovation and personal identity that transcend relative ranking? If fashion were truly no more than an exercise in status display, a consumer would have no way of forming a preference for one equally expensive, well-known, logoed handbag over the next—and yet such individual preferences clearly exist. In the decades since historian Valerie Steele lamented the academy's inattention to fashion in "The F-Word,"[28] scholars outside of legal academia have begun to identify a myriad of ways in which fashion reflects interests and values beyond a status game, though fashion is still developing as a mainstream academic discipline. The very qualities that are receiving the most attention in cutting-edge work outside the legal academy, however, fail to penetrate the overt legal characterization of the fashion world as a frivolous scramble to show one's comparative worth.

Veblen's limited treatment of fashion may have suited the argument that he proposed more than a century ago, during an era of the fashion industry that would be unrecognizable to modern consumers, but repeatedly recasting an archaic theory in the language of market failure, equitable distribution, or positional goods does not give it new depth or persuasive force. The same is true of other outmoded models, such as economist Paul Nystrom's 1928 description of the fashion cycle.[29] While it is conceivable that the legal academy is simply sticking with familiar theories learned decades ago, the onrush of new commentators to the subject of intellectual property and fashion design would suggest that other factors are at work.

One reason for the lag may be the recent nature of the legal academy's interest in fashion as a sustained object of study. Efforts to secure design protection in the first half of the twentieth century produced a handful of articles on that particular topic;[30] the

---

[28] Valerie Steele, *The F-Word*, LINGUA FRANCA, April 1991.

[29] PAUL NYSTROM, THE ECONOMICS OF FASHION 18–29 (1928). As Nystrom observed, the fashion cycle is a model for understanding "the rise, culmination and decline in popular acceptance of a style," with a new style arising in its place. *Id.* at 18.

[30] *See, e.g.*, Note, *Self-Protection of Design Creation in the Millinery Industry*, 49 YALE L.J. 1290 (1939–40); Rudolf Callman, *Style and Design Piracy*, 22 J. PATENT OFFICE SOC. 557 (1940); Maurice A. Weikert, *Design Piracy*, 19 IND. L.J. 235 (1943–44).

revival of attention in recent years to a certain degree shows the effects of being stuck in amber.

A related issue is the legal academy's lack of an intuitive grasp of fashion fundamentals from the inside out. An environment open to opining on the originality of designs without an organic familiarity with fashion culture, the history of costume and style, aesthetics, the business of fashion, or the elements of garment construction is highly conducive to analytical clichés. It also creates an opening for miscues that undermine the academy's already tangential authority within the fashion community, such as panels on which scholars unwittingly demonstrate the limits to their knowledge of Hermeez, Lewbooteen, and Versayss.[31]

The passage of time offers hope of at least a partial correction of these problems, but preoccupation with status and social rank may very well continue to hinder development of a common legal academic awareness of the significance of style as more nuanced than at best a mere metric of success and at worst a social evil.[32] Persistent use of reductionist stereotypes to negate fashion's value is a telling sign that envy has exerted an influence on legal scholarship related to the fashion world, at least to the extent that fashion logos—and by extension most designs, designers, consumers, and other elements of fashion—can be dismissed as "toxic waste."[33]

Within law schools fashion has a valence distinct from other areas of the university, especially when it comes to the perception of status. A theme in the understanding of envy that has remained consistent from Aristotle through Nozick and contemporary cognitive theory is the effect of a shared context for comparison. For instance, the propensity of a professor of medieval history to nurture substantial envy of someone wearing a Prada suit is likely to be rather low, since the typical grad student who sets out to study thirteen-century texts understands that this is not a career choice calculated to finance a wardrobe of luxury goods, nor is the history department an environment in which such items are frequently seen on fellow students or professorial colleagues.

The legal academy, though, is a different environment. A lawyer who becomes a law professor is regularly confronted with visual reminders of more economically rewarding or otherwise upwardly mobile roads not taken within the legal profession. Students who once cowered in class may ascend through the associate ranks to become wealthy law firm partners in bespoke suits, while others appear in alumni publications wearing distinguished judicial robes. Within law faculties themselves, salaries are higher and have a wider range

---

[31] Yes, I've heard these mispronunciations of Hermès, Louboutin, Versace and others, publicly and loudly, despite their centrality to the panelists' presentations in each case, and no, I won't name names.

[32] *See generally* DEBORAH L. RHODE, THE BEAUTY BIAS: THE INJUSTICE OF APPEARANCE IN LIFE AND LAW (2010) (criticizing the social importance of women's physical appearance—albeit with a red stiletto pump adorning the book's cover).

[33] Barton Beebe, Panel discussion at the Penn Intellectual Property Group Annual Symposium, University of Pennsylvania Law School, March 20, 2012.

than in most academic departments, and some professors engage in well-compensated consulting work that further tips the scales.

The legal academy has adapted to this environment by developing a substitute array of tiered metrics, clustering primarily around the nodes of education, affiliation, and publication. At the same time a vibrant culture of communicating and comparing relative worth has emerged, ranging from conference gossip to Brian Leiter's Law School Reports blog.[34]

While the markers of status for law professors are rather conspicuous within the legal academy, outside academia these intellectual insignia are abstract and for the most part invisible. Clothing, and in particular the expensive luxury goods associated with those who have considerable wealth and achievement, presents a visible and direct challenge to the status of legal scholars once they step outside of their more familiar milieu. As predicted by envy theory, academics respond aggressively to this implicit judgment on their own adequacy and reminder of their lack of wealth by rhetorically reducing fashion's creative expression to little more than a meaningless status marker that is wholly undeserving of protection in an egalitarian, meritocratic society.

With regard to scholarly analysis, then, the legal academic medium is the message: the orientation toward social comparison within this highly stratified professional environment has shaped the content of its scholarship in manifest ways. The predilection for viewing fashion in terms of class and privilege is a case in point, and obsession with status does not stop with items of apparel and accessories that are costly. Attire that exhibits a creative edge not only confounds the legal academy's system of rankings, but it also presents this image to the world in a direct visual encounter that professors cannot hope to rival until résumé T-shirts become a trend.

The impact of this encounter is evident in print. The complexity of fashion—beauty, meaning, identity; the interplay of designer and wearer; elements that cross and transcend class divides—is limited and distorted into an irrational status game and the undemocratic defense of privilege, thus depriving fashion of any advantages that undermine the academy's own claims to superior expertise and status.

IV. From Sinners to Saints: Toward a Scholarly Engagement with Envy

The juxtaposition of envy theory, intellectual property, and fashion law scholarship abounds with unrealized potential, an abundance of textual, tactile, and image-based data that provide a unique opportunity to advance understanding of how a common human impulse relates to public policy. What the quality of the legal academy's

---

[34] The prevalence of ranking is such that it is occasionally the basis of self-deprecating humor. *See, e.g.,* Brian Leiter, *"Why Tolerate Religion?" Has Clearly Touched a Nerve: Some Comments on Michael McConnell's Review*, Brian Leiter's Law School Reports, December 18, 2013, http://leiterlawschool.typepad.com/leiter/2013/12/why-tolerate-religion-has-clearly-touched-a-nerve.html ("The second most distinguished and accomplished conservative scholar of law and religion [yes, I rank those too]....").

contribution will be on this score, however, depends to a significant extent on its ability to step outside itself. Rather than projecting the signature status-seeking motivations of legal academia onto a popular phenomenon, the scholarly community has an opportunity to engage in rigorous Socratic scrutiny of its own unexamined assumptions.

An initial topic ripe for sustained examination is the concept of luxury itself. Contrary to what one might conclude from some descriptions of the fashion industry in legal scholarship, clothing, creative fashion, and luxury are not synonymous; at the conference that was the genesis of this collection, even the most confirmed critics delivered their papers while wearing clothes. Not only can an unreflective focus on fashion transform the status-conscious subtext of legal academic culture into a rather conspicuous text, leaving our Freudian slip showing, but an assessment of luxury concerned primarily with either negating or gaining access to others' distinction also tends to overlook a range of other ways in which luxury is expressed and interpreted.

With respect to fashion as a field of study apart from a narrow focus on luxury, however defined, sensitivity to the influence of envy can also serve as a spur toward more empathic engagement.[35] Fashion is a subject upon which people all too often feel free to opine without attempting to understand, a state of affairs that provides an ideal context for academic inquiry to demonstrate its own worth.

Beyond the possibilities for scholarship as an end in itself, understanding envy in public and academic life also has the potential to shed light on the persistent problem of intellectual property protection. Over the past century, reductionist stereotypes of fashion as a recursive and creatively bankrupt medium or a mere status marker have been a significant factor in first limiting the application of extant U.S. intellectual property laws to fashion and, second, delaying the passage of corrective design-specific legislation. The resulting environment has left creators and consumers to rely heavily on the third, extralegal option of designing their own defenses, a phenomenon that I have on frequent occasions since 2005 referred to as self-help.[36] Stakeholders in fashion originality have responded to the gaps in protection with an array of tactics that warrant further study as evidence of the distorting effects of the current state of the law and resources for optimizing legal reform. Among the patterns of self-help that I have catalogued are evolution of technological means of ascertaining authenticity, engagement with social norms, use of humor and media messages, strategic leveraging of consumer behavior, defensive choices regarding technique and quality, and adaptation of business structures. While a detailed discussion of the legal and extralegal landscape of fashion and intellectual property law lies beyond the scope of this chapter, an examination of envy plays a key role in understanding its peculiar nature.

---

[35] *See, e.g.,* NINIVAGGI, *supra* note 9, at 287.

[36] *See, e.g.,* Susan Scafidi, *Intellectual Property and Fashion Design, in* 1 INTELLECTUAL PROPERTY AND INFORMATION WEALTH 115 (Peter K. Yu ed., 2006) ("Chief among these self-help efforts to control design piracy was the establishment of the Fashion Originators' Guild of America in 1932").

In addition to revealing the contours of a legal lacuna and its consequences, academic analysis of envy and its effects has the potential to strengthen the theoretical basis for fashion design protection in whatever form it takes. For instance, the various models for integrating envy into theories of justice in political philosophy have their differences, but their core methodology and reasoning point to a possible means of rationalizing statutory reform that provides fashion designs with a more narrowly tailored scope of protection than standard copyright. Accommodating the human phenomenon of envy can provide grounds for a strategic concession to political reality while acknowledging fashion's creative force.

Even on a personal level, models of envy point to ways in which the legal academy can ameliorate its response to the expertise and values woven into cutting-edge clothes. It is not necessary to buy expensive designer goods to be fashionable; indeed, style connoisseurs have long been aware that looking only at labels is a primrose path to fashion victimhood. Steele's indictment of academics as the "worst-dressed middle-class occupational group in the United States"[37] still rings true years later, as does a subsequent conversation in which she challenged me to imagine a typical law partner and a typical hairdresser's assistant, and then to note which likely had more money to spend on her outfit and which wore the more personally expressive and creative ensemble. Instead of obsessing over a fictive status competition in which the person with the most costly labels wins, and counterfeits and knockoffs persist as an envious but fundamentally uncreative response to the original, it is far better to express one's own personal style with the innovative flair that the best fashion celebrates.

[37] Steele, *supra* note 28, at 16.

V The Globalization of Luxury Brands

13 Let Them Eat Fake Cake

THE RATIONAL WEAKNESS OF CHINA'S ANTI-COUNTERFEITING POLICY

Kal Raustiala* and Christopher Jon Sprigman**

THE LUXURY JEWELER and watchmaker Cartier has four boutiques in New York City. Given New York's great concentration of wealth, and its position at the center of the world's fashion industry, this is unsurprising. What may be surprising is that in Beijing, Cartier has six boutiques. And in Hong Kong, Cartier has eleven. Cartier's sizable presence in China is not anomalous. Luxury brands abound in China today; American and European luxury-goods firms are vigorously pursuing Chinese customers, with more and grander stores and boutiques opening every year. By many measures China is now the world's largest market for luxury goods.[1]

---

* Professor, UCLA School of Law; Director, UCLA Ronald W. Burkle Center for International Relations.

** Professor, New York University School of Law and Co-Director, Engelberg Center on Innovation Law and Policy. Thanks to Orly Lobel for suggesting the title of this chapter. We thank Tom Plate, Haochen Sun, Alex Wang, and Peter Yu for excellent comments on earlier drafts, and Isabella Hsu for very able research assistance. Thanks also to The Filomen D'Agostino and Max E. Greenberg Research Fund for a grant that supported this research.

[1] *Beyond Bling*, ECONOMIST, June 8, 2013, *available at* http://www.economist.com/NEWS/BUSINESS/21579015-LIFE-GETTING-HARDER-PURVEYORS-LUXURY-CHINA-GROWTH-PROSPECTS-ARE-STILL.

At the same time, however, the Middle Kingdom remains the Knockoff Kingdom. The Chinese are great producers and consumers of counterfeit and copied goods, and efforts to curtail counterfeiting are a central focus of many Western firms and governments. In the United States, for example, the 2013 report of the blue-ribbon Commission on the Theft of American Intellectual Property, co-chaired by former American Ambassador to China Jon Huntsman, focused extensively on China. The Commission declared that "China is the world's largest source of IP [intellectual property] theft."[2] According to the Commission, China's share of world IP theft reaches nearly 80%.[3]

How did China become the world's leader in luxury-goods sales—a category that relies heavily on IP rights for its market value—while at the same time achieving unchallenged global dominance in "IP theft"? How can authentic luxury products, with their often-stratospheric prices, have such astonishing market success in China when knockoff versions are so easily produced and so widely available?

In this chapter we explore these questions. We begin by describing China's approach to IP and its thriving luxury-goods market.[4] We then examine China's equally robust knockoff economy, and explore how copying and counterfeiting occur in China. Finally, we speculate about how the success in China of both legitimate branded luxury goods and counterfeits can be reconciled. We argue that much of the harm assumed to flow from counterfeits is difficult to demonstrate empirically in the luxury-goods sector, and there are good theoretical reasons to doubt its magnitude. Indeed, the conventional wisdom about the harm caused by counterfeits is more often a matter of inference than evidence. And there is some evidence, including evidence from China itself, that counterfeits can *strengthen* brands as well as undercut them.

To be clear, we do not argue that counterfeits are harmless—only that the standard case against them is surprisingly weak. As a result, the case for vigorous public enforcement of trademark law to stem the tide of luxury-goods counterfeits is also weak, and especially so in China. From a Chinese perspective counterfeits have many virtues. China is a country where both the economy and income inequality are expanding rapidly, and where the growing gap between rich and poor contributes to social unrest that troubles the country's leadership. In this context, a tolerance for counterfeits and what are sometimes known as "shanzhai" goods can serve important social and political goals.[5] These social and political effects may outweigh whatever harms may stem from counterfeits—especially considering that most of that harm, at present and for the

---

[2] National Bureau of Asian Research, The Report of the Commission on the Theft of American Intellectual Property 2 (2013).

[3] *See id.* at 3.

[4] We primarily look at luxury apparel and accessories, but at times we consider other luxury products, such as fine wines or automobiles. These markets are often so distinct, however, that it can be difficult to generalize across them.

[5] We say more about *shanzhai* below.

foreseeable future, falls on foreign manufacturers. China's tolerance for knockoffs, in short, is a rational policy.

I. Intellectual Property in China

China's comparatively weak enforcement of its intellectual property laws and the widespread copying and counterfeiting that takes place in China have long confounded the United States and other Western governments. China has a storied history of innovation—including truly groundbreaking technologies such as gunpowder and printing—but contemporary China is much better known for knockoffs than breakthroughs. This impression is not entirely fair or accurate; many contemporary Chinese firms are quite inventive.[6] But China has not been a major source of truly transformative technologies in many centuries, nor do more than a handful of Chinese brands command attention in the global marketplace.

While China has joined the World Trade Organization and is party to more than a dozen multilateral IP treaties, copying remains a common activity largely untouched by the central government.[7] This is not because of any lack of formal law against copying and counterfeiting. China has complied with World Trade Organization rules requiring member states to adopt the "minimum standards" contained in the Trade-Related Aspects of Intellectual Property Rights agreement, or TRIPs. These standards largely reflect the stringent Western approach to IP protection. But China's *implementation* of these treaty rules has hardly satisfied American officials. The country's enforcement effort pales in comparison to the scope of IP infringement taking place. This gap has received attention at the highest levels in the United States. Briefing reporters at the White House in February 2013, then-Undersecretary of State Robert Hormats called China's treatment of IP "a serious and highly troubling issue."[8]

American concern is tied to the scale and scope of copying in China, but also to a specific Chinese policy of "indigenous innovation"—a policy that American business has seen as a green light for copying. According to past statements of the Chinese government, indigenous innovation can include "enhancing original innovation through co-innovation and re-innovation based on the assimilation of imported technologies." In other words, this means innovation through copying.[9] Combined with Beijing's

---

[6] Kal Raustiala & Christopher Sprigman, *Fake It Till You Make It*, FOREIGN AFFAIRS, (July/Aug. 2013), *available at* http://www.foreignaffairs.com/articles/139452/kal-raustiala-and-christopher-sprigman/fake-it-till-you-make-it

[7] *See, e.g., Summary Table of Membership of the World Intellectual Property Organization (WIPO) and the Treaties Administered by WIPO, plus UPOV, WTO, and UN*, WORLD INTELLECTUAL PROPERTY ORGANIZATION, http://www.wipo.int/treaties/en/summary.jsp (last visited Jan. 28, 2014, 10:46 PM).

[8] Raustiala & Sprigman, *supra* note 6.

[9] Raustiala & Sprigman, *supra* note 6, at 26.

relatively unsuccessful efforts to enforce existing rules, indigenous innovation is seen by many in the West as one more indicator that China is in fact committed to obtaining foreign IP without paying for it. Given the vast scale of the Chinese market, the United States government considers it vital to rein in Chinese copying, and it has exhorted China—and sued it before the World Trade Organization—to change its ways. Other nations have acted similarly.[10]

What is the source of China's ambivalence toward (or, as some would say, flouting of) IP rights? Many analysts point to cultural factors, in particular the powerful legacy of Confucian thinking. According to this view, China has a distinctive historical relationship to copying that puts it at odds with the model of private ownership of creative goods that is deeply embedded in contemporary Western, and by extension international, IP law. Analyses of China's uneasy relationship to IP often quote Confucius's famous dictum that "I transmit rather than create." This statement became, it is sometimes suggested, an influential guiding principle in later centuries; as one scholar of China has argued, "the incorporation of elements of past works in one's own was not undertaken with the intent to steal another author's ideas. Rather, *imitation was the means for authors to demonstrate their knowledge and mastery of history*; it was a form of tribute to their predecessors."[11] A similar analysis states flatly that IP law as it has been conceived in the West "goes firmly against the grain of Asian culture, which supports the concept of sharing, not protecting, individual creative work."[12] In short, according to some commentators, IP is a "cultural phenomenon as well as an economic one." Countries (such as China) with a "collective" culture—"one that emphasizes sharing over individual ownership rights"—have significantly higher rates of copying and counterfeiting than do countries with "individualist" cultures.[13] Copying in these contexts is as much sharing as it is stealing.

William Alford, in his influential *To Steal a Book Is an Elegant Offense*, suggests that this relativist argument is oversimplified. But he broadly agrees that the past was and remains a very important source of legitimacy in traditional China, and that this reverence for the past has important implications for how copying is perceived and valued today. "The indispensability of the past, for personal moral growth," Alford writes, "dictated that there be broad access to the common heritage of all Chinese." This, and

---

[10] *See Dispute DS362: China-Measures Affecting the Protection and Enforcement of Intellectual Property Rights*, WTO, http://www.wto.org/english/tratop_e/dispu_e/cases_e/ds362_e.htm (last visited Jan. 28, 2014). Among others, Argentina, Australia, Canada, the European Communities, India, Taiwan, Turkey, and Thailand all joined the suit against China as third parties.

[11] Thomas Tze-Hun Chou, *Private Copyright Investment in* China, 1 J. SMALL & EMERGING BUS. L. 375, 393 (1997) (emphasis added).

[12] W. R. Swinyard et al., *The Morality of Software Piracy: A Cross-Cultural Analysis*, 9 J. BUS. ETHICS 655, 662 (1990).

[13] Donald B. Marron & David G. Steel, *Which Countries Protect Intellectual Property? The Case of Software Piracy*, 38 ECON. INQUIRY 159, 172 (2000).

other factors, "militated against thinking of the fruits of intellectual endeavor as private property."[14] Like other analysts of China, Alford contrasts this perspective with the West, where the seventeenth and eighteenth centuries "witnessed the development of an approach toward intellectual property in Europe that had no counterpart in imperial Chinese history."[15] He notes as well that many great Chinese painters tolerated or even welcomed forgery of their work "because such copying, in effect, bore witness to the quality of the work copied and to its creator's degree of understanding and civility."[16] This notion—that a copy is a form of homage, one that actually raises the value and importance of the original—is critically important, as we will discuss further below, though not only for the reasons that Alford and others have proposed.

China's reverence for the past has not always been consistently felt, of course, and this makes easy linkages between Confucian precepts and contemporary policy and practice suspect. After 1949, Mao expressly sought to discredit the past as a source of legitimacy, seeing China's ancient cultural legacy as a source of oppression and backwardness. Confucius himself even fell into disfavor. During the Cultural Revolution that followed, the "Four Olds"—Old Customs, Old Habits, Old Culture, and Old Ideas—were vilified. But this wholesale rejection of the old wisdom and ways did not mean the end of copying in China. Nor did it entail the embrace of Western individualist notions of intellectual property—indeed, property of all kinds was viewed as anathema in Maoist China. It was only in the aftermath of the Cultural Revolution, as Mao's influence waned and China began to open up again to the West, that Chinese leaders began slowly to embrace Western approaches to IP, at least on paper. China passed its first post-revolutionary patent and trademark laws in the 1980s and its first copyright law in 1990. Simultaneously, the Chinese leadership laid the groundwork for the country's extraordinary economic growth. And this economic growth in turn fueled China's vibrant—many would say rampant—contemporary culture of copying.[17]

II. Economy and Luxury

Deng Xiaoping may not have actually said it, but the phrase often associated with him—"to get rich is glorious"—signaled to post–Maoist China that things had changed markedly, and that an unleashing of the entrepreneurial and acquisitive talent that had long

[14] William P. Alford, To Steal a Book Is an Elegant Offense 20 (1995).

[15] *Id.* at 18.

[16] *Id.* at 29.

[17] Today China's past is again a source of pride. Even Confucius is back as a favored sage; in 2011 his statue was placed in Tiananmen Square. Confucius's statue was apparently removed, for reasons that are unclear, four months later. But the sage remains largely in favor among Chinese leaders. *See, e.g.*, Chris Buckley, *Xi Pays Homage to Confucius, a Figure Back in Favor*, N.Y. Times (Nov. 26, 2013, 11:34 PM), http://sinosphere.blogs.nytimes.com/2013/11/26/xi-pays-homage-to-confucius-a-figure-back-in-favor/.

marked diasporic China was about to unfold in the motherland.[18] In the decades since Deng's supposed dictum China has experienced unprecedentedly rapid development. China's per-capita GDP in 1993 was $410. Two decades years later it was nearly $6,000.[19] That astonishing rise explains something about China's embrace of luxury goods; a nation as poor as China was in 1993 had little capacity for luxury-goods consumption.

Yet supplying the means is not the same as supplying the motive. Scandinavia is very wealthy—much more so than China on a per capita basis—but lacks a single Cartier boutique. Luxury goods appear to have greater cultural salience in China than in many other places with more longstanding wealth. At one level this is surprising: China is a nominally communist country where in the not too distant past the dour Mao jacket ruled. At another level, however, it is not just the economy that is changing: mores about wealth and its display have also changed markedly. As the Chinese economy has grown at unprecedented rates, and many but by no means all Chinese have become wealthy, interest in signifiers of luxury and markers of class distinction has grown.

Still, some observers believe the Chinese love of luxury, much like its proclivity for copying, is driven by distinctive cultural factors. For example, Gao et al. argue that "consumers in Asia purchase luxury goods to secure social recognition and to show their status because the culture emphasizes hierarchy and status."[20] The concept of "face" or *mianzi* looms large in many of these culturally based analyses. As another observer argues, "Due to the heavy influence of face, Asian consumers must purchase luxury products to enhance, maintain or save their face. Therefore, the conceptualisation of face and face consumption provides a useful way to understand why Asian consumers, on the one hand, are very thrifty in their everyday life and consumption but, on the other hand, spend (and sometimes waste) a large amount of money on luxury consumption."[21] From this perspective, a culturally determined obsession with saving face and building face pushes the Chinese to seek out luxury goods that are visible and recognizable to others—making the cash registers ring at Chanel and Armani.

Obviously, buying luxury goods requires means, but does the concept of *mianzi* provide a distinctly Chinese motive? In other words, is it true that there is an exceptional Chinese, or Asian, obsession with face—or in more familiar Western terms, with

---

[18] On the likely spuriousness of Deng's famous dictum, see Evelyn Iritani, *Great Idea But Don't Quote Him*, L.A. TIMES (Sep. 9, 2004), http://articles.latimes.com/2004/sep/09/business/fi-deng9.

[19] *Data-China*, THE WORLD BANK, http://data.worldbank.org/country/china (last visited Jan. 30, 2014). Even at $6,000, China is poorer per capita than Iraq, a place rarely associated with vibrant luxury-goods markets. In short, there clearly is more than sheer economics at play.

[20] Bopeng Zhang & Jung-Hwan Kim, *Luxury Fashion Consumption in China: Factors Affecting Attitude and Purchase Intent*, 20 J. RETAILING & CONSUMER SERVICES 68, 70 (2013) (citing Norton L. Gao et al., *Potential Niche Markets for Luxury Fashion Goods in China*, 13 J. FASHION MARKETING & MANAGEMENT 514, 514–26 (2009)).

[21] Julie J. Li & Chenting Su, *How* Face *Influences Consumption: A Comparative Study of American and Chinese Consumers*, 49 INT'L J. MARKET RES. 237, 251–52 (2007).

reputation and status? The argument that there is something special in Chinese culture, rather than in China's stage of economic development, that focuses the attention of Chinese consumers on luxury goods can, as with cultural explanations of the Chinese embrace of copying, easily be taken too far. China has no lock on status-seeking; indeed, one can go back to Thorstein Veblen's landmark 1899 analysis of new wealth in Gilded Age America and find many similarities with contemporary analyses of China, even though the cultures are extremely different. Veblen, who coined the term "conspicuous consumption," did not ground the acquisitive and showboating behavior he observed at that time in particularistic American cultural traits. Rather, Veblen stressed seemingly universal desires to signal wealth and standing in a social context (the roiling, rapidly urbanizing, and industrializing post–Civil War United States) in which traditional markers of status were in decline.

Veblen's insights—and the recent history of Russia, Brazil, and other societies in which great wealth and great inequality have gone hand in hand—suggests that perhaps culturally specific concepts such as *mianzi*, while surely relevant, are not sufficient to explain China's remarkable appetite for luxury. Just as important or perhaps more so is China's dislocatingly rapid economic growth—growth that produces a new and socially insecure upper class that in turn seeks to mark and cement its rising status through readily identifiable luxury brands. China today does share many features with these other rapidly developing countries. Perhaps the brash desire of the newly wealthy to show off is simply part and parcel of acquiring great wealth—and differentiating oneself from those who haven't attained it. In short, *mianzi* may well reflect distinctively Chinese, or East Asian, cultural concerns. But it may also largely be a regional gloss on the broader concept of status, which seems to be an almost universally human obsession. Either way, what is clear is that for China's huge numbers of the newly rich, or newly middle class, Western brands often serve as instant and very desirable social signifiers of success.

Still, contemporary China does have some distinctive features that merit attention—including one that Veblen's late nineteenth-century America, for all its parallels, lacked: a very low birthrate. The result is what is sometimes called the "one-child generation." As one study notes, "Between 1979 and 1990, 227 million Chinese" were born into the one-child generation. One of the consequences of China's legally enforced one-child policy is the "'little emperors family structure,' in which every child born is indulged by 'six-pockets' (two parents and four grandparents). In the view of some commentators, this phenomenon has created 'little emperors' who are more concerned with materialism, brands, and self-gratification."[22] While its impact is hard to measure, it is at least plausible that China's one-child policy, which is most strictly enforced in major

---

[22] Ashmun Lalida, *Identity and Branding: Consumer Behavior and the Shaping of the Self—A Cross-Cultural Analysis of East Asian and American Luxury Consumers* (June 2012) (Master of Arts in Liberal Studies thesis, Dartmouth College).

cities, has exacerbated trends toward materialism and conspicuous consumption in the younger generations, especially in a context of increasing affluence.

A second special, though hardly unique, feature of China is the very high rate of income inequality. According to a recent report from *Reuters,* China has 2.7 million (U.S. dollar) millionaires and an astounding 251 billionaires.[23] By comparison, according to *Forbes* magazine, the United States, which itself is quite unequal, and which enjoys per capita GDP more than eight times larger than China's,[24] has 442 billionaires.[25] Yet despite the large number of billionaires and millionaires, 13% of China's people live on less than $1.25 per day.[26] And China's per capita disposable income is approximately $3,000 per year, compared with approximately $39,000 per year in the United States. So while China's vast size and burgeoning class of wealthy citizens make it a remarkably lucrative market for luxury retailers, in fact most of the country is still very poor by any standard. For the majority of Chinese, luxury goods are fantastical items that are simply unattainable at anything like market prices.

Corruption is a third feature of contemporary China that may have implications for luxury-goods markets, though again it is not factor that it is unique to China. Nor is China especially corrupt—Transparency International's index ranks China at 80 out of 177 ranked nations for 2013; better than average, certainly better than neighboring Asian giant India, and only about 10 places behind iconic luxury-good source Italy.[27] Still, China-watchers often note that China's political class is widely corrupt and that gift-giving in the guise of payoffs and bribes is a regular feature of Chinese business life.[28] Luxury goods form, it is said, a large fraction of these gifts—though it is obviously difficult to distinguish legitimate gifts from disguised bribes. *The Economist* reported in 2014 that President Xi Jinping's anti-graft campaign has been showing results, and speculated that luxury-goods sales may be a victim. "A number of luxury brands have reported sharp falls in revenues," wrote *The Economist*. "Rémy Cointreau saw sales of its flagship cognac fall by more than 30% in the last three months of 2013 over the previous year, mostly owing to falling Chinese demand."[29]

---

[23] Kevin Yao & Aileen Wang, *China Lets Gini Out of the Bottle; Wide Wealth Gap*, REUTERS, (Jan. 18, 2013, 3:30 AM), http://www.reuters.com/article/2013/01/18/us-china-economy-income-gap-idUSBRE90H06L20130118.

[24] *Data-GDP Per Capita (Current US$)*, THE WORLD BANK, http://data.worldbank.org/indicator/NY.GDP.PCAP.CD, (last visited Jan. 30, 2014).

[25] Erin Carlyle, Full List: U.S. Billionaires of 2013, FORBES (Mar. 6, 2013, 8:58 AM), http://www.forbes.com/sites/erincarlyle/2013/03/06/full-list-u-s-billionaires-of-2013/.

[26] *Data- Poverty Headcount Ratio at $1.25 a Day (PPP)(% of population)*, THE WORLD BANK, http://data.worldbank.org/indicator/SI.POV.DDAY, (last visited Jan. 30, 2014).

[27] *Corruption Perceptions Index 2013*, TRANSPARENCY INT'L, http://cpi.transparency.org/cpi2013/results/ (last visited Feb. 18, 2014).

[28] We thank Haochen Sun for stressing this point to us.

[29] *Less Party Time*, ECONOMIST, Jan. 25, 2014, *available at* http://www.economist.com/news/china/21595029-communist-partys-anti-graft-campaign-has-had-surprising-impact-new-report-shows-how. If this is broadly accurate, China's luxury goods market has been somewhat bolstered by the need to supply readily identifiable and coveted gifts, and if President Xi's efforts are successful, perhaps this market may

A fourth noteworthy feature about contemporary China is that it is rapidly and dramatically urbanizing. Again, urbanization is not unique to China; many developing and middle-income countries are rapidly urbanizing as well. But more than half of Chinese live in cities today, whereas less than one in five did in the 1970s.[30] Beijing, Shanghai, and the greater Hong Kong/Guangzhou conurbation are vast cities well known in the West. Yet equally large, if not larger, are Chongqing, Tianjin, and Wuhan. Indeed, China has 10 cities with urban populations over six million. Large, dense cities, with their associated markets, multilayered connections both locally and to the outside world, and endless scope for individuals to watch and be watched by throngs of strangers, are perfect petri dishes for status competition, *mianzi*-obsession, and brand-building. The juxtaposition of urban life, new wealth, and conspicuous consumption in contemporary China are amply illustrated by two of the hit films of the summer of 2013: *Tiny Times 1* and *2*. Both films chronicle the lives of four girls, *Sex in the City*-style, as they engage in an "overt celebration of materialism" in fast-paced Shanghai. As one reviewer explained, the books upon which the popular films are based

> are stuffed with English-language brand names like Chanel and Gucci and choice phrases. ("Economy class kills me!" and "I hate Beijing!") [The] films show the actual designer goods and include dialogue that has also riled commentators, like this exchange in "Tiny Times 1" between two star-crossed young lovers: "I like you," the young man says, "not because you've had a driver since you were little, and not because you have designer bags, and definitely not because you gave me expensive boots. Even if you didn't have a cent, I would still like you." The woman then turns on him: "Let me tell you, love without materialism is just a pile of sand!"[31]

III. *Shanzhai*

There is one additional distinctive aspect of contemporary China that deserves more extensive attention: the singular Chinese concept of *shanzhai*. *Shanzhai* literally translates as "mountain stronghold" or "bandit stronghold." In contemporary usage, however, it refers to low-cost knockoffs, such as buildings (including those of the ersatz central European villages that have cropped up in Chinese suburbs), stores (such as the fake Apple store in Kunming that sold real but refurbished Apple products), and even events (such as the imitation Olympic torch relay that rural villagers in China organized when

---

slump or at least show much slower growth. We haven't seen broad-based data to bear out this hypothesis, but it is worthy of further study.

[30] John Pomfret, In *Search of the Real China: Outsiders Still See What They Want to See*, FOREIGN AFFAIRS, Nov./Dec. 2013, at 152.

[31] Sheila Melvin, *A Film-Fueled Culture Clash Over Values in China*, N.Y. TIMES, Sep. 3, 2013, http://www.nytimes.com/2013/09/04/movies/in-tiny-times-movies-material-girls-have-a-nation-tsking.html?_r=0.

the official relay passed over their regions).[32] *Shanzhai* is significant for understanding both luxury goods and counterfeits in China because *shanzhai* culture links the desire for wealth to copying of luxury goods, and makes production and consumption of counterfeits more socially legitimate than they might be otherwise. *Shanzhai* once connoted shoddy imitations of desirable originals. But like so much else in China, the term's meaning has undergone change as China itself changes. As *The Wall Street Journal* recently noted, "Once a term used to suggest something cheap or inferior, *shanzhai* now suggests to many a certain Chinese cleverness and ingenuity." *Shanzhai* cellphones, consumer household products, fashion items, and even fast food restaurants abound in China, and today are often pointed to with pride.

The popular appreciation of *shanzhai* products poses a challenge for anti-counterfeiting efforts. And indeed, far from cracking down on the phenomenon, the Chinese government seems to believe that *shanzhai*-style creativity is something to cultivate. In 2009, an official from China's National Copyright Administration declared that "*shanzhai* shows the cultural creativity of the common people." He added, "It fits a market need and people like it." There is a certain convenience to this realization: Chinese authorities seem to recognize that *shanzhai* is socially embedded and unlikely to disappear. But *shanzhai* offers some additional benefits to Beijing. A vibrant culture of copying has political value in a highly unequal society such as China's; by allowing the less well off to access versions of the products that only the wealthy can afford in their original form, the widespread availability of *shanzhai* products may be useful as a brake on the social unrest that contemporary China's high level of social inequality tends to create. In short, the relative freedom to copy may help ease or at least mask the nation's yawning economic divide.

Yet like so much in China, *shanzhai* is not simply an economic phenomenon. It also functions as an unusual form of cultural resistance to authority—albeit one that, unlike the popular political uprisings that led to the massacre in Tiananmen, or recently occurred in Hong Kong, appears to pose little direct threat to the hegemony of the Communist Party. Yu Hua, the Chinese writer, describes this in his best-selling book *China in Ten Words*. He details the copycat Internet news show that parodies the government's official evening news broadcast; copycat entertainment shows that ape the government's televised Spring Festival gala; and the copycat songs, copycat announcers, and copycat stars and starlets that populate them. "From this," Yu writes, "we can see that the copycat phenomenon has a certain positive significance in China today. Seen in this way, it represents a challenge of the grassroots to the elite, of the popular to the official, or the weak to the strong."[33]

---

[32] *See, e.g.*, Bianca Bosker, Original Copies: Architectural Mimicry in Contemporary China (2013); Haochen Sun Haochen Sun, *Can Louis Vuitton Dance with HiPhone? Rethinking the Idea of Social Justice in Intellectual Property Law*, 15 U. Pa. J. L. & Soc. Change 387 (2012)

[33] Yu Hua, China in Ten Words 188 (Allan H. Barr trans., 2012).

This may be one reason the Chinese government has chosen to tolerate and at times even embrace *shanzhai*. To oppose it too overtly might only reinforce the sense that it is a challenge to established hierarchies. Another reason Chinese leaders may tolerate *shanzhai* is that they are not the only or even primary target. *Shanzhai* can also be a way for ordinary Chinese to challenge global authority, in particular the continuing (and often irritating, to Chinese eyes) economic dominance of the West.

Xiaomi, for instance, is one of China's fastest-growing technology companies. Less than four years old, Xiaomi has sold nearly seven million smartphones and raked in more than ten billion yuan ($1.6 billion)—impressive numbers for a company that sold its first smartphone in August 2011. Xiaomi's phones look familiar to Westerners because many of the company's designs are *shanzhai* versions of Apple's coveted iPhone. And design is not the only cue that Xiaomi takes from Apple. At a recent product launch, Lei Jun, the head of Xiaomi, stood alone onstage in a black shirt, jeans, and black Converse sneakers—déjà vu for anyone who ever saw the late Steve Jobs, the founder and former CEO of Apple, introduce new products at a Macworld convention. Lei's message was clear: Xiaomi, and its products, are just as cool as Apple. And Chinese consumers have happily embraced Xiaomi's products without any illusions about their provenance. In a telling turn of phrase, a Shanghai university student recently told *The New York Times* "Xiaomi is the real fake."[34] With its *shanzhai* smartphones and *shanzhai* Steve Jobs, firms like Xiaomi not only serve to highlight contemporary Chinese ingenuity, but also to show that China can be just as good at creating cutting-edge consumer products as America.[35]

Shanzhai is not without its critics, of course, and not only in the offices of the U.S. Chamber of Commerce. *Shanzhai* culture in China may demonstrate resilience and resistance. Yet, Yu Hua argues, it is also a symptom of a sort of nationwide nervous breakdown, brought on by the enormous tensions created by a society that simultaneously practices economic openness and political repression:

> It seems to me that the emergence—and the unstoppable momentum—of the copycat phenomenon is an inevitable consequence of this lopsided development. The ubiquity and sharpness of social contradictions have provoked a confusion in people's value systems and worldview, thus giving birth to the copycat effect, when all kinds of social emotions accumulate over time and find only limited channels of release, transmuted constantly into seemingly farcical acts of rebellion that have certain anti-authoritarian, anti-mainstream, and anti-monopoly elements. The force and scale of copycatting demonstrate that the whole nation has taken to it as a form of performance art.[36]

---

[34] Sue-Lin Wong, *Challenging Apple by Imitation*, N.Y. TIMES, Oct. 29, 2012, http://www.nytimes.com/2012/10/29/technology/challenging-apple-by-imitation.html.

[35] We thank Peter Yu for stressing this point to us.

[36] YU HUA, supra note 33, at 189.

For all of *shanzhai*'s political roots and reverberations, however, its most overt consequences are found in the country's consumer economy. Many *shanzhai* products are, not surprisingly, purely imitative. But we also see Chinese firms that mix imitation with innovation, and these products are the ones that often elicit pride in the ingenuity embedded in *shanzhai* offerings. Xiaomi's phones are an excellent example. Xiaomi is clearly riffing on Apple in many aspects of its product and image. Yet it is not just a simple knockoff of Apple. Xiaomi's success, in fact, hinges on the company being quite *unlike* Apple in some important respects.

For one, Xiaomi's phones typically cost about half that of its rival's. Even more important, Xiaomi has a very different attitude toward innovation. Apple is known for its closed approach to product development. The company believes that it knows what its customers want before they do, so Apple's design process is essentially dictatorial. Xiaomi's design process, by contrast, is quite democratic. Every Friday, Xiaomi releases a new round of software updates for its mobile operating system, which is based on Google's open-source Android software. Within hours, thousands of users flock to Xiaomi's online forums to suggest new features, functions, and designs and to identify and resolve software bugs. Xiaomi has relied on user input to determine how much memory to install on its phones, how important the phone's thickness is to users, and whether its phones should allow users to take photos without pushing a button. Lei might dress like Jobs, but he runs his company very differently.

Xiaomi is hardly China's only *shanzhai*-style innovator. Weibo, the country's most popular social networking service, boasts hundreds of millions of users. Launched in 2009, three years after Twitter, Weibo is widely viewed as a Twitter clone. Since its launch, however, it has added a clutch of features that distinguish it from Twitter, including a more interactive system for commenting. Such improvements make Weibo arguably more functional, and more fun, than the service it copied. Another Chinese value-adding knockoff is Youku, which is just one of a number of Chinese copies of YouTube. (*Youku* translates as "excellent" or "cool.") Unlike YouTube, Youku allows users to upload videos of any length without copyright verification. That means that Youku hosts hundreds of thousands of hours of unauthorized programming. But the service has also partnered with more than 1,500 professional content providers to deliver authorized videos, and the Chinese service is further along than its U.S. rival in delivering original content. Indeed, Youku has emerged as a serious competitor to traditional broadcast TV in China—a feat that YouTube must envy.

In sum, China's vibrant *shanzhai* culture spans a range of activities from the homemade to the high tech to the (literal) high-rise. Copying is celebrated as much, or perhaps more, than it is condemned, and China continues to innovate even as it imitates. Much of this *shanzhai* activity is unrelated to luxury goods. But it has resonance for luxury products, because it taps into the larger social and economic and even political context in which copying and counterfeiting occur in contemporary China.

IV. The Chinese Challenge to the Conventional Wisdom on Counterfeits

Embedded in many domestic legal systems around the world, in international IP agreements, and in international trade accords alike is a simple notion: counterfeits undercut, outcompete, and ultimately harm originals. We will call this the *substitution effect*. Counterfeits are usually far cheaper than originals. And while quality differences between originals and copies may be equally large, those quality differences may not matter to, or even be observable to, many consumers or onlookers. For some, the knockoff is a serviceable and even attractive substitute for the high-priced original. And so, the conventional wisdom maintains, by offering a cheaper alternative that may be hard to distinguish from the original (at least to the untrained eye—or at a distance), counterfeits substitute for sales from originals, cause consumer confusion, and degrade the value of a brand.[37]

This, in a nutshell, is why counterfeits are thought to be bad, and why strong enforcement of IP law is thought to be essential. When American officials berate China over copying, this basic set of arguments undergirds their critique. To be sure, the conventional story about copying's dangers is intuitive and widely accepted. Yet there is good reason to doubt important parts of it, both with regard to copying in the West and, perhaps even more so, for copying in China. This is not to say the conventional wisdom is wholly wrong—only that it is largely unproven, and that there is significant reason to question whether the negative effects of counterfeits are as severe or as widespread as it assumes.[38]

Our skepticism is grounded in several difficulties with this conventional wisdom. Whether, and if so, how much, counterfeits substitute for sales from originals is an empirical question. Yet there is surprisingly little rigorous research into its scale. And there is good reason to doubt that the scale of the substitution effect is very great especially for luxury goods. As we explain below, genuine luxury goods and counterfeits often occupy different markets altogether, with the market for counterfeits populated by buyers who lack the resources (for now, if not forever) to purchase the original. Counterfeit sales in this setting are not "lost sales;" they are simply different sales.

Nor, in most instances, are counterfeit luxury goods likely to confuse consumers into thinking they are buying originals. This is true whether at the critical point of sale or at the murkier and more controversial "post-sale" stage. Given the many ways in which

---

[37] In the context of copyright and patent, excessive copying in turn is said to lead to reduced innovation, because who will innovate if others will steal the fruits of their innovation? In the trademark context, however, even the conventional wisdom rarely accords great weight to innovation as a harm from counterfeiting. Indeed, as we will discuss further below, articulating the precise social harm from counterfeiting trademarks is more difficult than many recognize.

[38] For a longer exposition of this basic argument see Kal Raustiala & Christopher Sprigman, The Knockoff Economy: How Imitation Sparks Innovation (2012).

counterfeit purchases differ from purchases of originals, there is little reason to think that many consumers who purchase counterfeit luxury goods are unsure about what they're buying. It is more likely that most counterfeit buyers want counterfeits and can't afford, or would never pay for, originals.

Taken together, these factors cast doubt on the magnitude of the substitution effect, as well as on the scale of consumer confusion that counterfeits create. Equally significant, there is suggestive evidence that counterfeits sometimes create *benefits* for producers of originals.[39] Counterfeits can serve as advertisements for originals, helping to grow sales, and they can serve as trial versions for those who do have the means, or who are likely to have the means in the future, to purchase original products. We say more about how counterfeits can actually help originals below. But if the potential benefits to producers from counterfeiting are not trivial, and if the harm from counterfeits to consumers and producers is more limited than commonly supposed, we ought to question whether counterfeits have a significant negative impact overall on originals. And when the social welfare effects for poorer consumers are taken into account—that is, the value they receive from being able to purchase inexpensive copies of items they desire—the effect of counterfeits may at times be, on net, positive.

A more definitive answer to the seeming puzzle of China's place both as the world's leading luxury-goods market and the world's leading counterfeiter will have to await further study. But at the very least, as we describe below that the case for strict enforcement of anti-counterfeiting law is not overwhelming—nor close to being proven. All this makes China's relaxed approach to IP enforcement a plausibly rational strategy—especially with regard to luxury goods. Even as Chinese producers increasingly move into higher value goods and begin, perhaps, to create luxury marks that resonate for wider audiences, we expect China to resist the West's call to impose very strict enforcement of IP rights. Moreover, these arguments suggest why and how a robust market in counterfeits can comfortably coexist with a robust market in originals.[40]

A. DO COUNTERFEITS OUTCOMPETE ORIGINALS?

It is a bedrock assumption of the conventional wisdom about IP that counterfeits, which are virtually always cheaper, outcompete originals. If two items are the same but for price, it follows from basic economic theory that the cheaper one will prevail in the marketplace. Yet upon closer inspection, this simple logic doesn't always hold in the real world. (And of course in the luxury-goods market, the logic sometimes fails altogether.

---

[39] For an early and insightful version of this argument, see Jonathan Barnett, *Shopping for Gucci on Canal Street: Reflections on Status Consumption, Intellectual Property and the Incentive Thesis*, 91 VA. L. REV. 1381 (2005).

[40] *See also* Raustiala & Sprigman, *supra* note 6.

Economists use the phrase "Veblen goods" for those items, such as luxury perfumes, that exhibit *increased* demand as their price rises.)[41]

One key question in this inquiry is whether consumers who purchase copies have the means to purchase the original. The more this is true, the more the counterfeit is likely to actually substitute for the original. And the more the counterfeit is a substitute, the more (given conventional economic assumptions) sales are likely to be diverted. While this seems like common sense, the evidence in favor of this proposition is surprisingly meager. Even in markets where the originals are quite inexpensive and copies are very similar—and perhaps even identical—to the original, the impact of counterfeits on sales of originals is not unequivocally negative. Perhaps the most striking example is digital music downloads, an industry that has faced very large-scale piracy. One recent study indeed found harm to original music sales from pirated downloads,[42] while another study (conducted by the EU's research arm and using Internet clickstream data) found no harm to originals. Indeed, this study found a slight *increase* in legal sales associated with online music piracy.[43] In short, even though digital copies are excellent substitutes for originals, it is not clear that there is empirical support for the notion that copies negatively impact the sales of originals.

For luxury goods, there is even more reason for skepticism about the magnitude of the substitution effect. By definition, luxury goods are expensive—sometimes astonishingly so.[44] Even in the United States the vast majority of consumers cannot afford them, unless they devote very large fractions of their income to these purchases (necessarily forgoing a host of other, more quotidian purchases). So for many consumers, the choice between original and counterfeit is no choice at all. This is all the more true in China. Given the widespread poverty and extremely high levels of income inequality, many Chinese consumers who purchase counterfeits will lack the resources to purchase original luxury goods. This is true even though counterfeits typically feature markedly inferior materials and workmanship that even the untutored consumer can readily discern. For most consumers, in short, counterfeits are an obtainable *alternative* for the genuine branded article. They are not, however, a *substitute*.[45] These consumers could never buy the original in the first place.

---

[41] H. Leibenstein, *Bandwagon, Snob, and Veblen Effects in the Theory of Consumers' Demand*, 64 Q.J. Econ. 183 (1950).

[42] Rafael Rob & Joel Waldfogel, *Piracy on the High C's: Music Downloading, Sales Displacement, and Social Welfare in a Sample of College Students*, 49 J.L. & Econ. 29, 29–62 (2006), *available at* http://www.nber.org/papers/w10874.

[43] Luis Aguiar & Bertin Martens, Digital Music Consumption on the Internet: Evidence From Clickstream Data, EU Joint Research Centre, Institute for Prospective Technological Studies (2013), *available at* http://ftp.jrc.es/EURdoc/JRC79605.pdf.

[44] Hermès's iconic Birkin handbag, for instance, can cost well over $20,000 for some models; a Kiton men's cashmere blazer currently sold at Neiman Marcus costs $6,495.

[45] Barnett, *supra* note 40.

In other words, in China, as elsewhere, originals and counterfeit luxury goods may largely occupy different market niches. The more this is true, the more the presence of counterfeits will have little direct effect on sales of legitimate branded luxury goods. Just like a fast food restaurant that opens down the street from a temple of expensive cuisine, the consumer bases are completely different. One hardly impacts the market of the other.[46]

B. DO COUNTERFEITS CONFUSE CONSUMERS?

The main goal of trademark law, in both the United States and China, is to prohibit uses of a mark that are likely to *confuse consumers* about the source of a particular branded product or service. In other words, we protect marks not primarily to protect the interests of the mark holders (though that is undeniably often a factor in practice) but to protect the consumer. The consumer who wants to buy a Birkin bag can use the Hermès mark as a guide; those products displaying the mark are the real thing and those that simply look like the Birkin bag but have a different mark are a copy. The policing of trademarks helps consumers find the products they want faster and easier. Hence trademark law's fundamental purpose is consumer protection.[47]

By definition, luxury-goods counterfeits use others' marks without authorization. But do they cause consumer confusion? In other words, do consumers know that fakes are fakes when they purchase them? This issue is a critical aspect of any inquiry into the substitution effect, since the more consumers believe—mistakenly—that a counterfeit is an original, the more sales are likely to be diverted, harming the original. (Though logically, were this true, we would expect more often than we do to see counterfeit prices that are not tiny fractions of the real price but instead much closer to the real price—since consumers in this scenario, by definition, think they are buying the real thing, knockoff sellers could charge prices closer to the market price in originals.)

---

[46] A harder question is whether, and if so much, of those very privileged few who can afford the original choose instead to buy counterfeits. This is an empirical question that surely varies market by market. We will say more on this below.

[47] We note that Chinese trademark law defines "infringement" quite broadly, subjecting counterfeiting and even the unauthorized use of similar marks to what looks, at least on the face of the Chinese trademark statute, like per se liability. *See* Trademark Law of the People's Republic of China (as amended up to Decision of October 27, 2001, of the Standing Comm. Nat'l People's Cong., Revising the Trademark Law of the People's Republic of China), *available at* http://www.wipo.int/wipolex/en/text.jsp?file_id=131395. That said, Chinese courts interpreting the 2001 Chinese trademark law have implemented a consumer confusion test for trademark infringement. *See* Luckie Hong, *China's Dilution of the Dilution Doctrine*, WORLD TRADEMARK REV., Apr./May 2009, at 24.

Trademark law also often prohibits uses that may *dilute* the selling power of famous marks. We'll talk about this interesting and complex issue separately below. It is unclear whether Chinese law recognizes a separate cause of action for trademark dilution. See *id.*

How likely is it that a Louis Vuitton counterfeit confuses a consumer into thinking she is about to purchase a real Louis Vuitton item? Whether we're talking about American or Chinese consumers, it is conceivable that some of them—probably a very small number—purchase counterfeit luxury goods thinking they are buying the original. This might happen where the counterfeit is an unusually good copy of the original.[48] But for luxury goods, many of which are made with expensive materials and workmanship and are therefore difficult to copy both cheaply and with precision, high-end knockoffs of the type that are likely to fool most consumers are very rare. Those that do exist are priced fairly high as a result.[49] Much more common are knockoffs that any reasonable buyer would know right away are fake—obviously inferior copies with cheaper materials, shoddy workmanship, and sometimes completely different designs. For some luxury products that cannot be evaluated pre-purchase—such as rare Bordeaux wines, unusual Scotch, or very old Maotai—it is far easier to imagine consumer confusion, and so the case for government regulation is stronger. But for most luxury fashion and accessories, the products can be touched and tried on and their quality easily discerned before purchase.

Moreover, inferences about counterfeits are not based simply on the product, but also on the seller. Whether high or low quality, counterfeits are very rarely if ever sold in a brand's own boutique; nor are they likely to be sold in any high-end retailer. Hence the context of the purchase will almost always give away the provenance of the good. In short, although the story may be different with fake pharmaceuticals or auto parts, for luxury goods the incidence of consumer confusion at the point of sale is likely to be quite low. If counterfeit luxury goods do not often confuse consumers, they are unlikely to interfere very much with the ability of trademarks to designate source. As a consequence, strict enforcement of anti-counterfeiting laws, at least in the area of luxury goods, does not line up very well with the primary underlying justification for trademark law.

If there is very little likelihood of consumer confusion at the point of sale, perhaps there may be what is sometimes called "post-sale" confusion. Accepted in some jurisdictions and not others,[50] the concept of post-sale confusion is controversial among

---

[48] Elizabeth Holmes, *The Finer Art of Faking It*, Wall Street Journal (June 30, 2011), http://online.wsj.com/news/articles/SB10001424052702304791204576401534146929212.

[49] *Id.*

[50] The relevant Chinese statute does not discuss post-sale confusion. However, Beebe suggests that Chinese courts may be using a version of it:

> To take an example from recent Chinese case law, the buyer of knockoff Gucci shoes at the Shanghai No. 1 Yaohan Department Store is certainly not confused as to their true source, particularly since the shoes prominently bear the trademark "Senda" (a well-known Chinese shoe manufacturer) on the insole and are sold at a relatively moderate price from the "Senda" counter in the department store. Nevertheless, as the Chinese court explained:
>
> > [W]hile the consumers are actually wearing the shoes, by-standers are unable to see the "Senda-woman" label covered by the feet; but [Gucci's] double-G interlock pattern on the upper cloth can be recognized clearly, which would lead to the mistaken belief by third parties of the

trademark experts. It posits that brand owners can be harmed if consumers see a counterfeit good being worn or carried or used *after the sale*. The theory is that these observers will mistake it for the branded original and then draw a negative inference about it. That is simple enough to state, yet the precise mechanism of harm, and the circumstances that can lead to harm, are far from clear.

Suppose a consumer sees a stranger wearing a fake pair of Lanvin sneakers and believes that they are the genuine item. How is the brand owner harmed? It might be that the fake Lanvin sneakers are shoddily made[51] and that the consumer perceives that and has a lower opinion of the brand owner's product thereafter. But for that to be true, there are some specific conditions that must be met. First, the observer must see the shoes well enough to perceive them as Lanvin. And he must see them well enough to perceive that they are low quality. But he must also *not* perceive them well enough to understand that the low-quality sneakers are in fact fakes. In other words, there must be just enough perception that the observer draws a negative inference about a specific brand, but not enough that they recognize the item is in fact a counterfeit.

There is little empirical study of these mechanisms. And given that post-sale confusion requires a Goldilocks-like level of perception by others, there is little reason to believe that post-sale confusion is a major problem for luxury-goods firms. Moreover, there are other consequences of post-sale confusion—and indeed, of any post-sale exposure to luxury-goods counterfeits, whether the observer is confused or not—that are potentially *beneficial* to brand owners. We'll describe these later; for now it will suffice to say that from a policy perspective any positive effects flowing from consumers' post-sale experience with counterfeits must be balanced against the (probably quite slight) harm from post-sale confusion.

While the magnitude of post-sale confusion is questionable, consider another possible form of harm to the original brand that is sometimes suggested: that counterfeits degrade the brand by diffusing the brand or logo into the larger community, robbing it of its exclusivity. To understand this, imagine that some set of observers see the fake Lanvin sneakers worn on another person, know they are fake, and infer that Lanvin, as a brand, is now being adopted by lower-class consumers. The very existence of (hypothetically) cheap counterfeit Lanvin sneakers shows that the Lanvin brand is not only coveted by the fashion-conscious high end, but by a larger and more ordinary swath of society—large enough to create a market in fakes.

---

actual brand of the products bought by purchasers. This situation would undoubtedly reduce the value of the double-G interlock pattern trademark and affect its commending function.

Barton Beebe, *Intellectual Property Law and the Sumptuary Code*, 123 HARV. L. REV. 809, 851 (quoting Guccio Gucci S.P.A. v. Jiangsu Senda Group Co., (2007) Case 78 of Pu Min San (Zhi) Chu Zi, at *6 (People's Ct. of Shanghai Pudong New Dist., Apr. 7, 2008)). We thank Haochen Sun for pointing out this example.

[51] Of course some luxury goods are shoddily made, especially in high-end fashion, or even designed to look shoddily made, but we'll assume, as is often the case, that luxury goods are actually well made.

None of this speaks to *confusion* about the brand, however. Indeed, quite the opposite: this line of reasoning requires a fairly detailed knowledge of the brand and its place in the fashion/status firmament. But to take this form of "harm" seriously introduces a larger issue we discuss further below: how trademark protection often has as its undeclared mission not the protection of consumers, which has almost nothing to do with this scenario, but instead the protection of producer interests and the bolstering of class distinction.[52]

C. DO COUNTERFEITS DILUTE THE VALUE OF BRANDS?

Thus far we have argued that, at least in the context of luxury goods, counterfeits are unlikely to cause much direct harm via consumer confusion and displacement of sales—whether at the point of sale, which is the point that really matters, or even in the (far more disputed) post-sale context. But that does not exhaust the inquiry. We must also ask whether counterfeits have an *indirect* effect on branded goods. The conventional answer is yes, and we agree with it. However, there is not just one indirect effect; there are several. And on balance, there is good reason to think the overall indirect effect is likely to be very small or even, in some cases, *positive*.

Although trademark law is primarily concerned with consumer confusion, trademark rules also address what is known in American law as dilution of a trademark's distinctiveness via either "blurring" or "tarnishment." A trademark is said to suffer dilution by blurring when an unauthorized use of a mark harms consumers' ability to associate that mark with a particular product or service. This can occur, for example, when a famous mark is used on a product different from its ordinary usage. So, for example, dilution by blurring may occur if Cadillac, a famous mark for automobiles, were applied to watches. Consumers encountering the Cadillac watch may, the argument goes, now find it more difficult to make the association between Cadillac and automobiles. But very little of the luxury-goods counterfeit trade in China raises the possibility of dilution by blurring. For the most part, Chinese luxury-goods counterfeits are recognizable (albeit imperfect) imitations of a legitimate branded good: rather than a Tom Ford toaster, fake Tom Ford sunglasses. Counterfeits like these are very unlikely to "blur" the association of the luxury-goods mark and the products to which they are applied. The entire purpose of a counterfeit luxury good is *to call precisely that association to mind.*

---

[52] On this larger point see Beebe, *supra* note 51, at 813–14. The one way such a rule could be seen as consumer-protective is as protecting consumer investment in exclusivity; that is, consumers pay a premium for Lanvin sneakers (a casual suede pair, available on the website Mr. Porter, lists for $575) not because they are fantastic athletic wear but because of the status that accrues to the Lanvin wearer. Degrading that status through knockoffs will in turn cause the value of the consumer's investment in the status-conferring item to drop. Perhaps that is a reason to police post-sale confusion, but it has not been one widely articulated, or defended, to date. In any event, to be justified, the analysis cannot be restricted to the possible reduction of wealthy consumers' investment. To be a true social welfare analysis, and not simply a measure of the preferences of rich people, it must also consider the welfare gains of less affluent consumers who are priced into some simulacrum of status consumption by the presence of fakes. The balance between status losses at the top and status gains for everyone else is not susceptible to theoretical analysis—it must be measured empirically.

Counterfeiting of luxury goods, whether in China or elsewhere, is also unlikely to lead to what trademark law recognizes as dilution by "tarnishment." A brand is said to be tarnished if it is weakened by unflattering associations. Tarnishment can stem from unauthorized use of the mark on other products, or, much more controversially, perhaps by adoption by certain consumers—as in our Lanvin sneaker example above. Tarnishment of this kind is rarely discussed because it is awkward to state. But when the managing director of Roederer Cristal champagne was asked by *The Economist* magazine whether the well-known association between the brand and hip hop could hurt the brand, he controversially replied "that's a good question, but what can we do?"[53] More typically, claims of tarnishment come from use, even parodic use, by another firm with another product.[54] An American case involving the globally well-known Victoria's Secret brand illustrates this mechanism.[55] In that case, lingerie giant Victoria's Secret claimed, successfully, that a small and local lingerie and sex toys shop named "Victor's Little Secret" tarnished the Victoria's Secret brand—apparently by associating the brand owner's comparatively tame lingerie with a more frankly sexual aesthetic.

For the most part, however, unsavory association is not the sort of harm that luxury brands face from counterfeits. The real concern for luxury brands, rather, is that the presence of counterfeits will weaken the brand by diminishing the degree to which consumers perceive it as *exclusive or rare*. By this reasoning, Patek Philippe watches are more valuable if only obviously wealthy or well-connected people carry them. If ordinary consumers can have passable fake Patek Philippe watches, and will be publicly seen wearing them, then the real thing will no longer enjoy the exclusivity premium it once did.[56] Again, there is no confusion at sale or post sale; the concern, rather, is the perception that, due to counterfeits, a brand is embraced by downmarket consumers and more widely available than either the producer or the consumers of the original prefer.

Brand owners' desire to maintain product exclusivity is not irrational. Exclusivity is the major source of value in most, if not all, luxury-goods brands. Luxury products from well-known brands confer status on their owners because they are expensive or rare. To be sure, that status may be very contextual: for some audiences in some places a given brand may confer no status, or low status, whereas for others, it confers significant status. Status signals depend on a larger set of social and cultural norms, as well as a baseline context of market depth (how great a variety of products competing for status?) and density (how visible is status consumption to others?) and connection to the larger world (how powerfully are status signals reinforced from the outside?).

---

[53] *Bubbles and Bling*, THE ECONOMIST, May 8, 2006, *available at* http://www.economist.com/node/6905921. In a sense, as we discuss above, our hypothetical example of fake Lanvin sneakers noted (negatively) by a fashion-conscious observer is a species of tarnishment, though not one endorsed by any court we are aware of. It is probably a bridge too far for a court to acknowledge that a brand such as Cristal could be tarnished by having even the original item purchased and publicly displayed or consumed by putatively undesirable groups.

[54] *See* Louis Vuitton Malletier S.A., v. Haute Diggity Dog, LLC, 507 F.3d 252 (4th Cir. 2007).

[55] *V Secret Catalogue, Inc. v. Moseley*, 558 F. Supp. 2d 734 (W.D. Ky. 2008).

[56] Beebe, *supra* note 51, at 852–54.

Still, does all this mean the presence of counterfeits inevitably *diminishes* exclusivity? As we have shown, there is substantial reason for doubt. The harm to exclusivity from counterfeits is not as straightforward, nor as obvious, as the conventional wisdom suggests. And as we describe in the next section, there is even evidence suggesting that under some conditions counterfeits can *bolster* consumers' perception of a brand's desirability. Similarly, while tarnishment and blurring may be reasonable targets of trademark law, when tarnishment is caused by the poor wearing brands associated with the rich, it is a much harder case to justify the intervention of the legal system. All these factors help explain why China has not traditionally viewed counterfeits as a major problem to be solved—and why that stance is rational in a nation riven by inequality and fearful of social unrest.

V. The Advertising Effect and the Gateway Effect

Thus far we have discussed why counterfeits may not harm originals very much. The notion that counterfeits may actually *help* originals is more far-reaching. It comes in at least two forms: that counterfeits can serve as effective advertisements for originals, and that counterfeits can serve as gateways to originals, providing a trial run for those who are unsure if they want to splurge on the real thing.

A 2011 study by economist Yi Qian, for example, looked at data from 31 branded shoe companies, as well as a number of counterfeiters, operating in China in 1993–2004.[57] Qian took advantage of a natural experiment that allowed her to test how counterfeits and their originals fared under different systems of IP enforcement. The study found that for low-end items, counterfeits did cause some harm; the substitution effect was present. Yet counterfeiting had a surprisingly *positive* effect on the sales of high-end items in China. For these products, the tendency of counterfeits to advertise the desirability of the branded product—what we call the "advertising effect"—outweighed any substitution effect. Thanks to the advertising effect, counterfeits served to strengthen high-end brands and their sales numbers.

A study by Bonghee Yoo and Seung-Hee Lee of 324 female college students in South Korea likewise found interesting interactions between counterfeit luxury products and originals. Rather than decrease the likelihood of purchasing originals, Yoo and Lee's research indicated that counterfeit purchases seem to fuel it. In their words, luxury-goods firms

> should investigate the possibility that they might benefit from counterfeits. Purchase intention of luxury fashion counterfeits positively affects purchase intention of

---

[57] Yi Qian, *Counterfeiters: Foes or Friends? How Do Counterfeits Affect Different Product Quality Tiers* (Nat'l Bureau of Econ. Research, Working Paper No. w16785), *available at* http://papers.ssrn.com/sol3/papers.cfm?abstract_id=1759857##.

> originals.... *This finding clearly implies that counterfeit consumers are very likely to become ultimate consumers for originals and do not return to counterfeits*, a likelihood that is consistently found in pirated software or illegal music file download research, where counterfeits aid a full and fast market penetration of the originals.... Likewise, fashion counterfeits might function as a risk free trial version, generate interest among consumers, and make them spread positive word of mouth to other consumers.[58]

We see similar evidence in studies in the United States. Research by Renee Gosline looked at people who knowingly purchased counterfeit luxury items, like handbags and sunglasses, at so-called "purse parties." These consumers were under no illusion that their purchases were originals; the parties and their hosts were open about the provenance of the goods. Yet this did not clearly lead to reduced sales over time. Indeed, Gosline found that counterfeits do not hurt the sales of luxury brands so long as consumers can reliably distinguish between them. On the contrary, and consistent with Yoo and Lee's findings, counterfeits in the study often used as "trial versions" of the high-end genuine branded item. After trying the counterfeit version, over 40% of counterfeit handbag consumers ultimately purchased the real brand.

The Qian, Yoo and Lee, and Gosline studies all suggest that in both the United States and Asia fake luxury goods can serve as an effective form of advertising that actually spurs, rather than squelches, the market for originals. People who buy fakes have a significant probability of being converted to the brand and buying the real thing once they can afford to do so. Copies, in short, can act as a kind of "gateway drug" that leads to consumption of the harder (or at least, more expensive) stuff. What's more, every time consumers go out with their fake item, they're publicly displaying the desirability of the brand.[59] In short, these studies suggest that China may be living through a time where a boom in counterfeits is a sign of a coming boom in branded luxury goods.[60]

---

[58] Bonghee Yoo & Seung-Hee Lee, *Buy Genuine Luxury Goods Products or Counterfeits?*, 36 ADVANCES CONSUMER RES. 280, 285 (2009) (emphasis added).

[59] Whether visible copies signal desirability and help raise demand or, rather (or perhaps in addition), shift demand from wealthier consumers to poorer ones is an empirical question. Both arguments appear plausible, and indeed both may be true with the key issue being the brand's willingness to expand downmarket in pursuit of greater numbers of customers at the risk of losing overall brand appeal in the longer run. The classic example of the risks of this trajectory is Halston in the 1970s, who in a move widely seen in the fashion industry as disastrous "cashed in on his famous name, cutting a deal with J. C. Penney in 1983 to sell cut-rate clothes." But, the story goes, "the association cost him dearly: Bergdorf dropped him, and the average Jane didn't seem too enthused, either." Halston's brand never recovered. Laura M. Holson, *The Men (and Women) Who Would be Halston*, N.Y. TIMES, Sept 2, 2011, at ST1, *available at* http://www.nytimes.com/2011/09/04/fashion/the-men-and-women-who-would-be-halston.html?pagewanted=all&_r=0.

[60] See Haochen Sun, *Can Louis Vuitton Dance with HiPhone? Rethinking the Idea of Social Justice in Intellectual Property Law*, 15 U. PA. J. L. & SOC. CHANGE 387, 426 (2012) ("Even though many *shanzhai* companies copy products made by luxury brands, they actually have little impact on the market share of luxury companies. Rather, the luxury market ... achieved an unprecedented rapid growth in China at the same time that the *shanzhai* phenomenon grew from its infancy to nation-wide popularity").

While highly suggestive and intriguing, these studies are of course not definitive; much more research is needed. The important point is that the overall effect of counterfeits in China for luxury brands is unclear, and that there is at least some compelling evidence suggesting that the overall effect could be muted or even positive. And that raises significant public policy issues, both for the West and for China. Should the Chinese government devote substantial resources to a problem of such uncertain dimensions? Should the United States expend substantial political capital on efforts to induce the Chinese government to focus more aggressively on anti-counterfeiting enforcement with regard to consumer products like mobile phones and luxury items like handbags and footwear?[61]

The Chinese leadership, like any government, faces conflicting political pressures with regard to enforcement. On the one hand, Beijing may want to blunt the effects of high or rising economic inequality and, as a result, may tolerate a relatively high level of counterfeiting as a way to allow the lower- and middle-class citizens access to coveted goods—or at least simulacra of those goods—they could otherwise not afford. As Barton Beebe has compellingly argued, IP law often functions as a new sort of sumptuary code, reinforcing class distinctions via legal means.[62] Protecting the interests (or distinctiveness) of elites, as sumptuary codes do, can be unpopular, especially in extremely unequal and rapidly changing societies like China. On the other hand, governments also face political pressures—sometimes quite intense—to protect IP rights. Rights-holders are often powerful actors with access and resources to bring to bear to vindicate their preferred policies. Of course, when the IP rights holders are almost uniformly foreigners, as is true for luxury products in China, those pressures are far less strong. The rational balance to be struck is to be more protective of consumers' interest in access to goods than of producers' interest in protecting market share. And this is indeed what we see in today's China.

Class distinctions and economic inequality, in short, are inevitably at the heart of trademark protection in the luxury context. These factors are especially complex in China. Indeed, the tremendous inequality between China's major cities and its vast hinterland has created marked disparities in the luxury market. A recent news report, for example, suggests that China's crackdown on corruption among government officials has diminished interest in some of the most readily identified luxury brands. "Prada is among a few premium brands reporting solid growth in the world's second largest luxury market even as a government campaign against conspicuous spending and gift-giving hurts firms with instantly recognizable brands like LVMH, Compagnie Financiere Richemont and Kering SA. The logos on Prada's deluxe leather handbags, wallets and shoes are, by and large, low-key and these days, discretion is a wise strategy

---

[61] *See* Raustiala & Sprigman, *supra* note 6.

[62] *See* Beebe, *supra* note 51, at 812–13.

in China."[63] The story suggests further that "The shift away from in-your-face luxury brands is most prominent in big cities such as Shanghai and Beijing, where many companies have their biggest stores and where customer tastes are rapidly evolving. Logos, however, are still very popular in China's vast interior, where luxury labels are still a novelty, analysts say."

Marketing analysts have called this strategy "abranding." As one study puts it, abranding, which was common among the most affluent subjects in their study, has as its goal

> to conceal consumption habits from the lay gaze of distant others. Underlying this behavior was a rampant desire to perpetuate social distance by restricting the knowledge others had about these consumers (Simmel 1950). Consumers in this group did not recognize a distinction between those buying counterfeits and any other consumer who wants to emulate the rich. Affluent consumers—uneasy with the idea that previously disenfranchised consumers wanted to emulate them—appeared to gravitate preemptively toward brands that lower-income consumers find difficult to detect.[64]

As any trip to a major Chinese city will confirm, what Veblen originally perceived as the driver of conspicuous consumption—status competition—is clearly alive and well in China. But whether the presence of counterfeit luxury goods has the straightforwardly harmful effect on original brands that the conventional view of trademark supposes is not so clear. The key to market success of a luxury good is the brand's ability to credibly signal wealth, taste, and style to others. Counterfeit goods trade on that signal, but whether in the process they also *impair or diminish* is a question that has yet to be satisfactorily answered.

VI. Conclusion

China is by some measures the largest market in the world for luxury goods, and luxury goods constitute a category famously dependent on intellectual property for its value. China is also the undisputed world champion of counterfeiting. How these two facts coexist—and why—has been our focus in this chapter.

Because so little empirical work on the relationship between IP and copying has been done in China, our arguments are necessarily preliminary. But they draw on a more

---

[63] *In China, the Devil Doesn't Wear Prada*, LIVE MINT & WALL ST. J. (Sep. 17, 2013, 8:39 AM), http://www.livemint.com/Consumer/9P3VsUHCdyexHEauBDoe7I/In-China-the-Devil-doesnt-wear-Prada.html.

[64] Suraj Commuri, *The Impact of Counterfeiting on Genuine-Item Consumers' Brand Relationships*, 73 J. MARKETING 86, 86 (2009).

fundamental and well-grounded claim, which is that counterfeits and copies are not nearly as harmful as the conventional wisdom suggests.

There is no compelling reason to reject this logic for China. But there are some additional factors or twists that we believe make the Chinese case distinctive. One is that unprecedented economic growth over the last three decades has produced, even in a supposedly Communist society, enormous income differences. This creates both great pressure for the newly wealthy to engage in Veblenesque conspicuous consumption, but also a vast market of poor and middle-class Chinese who can only aspire to afford counterfeited facsimiles of the fancy goods they desire. China's rapid urbanization adds to this by providing dense spaces for status competition to unfold. At the same time, many have argued that China has a literary and artistic tradition that is quite forgiving and even positive about copying, and a vibrant contemporary *shanzhai* culture that celebrates the clever copy as a triumph of ingenuity and creativity.

Adding to this is a set of dynamics that are not unique to China, but that serve to underscore the ways in which counterfeits can help as well as harm luxury brands. As research in the United States, China, and South Korea have shown, counterfeits can serve as advertisements, highlighting the desirability and trendiness of particular brands and associated styles. Counterfeits can also serve as gateways, allowing customers with the means to purchase the original luxury item a low-cost way to "try on" a purchase and essentially sample the marketplace. These studies turn the conventional wisdom on its head, and highlight the complex relationship between original and knockoff.

Together, these considerations make the Chinese tolerance of knockoffs easier to understand, and provide a rational basis for China's continuing resistance to the pressure from the West for more aggressive policing of counterfeits. There is little reason to believe that China's luxury-goods market, or its counterfeit market, will change anytime soon; China remains a largely poor country despite its astounding growth rate and notwithstanding its large number of newly minted millionaires. These considerations also suggest—although they do not yet prove—that counterfeit and original can coexist more readily than conventional wisdom allows. In other words, one compelling explanation for the simultaneous and astonishing success of both legitimate luxury goods and counterfeits in China is that there is nothing surprising at all. Counterfeits do not injure the branded goods they imitate—at least not substantially—and it is in the interest of the Chinese government to permit both the luxury boom and the associated boom in luxury fakes to continue.

14 A Perspective from Asia

SPECIAL PROTECTION FOR LUXURY BRANDS—LEGAL SENSE OR NONSENSE?

David Llewelyn*

I. Introduction

Among the siren calls heard in recent times for ever-broader legal protection of intellectual property rights is that from those who peddle the type of "luxury" goods that Hollywood actors take with them on riverboat journeys in Cambodia: actor Angelina Jolie is one of three "Core Values personalities" (the others are singer Bono and actor Sean Connery) featured in advertising for international fashion house Louis Vuitton, part of the LVMH conglomerate that owns many self-styled "luxury brands."

In September 2012 the European Commission acknowledged "luxury" as a sector in its own right. Armando Branchini, president of lobbying group the European Cultural and Creative Industries Alliance (ECCIA), was quoted in the Financial Times' Special Report on Business of Luxury[1] as saying that this is "our first public achievement" and the first time the Commission had "recognised the high-end industry as the pillar of cultural and creative industries." ECCIA was set up in 2010 by national organizations for

* Deputy Dean & Professor (Practice), School of Law, Singapore Management University; Professor of Intellectual Property Law, Dickson Poon School of Law, King's College London.

1 FINANCIAL TIMES SPECIAL REPORT, THE BUSINESS OF LUXURY I (2013).

the luxury sector Comité Colbert (France), Meisterkreis (Germany), Altagamma (Italy), Circulo Fortuny (Spain), and Walpole (UK).

The arguments in favor of broader legal protection for luxury brands can be reduced to a simple one: "we spend more money than most on advertising and promoting our products, therefore the law should protect us more." This, or a variant of it, is also heard frequently in discussions on the extent to which well-known or famous marks should be accorded more extensive protection than given to other trademarks: the terms "luxury brand" and "well-known mark" are all too often elided or used interchangeably, even though many of the former do not fall in the latter category, however it is defined.

A recent textbook by two leading law academics, Annette Kur and Thomas Dreier, *European Intellectual Property Law*,[2] puts it thus:

> [a]n economic justification [for extended protection] is found in the fact that reputation enjoyed by a mark is regularly the fruit of intense investment, for which further incentives are provided by the additional protection granted.

Interestingly, the learned authors make no mention of the economic impact of that extended protection: for every would-be plaintiff there is always at least one defendant, and many of them are engaging in activities that a neutral observer would regard as fair competition. Indeed, it would not be unreasonable for such an observer to conclude, all things considered, that there is more than sufficient legal protection already for the owners of luxury brands and to extend it even further lacks any coherent legal or economic basis.

When any area of the law starts to lose its coherence the danger is that underlying, and important, rationales start to get lost or abandoned: eventually the whole area lacks a raison d'être beyond "that's the way it is." Anyone who believes in the importance of a balanced system of intellectual property laws to encourage creativity and innovation needs to be aware of the danger to such a system that is posed by the siren calls for yet more expansion of those laws.

II. The Fake Problem

Many luxury brands have a serious problem with fakes and this leads to demands for more extensive legal protection. Indeed, no one interested in a coherent and balanced system for the protection of intellectual property rights can disagree with two basic propositions, that

(a) fakes bearing another's trademark (or one indistinguishably similar to it)—perhaps we should describe them as "copies that deceive"—should constitute

---

[2] Annette Kur & Thomas Dreier, European Intellectual Property Law 212 (2013).

infringements of the law, whether of trademark law or some closely allied field such as passing off or unfair competition; and

(b) such infringements should be as easy for the right owner to prevent as the interests of justice allow.

In fact, the laws of most countries comply with proposition (a): behind much criticism is a perception that proposition (b) is not the case and, where that is so, future investment in the creation and burnishing of brands is jeopardized. The bigger the historical investment in brand-building, the greater the critics seem to view the perceived threat.

III. Infringements Versus Counterfeits

However, the problem of luxury-brand "fakes" or "counterfeits" (terms that mean different things to different people) is too often thrown into the mix of the legal debate as to what should constitute "trademark infringement" or "passing off" (in common law countries), despite it being clear that a fake is almost always both an infringement and passing off under the existing laws of most countries. That debate raises important issues as to the dividing line between legitimate competition and the enforcement of private rights, which the question of how to deal with fakes serves only to obfuscate.

For example, in a recent article by Jennifer Darcy on the fashion industry and "fake goods"—the terms "fake goods" and "counterfeit luxury goods" seem to be used interchangeably by her—she notes: "many brands have had to resort to costly litigation to assert their IP rights, which is not always successful."[3] Ms. Darcy makes this comment, which presumably is meant to elicit sympathy and an immediate rush for further legislation, before describing the litigation in which, relying on its well-known three-stripe mark, Adidas sued, in separate actions, two third parties (Marca Mode and Fitnessworld) who were using two stripes on their products. The European Court of Justice held, on references from the Dutch courts, in the first,[4] that this *could* constitute infringement under article 5(1)(b) of the Trade Mark Directive as "confusion cannot be ruled out" and, in the second,[5] that it *may* constitute "dilution" under article 5(2) (emphasis added in both instances).

It is important to note, which Ms. Darcy does not, that the Court of Justice also held that if, on the facts, the public views the sign as an embellishment it would not be an infringement: this would seem to suggest, contrary to Darcy's black-and-white view (which seems to accept unquestioningly that Marca Mode's and Fitnessworld's goods

---

[3] Jennifer Darcy, *Under-Regulated or Under-Enforced: Intellectual Property, the Fashion Industry and Fake Goods* EIPR, 35, 82 (2013).

[4] Marca Mode CV v. Adidas. AG [2000] ETMR 723 at 42.

[5] Adidas-Salomon AG v. Fitnessworld C-408/01 [2004] ETMR 10 at 41.

bearing two stripes are "counterfeits"), that the case could go either way depending on the national court's findings on the facts. This is surely a good reason for requiring of a legal system that it have processes that ensure an appropriately rigorous assessment of both law and fact, rather than accepting without demur wide-ranging allegations of infringement from deep-pocketed trademark proprietors.

> For example, on the other side of the Atlantic, the Southern District Court of New York rejected the claim of trade mark infringement brought by Louis Vuitton against Warner Brothers arising from the use in the film *The Hangover: Part II* of a bag that one of the main characters refers to as being made by Louis Vuitton (although the first part of the well-known brand is mispronounced "Lewis"). The court preferred the First Amendment's protection of artistic works to this assertion of private rights.
>
> In the interests of fairness, this should be contrasted with the decision of a Paris court in November 2007 which ordered Sony BMG and MTV Online to stop broadcasting or marketing the video for Britney Spears' "Do Something" and fined them 80,000 euros ($117,000) each. In the opening scenes of the video, Spears appeared in the driver's seat of a hot pink Hummer floating on make-believe clouds. One shot showed fingers drumming on a dashboard covered with what apparently looked like Louis Vuitton's "Cherry Blossoms" design: dark pink blossoms on a pale pink background, embossed with the "LV" logo.

IV. The Fake Market

It is also telling that Ms. Darcy, as do many other commentators, throws around estimates of the size of the market for counterfeits like confetti: characterizing Marca Mode's and Fitnessworld's products (which were so close to the line of infringement/no infringement that both cases ended up before the European Court of Justice) as "fake products" or "counterfeits" may explain the US$600 billion figure that she cites[6] as the value of the counterfeit luxury goods trade. She refers also to *Harper's Bazaar* magazine's estimate of an annual loss of US$512 billion of global sales and losses of 750,000 jobs and US$250 billion to companies in the USA alone (which must lead to the question "how was that remarkably precise figure of US$512 billion arrived at when other figures bandied about seem to be rounded up to the nearest $10 billion at least?").

Surely, the scourge of counterfeiting is bad enough without using exaggerated figures and over-broad definitions of what constitutes a counterfeit, which have the regrettable result of diminishing the seriousness with which the problem should be viewed and

[6] Darcy, *supra* note 3.

combated. Sadly, what comes to mind is the story of the boy who cried "Wolf!" one time too many.

It is important always to remember that, as well as the very serious problem of (dare one say "real"?) counterfeits, there are many examples of good-faith use and legitimate copying, or gray imports of genuine goods (only a "counterfeit" in the mind of a specialist lawyer), that upset other people, who then make claims of infringement, some justified, some not. To repeat, eliding good-faith use and counterfeiting serves only to confuse. Not all unauthorized use of another's trademark can or should be stopped: the artwork of Andy Warhol is only one example that comes to mind of unauthorized use of luxury brands, think Chanel No. 5 and Apple's Mac as well as the more prosaic Campbell's Soup. Nor is all copying bad: many successful products and services, as well of course as great artworks, are built on and improve upon what there was before. Indeed, on an upbeat note, American academics Kal Raustiala and Christopher Sprigman, in a recent work *The Knockoff Economy: How Imitation Sparks Innovation*,[7] which includes extensive industry case studies, conclude that copying in the American fashion industry

> has never been more creative. All this copying has not killed the fashion industry. In fact, fashion not only survives despite copying; *it thrives due to copying*.[8]

V. Crying "Wolf!"

In the intellectual property law field generally, special pleading by specific interest groups or even individuals has resulted in a number of areas in which either logic or coherence (or both) is lacking.

One example that always raises a few eyebrows is the Vessel Hull Design Protection Act of 1998 in the United States that provides 10 years' legal protection for boat hulls. At least with this sui generis protection one could be forgiven for thinking that it is clear what a "vessel" is and what a "hull" is. But you would be wrong if you did so: to close a loophole some manufacturers took advantage of that opened as a result of the definitions in the original Act, the Act was amended in 2008 by the Vessel Hull Design Protection Amendments, signed into law by President Bush in October.

Before these amendments, the definition of "hull" included the deck: this meant that a manufacturer could copy exactly the hull of a competitor's boat but change the configuration of the deck and thereby avoid infringement. The amended Act protects "the design of a vessel hull, deck, or combination of a hull and deck, including a plug or mold." In addition, "hull" is defined as "the exterior frame or body of a vessel, exclusive

[7] Kal Raustiala & Christopher Sprigman, The Knockoff Economy: How Imitation Sparks Innovation (2012).

[8] *Id.at 156.*

of the deck, superstructure, masts, sails, yards, rigging, hardware, fixtures, and other attachments," and a "deck" is "the horizontal surface of a vessel that covers the hull, including exterior cabin and cockpit surface."

Prior to October 1, 2008, 381 designs had been registered under the 1998 legislation (an average of roughly 10 per annum); after that date 144 had been registered as at June 13, 2012 (an average of roughly 38 per annum).[9] Hence, the popularity of the protection seems to have increased somewhat from a very low base since the amendments, although in a February 8, 2013 forum post on the www.boatdesign.net website, "CutOnce" commented on the practical impact of the legislation:

> Putting it crudely, design litigation is a money contest, and the guy with the deepest pockets usually wins. Huge organizations can out-lawyer, delay and obfuscate most patent holders till they run out of money, and then snap up the assets at the insolvency sell-off for cents on the dollar. Right and wrong have little to do with defining who will eventually end up with the market.

Notwithstanding that, the question remains for the lobbyists who drive the agenda in so many parts of the IP arena: "if boat hulls, why not jewelry/dresses/buildings/shoes (delete and add to as applicable), especially if they are expensive?"

VI. Expanding Rights for an Expanding Market

In a 2006 article,[10] Kai Raustiala and Christopher Sprigman estimated the annual turnover globally in fashion apparel alone to be in the region of US$750 billion. Presumably a not insignificant proportion of such fashion apparel bears what many think of as a luxury brand, so, when the owners of those luxury brands tell the legislators that they need more and wider protection than is given to the common or garden trademark used on baked beans or shovels, the legislators tend to listen, even though they rarely understand. Hence the expanded protection, in recent times, under the laws of most countries, given to "well-known marks."

Special protection for well-known marks ("*marques notoires connue*," sometimes translated as "well-known and famous marks": for example, de Werra and Simon, eds. "*Marques notoires et de haute renommée: Well-known and famous trademarks*")[11] was introduced long ago at the international level by Article *6bis* of the Paris Convention

---

[9] Somewhat curiously, DVH No.0525, belonging to South Boats (Holdings) Limited, is described on the U.S. Copyright Office website as one of the June 13, 2012, registrations, although the actual certificate available on the website has a stamped registration date of July 13, 2012.

[10] Kai Raustiala & Christopher Sprigman, *The Piracy Paradox: Innovation and Intellectual Property in Fashion Design* U. Va. L. Rev. 1687 (2006).

[11] Actes de la Journée de Droit de la Propriété Intellectuelle du 15 février 2011 (Schulthess, Geneva).

(agreed at the Hague Revision Conference in 1925). However, this applied only to use in relation to goods identical or similar to those in respect of which the mark had become well known, and did not include services.

At the 1958 Lisbon Conference on the Paris Convention, the United States proposed that Article *6bis* be extended to dissimilar goods in the case of marks with an exceptional reputation but this proposal (and five others which had been voted on by the drafting committee) was not put to a vote in the full Conference.[12] Wadlow notes that the Programme of the International Bureau for the Conference considered in some detail the proposition that "there was already an international consensus against parasitic, but possibly non-confusing, use of highly renowned marks," and the 1898 *Kodak* case (a passing off case in which use on bicycles of the well-known mark "Kodak"—invented by George Eastman and used on his company's cameras and film—was restrained, 15 RPC 105) "took pride of place" in this consideration.[13] It is instructive to note that a distinction was drawn at this Conference between "*marques notoirement connue*" (or well-known marks), which Article *6bis* protects, and "*marques haute renommée*" (or especially famous marks, which Wadlow describes as "one degree higher than '*marques notoirement connue*'").[14] The addition of the proposed U.S. category, marks with an exceptional reputation, would have added a further layer of potential for confusion.

A year after Article *6bis* was added to the Paris Convention in 1925, the proponents of even more expansive protection for famous marks were awarded their academic seal of approval in the Anglo-American law world with publication of the seminal Harvard Law Review article on the concept of dilution written by Frank I. Schechter, *The Rational Basis of Trademark Protection*.[15] This proposed the adoption in the United States of the German law notion of *Verwässerung* (strictly, watering down) that had been applied the previous year by the *Landgericht* in Elberfeld[16] when ordering the cancellation of a mark, registered for steel railway products, that was identical to the "Odol" mark that the plaintiff not only invented but had used for more than 25 years on its mouthwash products.

Few would disagree with the *Landgericht* and Schechter that it would be unfair if "fanciful, arbitrary or coined"—or, as sometimes described, "invented"—trademarks like "Odol" could not be protected against third-party use, even on unrelated goods. Such use could be due only to a desire to benefit from the reputation created by the trademark's inventor and suggest falsely that there is some sort of a trade connection with the owner of the famous trademark. One thinks of the cross-examination that would ensue in an English or American court: "Would you tell the court why you chose to

---

[12] CHRISTOPHER WADLOW, THE LAW OF PASSING OFF, at para 2-057 (2011).

[13] *Id* at para 2-057, footnote 116.

[14] *Id.*at para 2-057, footnote 115.

[15] Frank I. Schechter, *The Rational Basis of Trademark Protection* 40 HARV. L. REV. 813.

[16] LG Elberfeld, September 14, 1924, *GRUR* 1924, 204–*Odol.*

use for your products this trademark [Odol/Exxon/Kodak] that was invented by the plaintiff and has no meaning at all in any language of which we are aware?" Of course, even in pre-1994 England (when trademark law was less protective than it became with the Trade Marks Act 1994) such behavior would have been enjoined without too much difficulty through a passing off action (as in *Kodak*) as long as the plaintiff had some goodwill in the jurisdiction. As a general matter, judges in passing off actions do not let the strict requirements of the tort prevent them from giving relief in cases where there is a clear intention to deceive: it can be seen from the judgment of Lord Diplock in the *Advocaat* case[17] that the tort is a flexible one.

Thus, as a matter of practice, a wide-ranging anti-dilution provision was (and is) unnecessary in the vast majority of cases where a famous mark has been used on dissimilar goods or services with an intent to deceive. To take the example put forward by Professor Burton Ong[18] of what he describes as "non-origin confusion" that in his view needs a special anti-dilution provision

> if ... an escort agency and a waste management services provider were to use "Mercedes Benz" as part of their business names, while making it very clear in their advertising materials that they are not related to, licensed by, or in any way affiliated with, the German car maker.

VII. A Luxury Sledgehammer

However, it is surely unnecessary to have resort to the "sledgehammer" anti-dilution remedy on which so much ink has been spilt and money wasted in order to prevent this type of behavior: there could be no reason to use the unique conjunction of "Mercedes" and "Benz" other than to deceive. In England this would certainly constitute passing off, regardless of any attempts the defendants might make to claim there was no deception because of the disclaimers (which are normally ignored by English courts as they do not believe they remove deception or its likelihood, as in *Parker-Knoll v. Knoll International*[19] (by both Wilberforce J. at first instance and the Court of Appeal)). On the other hand, if the escort agency in Professor Ong's hypothetical was called Mercedes Escort Agency, this would be unlikely to constitute passing off in the absence of other factors, perhaps the use of a three-pointed star as well: "Mercedes" is a relatively common Christian name of Spanish origin (as well as being the name of a place in at least five different countries) and was originally chosen by Emil Jellinek as the name of the new car developed for him by Daimler in 1900 because his daughter was known by that name

[17] J. Townend & Sons (Hull) Limited ("Advocaat") [1979] FSR 397.

[18] Burton Ong, *Interpreting Intellectual Property Statutes in Singapore* 24 SAcLJ 1032 (2012).

[19] Parker-Knoll v. Knoll International [1962] RPC 243.

(and in any case the Daimler name could not be used in France, where Jellinek wanted to sell the new car, as in that country the Daimler name belonged to Panhard & Levassor).

But where the unauthorized use is of an invented mark (like Mercedes-Benz or Rolls-Royce),[20] passing off is likely to be found, however weak the evidence. Thus, in Australia, sports goods company Nike International succeeded before the High Court[21] in its actions for passing off and under section 52 of the Trade Practices Act 1974 against a Spanish company Campomar that had registered the mark Nike for perfumes and was then using it on sports perfumes in a style of lettering very similar to that used by Nike International. Indeed, showing how far the tort can stretch in appropriate circumstances, in *Lego v. Lego M. Lemelstrich*,[22] the Danish maker of toy bricks persuaded the English High Court to restrain the defendant from using "Lego" on plastic garden sprinklers (although failed to do so in Australia). On this, Christopher Wadlow[23] comments that, first, "[c]onsidered as a head of damage in its own right, loss of exclusivity needs to be treated with caution" and, secondly, "much of the reasoning in *Lego* is unconvincing."[24]

VIII. Some Confusion

On the issue of whether loss of exclusivity could be a separate head of damage in a passing off action, which had received judicial approval in the *Elderflower Champagne* case,[25] from Bingham MR ("damage of an insidious and serious kind,"[26] Peter Gibson LJ ("blurring or erosion of the uniqueness")[27] and Mann LJ ("[t]he impairment is a gradual debasement, dilution or erosion of what is distinctive"),[28] Millett L.J. (as he then was) expressed serious concern in *Harrods Ltd. v. Harrodian School Ltd.*:[29]

> "Erosion of the distinctiveness of a brand name has been recognised as a form of damage to the goodwill of the business with which the name is connected in a number of cases, particularly in Australia and New Zealand; but unless care is

---

[20] "Rolls-Royce" was used by Schechter, in testimony before the House Committee on Patents (72d Cong., 1st sess.15 (1932)), as an example of a famous mark whose notoriety might be diluted if it were to be used by others on products unrelated to motor-cars. It is noteworthy that today the same mark is used by unrelated parties—BMW AG and Rolls-Royce Holdings PLC—for motor-cars and aircraft engines, apparently without harming the value of either for their respective proprietor or causing consumers noticeable distress.

[21] Campomar v. Nike International (2000) 46 IPR 481.

[22] Lego v. Lego M. Lemelstrich [1983] FSR 155.

[23] WADLOW, *supra* note 12, at para 4-046.

[24] WADLOW, *supra* note 12, at para 4-046.

[25] Taittinger and Others v. Allbev Ltd. and Another [1993] FSR 641.

[26] *Id.*

[27] *Id.*

[28] *Id.*

[29] Harrods Ltd. v. Harrodian School Ltd. [1996] RPC 697.

> taken this could mark an unacceptable extension to the tort of passing off. To date the law has not sought to protect the value of the brand name as such, but the value of the goodwill which it generates; and it insists on proof of confusion to justify its intervention. But the erosion of the distinctiveness of a brand name which occurs by reason of its degeneration into common use as a generic term is not necessarily dependent on confusion at all.... I have an intellectual difficulty in accepting the concept that the law insists upon the presence of both confusion and damage and yet recognises as sufficient a head of damage which does not depend on confusion."[30]

It must also be questioned how justified many complaints about loss of exclusivity are in the real world (as opposed to that inhabited by trademark lawyers): the real world where buyers of luxury products have no problem distinguishing between the unrelated marks "Gucci" and "Pucci," and don't think the worse of either because there is another luxury brand with only a letter difference. For example, the Jif lemon coexisted happily in the UK with Jif abrasive cleaner for many years and no one seems to have put the latter on their pancakes. It was only because of a wish to have a more global brand for its abrasive cleaner that Unilever changed "Jif" to "Cif" in the UK in 2000; it's still called Jif in Australia and New Zealand, but you don't see Aussies or Kiwis in London using lemon juice to clean their toilets.

Likewise, in Mostert's book, *Famous and Well-Known Marks* (1997), the following example of what would constitute "blurring" is used:

> If, for example, the TIFFANY mark has become well-known in connection with jewellery , and it is used on a multiplicity of other goods such as chocolates, clothing, a motion picture house, and a restaurant, the likelihood that the TIFFANY mark will still exclusively call to mind its owner's jewellery products becomes increasingly diminished.

But, surely, is not Tiffany a name that is used already by many other people and businesses? Would anyone be confused or think less of Tiffany jewellery if Cadbury's brought out a Tiffany bar of chocolate, as long as the color of the packaging was not similar to what Wikipedia describes as "the light medium robin egg blue color [*sic*] associated with Tiffany & Co, the New York jewelry company" (if it was, there would be clear passing off). Do the Tiffany Café in Furama City Centre in Singapore, the Tiffany Sports Lounge in St. Paul, Minnesota ("since 1971 friendship, laughter and service"), or the Korean TV star Stephanie Hwang whose stage name is Tiffany diminish in any meaningful way what Mostert claims to be the "exclusivity" of the TIFFANY jewellery mark?

---

[30] *Id.*

Or what if Donald Trump's daughter Tiffany starts a clothing range called "Tiffany"? Of course there is no such diminution, whether you call it "blurring" or "tarnishment." The reality is that there is no such exclusivity possessed by famous marks such as Tiffany, BP, Hermes, Coach, and Chloë, whereas there is for invented marks such as Odol, L'Oréal, Rolls-Royce, and Mercedes-Benz: the type of marks of which Schechter wrote. Yet the clamor seems to demand that they be treated as if there is.

In 1997 Sir Robin Jacob, one of the best known (or, dare one say it, famous) trademarks judges of the past century, commented to a Fordham Law School conference on IP of the clamor he was hearing even at that time (and it has become louder):

> [t]he Protectionist side, in my estimation, has been getting a louder and louder voice. It is embodied in the recent book "Famous and Well-Known Marks" [edited by Mostert, see above], which reviews the position in 15 countries. Why a louder voice? I am bound to say that I think it is because they have the richest and most organised lobby. I cannot see any other good reason. I cannot think that the conventional deception test has been inadequate in any way. What are the concrete instances of marks losing value or distinctiveness when trade mark rights were based simply on deceptiveness?

IX. A Detour to China

More than a century after its groundbreaking success against "Kodak" bicycles in England, referred to above, Eastman Kodak succeeded in China in its trademark infringement action against Suzhou Keda Hydraulic Elevators, which had been using "Kodak" on elevators: in the April 6, 2006, judgment of the Suzhou Intermediate People's Court[31] it was found that the plaintiff's mark was known to practically every household in China, and elsewhere, and therefore the defendant was trying to obtain illicit benefits through its use on elevators.

In China, to decide if a mark is well known is open to the Trademark Office

- either in opposition proceedings: for example, see Trademark Office decision No. 1963 of 2000 upholding an opposition by the owners of the Chinese version of the "SEVEN UP" soft drink mark (a subsidiary of PepsiCo Inc.) to the application to register the same mark for animal feed. It is important to note that the mark had been used in China on soft drinks for many years; or

[31] The Jiangsu Province Suzhou City Intermediate People's Court's Civil Judgment. No. Suzhongminsanchuzi 0213/2005.

- by the Trademark Review Board in the course of administrative proceedings for infringement brought before the Administration for Industry and Commerce (AIC);

and to the courts:

- the well-known status of a mark can arise either in infringement actions or on appeal from Trademark Office adjudications in oppositions. For example, in December 2012 the Beijing First Intermediate People's Court overturned a Trademark Review & Adjudication Board refusal of the opposition by the owner of the "Häagen-Dazs" trademark for ice cream to an application to register "Haager Dazs" for clothing, finding that the ice cream mark was well known and therefore the clothing mark should be refused.

Although there were no provisions on well-known marks in either the initial 1982 Trademark Law or the amended 1993 version, the Trademark Office accorded well-known mark status to a foreign mark, "Pizza Hut," for the first time in 1987, in an opposition against an application by an Australian company to register the mark for cakes. Two years later, it accorded the status to the first Chinese well-known trademark, "Tong Ren Tang," for a manufacturer of Chinese medicine.

In April 2009 the Supreme Court of the People's Republic of China issued an explanation setting out its views on some of the issues arising in disputes relating to well-known marks. Among the purposes of the Explanation was to clarify the provisions of Article 13 of the Chinese Trademark Law (introduced in October 2001), which provides the following:

> 13. A trademark which is applied for registration in relation to identical or similar goods shall not be registered or shall be prohibited from use, if it is a reproduction, an imitation or a translation, liable to create confusion, of a well-known mark which is not registered in China.
>
> A trademark which is applied for in relation to similar or dissimilar goods shall not be registered or shall be prohibited from use if it is a reproduction, an imitation or a translation, misleading the public, of a well-known mark which is registered in China, provided that the interests of the owner of the well-known mark are likely to be damaged by such use.

Article 13 is clearly aimed at protecting Article *6bis* types of marks against use likely to confuse, which is how their owners are damaged. In addition, the Supreme Court's Explanation makes it clear that "well known" means well known in China; notoriety outside China is not relevant (although, somewhat confusingly, it may be taken into account, as in the Trademark Office decision that held that "Disney" is a well-known mark and noted that "Disneyland" is known widely around the world).[32] Notwithstanding this, there are now a number of foreign-owned marks:

> A search of the listings on the China Trade Mark Office on February 21, 2013, revealed the following foreign-owned well-known marks: Martell, Sheraton, Yahoo!, Total, Honda, Apple Inc.'s apple device, the Toyota logo, Kenwood, Sony.

These marks have been accorded well-known status either by the courts or the Trademark Office, although perhaps unsurprisingly their number is dwarfed by locally owned marks given the status (of the 293 announced by the Trademark Office in January 2010, BMW was the only foreign-owned one). In fact, one can argue that the well-known mark craze has got out of control in China, where there are both "nationally famous marks" (*chiming shangbiao*) and "locally famous marks" (*zhuming shangbiao*) that together number in the thousands (by 2001, Zhejiang province alone had 465 "locally famous marks" awarded by the principal Administration for Industry and Commerce). Both the nationally famous and locally famous marks can be advertised and promoted using the fact that they have this status—in practical terms using it as an official seal of approval.

Certainly that was not the intention of the framers of Article *6bis* of the Paris Convention back in 1925, or Schechter a year later: what they wanted to prevent was unauthorized use of a well-known mark on dissimilar goods where it was likely to mislead people into thinking there was some form of trade connection when there was not.

X. Back to the Future: From "Well Known" under Article 6*bis* Onward

With the addition of Article *6bis* to the Paris Convention at the 1925 Hague Conference, protection was expanded for the owners of well-known marks. So far, so good. But trademark owners can never get too much of a good thing, and pressure was brought to bear for "more": perhaps Oliver Twist should become the patron saint of trademark proprietors? And, unlike in Dickensian London, in the modern IP world, what Oliver wants, Oliver usually gets. The EU trademark regime now gives expanded protection against unauthorized use on dissimilar goods not just to invented marks or even to famous or well-known marks but also to "marks with a reputation." And without a need to establish there is a likelihood of confusion: all that is required is potential free-riding or detriment to the owner of the mark with a reputation.[33]

---

[32] Decision No 585 of 2004.

[33] For more detail on this area, see David Llewelyn, *Protection of "Famous" Marks under Trademark Law and Passing Off*, *in* OVERLAPPING INTELLECTUAL PROPERTY RIGHTS (Neil Wilkof & Shamnad Basheer eds., 2012) at p231 et seq.

Despite its being relatively clear that what was intended to be protected were well-known marks, courts throughout the EU have read the provision and its wording and concluded, unsurprisingly, that it is not so limited. In the Max Planck Institute's Study on the Overall Functioning of the European Trade Mark System in 2011, it is stated that "marks which have attained a level of reputation that qualifies for extended protection [as marks with a reputation] would likewise have to be protected as well known marks within the meaning of Article *6bis* of the Paris Convention and vice versa."[34] If, by that, the Study means that "mark with a reputation" should be interpreted as, and limited to, "well known marks" that should be the correct analysis (and see also *Nieto Nuño v. Monlleó),*[35] but it does not reflect what happens in practice in national courts.

Indeed, in the *L'Oréal v. Bellure* case the plaintiff's marks relied upon were not even words or well-known logos but marks comprising the external cardboard packaging (with no brand name on it) for the goods, which were bottled perfumes bearing the word marks "Lancôme" and "Trésor." These packaging marks were accepted by the English High Court, apparently without hesitation, to be "marks with a reputation" even though they were never used (nor were they ever intended to be used) without the word marks on them. Such is the Alice in Wonderland world of European trademark law.

XI. Mixed Up

But it gets worse. In the *Whirlpool* case[36] the "mark with a reputation" was one that was accepted for registration only because it had the word "KitchenAid" on the drawing of the KitchenAid food mixer (and was therefore not *exclusively* an unregistrable shape under Article 7(1)(e)(ii) or (iii) of the CTM Regulation). This was despite the fact that the word was illegible when making an online search of the Trade Marks Register (and how else are honest traders to find out what marks are registered in order to ensure that what they are proposing does not infringe others' rights?) Lots of food mixers were sold under the mark "KitchenAid" and as a result the unregistrable (but—because of the illegible "KitchenAid"—actually registered) shape mark was now a "mark with a reputation," entitled to the extended protection that could trace its history back to that first proposal by Schechter for "fanciful, arbitrary or coined" marks all those years ago.

Fortunately, both the English High Court and Court of Appeal bent over backward to stop insult being added to injury, by refusing to find the "[unregistrable but registered] mark with a reputation" infringed by the defendant's similar-looking food mixer. After all, how different can the shape of food mixers be? And can a particular design of

---

[34] Max Planck Institute, Study on the Overall Functioning of the European Trade Mark System (2011) at para 2-132.

[35] Nieto Nuño v. Monlleó [2008] ETMR 222, CJEU.

[36] Whirlpool Corp. v. Kenwood Ltd. [2010] ETMR 7.

a food mixer really operate as an indication of trade origin, which remains the principal function of a trademark?

At the international level, Article 16 of the 1994 Trade-Related Aspects of Intellectual Property Rights (TRIPS) Agreement extends Article *6bis* Paris Convention protection, first, to services (Art.16(2)) and, secondly, to cover use in relation to goods and services that "are not similar to those in respect of which a trade mark is registered, provided that [such] use ... would indicate a connection between those goods or services and the owner of the registered trade mark and provided that the interests of the owner of the registered trademark are likely to be damaged by such use" (Art.16(3)).

In order to clarify (and possibly supplement) the Paris Convention and TRIPS Agreement provisions, the Standing Committee on the Law of Trade Marks of the World Intellectual Property Organisation (WIPO) considered it useful to draw up a Joint Recommendation Concerning Provisions on the Protection of Well Known Marks. This was then adopted by the respective Assemblies of the Paris Union and of WIPO in September 1999. These were guidelines, not rules, to assist in determining whether a mark can be considered well known,[37] and there was no attempt to provide a definition.

Some commentators contend that the Joint Recommendation was not purely explanatory but intended to expand the protection for well-known marks beyond even that provided in TRIPS. For example, see Burton Ong, *The Trade Mark Law Provisions of Bilateral Free Trade Agreements*,[38] in which the author discusses what he describes as the TRIPS-plus provisions contained in the US–Singapore Free Trade Agreement and EFTA–Singapore Free Trade Agreement that require giving effect to the Joint Recommendation. Professor Ong's view (developed in more detail in *Protecting Well-Known Trade Marks: Perspectives from Singapore*)[39] was expressly rejected by the Singapore Court of Appeal in *Novelty Pte. Ltd. v. Amanresorts Ltd.*,[40] a rejection that in turn Professor Ong has rejected (in *Interpreting Intellectual Property Statutes in Singapore.*)[41]

After the US–Singapore Free Trade Agreement in 2003, Singapore introduced into its law a supercharged well-known mark category. Section 55(3(b) of the Trade Marks Act gives protection to marks that are "well known to the public at large in Singapore"

---

[37] Standing Committee on the Law of Trade Marks of the World Intellectual Property Organisation, *Joint Recommendation Concerning Provisions on the Protection of Well Known Marks*, WORLD INTELLECTUAL PROPERTY ORGANISATION (2000), available at http://www.wipo.int/export/sites/www/freepublications/en/marks/833/pub833.pdf.

[38] *The Trade Mark Law Provisions of Bilateral Free Trade Agreements, in* TRADEMARK LAW AND THEORY: A HANDBOOK OF CONTEMPORARY RESEARCH (Graeme Dinwoodie & Mark Janis eds., 2008) at p229 et seq.

[39] Burton Ong, *Protecting Well-Known Trade Marks: Perspectives from Singapore* 95 TMR 1221 (2005).

[40] Novelty Pte. Ltd. v. Amanresorts Ltd. [2009] 3 SLR(R) 216.

[41] Burton Ong, *Interpreting Intellectual Property Statutes in Singapore* 24 SAcLJ 1020 (2012).

against non-confusing use on dissimilar goods. Marks that are merely "well known in Singapore" are protected only if there is a likelihood of confusion. This new protection is, in the words of the Singapore Court of Appeal, "the preserve of a rare, a privileged, few."[42]

XII. What Is a Luxury Brand?

If, as experience seems to show, it is difficult to get agreement on what is a well-known/famous/notorious mark and through whose eyes, it seems likely that reasonable people will disagree about what a luxury brand is. Is BMW (which has been accorded well-known mark status in China) a luxury brand, for example? What about BMW AG's other brand, Rolls-Royce, which is a trademark also used by an unrelated company on aircraft engines, without apparent impact on the sales of Rolls-Royce cars? If not, why not?

Or, moving to less technologically complicated products: the handbag. If one looks at the shops in Hong Kong's IFC upscale shopping mall, are the following luxury brands in a "Schechterian sense"?:

COACH—surely one of the least exclusive words in the "luxury brand" universe?

HOGAN—a Tod's Group brand which seems to have started in 1986 with a sneaker "inspired by" a cricket shoe but now has boutiques in the essential "luxury goods" centers of Florence, Milan, Paris, Seoul, Taipei, as well as Hong Kong, and collaborates with Karl Lagerfeld?

JUICY COUTURE—Amy Odell on NYMag.com reported in April 2010 that "A spot check of stores revealed that Saks Fifth Avenue dropped the Juicy Couture line at the New York flagship for fall; Bloomingdale's flagship cut way back on its Juicy department on the contemporary floor; Nordstrom passed on the apparel line for fall; Bergdorf Goodman no longer carries the line, and Neiman Marcus has dropped the line in several stores."? This raises the interesting *fashionista* question whether you can be a luxury brand if you are not sold in Bergdorf Goodman and Saks Fifth Avenue.

KWANPEN—a Singapore brand accused by some *fashionistas* of copying the Hermès Birkin and Kelly bags, although to judge from the fashion blogs few seem to be bothered enough to refuse to buy the recognizably high-quality products made by the Singaporean company?

[42] *Supra* note 40.

Are the following jewelry and accessories luxury brands in any sense meaningful to the trademark lawyer?

TIFFANY (a relatively common girl's name)?

OMEGA (a letter in the Greek alphabet adopted as its trade name by Omega Engineering of Switzerland, among many others)?

QEELIN?—Founded in 2004 by a Frenchman, Guillaume Brochard, who was previously with Tag Heuer and Louis Vuitton, and Dennis Chan (Chan Shui Lun), a Hong Kong designer, "Qeelin" sells expensive jewelry at prices similar to those in Cartier and Tiffany & Co. In December 2012 it became the first Chinese company to be bought by PPR, the world's third-largest "luxury group" behind French peer LVMH and Swiss company Richemont (which since 1998 has had a majority stake in Shanghai Tang). Interestingly, even though Qeelin was set up with the avowed aim of becoming a Chinese luxury jewelry brand (M. Brochard commented to the media that there was Tiffany in the United States, Cartier and Bulgari in Europe, Mikimoto in Japan, but no Chinese luxury brand), it opened first in Paris, then London and Hong Kong before moving into China, where it had seven stores at the time of the acquisition by PPR of a majority stake.

LINKS (what courts in Europe say there should be between a mark with a reputation and a third-party use before there can be infringement, but also a brand of cufflinks)?

What are viewed as luxury brands will surely depend on whom you ask: the answer from a person coming out of a Ferrari showroom in Hangzhou will be different from that given by a street vendor, and everyone between those two poles will have a different answer too. A 2012 article by Peter Shadbolt, *The Economic Necessity of Luxury*, makes the blunt statement: "When it comes to Asia's new markets, it is difficult to overdo luxury."[43] Apparently, this is particularly so for China.[44]

Presumably what is a luxury brand cannot depend on whether it is a niche product rather than a mass market product: for example, is Armani always a luxury brand ("Giorgio Armani" and "Armani Exchange" are featured annually at the Milan Fashion Week but "Armani Collezioni," "Armani Jeans," and "Armani Exchange" are not) or only when it's used on clothing in Giorgio Armani boutiques or on the perfumes marketed under license by L'Oréal's "Luxe" division rather than on Armani Jeans that are found in department stores?

On the other hand, it may well depend on where the person being asked the question has spent her life: as a matter of fact, the view of an inhabitant of Mumbai will

[43] Peter Shadbolt, *The Economic Necessity of Luxury*, ASIA BUSINESS INSIGHTS 55 (2012).

[44] Luca Solca, *Consumers Push Big Names to Account for Supply Chains*, THE FINANCIAL TIMES' SPECIAL REPORT ON BUSINESS OF LUXURY (2013) 5.

differ from that of a Chongqing resident or a Sydneysider. Of course, what the Comité Colbert—the association founded in 1954 by Jean-Jacques Guerlain[45] to celebrate *l'art de vivre française* that today represents the interests of 75 "French luxury brands"—would like us to believe is that the answer would be the same wherever you ask the question; and it may be, if it is posed to affluent-looking people walking near the Cartier, Chanel, or Louis Vuitton boutiques in Mumbai, Chongqing, and Sydney.

While considering the vagueness of the notion of "luxury brand," it is noteworthy that the Comité Colbert includes George V amongst its 75 "French luxury brands" membership; one wonders what Queen Elizabeth II, the granddaughter of King George V, thinks of that. It also includes John Lobb, a brand unconnected with the John Lobb handmade shoe business in London's St. James that is still run by descendants of the John Lobb who set up business in London in 1866 after previously selling his boots to prospectors in the Australian gold rush that started in the early 1850s. In 1976 the Paris business that had been set up in 1901 by the founder's younger son William Hunter Lobb (his elder brother John had been cast into the wilderness by his father after being discovered behaving dishonestly)[46] was bought by Hèrmes: *et voilà*, 37 years later it's a "French luxury brand." Another member is Le Ritz: presumably neither the well-known crackers nor the Ritz-Carlton group of hotels (which the Paris Ritz Hotel failed to stop using "their" name in a passing off action in Australia) would agree that "Ritz" is a French luxury brand.

XIII. Whining about Wine

The difficulty of categorizing such brands in trademark law terms is reminiscent of the controversy surrounding the 1855 Classification of Bordeaux wines. Put together in April 1855 by the Bordeaux wine brokers' union for the Universal Exhibition in Paris, the Classification of 58 châteaux into five "great growths" (*crus classé*) was based on the château's ability to produce outstanding wines consistently over the years.

The 1855 classification became, and remains, the authoritative source as to quality at the top end of Bordeaux's wine producers and has been changed officially only twice (although there are now 61 named properties, as three estates—"Léoville," "Pichon," and "Batailley"—have split into two or more châteaux, while two separate names—"Pouget" and "Pouget-Lassale"—have been combined into one, known simply as Ch. Pouget. In addition, Third Growth "Dubignon" has disappeared entirely, although its vineyards live on as part of other Margaux properties. Ch. Gloria is not a Cru Classé but its vineyards

[45] He was the son of Jacques, the third master perfumer of the House of Guerlain founded in 1828 and who, amongst others, created the "Shalimar" perfume. In 1994 the Guerlain family sold the business to LVMH.

[46] Brian Dobbs, The Last Shall Be First: The Colourful Story of John Lobb the Bootmakers of St James's (1972).

all come from plots of lands that were originally part of other Cru Classé estates). The two instances in which the classification was officially changed are:

– after a few months, in September 1855, Cantemerle was included among the Fifth Growths; and
– more than a century later, the promotion of Mouton Rothschild to "*premier cru classé*" status—for many years the Mouton label displayed the words "*Premier ne puis, second ne daigne, Mouton suis*" ("First I cannot be, Second I do not deign to be, Mouton I am"). At last, in 1973 Jacques Chirac, then the Agriculture Minister, signed a decree bestowing First Growth status on Mouton, and the old phrase was replaced by "*Premier je suis, second je fus. Mouton ne change*" ("First I am, Second I was, Mouton does not change").

But, as with the categorization of marks into

those with a reputation,
those well known,
those famous,
those locally famous,
those notorious,

the 1855 Classification has been the subject of intense debate ever since it was settled upon. For example, in 1960 the Russian-born wine writer and investor Alexis Lichine proposed a new categorization: *Outstanding Growths, Exceptional Growths, Great Growths, Superior Growths*, and *Good Growths*. According to M. Lichine, "The reaction was explosive outrage."[47] M. Lichine went ahead and published his own "*Classification des Grands Crus Rouge de Bordeaux*" in 1962, but the 1855 Classification still reigns supreme.

XIV. Conclusion: A Legal Hodgepodge

So, back in the world of trademarks for handbags, shoes, and watches, does "luxury brand" have any significance beyond being expensive and heavily advertised? Of course, this is not to suggest that luxury brands do not make valuable contributions to the economies of certain countries: that much is clear.[48] Indeed, one commentator has "calculated" that in 2011

---

[47] Frank J. Prial, *Wine: The Battle of 1855*, N.Y. Times, Aug. 20, 1989, which notes, "The list remains immutable, but the wine properties certainly have not."

[48] Part of the contribution to the French economy comes from the sale of Champagne. On March 20, 2013, the *Comité Interprofessionel du Vin de Champagne* (CIVC), the trade body representing producers of Champagne, succeeded in securing protection in China, as a geographical indication, for the word "Champagne" and its Chinese transliteration. The applications had been filed with the Administration of Quality Supervision Inspection and Quarantine (AQSIQ) in June 2012. A spokesman for CIVC

the French luxury industry had a positive trade balance of €34 billion, twice that of the French aerospace industry: "In other words, handbags, perfumes and spirits carry twice the weight of aeroplanes in terms of commercial balance. That demonstrates an extraordinary force for the French economy," according to Emmanuel Combe, affiliate professor at ESCP-Europe Business School in Paris.[49]

But, is it nevertheless sensible to have in the law all these different categories of trademark, with different levels of protection accorded to each?

In the words of Jennifer Darcy:

> The fashion industry is deserving of intellectual property protection owing to the investment and promotion that has contributed to its expansion and prosperity.[50]

If so, the law already seems to give it adequate protection against unauthorized use by others, which deceives or is likely to confuse as to trade connection, even if that confusion is fleeting in nature and quickly dispelled. After all, the courts in Britain, which have traditionally been reluctant to give wide protection, have accepted in a number of cases recently[51] that "initial interest confusion" (a notion developed in the United States) is sufficient for a finding of trademark infringement: in the earliest, the Court of Appeal in Northern Ireland even restrained a chain of Irish petrol stations called TOP from using the color green (the color in which the Irish rugby team play, the color of shamrocks, the color associated with environmentally friendly products) for the fascia of its forecourts in an infringement action brought by BP, which has registered a particular shade of green.[52] Additionally, where the brand is well known, it is protected against parasitic use that does not confuse.

The fair-minded observer will surely pause before moving even further down the road toward protecting investment per se, which seems to be the aim of at least some owners of so-called luxury brands. That observer will also recollect what happened to those sailors who listened to the siren calls and may worry about another shipwreck in the sea of IP rights.

(M. Thibault Le Mailloux) noted "Chinese law gives us protection that Russia and the US do not," describing the approach of these two countries as "anachronistic and without future."

[49] Quoted in *Business of Luxury—Strategic Industry Comes of Age, in* The Financial Times Special Report 6 (2013).

[50] Jennifer Darcy, *Under-Regulated or Under-Enforced: Intellectual Property, the Fashion Industry and Fake Goods*, 35 EIPR 82 (2013).

[51] The most important is the judgment of Arnold J. in Och-Ziff Management Europe Ltd. v. OCH Capital LLP [2010] EWHC 2599 (Ch).

[52] BP Amoco plc. v. John Kelly Ltd. [2002] FSR 5. Interestingly, in Staywell Hospitality Group Pty. Ltd. v. Starwood Hotels & Resorts Worldwide [2013] SGCA 65, the Court of Appeal in Singapore, after considering the US and UK authorities, rejected the suggestion that "initial interest confusion" be introduced into Singapore law, citing "policy concerns over extending the protection of these [trade mark infringement] provisions ... among these is that it can stifle competition without resulting benefit to consumer choice or access to information" (at para.114).

15 Cosmopolitanism and the Transnational Trademark

Sonia K. Katyal*

I. Introduction

In May of 2008, Nadia Plesner, a Danish art student, decided to do something about the lingering crisis in Darfur. She designed a T-shirt to raise money for the cause, depicting a starving Sudanese child holding a chihuahua in one hand and a Louis Vuitton bag in the other—in a classic appropriation of a famous photograph depicting Paris Hilton in a bikini. "I started this campaign because of the distorted way the media prioritizes between big and small world news," she explained. "How can Paris Hilton make more front covers than the genocide in Darfur?"[1] Shortly thereafter, she was served with a

* Chancellor's Professor of Law at University of California, Berkeley, and formerly Associate Dean for Research and Joseph M. McLaughlin Professor of Law, Fordham Law School. Special thanks to my outstanding research assistants, Reed Kristovich and Catherine Song, for their hard work, and Sarah Jaramillo in the Fordham Law Library for her very impressive help.

[1] Ernesto, *Louis Vuitton Sues Darfur Fundraiser for Copyright Infringement*, TORRENTFREAK (Apr. 25, 2008), http://torrentfreak.com/louis-vuitton-sues-darfur-fundraiser-for-copyright-infringement-080425 (quoting Nadia Plesner).

harshly written letter from the Intellectual Property Director for Louis Vuitton that read, in part:

> Although we applaud your efforts to raise awareness and funds to help Darfur, a most worthy cause, we cannot help noticing that the design ... includes the reproduction of a bag infringing on Louis Vuitton's Intellectual Property Rights, in particular the Louis Vuitton Monogram Multicolore Trademark to which it is confusingly similar. We are surprised of such a promotion of a counterfeit bag.

LVMH did not mince its words. The letter goes on to request that Plesner discontinue distributing the shirt immediately.[2]

Plesner eventually replied, explaining to LVMH's lawyer that she didn't use an exact replica of the bag, but rather meant for her depiction to simply evoke designer bags in general.[3] Nevertheless, LVMH decided to file suit against her, threatening thousands of dollars in damages. Shortly thereafter, the news quickly began to travel worldwide. Speaking to *New York Magazine*, Plesner argued that "[i]f I was making bags and copying the design, I would understand the problem," but since she was caricaturing it instead in a picture, she considered it part and parcel of her artistic freedom.[4] Roughly six months later, and after a major maelstrom in the media, the case finally settled for an undisclosed amount, and Plesner no longer distributes the shirt as a result.

The resolution of the case might have ended the standoff between LVMH and Plesner, but only for the moment. Interestingly, a year or so after the settlement, Plesner decided to reuse the very same image in a large piece of visual art called *Darfurnika*, a piece modeled after Picasso's *Guernica* (a famous 1937 piece protesting the bombing of the town with the same name). Plesner juxtaposed the image with a variety of global luxury brands, political symbols, and other elements from high fashion. Plesner explained that she decided to name the painting after Picasso's famous work after she discovered that *Guernica* was shrouded in blue cloth during a United Nations press conference on the war in Iraq in 2003. For her, *Guernica* represented the power of visual art to make connections between current political events and issues of social justice.

Plesner's own work draws obvious parallels between the power of political symbols, luxury symbols, and corporate symbols, noting how each one occupies a tremendous amount of prominence in our visual culture. Indeed, there is a triadic convergence of function between all three categories of symbols, because each type can personify *both* the brand creator as well as the audience that consumes them. Each of these

---

[2] Letter from Nathalie Moullé-Berteaux, Intellectual Property Director, Louis Vuitton Malletier, to Nadia Plesner (Feb. 13, 2008), *available at* http://www.clancco.com/LouisVuittonLetter.pdf.

[3] *See* Ernesto, *supra* note 1.

[4] *See* The Cut, *Art Student Nadia Plesner's Giant Louis Vuitton Copyright Suit*, N.Y. MAG. (May 6, 2008), http://nymag.com/daily/fashion/2008/05/art_student_nadia_pelsners_gia.html.

audiences—whether consumers of luxury goods, political actors, or artist/activists like Nadia Plesner—oppositional or otherwise, all integrate and respond to particular brands as part of their process of self expression.

Further, as this story demonstrates, the relationships between luxury brands, artistic expression, and global politics are constantly shifting and in flux. The transnational nature of social movements and global branding strategies has evoked significant questions about the proper role of intellectual property law, sovereignty, and speech within each sphere. Whereas earlier discussions of international social justice issues (like the crisis in Darfur) might have been restricted to human rights law or other forms of public international law, today's movements now unfold within the structures of the increasing globalization of intellectual property law, as well. In other words, private law—or specifically, trademark law—is now emerging to play a role in international social justice disputes alongside these longstanding public law approaches.

We have long been aware of the magnetic pull of global brands across the world. But what is also remarkable is how powerful that pull has become, even to those who oppose their prominence. As Plesner's case demonstrates, global luxury brands have become not just the lingua franca of transnational consumption, but also of the antibranding activists who resist it. Particularly when luxury brands acquire a level of global prominence in public culture, as LVMH has done, it is inevitable that its iconic imagery becomes even more susceptible to recoding and commentary. The more LVMH has invested in its brand, making it more and more ubiquitous in consumer culture, it becomes more and more vulnerable as a result, leading many individuals to use their brands and logos as a means of expressing their own identity or as a vehicle for commenting on consumerism, luxury, or branding in general. As a result, LVMH's logo isn't just a logo; precisely because of its ubiquity, it now stands for something else—luxury, elite excess, celebrity culture, and the like. As Plesner's case demonstrates, activists may seek to recode a brand for purposes that have little to do with LVMH's brand specifically. Yet in each of these cases, property principles and freedom of speech collide, with luxury brands as the backdrop, producing an impasse with variable and unpredictable results.

Clearly, unauthorized uses pose serious legal and ethical questions for global brand owners. Today, LVMH is one of the world's most valuable global brands. Like many luxury brands, LVMH, when faced with examples of unauthorized use, has a choice to make: it can either tolerate alternative commentary, or it can choose to threaten litigation over the unauthorized use of its trademarks. Either choice carries consequences, both positive and negative, but each decision that LVMH faces underscores how much our world has changed in the last several decades regarding the rise and prominence of global branding. Today, there is a multitude of what I call transnational brands: brands that began with national origins, but which have become global icons in the process.

The rise of transnational brands brings with it an attendant series of legal shifts in trademark law. Long considered the stepchild of intellectual property law, today trademark law has morphed into a powerful global legal phenomenon, revealing a foundational shift from national and regional systems to harmonized international regimes governing trademark law. A unitary system of trademark registration is emerging. However, even if a system of harmonized registration becomes the new normal, territorial systems of trademark enforcement—not to mention constitutional protections for freedom of expression—vary widely. Here, age-old questions regarding sovereignty, human rights, and artistic freedom have also begun to play a role in modern trademark disputes, both domestically and internationally. Yet as the Plesner case clearly demonstrates, as brands become global, transnational entities, they also engender modes of resistance from a number of different social movements. These movements, it seems, are just as transnational as the global branding strategies that are often their targets, demonstrating how questions of freedom of expression emerge alongside the circulation of transnational brands.

This chapter details how each of these areas are deeply intertwined with one another, and how they demonstrate the emergence of a broad phenomenon that I call trademark cosmopolitanism, which carries important implications for freedom of expression worldwide. I refer to the phenomenon of trademark cosmopolitanism to broadly sketch out four trajectories of transnational activities and their relationships to the various entities that play key roles in the global branding enterprise—namely, the consumer, the corporation, the politician, and the activist. The first set of activities involves what I call consumptive cosmopolitanism, and that refers to the purchasing and shopping practices of the global consumer and the ways in which these practices reflect a kind of globalized consciousness. The second set of activities, which are closely related to the first set, involves the emergence of a corporately oriented cosmopolitanism that stems from the global corporate social responsibility movement. The third kind of activity, which reflects a more macroeconomic set of considerations, involves the emergence of an institutionalized form of cosmopolitanism, which refers to the variety of government and nongovernment entities that have emerged to facilitate the creation, enforcement, and protection of transnational brands. The final set of transnational activities, however, typifies a more politicized form of cosmopolitanism that focuses on challenging, rather than consuming, the power of branding and multinational corporations.

All of these trajectories, I would argue, demonstrate broad and varied facets of a phenomenon I call trademark cosmopolitanism—underscoring the globalization of trademark law. In section II below, I describe the first three trajectories of trademark cosmopolitanism, and discuss the emergence of brands as global, transnational figures of speech, property, and increasingly, corporate ethics. In sections III and IV, I turn to the last trajectory and discuss how the rise of trademark cosmopolitanism also relates to the global antibranding movement, typified by the Plesner example. The interplay between the global brand; the global antibrand; and the language of ethics, cosmopolitanism, and corporate social responsibility, with all of the legal differences associated with sovereignty and speech, I would suggest, is one of the paramount issues for trademark scholars in the future.

II. The Rise of Trademark Cosmopolitanism

In 1992, Jeremy Waldron published an article, "Minority Cultures and the Cosmopolitan Alternative," which described the emergence of individuals who prefer that their cultural identities not be tied specifically to a set of rigidly defined borders.[5] Two years later, Martha Nussbaum published a groundbreaking essay, "Patriotism and Cosmopolitanism," where she argued in favor of a kind of moral universalism and the need for a cosmopolitan education that recognized that central features of human personhood transcended national boundaries.[6] At the same time, however, she also embraced a more robust notion of empathy. "By looking at ourselves in the lens of the other," she wrote, "we come to see what in our practices is local and non-necessary, what more broadly or deeply shared."

Those words were written almost twenty years ago, where Nussbaum described cosmopolitanism's roots as linked to Diogenes, the ancient Greek Cynic philosopher, who once proclaimed himself as "a citizen of the world," in response to a question about his geographic origin. In a sense, as Nussbaum explained, Diogenes meant that he eschewed a sense of identity that was defined solely by his local origins and memberships, that instead, his identity was defined by more universal aspirations. Much of this early view was later developed by the Stoics, who viewed everyone as belonging to a world community of humankind that was joined by basic ethical values and principles, like justice, dignity and respect.[7] As Nussbaum observed, through these globalized lenses, "[w]e recognize moral obligations to the rest of the world that are real, and that otherwise would go unrecognized."

Similar observations have been made by Stuart Hall,[8] anthropologist Craig Calhoun,[9] and others, all of whom embrace the notion of an emergent global citizenry, a kind of transnational consciousness that spanned borders and cultures and celebrated openness and solidarity.[10] Many have described cosmopolitanism as having essentially two strands—one about culture and the self, and another about justice—rejecting a kind

---

[5] *See* Jeremy Waldron, *Minority Cultures and the Cosmopolitan Alternative*, 25 U. MICH. J.L. REFORM 751, 754 (1991–1992).

[6] *See* Martha Nussbaum, *Patriotism and Cosmopolitanism*, BOS. REV. (Oct. 1, 1994), http://bostonreview.net/martha-nussbaum-patriotism-and-cosmopolitanism.

[7] *Id.* at 7–12.

[8] *See* Stuart Hall, *Political Belonging in a World of Multiple Identities, in* CONCEIVING COSMOPOLITANISM: THEORY, CONTEXT, AND PRACTICE 25, 26 (Steven Vertovec & Robin Cohen eds., 2002).

[9] *See* Craig Calhoun, *The Class Consciousness of Frequent Travellers: Towards a Critique of Actually Existing Cosmopolitanism, in* CONCEIVING COSMOPOLITANISM: THEORY, CONTEXT, AND PRACTICE 86, 102–9 (linking cosmopolitanism to the spread of democracy).

[10] Des Gasper, *Cosmopolitan Presumptions? On Martha Nussbaum and Her Commentators*, 37 DEV. & CHANGE 1227, 1229 (2006).

of relativism that strict nationalism might embrace.[11] Others describe it along the lines of a political or institutional formulation—focusing on the emergence of globalized institutions.[12]

Of course, much ink can be spilled about the importance of cosmopolitanism on political and legal theory. My focus here, however, is to briefly sketch out some of the ways in which dominant approaches to the study of both cosmopolitanism and transnationalism reveal new ways of situating our increasingly globalized systems of trademark regulation, and the ancillary ethical and moral questions that inevitably accompany this growth.

On a primary level, I would argue that Nussbaum and the current scholarship on cosmopolitanism have much to offer intellectual property scholars, many of whom are grounded in territorial frameworks that often fail to reckon with the erosion of sovereignty, the rise of global branding, and the ancillary rise of trademark harmonization in our current legal context. Currently, the field of trademark doctrine often remains closely tied to principles of territoriality and localized principles, despite the widespread embrace of transnational forces. As a result, the two forces often collide—a trademark system grounded in territoriality and the emergence of harmonized systems of branding, marketing, and registration.

Admittedly, given how broad the field of cosmopolitanism has become, and its vast history, it can mean a variety of things—everything from an attitude or a value, to a kind of global governance, to a set of views on social structures and beyond.[13] Yet trademarks and global brands are often a central vehicle by which these general approaches to cosmopolitanism specifically and symbolically unfold, and often the terrain under which conflicts over globalization and localization take place. As a result, trademark cosmopolitanism, one might argue, is thus inextricably linked to global flows of content, and as content and luxury brands circulate transnationally, so do the legal principles of intellectual property that underpin them. The same is true for the social and political movements that have also emerged surrounding the rise of global brands. Even the forces that oppose globalization and the rise of multinational corporations, I would argue, reflect a kind of cosmopolitan ethic that is worth further analysis and study. This phenomenon also includes a wide array of third parties who are, directly or indirectly, broadly implicated in the process of global branding, either because they support the process, like consumers, or because they oppose it, like anti-globalization activists. All of these

[11] *See, e.g.*, Thomas W. Pogge, *Cosmopolitanism and Sovereignty*, 103 ETHICS 48, 49 (1992) (distinguishing between legal and moral cosmopolitanism); Samuel Scheffler, *Conceptions of Cosmopolitanism*, 11 UTILITAS 255 (1999) (outlining two views of cosmopolitanism).

[12] *See* Gasper, *supra* note 10, at 1229.

[13] *See* Ian Woodward et al., *Attitudes Towards Globalization and Cosmopolitanism: Cultural Diversity, Personal Consumption and the National Economy*, 59 BRIT. J. SOC. 207, 208 (2008) (making this observation).

elements encompass descriptive and normative aspects to their approaches, and they also underwrite some of the most important challenges for trademark law in the future.

A. FROM NATIONAL BRAND TO GLOBAL ICON: CONSUMPTIVE COSMOPOLITANISM

In 1983, in a groundbreaking article for the *Harvard Business Review*, professor Theodore Levitt claimed in an article that a global market for standardized, uniform products and services had emerged.[14] To maximize the opportunities that this market presented, Levitt recommended selling standardized products in a wide variety of geographic contexts and markets. Commenting on Levitt's article, years later, brand scholars Douglas Holt and others explained that even though Levitt did not explicitly discuss branding, his ideas were interpreted to suggest the need for greater standardization and uniformity—not just among products, but among brand identities—giving rise to the growth of the global branding phenomenon.

Thirty years after Levitt's article was published, we see dramatic shifts in the standardization of both goods and of trademarks globally. Corporations, just like individuals, have adopted a global outlook and approach in many aspects of their day-to-day practices regarding brand management. Today, international branding comprises much more today than just a selection of brand names—remember the famous Chevy Nova story—where "No Va" translated into "no go" in Spanish—but it's also about auditory, visual, emotional brand design.[15] The process of global branding, for example, has been described to encompass everything from companies that use an identical marketing strategy across countries to others that utilize a similar brand with some variations in different markets.[16] Other definitions of global branding focus instead on the building of brand equity internationally, and still others focus on the harmonization of an international brand and marketing architecture.

In turn, just as brands now reflect a kind of global consciousness and design, globalization has also produced a generation of cosmopolitanist consumers. This emerging culture is not tied to a singular global brand, or a culture of homogeneity, but a global culture instead—enabling consumers to "see themselves in relation to other cultures as

---

[14] *See* Theodore Levitt, *The Globalization of Markets*, HARV. BUS. REV., May–June 1983, at 92, 92–102; *see also* Susan P. Douglas et al., *Integrating Branding Strategy Across Markets: Building International Brand Architecture*, 9 J. INT'L MARKETING, no. 2, 2001, at 97, 101; Douglas B. Holt et al., *How Global Brands Compete*, HARV. BUS. REV., Sept. 2004, at 68, 69 [hereinafter *Global Brands*].

[15] *See* Bernd Schmitt, *From the Special Issue Editor*, 10 J. INT'L MARKETING, SPECIAL ISSUE ON GLOBAL BRANDING, Summer 2002, at 2, 2–3 (containing excellent empirical papers on global trademarks and brands).

[16] *See, e.g.*, David A. Aaker & Erich Joachimsthaler, *The Lure of Global Branding*, HARV. BUS. REV., Nov.–Dec. 1999, at 137 (discussing the principles that successful global branding employs).

well as their own."[17] This is not to suggest that consumers share the same tastes, but rather, that they participate in a shared conversation that often centers on the presence and participation of global brands, particularly luxury brands. "Like entertainment stars, sports celebrities and politicians," Douglas Holt writes, "global brands have become a lingua franca for consumers all over the world."[18] Anecdotal evidence further demonstrates these conclusions—"Global brands make us feel like citizens of the world, and ... they somehow give us an identity," one Argentinian consumer observed.[19]

Reading some of the vast literature on global branding, one is struck by the immediate similarity of its descriptive and normative insights to the literature on cosmopolitanism. Some authors, for example, tend to focus on the notion of cosmopolitanism as a fundamental set of identities that involve a sense of "belonging ... to the world as a whole," a kind of global citizenry that reflects transnational perspectives.[20] Other authors tend to describe cosmopolitanism in terms of a set of identities, values, and attitudes that variously embrace notions of diverse world perspectives and a strong degree of openness to others. This type of cultural competence embraces global diversity in terms of food, music, self-presentation, and ethical worldviews.[21]

As the prior sentence suggests, part of the culture of cosmopolitanism is deeply tied to consumer practices of consumption, and it is also linked to visual brand culture as well. Our sense of the world around us—our very language and ways of thinking and framing our environments—are deeply inscribed, and circumscribed by the brands and advertising that inhabit our everyday world. Brands, like cosmopolitanist approaches, have symbolic, emotional, and cultural aspects. And as brands become more and more global in their design and interpretative reach, it makes sense that our cosmopolitan worldview becomes reflected through patterns of consumption and changes in consumer identity. Twenty years ago, global branding scholars argued that the less consumerized a market is, the more the emphasis is on the utilitarian aspects of a brand and its link to the marketplace. Today, all of that has shifted in favor of advertising that trends toward being more symbolic and emotional in order to connect to the consumer. Trademarks, today, are less about identifications of origin; instead, their earlier function has been surpassed by their growing role as "messengers" that convey a broad range of information to the public about the product, the company, the people behind the company, and the attributes of each.[22] As a result, the trademark represents both a global visual receptacle and a

---

17 Holt et al., *Global Brands, supra* note 14, at 70.

18 *Id.*, supra note 14, at 70.

19 Holt et al., *Global Brands, supra* note 14, at 71.

20 *See* Nancy E. Cook, *Canadian Development Workers, Transnational Encounters and Cultures of Cosmopolitanism*, 27 INT'L SOC. 3, 5–6 (2012) (suggesting three aspects—one normative, one political, and one cultural).

21 *See* Woodward et al., *supra* note 13, at 208.

22 Matthew James Elsmore, *The Implications of Intellectual Property Law for the Auditing and Protection of National and International Brands: Part III. Brands in Europe*, 15 MANAGERIAL AUDITING J. 209 (2000).

vehicle for all of the emotive and personality characteristics that advertisers hope to associate with a particular brand.[23] Obviously, as markets become globalized, brands—and individuals—do as well.

More recently, although the rush toward global branding has waned at different points, it has also given rise to a greater push toward localized customization to suit consumer tastes, a "glocal" strategy, as some have called it.[24] For example, Kraft General Foods markets Philadelphia Cream Cheese globally, but it differs its approach—so in the United States we are encouraged to eat it on bagels, but in Spain, they sell a salmon-flavored version; Germany gets a pear-flavored version; Italy, a tuna-flavored version. McDonald's does something similar—you can get wine with your burger in France or beer in Germany or an Indian potato burger in India.[25] All of this, of course, depends on the interplay between satisfying and constructing consumer preferences, depending upon the context.

Today, Coca-Cola soft drinks and Marlboro cigarettes are the top two global brands. Soft drinks, tobacco, pet foods, and snack foods are other areas with the greatest global brand presence.[26] Not only are global branding strategies economical from an efficiency perspective because they enable one company to use one advertising agency for its global reach but they also help centralize the messaging and personality that surrounds a global brand.[27] Further, not only do they enable the creation of a global brand identity, but they are also thought to offer a number of benefits to the consumer, namely credibility, authority, value, power, and the feeling of belonging to a global community.[28]

However, cosmopolitanism is not an enterprise free from critique and concern. Some scholars have critiqued cosmopolitanism for its close relationship to notions of empire, capitalism, and western idioms of thought, expressing concern that it facilitates "an improving conversion of the local other into the western universal."[29] One must be careful not to presume that both cosmopolitanism and globalization are always connected—as one author points out, it is both historically and empirically unwarranted to view globalization as a precondition for cosmopolitanism.[30] One can be globalized, but still desire insularity, nationalism, and parochialism—consequently lacking the definitive consciousness that cosmopolitanism brings.

---

[23] *See* Ming Hsieh, *Identifying Brand Image Dimensionality and Measuring the Degree of Brand Globalization: A Cross National Study*, 10 J. INT'L MARKETING, SPECIAL ISSUE ON GLOBAL BRANDING, Summer 2002, at 46, 59.

[24] Holt et al., *Global Brands, supra* note 14, at 69.

[25] Elsmore, *supra* note 22.

[26] Dennis Pitta, *Foundations for Building Share of Heart in Global Brands*, 17 J. PROD. & BRAND MGMT. 64 (2008).

[27] Aaker & Joachimsthaler, *supra* note 16, at 137.

[28] *See* Hsieh, *supra* note 23, at 60–61.

[29] Cook, *supra* note 20, at 5 (citation omitted).

[30] *See* Woodward et al., *supra* note 13, at 210.

Further, there remain substantial and quite valid concerns about the impact of globalization on cultural and consumer diversity.[31] Global consumer culture has been described as "a cultural identity not associated with a single country, but rather a larger group generally recognized as international and transcending individual national cultures."[32] There are, of course, distributional effects of these social formations—one scholar writes that the "rise of global consumption ideals, potentially makes the elite among Third World consumers into cosmopolitans who are more concerned with how they compare to the world's privileged consumers than they are to compare themselves locally."[33] Other anecdotal and theoretical treatments of this issue have emphasized the increasing homogeneity of the global consumer, to the point that localized cultures and tastes may play a secondary role to the dominance of global brand identity. Even empirical studies have suggested this to be the case.[34] Other studies argue, as a variation, that "increasing globalization has reduced the homogeneity of consumer behaviors *within* countries, while increasing communalities among consumers *across* countries."[35] Central to this process, nevertheless, is the desire to own the "consumption symbols" or goods from countries whose lifestyles are admired.[36] Here, brands, particularly luxury brands, become a central part of the sign of membership in a global cosmopolitan community, of membership in a "transnational commerce culture."[37]

B. THE RISE OF CORPORATE COSMOPOLITANISM

So far, I have outlined how a cosmopolitan worldview has become reflected in the process of global branding and transnational consumption, both by corporations and also by individuals. But for Nussbaum and others, cosmopolitanism is also deeply tied to a notion of ethics, a concept of duty to other individuals. Here, too, trademark law becomes intimately tied to the process of creating greater attention to corporate social responsibility, particularly in the creation of global brands.

As companies become more globalized and multinational in character, and the design and creation of brands have followed suit, consumers have also followed this trend, focusing their attention on the global business practices of the companies that

---

[31] See, for example, the work by SASKIA SASSEN, THE GLOBAL CITY (1991) and THE MOBILITY OF LABOR AND CAPITAL (1998); also GEORGE RITZER, THE MCDONALDIZATION OF SOCIETY (1993).

[32] *See* Dana Alden, Jan-Benedict Steenkamp, and Rajeev Batra, *Brand Positioning through Advertising in Asia, North America, and Europe: The Role of Global Consumer Culture*, 63 J. MKTG. 75, 80 (Jan. 1999).

[33] Mark Cleveland, Michel Laroche, and Nicolas Papadopoulous, *Cosmopolitanism, Consumer Ethnocentrism, and Materialism, An Eight Country Study of Antecedents and Outcomes*, 17 J. INT'L MKTG., 116, 120 (2009) (quoting Russell Belk, *Consumption Patterns of the New Elite in Zimbabwe, in* MARKETING CONTRIBUTIONS TO DEMOCRATIZATION at 13 (2000)).

[34] Bruce Keillor, Michael D' Amico, and Veronica Horton, *Global Consumer Tendencies*, 18 PSYCHOL. & MKTG., 1, 15 (January 2001).

[35] Mark Cleveland & Michel Laroche, *Acculturation to the Global Consumer Culture: Scale Development and Research Paradigm*, 60 J. BUS. RES. 249, 250 (2007).

[36] Cleveland et al., *supra* note 33, at 253.

[37] *See* Alden et al., *supra* note 32, at 77 (quoting Ulf Hannerz).

they patronize. While there is a vast literature on corporate social responsibility (CSR) and its various forms, I want to sketch out, briefly here, some of the complementarities between modern CSR approaches and the phenomenon of trademark cosmopolitanism that I have described so far.[38]

Although the term "corporate social responsibility" was coined by economist Howard Bowen a decade after Nuremberg, its modern formation tends to emphasize the need for corporations to consider the social and ecological impact of their practices on humanity as a whole, and without ceasing to remain a profit generating entity.[39] While the field of corporate social responsibility traditionally refers to the protection of human rights, labor rights, the environment, and non-corrupt business practices, among other considerations, it also connects deeply to notions of trademark cosmopolitanism for a variety of reasons.

First, as the previous section suggested, the brand's visuality often becomes the central repository for all the ancillary conflicts that surround a corporation—social, political, economic, and so forth. As a result, in order to protect their brands from public reproach, most companies now engage in proactive strategies that infuse the brand's personality with information about a company's desirable business practices and its commitment to social responsibility.[40] Information about corporate practices in each of these areas—human rights, labor, the environment, etc.—deeply affects the way in which the brand is viewed. Think, for example, of how companies like British Petroleum have had to rebrand themselves after evidence of their ethical or environmental practices came to light.

Second, it also connects to consumers' own cosmopolitanism, reflected in their global buying practices. As consumers view themselves as global citizens, they increasingly offer concern for the manufacturing practices of the companies that they patronize. For example, consider the maelstrom of media attention that focused on Apple after evidence of its iPhone manufacturing practices was exposed.[41] Third, and relatedly, the brand becomes the visual cue for the information that the consumer possesses about a company's labor practices. That is why the relationship between a company's brand managers and activist antibranding movements can be so contentious for trademark lawyers. By recoding brands in ways that highlight a company's connection to environmental degradation, unfair labor practices, or other issues of social justice, activists can further

---

[38] For more information on CSR see *Corporate Social Responsibility*, INT'L INST. FOR SUSTAINABLE DEV., http://www.iisd.org/business/issues/sr.aspx (last visited Sept. 29, 2013).

[39] *See* Jonathan Bellish, *Towards a More Realistic Vision of Corporate Social Responsibility Through the Lens of the Lex Mercatoria*, 40 DENV. J. INT'L L. & POL'Y 548, 560 (2012).

[40] *See* Douglas B. Holt et al., *How Model Behavior Brings Market Power: Consumers Associate Global Brands with Good Quality But Also Hold Global Companies to Higher Ethical Standards*, FIN. TIMES (Aug. 23, 2004), http://www.ft.com/cms/s/0/0e4c539c-f4a0-11d8-9911-00000e2511c8.html#axzz2fSAilHhN.

[41] *See, e.g.*, Bobbie Johnson, *Will Child Labour Claims Stop You Buying Apple?*, GUARDIAN (Mar. 1, 2010, 3:00 PM), http://www.theguardian.com/technology/blog/2010/mar/01/apple-ipod.

inform the public and—literally—alter the semiotic significance of a particular brand to the public. That is why branding often plays such a powerful role in disputes about corporate social responsibility. It also helps explain why the most prominent global brands often have the best reputations for corporate social responsibility.[42]

There are other, proactive branding strategies that further underscore a commitment to corporate social responsibility.[43] One of the key ways in which corporations address their corporate social responsibility is through the marketplace—including "rights-sensitive" branding strategies, codes of conduct, voluntary submissions to auditing practices, and shareholder pressure.[44] "Rights-sensitive" branding involves the practice of offering a particular selection of goods to consumers who are willing to pay a premium for ethically sourced materials—like Starbucks's "fair trade" coffees, Chiquita's "ethical banana" marketed in Europe, and the Kimberly process of reducing conflict diamonds in the marketplace. Other market-based solutions also have branding implications as well—Royal Dutch Shell, Nike, and others have adopted private codes of conduct that are often used to buttress their reputations on the global branding platform.[45]

Of course, that is not the only practical strategy of CSR visibility—other companies, like Shell Nigeria, Exxon Mobil, British Petroleum, and Union Carbide also engage in rebranding and CSR-type behavior after a major disaster, attempting to retain consumers by taking measures to restore their reputation.[46] Other companies engage in voluntary codes of conduct—Nike, Gap, Levi Strauss, and other companies employ inspectors who grade suppliers on labor standards and attempt to ensure fairer practices.[47] These practices are both represented and reinforced by massive advertising campaigns that are also infused with branding these companies' social responsibility and further informing the public of their activities. Here, the global brand is actively linked to the culture and ethics of cosmopolitanism, albeit indirectly, further underlining how trademarks provide the visual, symbolic vehicle to communicate such information.

C. THE ROLE OF INSTITUTIONALIZED COSMOPOLITANISM

Of course, trademark cosmopolitanism would be deeply ineffective if it were not for the way in which both legal and political systems have adjusted to facilitate the production of global brands to suit consumer preferences. Here, too, we can find key synergies with

---

[42] See, for example, Jacquelyn Smith, *The Companies with the Best CSR Reputations*, FORBES (Dec. 10, 2012, 11:59 PM), http://www.forbes.com/sites/jacquelynsmith/2012/12/10/the-companies-with-the-best-csr-reputations/.

[43] *See* Ellisha Nasruddin & Reevany Bustami, *The Yin and Yang of CSR Ethical Branding*, 12 ASIAN ACAD. MGMT. J. 83, 83–85 (2007).

[44] Bellish, *supra* note 39, at 567.

[45] *Supra* note 39 at 567–68.

[46] *Supra* note 39 at 573.

[47] *Supra* note 39 at 574.

traditional cosmopolitanist approaches, particularly those that focus on the growth of institutional frameworks. For example, one of the most prominent articulations of modern institutional cosmopolitanism stems from Immanuel Kant, who emphasized the idea of membership to the community of humanity as a whole.[48] Kant developed this idea in the context of a world federation that focused on cosmopolitanism as a form of right, along with the growth of world trade and a global public sphere.[49] In more contemporary times, Jack Goldsmith, in his writing on cosmopolitanism, similarly writes of a recent turn to a more institutionalized sense of cosmopolitanism—the idea that duties attach to domestic institutions (e.g., national governments) and, derivatively to international institutions.[50]

These ideals also resonate in the complex world of international intellectual property. In just the past few decades, we have seen a massive rise in systems of intellectual property harmonization, along with the simultaneous rise of global branding and trademarking practices. While the two may or may not be causally related, they suggest that the institutional growth of transnational entities to regulate trademarks raise related questions regarding the aftereffects of globalization on both legal and political systems. The Paris Convention and TRIPS both obligate parties to create and provide minimum standards of protection for trademarks, but this process has been messy, costly, and deeply fraught with conflict for some nations, particularly across the developing world.[51]

Yet as applied to trademarks, the institutional afterlife of cosmopolitanism reveals a complex reordering of the notion of national borders, one that is largely scripted by the transnational circulation of global brands. Some brands, of course, begin as local markets and then expand internationally, and others are actually designed to be global at their outset. The emergence of transnational systems—TRIPS, the Madrid System, and Europe's Community Trademark system, among others—shift the process of branding from a national or local enterprise to one where companies must imagine, at the moment of brand creation, how their brands will fare on the worldwide stage. "At Novartis," for example, one spokesperson explains, "we only have global branding concepts. Our products are introduced at the global scale."[52]

---

[48] Pheng Cheah, *Cosmopolitanism*, 23 Theory, Culture & Soc'y 486, 487–89 (2006).

[49] *See id.* at 487.

[50] Jack Goldsmith, *Liberal Democracy and Cosmopolitan Duty*, 55 Stan. L. Rev. 1667, 1670 (2003). Others also have written about the cosmopolitanist elements in extraterritorial jurisdiction, which focuses on a broad concept of a legal duty to others. *See* William F. Helmken, *Legal Duty Beyond Borders: Value Pluralism and the Possibility of Cosmopolitan Law*, 4 Wash. U. Jurisprudence Rev. 151, 160 (2011).

[51] *See* Margaret Chon, *Intellectual Property and the Development Divide*, 27 Cardozo L. Rev. 2821, 2831–32 & n.80 (2006); Carlos M. Correa, *TRIPs: An Asymmetric Negotiation*, 1993 Third World Econ. 9, 10; Graeme B. Dinwoodie & Rochelle C. Dreyfuss, *Designing A Global Intellectual Property System Responsive to Change: The WTO, WIPO, and Beyond*, 46 Hous. L. Rev. 1187, 1188–89, 1201–4 (2009).

[52] Roya Ghafele, *Trademark Owner's Perspective on the Madrid System: Practical Experiences and Theoretical Underpinnings*, 3 J. Intell. Prop. L. & Prac. 160, 166 (2007).

Thus, just as global branding is now an integral part of any multinational marketing enterprise, global trademark registration is an essential part of the portfolio for any growing business. Empirical evidence has shown how trademarks have dramatically risen in power, as companies have chosen to engage in far more trademarking and branding activity than in prior years, suggesting that trademarks comprise a much greater proportion of countries' GDP.[53]

The increase in trademarking activity—coupled with the rise of global branding—has also spurred some significant international changes. More and more companies are choosing to register trademarks in other countries; WIPO has reported a significant increase in nonresident applications for trademarks, mostly from applicants who reside in higher income countries. Consider some statistics. According to WIPO, the number of trademarks has increased from 500,000 in 1985 to over 2 million in 2007.[54] From 2009 to 2010, for example, the world saw a 21.4% increase in the global registration of trademarks.[55] In turn, 2011 saw the highest number of international trademark applications ever filed under WIPO's Madrid system, with filings from Russia, the EU, and the United States in the lead for the most applications.[56]

Today, the Madrid Protocol remains the most powerful tool for brand owners to register their marks in other countries.[57] The Madrid System enables applicants to file a single registration, facilitating the global spread and growth of brands. Under the Madrid system, a firm that already has a trademark in one of the participating countries can apply to register that mark in other participating countries. The top users of the Madrid System utilize a global branding strategy, enabling them to market a single brand in multiple markets, reflecting both market power and dominance.[58] One business owner

[53] The expanding economic role for trademarks in national economies is dramatic. In Australia, for example, the number of marks per billion of dollars of GDP has doubled, from 50 in the early 1990s to 100 in 2002. Joanne Loundes & Mark Rogers, *The Rise of Trade Marking in Australia in the 1990s* 3 (Melb. Inst. of Applied Econ. and Soc. Res. Inst. of Austl., Working Paper No. 8/03, 2003), *cited in* Mitchell Smith, *Trade Marks and the Protection of Cultural Integrity* 2 (Apr. 27, 2009) (unpublished manuscript), http://papers.ssrn.com/sol3/papers.cfm?abstract_id=1395548.

[54] Loundes & Rogers, *supra* note 53, at 6 (citing *Statistics on Trademarks,* WIPO, http://www.wipo.int/ipstats/en/statistics/marks/) (last visited Sept. 20, 2013).

[55] *Intellectual Property Filings Worldwide Rebound Strongly in 2010*, WIPO 8, http://www.wipo.int/export/sites/www/ipstats/en/wipi/pdf/941_2011_highlights.pdf (last visited Sept. 20, 2013).

[56] *See Record International Trademark Filings in 2011*, WIPO (Mar. 12, 2012), http://www.wipo.int/pressroom/en/articles/2012/article_0004.html.

[57] Ghafele, *supra* note 52, at 161. The Madrid system is based on two treaties, the Madrid Agreement, which is called the Madrid Agreement Concerning the International Registration of Marks (Madrid Agreement), adopted in 1891, and the Protocol Relating to the Madrid Agreement, adopted in 1989 and in force since 1996. For articles on the Madrid Protocol, see generally Protocol Relating to the Madrid Agreement Concerning the International Registration of Marks, art. 4, *adopted on* June 27, 1989, S. Treaty Doc. No. 106-41, *available at* http://www.wipo.int/madrid/en/legal_texts/trtdocs_wo016.html; John M. Murphy, *Demystifying the Madrid Protocol,* Nw. J. Tech. & Intell. Prop. 1 (2004) (summarizing the Madrid Protocol and discussing it from a U.S. applicant and foreign applicant point of view).

[58] Mitchell Smith, *supra* note 53, at 7 (citing Ghafele, *supra* note 52, at 166).

said that Madrid is essential for a global branding strategy—"Through Madrid we can get quicker into markets. This means we gain time and the whole management of IP is different. There are not 50 different systems, but everything is much simpler."[59]

The advantages of the Madrid system are manifold—it reduces the costs associated with trademark registration, and streamlines the process. The Madrid system has been heralded for its low costs—Microsoft has claimed that costs have gone down 40% in its international filings.[60] Empiricists have also found a positive correlation between the growth of global trade and the rise of filings and renewals under the Madrid System.[61]

However much the Madrid system does to advance trademark cosmopolitanism, it is not perfect. The system is mostly a procedural one; it does not actually substantively examine the specific trademarks. Instead, the substantive application takes place in the originating country, otherwise known as the Country of Origin.[62] As a result, since trademark laws vary so widely, it is entirely possible to have a mark protected in one country but not in another. Similarly, these registrations are also deeply dependent on the home country—so that whatever happens to the national trademark, whether it is an amendment, cancellation, denial, or withdrawal, happens to the international one as well, although it is possible to convert some applications into national ones.[63] There is also not a lot of room for movement in terms of localizing or nationalizing global brands filed under the Madrid system—any slight change in the trademark's status usually requires a refile.[64]

However mixed some of the reviews may be of the Madrid System, it is patently clear that Madrid reflects, in some ways, an institutionalized cosmopolitanist outlook that bridges the link between corporations and government systems in the process of global branding. Even as it actively facilitates global branding, it is also intrinsically designed to overlook national differences in trademark registration, the protection of speech, and so on. Yet optimistic predictions of the rise of global trademarking can often belie a more complicated reality regarding the distributive effects of harmonization.[65] At the same time that this global trend has unfolded, for example, it is important to mention

---

[59] Ghafele, *supra* note 52, at 166.

[60] *See Transcript from the Video Interview with Microsoft on the Madrid System*, WIPO, http://www.wipo.int/madrid/en/transcript/microsoft.html.

[61] Ghafele, *supra* note 52, at 161–62. In 1985, there were only 50,000 nonresident trademark registrations, comprising 28% of the global trade marks registered; as compared with 760,000 such registrations in 2007, making up now 36% of those marks in 2007. Smith, *supra* note 53, at 6 (citing Eugenia Baroncelli et al., *The Global Distribution of Trademarks: Some Stylized Facts*, 28 WORLD ECON. 765 (2005)).

[62] *See* Rachelle H. Thompson, *Trademarks in International and Comparative Law: International Trademark Protection Strategy*, 19 J. CONTEMP. LEGAL ISSUES 479, 494 (2004).

[63] *See* Ghafele, *supra* note 52, at 164–65.

[64] *See supra* note 52 at 165.

[65] *See generally* Marshall A. Leaffer, *The New World of International Trademark Law*, 2 MARQ. INTELL. PROP. L. REV. 1 (1998).

that there are some islands of resistance to the global branding trend. One study on the Madrid Protocol has discovered, for example, that India and South Africa have demonstrated some forms of discrimination in the registration process against foreign firms.[66] This finding resonates with the research done by another scholar, who has found evidence of trademark protectionism in China, Hong Kong, India, and South Africa, noting that "discrimination is more likely to occur when products offered by foreign firms are of similar quality to the ones produced by domestic firms."[67]

Further, perhaps one of the greatest issues faced by the rise of trademark cosmopolitanism is how to reconcile the protection of intellectual property with the protection of other fundamental rights, like the freedom of expression. Some countries, like the United States, expressly protect freedom of expression as a fundamental right, and some courts offer specific protections for things like parody; and still other commonwealth countries, like the United Kingdom, New Zealand, and Australia, do not have a constitutional right to freedom of speech but recognize its existence in statutes or common law.[68] In addition, there has been very little discussion of the importance of protecting freedom of expression at the treaty negotiation level, suggesting that many of these issues are considered to be best left to the local and regional judicial systems to sort through. For example, according to Lisa Ramsey, the legislative history suggests that there was almost no discussion of the conflict between trademark rights and freedom of expression during the TRIPS negotiations.[69] Neither the Paris Convention, nor TRIPS, nor the Madrid Protocols have any formal declaration of a commitment to freedom of expression, suggesting that it never rose to a level of importance as a fundamental part of the international architecture of trademark law. International protections of copyright, in contrast, do have protections for freedom of expression built into them.[70] As the following sections suggest, this absence has deep significance for the activist movements that target multinational corporations and their practices, and generally for the flourishing of freedom of speech.

---

[66] Smith, *supra* note 53 at 8 (citing Eugenia Baroncelli et al., *Trademark Protection or Protectionism*, 15 REV. INT'L ECON. 126, 128 (2007)).

[67] Baroncelli et al., *supra* note 75, at 140.

[68] *See* Lisa P. Ramsey, *Free Speech and International Obligations to Protect Trademarks*, 35 YALE J. INT'L L. 405, 412 (2010).

[69] *Id.* at 415.

[70] *See* Martin Senftleben, *The Trademark Tower of Babel—Dilution Concepts in International, US and EC Trademark Law*, 40 INT'L REV. INTELL. PROP. & COMPETITION L. 45, 62 (2009). For example, whereas many sections of the Berne convention leave room for freedom of expression, trademark law only has a section in Article 17 that provides for "fair use of descriptive terms," but no reference to the protection of parody. *Id.* (quoting Agreement on Trade-Related Aspects of Intellectual Property Rights, Apr. 15, 1994, Marrakesh Agreement Establishing the World Trade Organization, Annex 1C, 1867 U.N.T.S. 154).

III. The Transnational Antibrand

As the previous section suggested, the emergence of trademark cosmopolitanism can often implicate questions about freedom of expression as a fundamental right, demonstrating another side to the phenomenon of global branding—global antibranding. In just the last few decades, a new movement of activists has sprung up internationally and domestically, engaging in artistic and political activity to challenge the expansion of the brand into public discourse.[71] Sometimes antibrands might target a certain brand for opposition; at other times (like Nadia Plesner's evocation of an LVMH bag to bring attention to Darfur), they might utilize a brand for the purposes of political, satirical, or humorous commentary on another subject. And yet, the ways in which these artists have done so have raised complicated questions of identity, language, and control—setting up a clash between the international standards for freedom of speech and intellectual property.[72]

Transnational activism of this sort is deeply connected to the rise of trademark cosmopolitanism, even if there is not always a perfect identicality between the two are not identical. The rise of the global antibranding movement is intimately tied to the rise of global branding: one cannot have one without the other, and the proportional growth of the antibrand is tied to the growth of the brand. Many of the activities of antibrand activists, therefore, are deeply tied to targeting corporate social responsibility practices—drawing attention to current events or using brands to comment on issues involving racial inequities, distributive injustice, labor issues, and the like. In other words, the same elements that contribute to the global consumption of brands can often contribute to global anti-consumption of them as well. As Rosemary Coombe has written, "[p]rotests against sweatshop labour practices, and the movement of big box stores and fast food franchises into communities, suggest that the trademark now provides a site and a symbol around which to resist forms of commodification that people find contrary to their understandings of community and social justice."[73]

---

[71] For more on this phenomenon, see Sonia Katyal, *Semiotic Disobedience*, 84 WASH. U. L. REV. 489, 492, 499–512 (2006), and Sonia Katyal, *Stealth Marketing and Antibranding: The Love That Dare Not Speak Its Name*, 58 BUFF. L. REV. 795, 797–98 (2010) [hereinafter *Antibranding*].

[72] Katyal, *Antibranding*, *supra* note 71, at 797–98.

[73] Matthew Rimmer, *The Black Label: Trademark Dilution, Culture Jamming, and the No Logo Movement*, 5 SCRIPT-ED 70, 80 (2008) (quoting Rosemary J. Coombe, *The Politics of Intellectual Property*, The Joint Graduate Programme in Communication and Culture, http://www.finestone.ca/aa/comcult/faculty/coombe.html). Coombe's work is foundational to understanding the relationship between trademarks and social movements. *See* ROSEMARY J. COOMBE, THE CULTURAL LIFE OF INTELLECTUAL PROPERTIES: AUTHORSHIP, APPROPRIATION, AND THE LAW 7 (1998); Sidney Tarrow, *Rooted Cosmopolitans and Transnational Activists*, *in* THE NEW TRANSNATIONAL 1, 43–45.

A. THE RISE OF COSMOPOLITAN POLITICAL SOLIDARITY

Benedict Anderson's famous book *Imagined Communities* powerfully postulated that a nation is conceived not as a reality but as a collective work of imagination that has emerged from the circulation of capital and the rise of print communication.[74] From this starting point, a number of scholars relied on Anderson for a deeper study of nationalism and the territorial impulse.[75] Writing on Anderson, Partha Chatterjee writes that the newspaper, the novel, and other forms of print media "afford the opportunity for individuals to imagine themselves as members of larger than face-to-face solidarities, of choosing to act on behalf of those solidarities, of transcending by an act of political imagination the limits imposed by traditional practices."[76]

Some have argued, and I would agree, that Anderson's observations can profitably extend to today's global circulation of media, and relatedly, to the emergence of cosmopolitan forms of solidarity.[77] After all, if print media helped individual citizens imagine the nation, then why can't the rapid circulation of new media help individuals imagine a similar kind of imagination of a collective, cosmopolitanist global identity? And why cannot the same be true of the transnational consumption of global branding, as well? Does the transnational circulation of brands signify a new global order, an imagined community of consumers—and an imagined community of global activists? As Arjun Appadurai observes, these transnational solidarities are crafted from, not nationalism, but from a commonality of tastes, of pleasures, and of politics, what Appadurai calls "communit[ies] of sentiment."[78]

Even as a purely non-legal matter, I would also argue that Anderson's construction of the imagined community perfectly tracks similar observations regarding the cosmopolitanist trajectories of *both* global consumption and anti-global activism.[79] In the case of global consumption, as I suggested in section II, we see a cosmopolitanist trajectory that embraces the increasing unification of global brands that operate to help individuals imagine themselves as part of a broader global community of other consumers. But in the case of the anti-globalization activist, the lingua franca of the antibrand operates

---

[74] *See* BENEDICT ANDERSON, IMAGINED COMMUNITIES: REFLECTIONS ON THE ORIGIN AND SPREAD OF NATIONALISM 30 (1991).

[75] *See, for example,* WILL KYMLICKA, MULTICULTURAL CITIZENSHIP: A LIBERAL THEORY OF MINORITY RIGHTS 90 (1995).

[76] Partha Chatterjee, *Anderson's Utopia*, 29 DIACRITICS, Winter 1999, at 128, 128.

[77] Maria Kyriakidou, *Imagining Ourselves Beyond the Nation? Exploring Cosmopolitanism in Relation to Media Coverage of Distant Suffering*, 9 STUD. ETHNICITY & NATIONALISM 481, 485 (2009); *see generally* ARJUN APPADURAI, MODERNITY AT LARGE: CULTURAL DIMENSIONS OF GLOBALIZATION (1996) [hereinafter MODERNITY]; Bruce Robbins, *Introduction Part I: Actually Existing Cosmopolitanism, in* COSMOPOLITICS: THINKING AND FEELING BEYOND THE NATION 7 (Pheng Cheah & Bruce Robbins eds., 1998) (discussing Anderson as part of an overall change in the definition of cosmopolitanism).

[78] Kyriakidou, *supra* note 77, at 485 (quoting MODERNITY, *supra* note 78, at 8).

[79] *See* TARROW, *supra* note 73, at 41–42.

similarly, just in reverse. As scholars have argued, many transnational activists presume a kind of cosmopolitan solidarity across borders that transforms "national citizens into global citizens by creating obligations toward people suffering outside the nation."[80]

There is also a fascinating parallel between the cosmopolitanist consumption that I detailed in section II and the antibranding activists I detail in this section and elsewhere.[81] Like consumers of global brands, many cosmopolitan activists accept multiplicities of roots and plural loyalties, and although they move outside of their spatial origins, they continue to be linked to a concept of place and the resources and opportunities that place offers them.[82] As a result, the imagined community, here, is not a community of consumers but of activists who are often deeply critical of the practices of multinational corporations and global branding. These activists are defined as transnational because they mobilize domestic and international resources in order to advance claims on behalf of external actors or in favor of goals they may hold in common with other transnational allies. These individuals typify the trend of "activism beyond borders," and they comprise groups of immigrant and labor activists, ecologists, and other political actors who may exist loosely outside of state formation.[83]

Indeed, as Douglas Holt has explained, at times, global branding has lost its luster precisely because multinational corporations have become vulnerable to charges from anti-globalization activists. "Who can forget," Holt writes, "the images of angry demonstrators smashing the windows of a McDonald's outlet in Davos, Switzerland, or stomping Coke cans in Seattle?"[84] Labor, pollution, and cultural imperialism concerns operate at the forefront of activist agendas, which tend to coalesce around the global branding enterprise.[85] As the journalist Naomi Klein recounts in her book, NO LOGO, the antibranding movement operates at the cross-section between art, labor, and anti-globalization.[86] By targeting companies that have invested millions in building strong global brands, antibranders seek to expose potential hypocrisy between corporate philosophy and corporate activity to the average consumer.[87] Indeed, evidence has suggested that in countries with weak or underenforced environmental regulations, companies tend to adopt private regulatory programs only when their overseas clients and shareholders demand it.[88] As a result, antibranding activism often exploits the same tools

---

[80] Kyriakidou, *supra* note 77, at 482 (emphasis omitted) (internal quotation marks omitted) (quoting Kate Nash, *Global Citizenship as Show Business: The Cultural Politics of Make Poverty History*, 30 MEDIA, CULTURE & SOC'Y 167, 168 (2008)).

[81] *See* Katyal, *Antibranding, supra* note 71.

[82] *See* TARROW, *supra* note 73, at 42.

[83] *Supra* note 73 at 9–10 (quoting MARGARET E. KECK & KATHRYN SIKKINK, ACTIVISTS BEYOND BORDERS: ADVOCACY NETWORKS IN INTERNATIONAL POLITICS, at xii (1998)).

[84] Holt et al., *Global Brands, supra* note 14, at 69.

[85] Supra note 14, at 69–70.

[86] Rimmer, *supra* note 74, at 78–80.

[87] Katyal, *Antibranding, supra* note 71, at 811–12.

[88] Daniel Berliner & Aseem Prakash, *Signaling Environmental Stewardship in the Shadow of Weak Governance: The Global Diffusion of ISO 14001*, 47 LAW & SOC'Y REV. 345, 367–68 (2013).

used in advertising—powerful visuals, brand recognition, catchy slogans, and emotionally scripted language—to get their message out to the public.

It is therefore no surprise that much of the world's most prominent trademark cases regarding antibranding has come from one of the largest and most international environmental action groups: Greenpeace. In 2010, Greenpeace, an environmental awareness group, in response to the British Petroleum oil spill in the Gulf, announced a contest to "Redesign BP's logo," explaining:

> A few years ago, BP rebranded themselves as "beyond petroleum." And yet BP is pursuing ... deepwater drilling, despite the massive environmental damage that's being caused by their business.
>
> That's why we want you to rebrand them.

The campaign concludes, "BP's slick green logo doesn't suit a company that engages in dangerous offshore drilling. We're inviting you to design them a new logo that's more suitable for their dirty business."[89] Greenpeace's work was particularly effective at changing the semiotic import of British Petroleum's massive advertising campaign to highlight its focus on clean energy. After a few of these graphic interventions, it was hard to see British Petroleum's advertising campaign in the light it had originally intended.

In addition to a growing concern about corporate social responsibility, a second factor has added to the growth in antibranding: the increasing force of "consumer sovereignty," which has led many consumers to respond and publicize their complaints against particular corporations.[90] These dynamics have reframed the relationship between advertising and consumers into a much more dialogic relationship, as opposed to a one-way relationship of corporate inculcation. "Ethical shareholders, culture jammers, street reclaimers, McUnion organizers, human rights hacktivists, school-logo fighters and Internet corporate watchdogs are at the early stages of demanding a citizen-centered alternative to the international rule of the brands," Naomi Klein writes in NO LOGO.[91] In many cases, antibranding activists have decidedly turned to the advertising executives' own arsenal of tools to address consumer concerns, using appropriative strategies to address the increasing dominance of branding strategies in both private and public space.

Many of these practices intrinsically raise trademark concerns, however. Consider, again, the story of Nadia Plesner and her relationship to the crisis in Darfur. Plesner's ability to use LVMH bags as a floating signifier of political import is also, in part, a function of the same variety of elements that facilitate brand transnationalism.[92] Yet Plesner

---

[89] *Redesign BP's Logo*, GREENPEACE (June 15, 2010), http://www.greenpeace.org/usa/news/gulf-oil-spill/bp-logo.

[90] *See* Robert Lande, *Consumer Choice as the Ultimate Goal of Antitrust*, 62 U. PITT. L. REV. 503, 503 (2001).

[91] Rimmer, *supra* note 73, at 79 (quoting NAOMI KLEIN, NO LOGO: TAKING AIM AT THE BRAND BULLIES 445–46 (2009)).

[92] *See generally* TARROW, *supra* note 73, at 35–56.

felt, like many cosmopolitanists, a moral duty to draw attention to the crisis—a keen desire born from a foundational belief in the shared responsibility of humankind. Every aspect of her political expression—from the conceptualization of the project, to its execution, to her attempts to secure legal protection for her expression—was tied to other localities.[93] Further, Plesner's intent in drawing a transhistorical connection between Picasso's antiwar position and her own critique of celebrity branding, luxury, and contemporary political culture was also meant to place use of the LVMH logo at the center of her expression. Whereas Picasso's earlier iconoclastic work of art targeted governments, Plesner's work drew attention to the need for targeting global luxury brands and the consumptive practices that exalted them. Moreover, as the legal dispute over Nadia Plesner's work demonstrated, much of the conflict played out in reference to the global visibility of LVMH's brand—which operated as a symbol and vessel for commentary on the global presence of luxury brands, cosmopolitanist consumption, and the need for international social justice and awareness.

There was no doubt that Plesner's use of the image was deliberately provocative, in that she had already been sued by Louis Vuitton. But it is also fascinating that Louis Vuitton chose to pursue a case against her when its previous threats against her led to such criticism in the press.[94] The court's reaction, though, was fascinating. Both parties relied on different sections of the European Convention on Human Rights; Plesner relied on the right of freedom of expression and Louis Vuitton relied on the fundamental right to property (and relatedly, intellectual property).[95] At first, the lower court ruled in favor of LVMH in its bid for a preliminary injunction, ruling in favor of its intellectual property rights. It concluded that a subsequent use of the picture in an announcement for the artist's upcoming exhibition was an "eye-catcher," and thus unjustified because

[93] She kept a widely read blog on the creation of her painting, *Darfunika*, making daily updates to the painting that were explicitly linked to the ever-changing political conditions in the Sudan. *See* Lucie Guibault, *The Netherlands: Darfunica, Miffy and the Right to Parody!*, 2 J. Intell. Prop. Infor. Tech. & e-Commerce L. 236, 244 (2011) (quoting from the translated decision Nadia Plesner Joensen v. Louis Vuitton Malletier SA, District Court of the Hague, May 4, 2011, IER 2011/39, *available at* http://www.nadiaplesner. com/upl/website/simple-living-darfurnica1/VerdictEnglish.pdf).

[94] There was, however, a key reason for LVMH's choice to sue. Contrary to the settlement in 2008, this time, Plesner—probably in a show of provocation to LVMH—planned to market sales of T-shirts and other goods that depicted the same image that LVMH had already objected to. When they discovered Plesner's commercial plans, LVMH was, understandably, quite incensed. After the piece was finished, LVMH again decided to seek action to stop the work from being shown, this time from a court in The Hague.

[95] Guibault, *supra* note 93, at 236. Note that LVMH argued that its fundamental right to property was violated, under the European Convention on Human Rights, and extended this fundamental right to intellectual property, which the European Court of Human Rights (ECHR) did in the Anheuser/Busch decision. Plesner's freedom of expression claim, in contrast, comes from Article 10 of the ECHR, which protects the right to hold opinions and to receive and impart ideas. *See* Guibault, *supra* note 93, at 245. For further discussion on Article 10, see Coenraad Visser, *The Location of the Parody Defence in Copyright Law: Some Comparative Perspectives*, 38 CILSA 321, 339–41 (2005).

it functioned as an advertisement for the artist's own work.[96] But a few months later, the same court reversed its position after fully adjudicating the issue, deciding to rule in favor of Plesner's freedom of expression instead. In an insightful citation, the court explained that property rights should take a secondary role to the protection of freedom of speech, noting, "[o]pposite Louis Vuitton's fundamental right to peaceful enjoyment of its exclusive rights to the use of the design, there is, according to established case law of the European Court of Human Rights, the fundamental right of Plesner that is high in a democratic society's propriety list to express her opinion through her art."[97]

Central, of course, to the court's determination was its conclusion that Plesner's activities, contrary to LVMH's arguments, did not take place in the commercial realm. "[A]rtists enjoy a considerable protection with regard to their artistic freedom, in which, in principle, art may 'offend, shock or disturb.'... Plesner's intention with 'Simple Living' is not (or was not) to free ride with Louis Vuitton's reputation in a commercial sense," the court concluded.[98] Instead, it found that Plesner's juxtaposition of LVMH logos and glamorous images with the crisis in Darfur was consistent with her critique of luxury and affluence in a time of famine. Indeed, the court explained her motivation as follows:

> she wished to draw attention to the poignant difference between luxury and affluence on the one hand, and poverty and famine in Darfur on the other hand. She has expressed the aspect of luxury by using the Design of the [LVMH] application in her work of art. She has succeeded in her purpose. Partly because of her work of art, the genocide in Darfur came to the attention of the general public in 2008.

It compared Plesner's symbolic brand appropriation to that of a newspaper, ascribing it an informational function by concluding that "a newspaper should not have a lesser far-reaching protection of the freedom of speech" because it pursues profits with the articles it publishes.[99] Significantly, in a curt line or two, the court ordered LV to pay Plesner's legal fees, and also quashed the previous order with retroactive effect, meaning that any penalties that Plesner faced would no longer be due.[100]

---

96 *See* Guibault, *supra* note 93, at 244 (quoting from a translation of the decision).

97 *See supra* note 93, at 246.

98 *See supra* note 93, at 246.

99 *See supra* note 93, at 247.

100 *See supra* note 93, at 248. Thrilled with the decision, Plesner told EYETEETH, a blog, that "[t]oday is a great day for art.... If I had lost this, I believe it would have caused many artists to censor their own work to avoid legal trouble. Now we have won back our freedom to make reference to the modern society we live in." *Nadia Plesner on Louis Vuitton Case: "This Is a Great Day for Art,"* EYETEETH (May 4, 2011, 11:22 AM), http://eyeteeth.blogspot.com/2011/05/nadia-plesner-on-louis-vuitton-case.html.

B. FUNDAMENTAL RIGHTS, COMMODITY, AND COMMERCIALITY: THREE KEY THEMES

Decades ago, Beaumarchais wrote, "Provided that, in my writings, I speak neither of the authorities, nor of religion, nor of politics, nor of morals, nor of the people in power, nor of the bodies in credit, nor of the opera, nor of other performances, nor of anyone who believes in anything, I shall be free to print whatsoever I choose, subject to inspection by two or three censors."[101] This famous quote, one trademark scholar argued, is especially pertinent in this day and age, noting that "it would probably now be necessary to add trade marks to the list of subjects that must be treated with delicacy and, in place of the censor, the large companies that hold these trade marks."[102]

In some ways, the antibranding activism that has evolved in the last decade or so reflects so much of the globalization that it often opposes. The problem that our antibranding movements demonstrate, however, is that while brands—and even antibrands—are now global and cosmopolitanist in character, the doctrinal architecture that protects them and enables them to flourish is not. As a result, the existing case law reflects an emerging confusion regarding how trademarks are viewed, both internationally and domestically, and whether antibrands are constitutionally protected. How do we balance protection of trademark property with protection for freedom of speech? Many cases take approaches that are similar to the Plesner case; where a court might begin by awarding relief to the trademark owner, but then take the opposite holding on appeal, usually after global media attention ensues and the appeals court has a chance to consider other approaches.

Cases like Plesner's, I would argue, illustrate yet another aspect of trademark cosmopolitanism, because they underscore the increasing globalization of brands as well as the jurisprudential frameworks that govern them. My principal argument is that just as we are seeing the emergence of a global branding movement, we are also seeing a global antibranding movement. However, national disparities regarding whether parody is a constitutionally protected freedom carry dramatic implications for the movement's future, raising critical questions about the future of reconciling trademark cosmopolitanism with the freedom of political and artistic expression.

Plesner's case, for example, relied almost exclusively on human rights reasoning. Whatever the result, this case, I think, suggests some areas that are ripe for further consideration, particularly given the global nature of each dispute. Consider three main areas of tension, illustrated by this case. The first major theme involves the fundamental question of which right matters more: the right to freedom of speech, and relatedly, the right to parody, or the right

---

[101] *See* Christophe Geiger, *"Constitutionalising" Intellectual Property Law? The Influence of Fundamental Rights on Intellectual Property in the European Union*, 37 INT'L REV. INTELL. PROP. & COMPETITION L. 371, 371 (2006) (quoting Beaumarchais) [hereinafter *Constitutionalising*]; see also Christophe Geiger, *Trade Marks and Freedom of Expression—The Proportionality of Criticism*, 38 INT'L REV. INTELL. PROP. 317 (2007) [hereinafter *Trade Marks*].

[102] *See supra* note 101 at 371.

to intellectual property. Underlying this question, I would suggest, is an architectural question about how to situate the protection of intellectual property alongside the creation and protection of other fundamental rights.[103] Is intellectual property a fundamental right, akin to other fundamental rights, or should it be treated as secondary to these other rights? And if intellectual property is considered to be a fundamental right, then how does that right square with that of the right to freedom of speech? The Charter of Fundamental Rights of the European Union states in Article 17 section 2 that "Intellectual property shall be protected," and further that it "stands as an end in itself."[104] However, if the world is moving toward a more unitary regime for trademark registrations, it becomes necessary to confront the diversity of speech protections within other nation states. Some countries, like the United States, expressly protect freedom of expression as a fundamental right, whereas certain commonwealth countries, such as the United Kingdom, New Zealand, and Australia, do not have a constitutional right to freedom of speech but recognize its existence in statutes or common law.[105]

Robert Burrell and Dev Gangjee have pointed out that the concept of freedom of expression in the United States, with its attendant suspicion of government, may make transplanting its legal principles quite difficult in jurisdictions that have different approaches to freedom of speech.[106] Speech is much more protected in the United States than in other jurisdictions like Germany, France, and South Africa, which explains in part why the commercial or noncommercial nature of the speech became so significant. There is also some suggestion that commercial courts are ill-equipped to be addressing constitutional matters, given the complexity of constitutional matters and the difficulty of transplanting legal concepts. There is also another excellent point raised by Gangjee and Burrell—a debate about constitutional rights framed by a conflict between property and speech—which just gets us nowhere because there is no "trumping" quality of either one.[107]

Then there is also the question of how to employ human rights principles in such disputes. Recall that the case involving Plesner, for example, was resolved not on trademark grounds—but on human rights principles. In Germany, too, in one case, the defendant altered the Marlboro trademark to deliver a nonsmoking message; the court cited the basic human right of freedom of expression in protecting the work.[108] This factor suggests yet another layer of complexity to trademark cosmopolitanism, because characterizing intellectual property as a fundamental right does not necessarily garner its primacy against other rights, like freedom of expression worldwide. Some have argued that

---

103 *See also* Geiger, *supra* note 101, at 371.

104 Geiger, *supra* note 101, at 376.

105 Ramsey, *supra* note 68, at 412.

106 Robert Burrell & Dev Gangjee, *Trade Marks and Freedom of Expression—A Call for Caution*, 41 Int'l Rev. Intell. Prop. & Competition L. 544, 558 (2010).

107 *Id.* at 559.

108 *See* Andreas Rahmatian, Trade Marks and Human Rights, in 18 INTELLECTUAL PROPERTY AND HUMAN RIGHTS 335, 349 (Paul Torremans ed., 2008 (discussing these cases).

human rights law operates as a "corrective" when IP rights might be used "excessively" or "contrary to their functions"—and that these protections operate when other "safety valves" in IP have failed, such as fair use, fair dealing, and other exceptions and limitations.[109] But, at the same time, there is growing evidence that the protection of intellectual property itself is now viewed as a human right—in one case before the European Court of Human Rights, involving the mark "Budweiser," the Court decided to classify trademarks as a type of "property right" for the purpose of human rights analysis.[110] As a result, it makes it difficult to see how relying on fundamental rights analysis assists in resolving tough cases.

Some scholars have argued, on this point, that thinking about IP as a fundamental right ensures that it receives an important place in the relevant national constitution, ensuring that it ranks highly in any rights hierarchy. It also makes further justification of IP unnecessary since it is viewed as a fundamental right. Finally, as Christopher Geiger has suggested, if IP is considered to be a fundamental right, it becomes linked to "ethical values," which are often considered to enjoy "widespread consent and acknowledgment under international law."[111]

Yet classifying IP as a fundamental right gives us very little insight as to how to balance such a right against other fundamental rights, like freedom of speech.[112] Particularly in countries where there is no fundamental right to freedom of speech, the very act of classifying IP in this manner raises the risk of further alienating speech interests in favor of the primacy of intellectual property.[113] Further, as Lawrence Helfer has explained, if intellectual property owners choose to invoke human rights law in order to garner additional protections, they would be likely to face stiff resistance from users and consumers, who would in turn draw upon *other* fundamental rights in order to articulate a competing vision that focuses on the need to restrict, rather than expand, intellectual property rights in order to protect fundamental freedoms.[114] So, for example, national courts in

---

[109] *See* Laurence R. Helfer, *Toward a Human Rights Framework for Intellectual Property*, 40 U.C. DAVIS L. REV. 971, 1017 (2007) [hereinafter *Human Rights Framework*].

[110] Anheuser-Busch, Inc. v. Portugal, 2007-I Eur. Ct. H.R. 39, 67, paras. 72–78. For more discussion of this case, see Megan M. Carpenter, *Trademarks and Human Rights: Oil and Water? Or Chocolate and Peanut Butter?*, 99 TRADEMARK REP. 892, 908–9 (2009); Laurence R. Helfer, *The New Innovation Frontier? Intellectual Property and the European Court of Human Rights*, 49 HARV. INT'L L.J. 1, 12 (2008); Helfer, *Human Rights Framework, supra* note 110, at 1016; Mirela V. Hristova, *Are Intellectual Property Rights Human Rights? Patent Protection and the Right to Health*, 93 J. PAT. & TRADEMARK OFF. SOC'Y 339, 353 (2011); Katja Weckstrom, *The Lawfulness of Criticizing Big Business: Comparing Approaches to the Balancing of Societal Interests Behind Trademark Protection*, 11 LEWIS & CLARK L. REV. 671, 676 (2007); Mary W. S. Wong, *Toward an Alternative Normative Framework for Copyright: From Private Property to Human Rights*, 26 CARDOZO ARTS & ENT. L.J. 775, 810 (2009).

[111] *See* Geiger, *supra* note 101, at 388.

[112] *See* Rahmatian, *supra* note 108 , at 347–48.

[113] Geiger, *supra* note 101, at 386.

[114] *See* Helfer, *Human Rights Framework, supra* note 109, at 1017.

Europe have been using the right to freedom of expression, protected by the European Convention, toward this end, particularly in the area of copyright to protect the creation of exceptions to the law.[115]

Another main theme involves the question of whether these disputes concerning antibranding are best explored through the lens of the classic division between speech and property, or whether it makes sense to turn to other areas of law, such as the internal architecture of trademark law, to resolve these disputes. And, as a related matter, how much should claims like defamation and disparagement be employed as part of the dispute? Is there a benefit to not looking solely to fundamental rights to address parody, but instead by crafting exceptions *within* trademark law instead? Does only allowing a defendant recourse to fundamental rights to speech allow the property right of trademarks to grow even further, without having internal safety valves in its architecture?

Part of this question, of course, addresses the context of the protection of parody in other jurisdictions. Constitutionalizing the right to antibrand, for example, might actually suggest that the right is comparable to that of an intellectual property right—which is interesting, given that in the United States, fair use is not considered to be a constitutional right, but rather seems to be characterized as a privilege.[116] The more a jurisdiction protects parody and freedom of speech, or the more uncertain of the outcome, one might argue, the more likely it will be that a plaintiff will seek to bring in other areas of law to restrict the defendant's speech, like defamation and disparagement, or moral rights, to defend its intellectual property. As a result, other areas of law become employed in the service of trademark law, reflecting areas that trademark law has really failed to conclusively address. For example, in the UK, the author of a parodied work can also bring an action for derogatory treatment—that it distorted or mutilated the work, or that it was prejudicial to the IP owner's honor or reputation.[117]

Even in the UK, where there are no specific mentions of the right to parody within the statutory language, scholars have argued that the trademark statute (which protects marks against unfair advantage or detriment "without due cause") suggests some possibility that the term "due cause" might provide some support for parody.[118] Others have suggested the use of the "fair dealing" exception to protect parody in the copyright context.[119] (The same is also true in South Africa, where fair dealing is used instead of "fair use.") And still other cases have protected parody on the grounds that the plaintiff has failed to show a likelihood of confusion.[120]

---

[115] *See Helfer, supra* note 109, at 1017.

[116] Geiger, *supra* note 101, at 401.

[117] Visser, *supra* note 95, at 337.

[118] *See* MOHAMMAD AMIN NASER, REVISITING THE PHILOSOPHICAL FOUNDATIONS OF TRADEMARKS IN THE US AND UK 206–7 (2010).

[119] *See* Visser, *supra* note 95, at 337.

[120] Ellen Gredley & Spyros Maniatis, *Parody: A Fatal Attraction? Part 2: Trademark Parodies*, 19 EUR. INTELL. PROP. REV. 412, 418 (1997); Ramsey, *supra* note 68, at 414, n.44–46.

In the context of antibranding, as Plesner's case demonstrates, it may not always be necessary to carve out specific protections for parody if there are other means of protection available. Often, these other means can come from other constitutional principles, or even other parts of the trademark architecture of that jurisdiction. In a German case, for example, the Supreme Court defended a postcard publisher that produced a satirical image that alluded to the trademark MILKA (a chocolate company) and also employed the distinctive lilac color in its artwork.[121] Yet although the Court classified the use as a trademark use, and also noted that the use of the lilac color did evoke MILKA's reputation, it opted to protect the use—not under freedom of expression or human rights principles per se—but under what has been described as a "constitutional right of freedom of the arts," a specific version of the right to freedom of expression.[122] Here, even though it recognized that the defendant was referencing the plaintiff's reputation, it chose to honor the principle of artistic freedom over intellectual property rights, noting "if the postcard (the media of the parody) does not debase the claimant's trade mark and if it is not proved that the defendant acted exclusively for a commercial purpose, the protection of artistic freedom has to prevail in the present litigation over the protection of property rights of Article 14(1) of the German Basic Law."[123]

An additional area of dispute, stemming from this last point, involves the question of whether the antibrand should be treated differently than a brand. Often antibrands can be sold, as well as circulated, raising questions of what to do when there are expressive as well as commercial interests at present. Not dissimilarly to the United States, it appears that parody is protected so long as it does not conflict with the commercial interests of the plaintiff, so long as the mark is being used for critique or parody.[124] Of course, there are costs with an approach that focuses solely on trademark use, since it's not always entirely clear what a use "in the course of trade" can comprise.[125] Yet scholars have expressed fear that the line between commercial and noncommercial expression (parody and the like) becomes extraordinarily blurred, given the expansion of trademark rights as property rights, a risk that only became exacerbated by the Arsenal Football Club of the European Court of Justice.[126]

But there are also a number of cases that involve the sale of goods that represent parodies or antibrands. Here, the case law is decidedly more mixed internationally, especially in the United States, where case law has lined up on either side. The same is true internationally, where the case law is also split. For example, despite the Plesner outcome, a German court had issued an injunction against the sale of shirts that had the Shell logo

---

[121] Rahmatian, *supra* note 108 , at 349 (discussing this case).

[122] Rahmatian, *supra* note 108 , at 349

[123] Geiger, *supra* note 101, at 396 (quoting case).

[124] *See* Rahmatian, *supra* note 108 , at 352.

[125] *See Rahmatian, supra* note 108 at 351.

[126] *See Rahmatian, supra* note 108, at 351.

with a skull, finding that the use was commercial and therefore fell within the Protection against Unfair Competition Act.[127] At times in trademark-related cases, courts have even attributed commercial motivations to media that has traditionally received the highest level of constitutional protections—like newspapers and other forms of editorial media. In one such case from the United Kingdom, a court even interpreted "use in the course of trade" to include a magazine's use of the logo of Philips Company that substituted the logo's stars with Nazi swastikas to draw attention to a story it was publishing on the company's activities during the Second World War.[128] The use was considered to be commercial in the sense that it was intended to increase sales of the magazine, but the risks to the concept of freedom of expression were obvious.

There are, however, a number of options to address the absence of clear protections for parody. States can easily specifically exempt noncommercial expression and political speech, and interpret parody as falling within these parameters.[129] Or states can choose to refrain from enacting strong dilution laws.[130] Still another option is for courts in member states to decline to award injunctive relief, opting instead to focus on damages in order to preserve the interest in freedom of speech, or require the use of disclaimers to obviate confusion.[131] A final option could be for member states to enact statutes that punish the filing of lawsuits for the purposes of censorship or intimidation, or to enact fee-shifting provisions that would force overly aggressive trademark owners to reconsider filing suit in nonmeritorious suits.

A final suggestion could be a broad one. Member states could amend the Paris Convention or TRIPS to state a direct commitment to "freedom of expression" when implementing their trademark protections. Although the obligation to protect freedom of expression is already part of the international treaty world, and certainly relevant to the interpretation of treaty terms, a more specific declaration for freedom of speech might be vital to ensuring a greater balance.[132]

---

[127] See Emmanuel Baud, The Damage Done, TRADEMARK WORLD, Apr. 2005, at 32.

[128] Gredley & Maniatis, *supra* note 120, at 418.

[129] *See* Ramsey, *supra* note 68, at 409. TRIPS Article 16 (1), for example, requires states to prevent uses of marks that cause a likelihood of confusion "in the course of trade." However, TRIPS Article 17 permits states to enact "limited exceptions" to trademark rights—these could easily include nontrademark or nominative uses, parodies, satire, and other commentaries. Ramsey, *supra* note 68, at 409.

[130] Ramsey, *supra* note 68, at 409–10. Since Article 16(3) of TRIPS requires only that member states prohibit third-party registrations or uses of "well known" trademarks to "indicate a connection between [the third party's] goods or services and the owner of the registered trademark," there is room for underenforcement or to avoid enacting dilution statutes altogether.

[131] Ramsey, *supra* note 68, at 434.

[132] *See* Ramsey, *supra* note 68, at 409.

IV. Conclusion

I have suggested a link between contemporary accounts of cosmopolitanism and the growing case law on both global branding and antibranding. As I have discussed, the world of global trademarks can be characterized in terms of a major shift from national to global branding strategies.

Many cosmopolitanist ideals, I have suggested, have taken root in a variety of different political, economic, and social contexts, including intellectual property regulation and the international trademark system. In the trademark context, I would argue each of these areas has a variety of different facets, some that are more culturally oriented, which are focused on the emergence of global brands and an accompanying transnational culture of consumption; others are more doctrinally or institutionally oriented and center on designing a legal architecture that focuses on harmonization.

At the same time, trademark lawyers often extol the virtues of harmonization and globalization without grappling with its complex dynamics as applied to the localized interpretation and expression of intellectual property protections. We see this particularly in the growing set of case law regarding the conflicts between the transnational brand, activist movements, and freedom of speech. As I have suggested, the dyadic relationship between the global branding and antibranding movements has exposed both the idealism and the fragility of cosmopolitanist ideals, offering us significant challenges for the future.

Index

www.ingramcontent.com/pod-product-compliance
Ingram Content Group UK Ltd.
Pitfield, Milton Keynes, MK11 3LW, UK
UKHW020843150926
475595UK00004B/137